ISSN 1538-6678

CAPITAL PUNISHMENT

CRUEL AND UNUSUAL?

Kim Masters Evans

INFORMATION PLUS® REFERENCE SERIES
Formerly published by Information Plus, Wylie, Texas

GALE
CENGAGE Learning™

Detroit • New York • San Francisco • New Haven, Conn • Waterville, Maine • London

GALE
CENGAGE Learning™

Capital Punishment: Cruel and Unusual?

Kim Masters Evans
Paula Kepos, Series Editor

Project Editors: Kathleen J. Edgar, Elizabeth Manar

Permissions: Barb McNeil, Jackie Jones

Composition and Electronic Capture: Evi Abou-El-Seoud

Manufacturing: Cynde Bishop

Gale
27500 Drake Rd.
Farmington Hills, MI 48331-3535

ISBN-13: 978-0-7876-5103-9 (set)   ISBN-10: 0-7876-5103-6 (set)
ISBN-13: 978-1-4144-0747-0   ISBN-10: 1-4144-0747-5

ISSN 1538-6678

This title is also available as an e-book.
ISBN-13: 978-1-4144-3828-3 (set)
ISBN-10: 1-4144-3828-1 (set)
Contact your Gale sales representative for ordering information.

Printed in the United States of America
1 2 3 4 5 6 7 12 11 10 09 08

CAPITAL PUNISHMENT
CRUEL AND UNUSUAL?

TABLE OF CONTENTS

PREFACE vii

CHAPTER 1

A Continuing Conflict: A History of Capital Punishment in the United States 1

This chapter presents an overview of capital punishment in the United States from the colonial period to the present day. Federal death penalty legislation, crimes punishable by death, constitutional legality of the death penalty, and worldwide trends are also covered.

CHAPTER 2

Supreme Court Rulings: Constitutionality of the Death Penalty, Guidelines for Judges and Juries, Jury Selection, and Sentencing Procedures. 13

Court cases and legal decisions regarding the constitutionality of the death penalty are presented in this chapter. Also discussed are judgments concerning the proper imposition of the death penalty; guidelines for judges and jurors, including the consideration of lesser charges; the jury selection process in capital cases; the admissibility of parole information; and sentencing procedures.

CHAPTER 3

Supreme Court Rulings: Circumstances That Do and Do Not Warrant the Death Penalty, Right to Effective Counsel, Appeals Based on New Evidence, and Constitutionality of Execution Methods. 25

This chapter presents capital punishment cases and legal decisions regarding rape and kidnapping, criminal intent, the right to counsel, prosecution errors (including coerced confessions and presumption of malice), types of evidence on which appeals may be based, and court challenges to execution methods.

CHAPTER 4

Supreme Court Rulings: Mitigating Circumstances, Youth, Insanity, Mental Retardation, the Admissibility of Victim Impact Statements, and the Influence of Race in Capital Cases. 37

Chapter 4 investigates court cases and legal decisions regarding mitigating factors, minors and the death sentence, the role of psychiatrists (including validity of testimony, a prisoner's right to an examination, and proving insanity), and the competency standard. Information about cases considering the execution of insane and mentally retarded people is also included, along with racial issues in capital cases.

CHAPTER 5

Death Penalty Laws: Offenses, Sentences, Appeals, and Execution Methods 51

The first section of this chapter defines the types of offenses that are considered capital crimes. The second section discusses the appeals process and methods of execution. Additional topics include the minimum age for execution, the execution of mentally retarded people, implementation of the federal death penalty in non-death penalty states, and witnesses at executions.

CHAPTER 6

Statistics: Death Sentences, Capital Case Costs, and Executions 61

This chapter presents and discusses historical statistics on prisoners under the sentence of death, the costs associated with capital cases, and prisoners who have been executed. Details are presented about the demographic characteristics—such as age, sex, and criminal history—of prisoners who have been sentenced to death and who have been executed.

CHAPTER 7

Issues of Fairness: Racial Bias and Quality of Legal Representation 75

Two of the most contentious issues associated with capital punishment are claims that racial bias and poor legal representation unfairly affect minority and poor defendants in death penalty cases. This chapter presents statistics and describes studies that have been performed to explore the extent to which race and legal representation affect the outcomes of death penalty trials.

CHAPTER 8

Exonerations, Moratoriums, and Reforms 85

This chapter discusses recent trends in exonerations of death row inmates and why exonerations occur. Claims that a large number of death row inmates have been found innocent are hotly disputed by capital punishment supporters. Nevertheless, several states have implemented death penalty moratoriums to allow time for additional study of factors affecting the fairness and validity of capital punishment sentences. Also described are reforms recommended and/or implemented in death penalty states to alleviate perceived problems in the capital punishment system.

CHAPTER 9

Public Attitudes toward Capital Punishment 97

Public opinion surveys regarding capital punishment are presented in this chapter. Areas covered include support for the death penalty, acceptable penalties for murder, crimes deserving the death penalty, death penalty versus life imprisonment without parole, reasons for supporting capital punishment, rate of imposition, and the death penalty as a deterrent.

CHAPTER 10

Capital Punishment around the World 107

This chapter offers an international consideration of the death penalty. Information includes United Nations resolutions regarding capital punishment, statistics on countries that have retained capital punishment and those that have abolished it, rulings on U.S. death penalty cases by the International Court of Justice, and international views on minors and the death penalty.

CHAPTER 11

The Debate: Capital Punishment Should Be
Maintained 119

This chapter contains statements in support of capital punishment in the United States. Excerpts from testimony in federal hearings on the death penalty are provided by Ann Scott (the mother of a murder victim), John McAdams (a professor of political science),

Paul H. Rubin (a professor of economics and law), William G. Otis (former chief of the appellate division in the U.S. Attorney's Office), and David B. Muhlhausen (a policy analyst with the Heritage Foundation). In addition, this chapter includes a statement made by Justice Antonin Scalia of the U.S. Supreme Court arguing that the death penalty should be maintained.

CHAPTER 12

The Debate: Capital Punishment Should Be
Abolished 127

This chapter contains excerpts of testimony by capital punishment opponents at federal hearings on the death penalty. Statements from Vicki A. Schieber (the mother of a murder victim), Stephen B. Bright (the Southern Center for Human Rights), Jeffrey Fagan (professor of law and public health), Hilary O. Shelton (National Association for the Advancement of Colored People), and Aníbal Acevedo Vilá (governor of the Commonwealth of Puerto Rico) are included. Also provided is a statement by Senator Russell Feingold arguing that the U.S. system of capital punishment should be abolished.

**IMPORTANT NAMES
AND ADDRESSES** 135

RESOURCES 137

INDEX 139

PREFACE

Capital Punishment: Cruel and Unusual? is part of the *Information Plus Reference Series*. The purpose of each volume of the series is to present the latest facts on a topic of pressing concern in modern American life. These topics include today's most controversial and most studied social issues: abortion, capital punishment, care for the elderly, crime, the environment, health care, immigration, minorities, national security, social welfare, women, youth, and many more. Although written especially for the high school and undergraduate student, this series is an excellent resource for anyone in need of factual information on current affairs.

By presenting the facts, it is the intention of Gale, a part of Cengage Learning, to provide its readers with everything they need to reach an informed opinion on current issues. To that end, there is a particular emphasis in this series on the presentation of scientific studies, surveys, and statistics. These data are generally presented in the form of tables, charts, and other graphics placed within the text of each book. Every graphic is directly referred to and carefully explained in the text. The source of each graphic is presented within the graphic itself. The data used in these graphics are drawn from the most reputable and reliable sources, in particular from the various branches of the U.S. government and from major independent polling organizations. Every effort has been made to secure the most recent information available. The reader should bear in mind that many major studies take years to conduct, and that additional years often pass before the data from these studies are made available to the public. Therefore, in many cases the most recent information available in 2008 dated from 2005 or 2006. Older statistics are sometimes presented as well if they are of particular interest and no more-recent information exists.

Although statistics are a major focus of the *Information Plus Reference Series*, they are by no means its only

content. Each book also presents the widely held positions and important ideas that shape how the book's subject is discussed in the United States. These positions are explained in detail and, where possible, in the words of their proponents. Some of the other material to be found in these books includes: historical background; descriptions of major events related to the subject; relevant laws and court cases; and examples of how these issues play out in American life. Some books also feature primary documents or have pro and con debate sections giving the words and opinions of prominent Americans on both sides of a controversial topic. All material is presented in an even-handed and unbiased manner; the reader will never be encouraged to accept one view of an issue over another.

HOW TO USE THIS BOOK

Few topics are as controversial as capital punishment. Capital punishment has been debated in America since the colonial period and is currently a worldwide issue. This book includes the history of capital punishment plus discussions of numerous court cases, legal decisions, and historical statistics. Also included is information about execution methods, minors and the death penalty, public attitudes, and capital punishment around the world.

Capital Punishment: Cruel and Unusual? consists of twelve chapters and three appendixes. Each of the chapters is devoted to a particular aspect of capital punishment. For a summary of the information covered in each chapter, please see the synopses provided in the Table of Contents at the front of the book. Chapters generally begin with an overview of the basic facts and background information on the chapter's topic, then proceed to examine subtopics of particular interest. For example, Chapter 7: Issues of Fairness: Racial Bias and Quality of Legal Representation begins with a discussion of whether racial bias plays a role in who receives the death penalty, then details the findings of various studies. The chapter then moves on to the topic of legal representation and whether all those facing the death penalty receive the same quality of representation. Readers can find their way through a chapter by looking for the section and subsection headings, which are clearly set off from the text. Or, they can refer to the book's extensive Index if they already know what they are looking for.

Statistical Information

The tables and figures featured throughout *Capital Punishment: Cruel and Unusual?* will be of particular use to the reader in learning about this issue. The tables and figures represent an extensive collection of the most recent and important statistics on capital punishment and related issues—for example, graphics in the book cover jurisdictions with and without the death penalty; public opinion concerning capital punishment; capital offenses by state; federal laws that provide for the death penalty; demographic characteristics of prisoners under sentence of death; and number of executions and methods used by state. Gale believes that making this information available to the reader is the most important way in which we fulfill the goal of this book: to help readers understand the issues and controversies surrounding capital punishment in the United States and reach their own conclusions about them.

Each table or figure has a unique identifier appearing above it for ease of identification and reference. Titles for the tables and figures explain their purpose. At the end of each table or figure, the original source of the data is provided.

In order to help readers understand these often complicated statistics, all tables and figures are explained in the text. References in the text direct the reader to the relevant statistics. Furthermore, the contents of all tables and figures are fully indexed. Please see the opening section of the Index at the back of this volume for a description of how to find tables and figures within it.

Appendixes

In addition to the main body text and images, *Capital Punishment: Cruel and Unusual?* has three appendixes. The first is the Important Names and Addresses directory. Here the reader will find contact information for a number of government and private organizations that can provide further information on aspects of capital punishment. The second appendix is the Resources section, which can also assist the reader in conducting his or her own research. In this section, the author and editors of *Capital Punishment: Cruel and Unusual?* describe some of the sources that were most useful during the compilation of this book. The final appendix is the Index, making it even easier to find specific topics in this book.

ADVISORY BOARD CONTRIBUTIONS

The staff of Information Plus would like to extend its heartfelt appreciation to the Information Plus Advisory Board. This dedicated group of media professionals provides feedback on the series on an ongoing basis. Their comments allow the editorial staff who work on the project to continually make the series better and more user-friendly. Our top priorities are to produce the highest-quality and most useful books possible, and the Advisory Board's contributions to this process are invaluable.

The members of the Information Plus Advisory Board are:

- Kathleen R. Bonn, Librarian, Newbury Park High School, Newbury Park, California

- Madelyn Garner, Librarian, San Jacinto College–North Campus, Houston, Texas

- Anne Oxenrider, Media Specialist, Dundee High School, Dundee, Michigan

- Charles R. Rodgers, Director of Libraries, Pasco-Hernando Community College, Dade City, Florida

- James N. Zitzelsberger, Library Media Department Chairman, Oshkosh West High School, Oshkosh, Wisconsin

COMMENTS AND SUGGESTIONS

The editors of the *Information Plus Reference Series* welcome your feedback on *Capital Punishment: Cruel and Unusual?* Please direct all correspondence to:

Editors
Information Plus Reference Series
27500 Drake Rd.
Farmington Hills, MI 48331-3535

CHAPTER 1

A CONTINUING CONFLICT: A HISTORY OF CAPITAL PUNISHMENT IN THE UNITED STATES

Capital punishment is the ultimate punishment—death—administered by the government for the commission of serious crimes. The word *capital* comes from the Latin word *capitalis*, meaning "of the head." Throughout history societies have considered some crimes so appalling that the death penalty has been prescribed for them. Over time changing moral values and ideas about government power have limited the number and types of offenses deemed worthy of death. Many countries have eliminated capital punishment completely, dismissing it as an inhumane response to criminal behavior. The United States is one of only a handful of modern societies that still administers the death penalty. This distinction from this nation's peers is not easily explainable. It arises from a complicated mix of social, legal, and political factors that shape American ideas about justice and the role of government in matters of law and order.

Capital punishment enjoys popular support in the United States. Figure 1.1 shows the results of a poll conducted in June 2007 by the Gallup Organization. Approximately two-thirds (65%) of respondents favored the death penalty at that time, compared to 31% who opposed it. Nonetheless, the topic is rife with controversy. Proponents and opponents of the death penalty are passionate in their beliefs. People on both sides of the debate often use philosophical, moral, and religious reasoning to justify their positions. This makes capital punishment a highly charged issue in which emotional opinions can outweigh all other arguments.

The U.S. system of governance is based on the separation of federal and state powers. This means that individual states decide for themselves if they want to practice capital punishment. As of August 2007 the death penalty was approved by the statutes of the federal government (including the U.S. military) and thirty-eight states. (See Table 1.1.) The legality of capital punishment has historically hinged on the interpretation of the short,

but monumental, statement that comprises the Eighth Amendment to the U.S. Constitution: "Excessive bail shall not be required, nor excessive fines imposed, nor cruel and unusual punishments inflicted." Is capital punishment cruel and unusual or not? American society has struggled with this question since the founding of the nation and continues to do so in the twenty-first century.

THE COLONIAL PERIOD

Since the first European settlers arrived in North America, the death penalty has been accepted as just punishment for a variety of offenses. In fact, the earliest recorded execution occurred in 1608, only a year after the English constructed their first settlement in Jamestown, Virginia. Captain George Kendall, one of the original leaders of the Virginia colony, was convicted of mutiny by a jury of his peers and sentenced to death by shooting in Jamestown. In 1632 Jane Champion, a slave, became the first woman to be put to death in the new colonies. She was hanged in James City, Virginia, for the murders of her master's children.

The English Penal Code applied to the British colonies from the beginning and listed fourteen capital offenses. Actual practice, however, varied from colony to colony. In the early days of the Massachusetts Bay Colony, twelve crimes warranted the death penalty: idolatry (worship of an image, idea, or object), witchcraft, blasphemy (expressing disrespect for religious beliefs), rape, statutory rape (nonforcible sexual intercourse with a person who is under the statutory age of consent), kidnapping, perjury (lying under oath) in a trial involving a possible death sentence, rebellion, murder, assault in sudden anger, adultery, and buggery (sodomy). In the statute each crime was accompanied by a quotation justifying capital punishment from the Old Testament of the Bible. Eventually, arson, treason, and grand larceny were added.

FIGURE 1.1

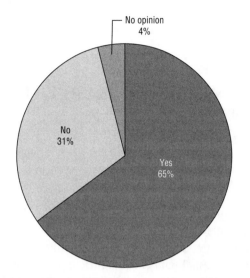

Public opinion on the death penalty for murder, June 2007

ARE YOU IN FAVOR OF THE DEATH PENALTY FOR A PERSON CONVICTED OF MURDER?

No opinion
4%

No
31%

Yes
65%

SOURCE: Adapted from Lydia Saad, "Are you in favor of the death penalty for a person convicted of murder?" in *Racial Disagreement over Death Penalty Has Varied Historically*, The Gallup Organization, July 30, 2007, http://www.galluppoll.com/content/?ci=28243&pg=1 (accessed August 3, 2007). Copyright © 2007 by The Gallup Organization. Reproduced by permission of The Gallup Organization.

TABLE 1.1

Jurisdictions with and without the death penalty, August 2007

Jurisdictions with a Death Penalty	Jurisdictions without a Death Penalty
Federal government	Alaska
Alabama	District of Columbia
Arizona	Hawaii
Arkansas	Iowa
California	Maine
Colorado	Massachusetts
Connecticut	Michigan
Delaware	Minnesota
Florida	North Dakota
Georgia	Rhode Island
Idaho	Vermont
Illinois	West Virginia
Indiana	Wisconsin
Kansas	
Kentucky	
Louisiana	
Maryland	
Mississippi	
Missouri	
Montana	
Nebraska	
Nevada	
New Hampshire	
New Jersey	
New Mexico	
New York	
North Carolina	
Ohio	
Oklahoma	
Oregon	
Pennsylvania	
South Carolina	
South Dakota	
Tennessee	
Texas	
Utah	
Virginia	
Washington	
Wyoming	

SOURCE: Adapted from Tracy L. Snell, "Highlights. Status of the Death Penalty, December 31, 2005," in *Capital Punishment, 2005*, U.S. Department of Justice, Bureau of Justice Statistics, December 2006, http://www.ojp.usdoj.gov/bjs/pub/pdf/cp05.pdf (accessed July 23, 2007)

Virginia's early statutes were even stricter, based on biblical morality and military laws developed in the Netherlands. First enacted by the Jamestown governor Sir Thomas Gates (d. 1621) in 1610, the *Lawes Divine, Morall, and Martiall* were expanded in 1612 by Sir Thomas Dale (d. 1619). Life in the colony was hard, and many of the laws were enacted in response to harsh necessities. Capital offenses included unauthorized trading with Native Americans, gathering vegetables or fruits from a garden without permission, and giving false testimony under oath. In addition, the laws held that "he that shall rob the store of any commodities therein, of what quality soever, whether provisions of victuals, or of Arms, Trucking stuffe, Apparrell, Linnen, or Wollen, Hose or Shooes, Hats or Caps, Instruments or Tooles of Steele, Iron, etc. or shall rob from his fellow souldier, or neighbour, any thing that is his, victuals, apparell, household stuffe, toole, or what necessary else soever, by water or land, out of boate, house, or knapsack, shall bee punished with death."

The Quakers, who settled in the mid-Atlantic region, initially adopted much milder laws than those who settled in the Massachusetts, New York, and Virginia colonies. The Royal Charter for South Jersey (1646) did not permit capital punishment for any crime, and there was no execution until 1691. In Pennsylvania William Penn's (1644–1718) Great Act of 1682 limited the death penalty to treason and murder.

The methods of execution in the fledgling North American colonies could be especially brutal. M. Watt Espy and John Ortiz Smykla note in *Executions in the United States, 1608–2002: The ESPY File* (2005) that even though hanging was the preferred method, some criminals were burned alive or pressed to death by heavy stones. Probably the cruelest punishment was known as "breaking at the wheel," wherein the executioner would snap all the offender's arm and leg joints with a chisel and then weave the extremities through the spokes of a large wheel like meaty ribbons. The prisoner would then be left outside to die of blood loss and exposure.

These executions were held in public as a warning to others, and often a festival atmosphere prevailed. Crowds of onlookers gathered near the gallows, and merchants sold souvenirs. Some spectators got drunk, turning unruly and sometimes violent. After the execution, the body of the convict was sometimes left hanging above the square in a metal cage.

David G. Chardavoyne describes a typical nineteenth-century execution scene in *A Hanging in Detroit: Stephen Gifford Simmons and the Last Execution under Michigan Law* (2003). One of only two executions in Michigan before the death penalty was outlawed there in 1846, Simmons was hanged in September 1830 for murdering his pregnant wife. Chardavoyne explains that at the time, "public executions owed much of their continuing legitimacy to the use of ritual." The associated rituals could last for hours and included parading the condemned prisoner through the crowd with a coffin by his side and a noose around his neck, speeches by public officials and religious leaders denouncing the crime, and in some cases a repentance speech by the prisoner.

Over time, the colonies phased out the crueler methods of execution, and almost all death sentences were carried out by hanging. The colonies also rewrote their death penalty statutes to cover only serious crimes involving willful acts of violence or thievery. By the late 1700s typical death penalty crimes included arson, piracy, treason, murder, and horse stealing. Southern colonies executed people for slave stealing or aiding in a slave revolt. After the American Revolution (1775–1783), some states went further by adopting death penalty statutes similar to Pennsylvania's. New York built its first penitentiary in 1796. With a place to house burglars and nonviolent criminals, the state reduced its capital offenses from thirteen to two. Maryland, Vermont, Virginia, Kentucky, Ohio, and New Hampshire all followed suit by constructing large jails and cutting their capital offenses to just a few of the worst crimes.

THE DEATH PENALTY ABOLITION MOVEMENT

Even though the founders of the United States generally accepted the death penalty, many early Americans did oppose capital punishment. In the late eighteenth century Benjamin Rush (1746–1813), a physician who helped establish the slavery abolition movement, decried capital punishment. He attracted the support of Benjamin Franklin (1706–1790), and it was at Franklin's home in Philadelphia that Rush became one of the first Americans to propose a "House of Reform," a prison where criminals could be detained until they changed their antisocial behavior. Consequently, in 1790 the Walnut Street Jail, the primitive seed from which the U.S. penal system grew, was built in Philadelphia.

Rush published many pamphlets, the most notable of which was *Considerations on the Justice and Policy of Punishing Murder by Death* (1792). He argued that the biblical support given to capital punishment was questionable and that the threat of hanging did not deter crime. Influenced by the philosophy of the Enlightenment

(an intellectual movement in the seventeenth and eighteenth centuries), Rush believed the state exceeded its granted powers when it executed a citizen. Besides Franklin, Rush attracted many other Pennsylvanians to his cause, including William Bradford (1755–1795), the attorney general of Pennsylvania. Bradford suggested the idea of different degrees of murder, some of which did not warrant the death penalty. As a result, in 1794 Pennsylvania repealed the death penalty for all crimes except first-degree murder, which was defined as "willful, deliberate, and premeditated killing or murder committed during arson, rape, robbery, or burglary."

The Nineteenth Century

Rush's proposals attracted many followers, and petitions aiming to abolish all capital punishment were presented in New Jersey, New York, Massachusetts, and Ohio. No state reversed its laws, but the number of crimes punishable by death was often reduced.

The second quarter of the nineteenth century was a time of reform in the United States. Capital punishment opponents rode the tide of righteousness and indignation created by antisaloon and antislavery advocates. Abolitionist societies (organizations against the death penalty) sprang up, especially along the east coast. In 1845 the American Society for the Abolition of Capital Punishment was founded.

EARLY SUCCESSES FOR DEATH PENALTY OPPONENTS. The leaders of the anti-death penalty movement first strove to put an end to public executions. They largely succeeded; in 1828 the state of New York passed a law allowing county sheriffs to hold executions in private. The law, however, was not mandatory, and no sheriff took advantage of it. In 1835 the New York legislature passed another law requiring that all executions be held within the prison walls. The law further required that twelve citizens be chosen to witness the hanging and report on the execution through the state newspaper. In 1830 Connecticut became the first state to pass a law prohibiting all public executions. The Pennsylvania, Rhode Island, New Jersey, and Massachusetts legislatures all followed suit. Maine outlawed public executions and put a temporary moratorium in place in 1835 after one public execution brought in ten thousand people, many of whom became violent after the execution and had to be restrained by the police.

In the late 1840s Horace Greeley (1811–1872), the founder and editor of the *New York Tribune* and a leading advocate of most abolitionist causes, led the crusade against the death penalty. In 1846 Michigan became the first state to abolish the death penalty for all crimes except treason (until 1963), making it the first English-speaking jurisdiction in the world to abolish the death penalty for common crimes. Common crimes, also called ordinary crimes, are crimes committed during peacetime.

Ordinary crimes that could lead to the death penalty include murder, rape, and, in some countries, robbery or embezzlement of large sums of money. In comparison, exceptional crimes are military crimes committed during exceptional times, mainly wartime. Examples are treason, spying, or desertion (leaving the armed services without permission). The Michigan law took effect on March 1, 1847. In 1852 and 1853 Rhode Island and Wisconsin, respectively, became the first two states to outlaw the death penalty for all crimes. Most states began limiting the number of capital crimes. Outside the South, murder and treason became the only acts punishable by death.

Opponents of the death penalty initially benefited from abolitionist sentiment, but as the Civil War (1861–1865) neared, concern about the death penalty was lost amid the growing antislavery movement. It was not until after the Civil War that Maine and Iowa abolished the death penalty. Almost immediately, however, their legislatures reversed themselves and reinstated the death penalty. In 1887 Maine again reversed itself and abolished capital punishment. It has remained an abolitionist state ever since. Colorado abolished capital punishment in 1897, a decision apparently against the will of many of its citizens. At least twice, Coloradans lynched convicted murderers. In response, the state restored the death penalty in 1901.

Meanwhile, the federal government, following considerable debate in Congress, reduced the number of federal crimes punishable by death to treason, murder, and rape. In no instance was capital punishment to be mandatory.

INTRODUCTION OF ELECTROCUTION AS A METHOD OF EXECUTION. Electricity had become widespread by the end of the nineteenth century. As a demonstration of how dangerous alternating current (AC) electricity could be, the Edison Company electrocuted animals in public demonstrations. The Edison Company, which manufactured direct current (DC) electrical systems, wanted to discredit Westinghouse Company, the manufacturer of AC electrical systems. However, instead of steering people away from AC systems, the effective demonstrations only served to inspire state executioners. New York became the first state to tear down its gallows and erect an electric chair in 1890. The chair was first used on William Kemmler in 1890. Other states soon followed.

THE ANTI-DEATH PENALTY MOVEMENT DECLINES

At the start of the twentieth century, death penalty abolitionists again benefited from American reformism as the Progressives (liberal reformers) worked to correct perceived problems in the U.S. legal system. Between 1907 and 1917 nine states (Arizona, Kansas, Minnesota, Missouri, North Dakota, Oregon, South Dakota, Tennessee, and Washington) and Puerto Rico, a U.S. territory, abolished capital punishment. However, the momentum

did not last. By 1921, of the nine states, just Minnesota and North Dakota remained abolitionist. The Prohibition Era (1920–1933), characterized by frequent disdain for law and order, almost destroyed the abolitionist movement, as many Americans began to believe that the death penalty was the only proper punishment for gangsters who committed murder.

The movement's complete collapse was prevented by the determined efforts of the famed Clarence Darrow (1857–1938), the "attorney for the damned"; Lewis E. Lawes (1883–1947), the abolitionist warden of Sing Sing Prison in New York; and the American League to Abolish Capital Punishment (founded in 1927). Nonetheless, of the sixteen states and jurisdictions that outlawed capital punishment between 1845 and 1917, only six—Maine, Michigan, Minnesota, North Dakota, Rhode Island, and Wisconsin—and Puerto Rico had no major death penalty statute at the beginning of the 1950s. Between 1917 and 1957 no state abolished the death penalty.

The abolitionist movement made a mild comeback in the mid-1950s, and the issue was discussed in several state legislatures. In 1957 the U.S. territories of Alaska and Hawaii abolished the death penalty. In the states, however, the movement's singular success in Delaware (1958) was reversed three years later (1961), a major disappointment for death penalty opponents.

Modest Gains in the 1960s

The abolitionists were able to recover during the civil rights movement of the 1960s. In 1963 Michigan, which in 1847 had abolished capital punishment for all crimes except treason, finally outlawed the death penalty for that crime as well. Oregon (1964), Iowa (1965), and West Virginia (1965) all abolished capital punishment, whereas many other states sharply reduced the number of crimes punishable by death.

RESOLVING THE CONSTITUTIONAL ISSUES

Until the mid-twentieth century there was legally no question that the death penalty was acceptable under the U.S. Constitution. In 1958, however, the U.S. Supreme Court opened up the death penalty for reinterpretation when it ruled in *Trop v. Dulles* (356 U.S. 86) that the language of the Eighth Amendment (which states that criminals cannot be subjected to a cruel and unusual punishment) held the "evolving standards of decency that mark the progress of a maturing society." Opponents of capital punishment believed the death penalty should be declared unconstitutional in light of the *Trop* decision (which did not specifically address capital punishment). The abolitionists claimed that society had evolved to a point where the death penalty was cruel and unusual by the established "standards of decency." As such, the death penalty violated the Eighth Amendment of the Constitution.

TABLE 1.2

Major U.S. Supreme Court decisions involving the death penalty, selected years 1972–2005

Case	Year decided	Decision	Major effect
Furman v. Georgia	1972	5 to 4	The death penalty as administered by states at the time was deemed cruel and unusual punishment in violation of the Eighth and Fourteenth Amendments
Gregg v. Georgia, Proffit v. Florida, Jurek v. Texas	1976	7 to 2	New death penalty statutes in Georgia, Florida, and Texas ruled constitutional
Woodson v. North Carolina	1976	5 to 4	Mandatory death sentences ruled unconstitutional
Coker v. Georgia	1977	5 to 4	The death penalty may not be imposed for raping an adult woman if the victim does not die
Godfrey v. Georgia	1980	6 to 3	State statutes must clearly define the circumstances that qualify a crime as a capital crime
Spaziano v. Florida	1984	5 to 3	Upheld as constitutional a judge's decision to impose a death sentence despite jury's recommendation of life in prison
Ford v. Wainwright	1986	5 to 4	Inflicting the death penalty on the insane ruled unconstitutional
Murray v. Giarratano	1989	5 to 4	Defendants under sentence of death do not have a constitutional right to counsel during postconviction proceedings
Ring v. Arizona	2002	7 to 2	Only juries, not judges, can determine the presence of aggravating circumstances that warrant a death sentence
Atkins v. Virginia	2002	6 to 3	Inflicting the death penalty on the mentally retarded ruled unconstitutional
Roper v. Simmons	2005	5 to 4	Death sentences imposed against minors (i.e., those less than 18 years of age when crime committed) ruled unconstitutional

SOURCE: Created by Kim Masters Evans for The Gale Group, 2007

In 1963 Justice Arthur J. Goldberg (1908–1990), joined by Justices William O. Douglas (1898–1980) and William J. Brennan (1906–1997), dissenting from a rape case in which the defendant had been sentenced to death (*Rudolph v. Alabama*, 375 U.S. 889), raised the question of the legality of the death penalty. The filing of many lawsuits in the late 1960s led to an implied moratorium (a temporary suspension) on executions until the Court could decide whether the death penalty was constitutional.

In 1972 the high court finally handed down a landmark decision in *Furman v. Georgia* (408 U.S. 238), when it ruled that the death penalty violated the Eighth and Fourteenth Amendments (the right to due process) because of the arbitrary nature with which the death penalty was administered across the United States. The Court also laid down some guidelines for states to follow, declaring that a punishment was cruel and unusual if it was too severe, arbitrary, or offended society's sense of justice.

Before the late 1960s U.S. death penalty laws varied considerably from state to state and from region to region. Few national standards existed on how a murder trial should be conducted or which types of crimes deserved the death penalty. Specifically, *Furman* brought into question the laws of Georgia and a number of other states that allowed juries complete discretion in delivering a sentence. In these states, juries could declare a person guilty of a capital crime and then assign any punishment ranging from less than a month in jail to the penalty of death. Even though verdicts were swift, the punishments such juries meted out were frequently arbitrary and at times discriminatory against minorities.

CREATING A UNIFORM DEATH PENALTY SYSTEM ACROSS THE UNITED STATES

Within a year of the Supreme Court's ruling in *Furman*, thirty-five states had updated their laws regarding the death penalty. Many of these new statutes were brought before the high court in the mid-1970s. By issuing rulings on the constitutionality of these state statutes, the Court created a uniform death penalty system for the United States. Table 1.2 provides a summary of the major cases decided by the Court dealing with the death penalty since 1972.

States amended their laws once again after the Supreme Court issued the new rulings. Every state switched to a bifurcated (two-part) trial system, where the first trial is used to determine a defendant's guilt, and the second trial determines the sentence of a guilty defendant. Generally, only those convicted of first-degree murder were eligible for the death penalty. Most states also required the jury or judge in the sentencing phase of the trial to identify one or more aggravating factors (circumstances that may increase responsibility for a crime) beyond a reasonable doubt before they could sentence a person to death. State legislatures drafted lists of aggravating factors that could result in a penalty of death. Typical aggravating factors included murders committed during robberies, the murder of a pregnant woman, murder committed after a rape, and the murder of an on-duty firefighter or police officer. In the mid-1970s the long appeals process for capital cases was also established.

THE END OF THE NATIONWIDE MORATORIUM

With the Supreme Court–approved laws in place, the states resumed executions. In January 1977 the nationwide moratorium ended when the state of Utah executed Gary Gilmore. Gilmore had been convicted of killing Ben Bushnell, a motel manager in Provo, Utah, on July 20, 1976. Authorities had also charged him with the July 19 murder of Max Jensen, a gas station attendant, in Orem, Utah. Gilmore received the death penalty for the Bushnell murder. He refused to appeal his case, demanding

FIGURE 1.2

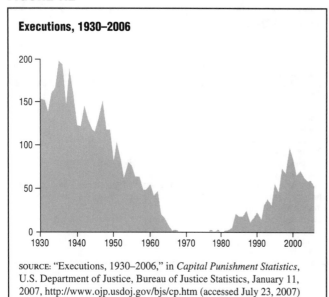

Executions, 1930–2006

SOURCE: "Executions, 1930–2006," in *Capital Punishment Statistics*, U.S. Department of Justice, Bureau of Justice Statistics, January 11, 2007, http://www.ojp.usdoj.gov/bjs/cp.htm (accessed July 23, 2007)

that his sentence be carried out swiftly. Gilmore requested the state supreme court to grant his wish because he did not want to spend his life on death row. The court granted his wish, but interventions by Gilmore's mother, as well as by anti-death penalty organizations, resulted in several stays (postponement) of execution. These organizations were concerned that the defendant's refusal to appeal his case and the court's agreement to carry out his wish might establish a precedent that would hurt the causes of other inmates. After several suicide attempts, Gilmore was finally executed by firing squad on January 17, 1977.

Several other states reinstated the death penalty after the Supreme Court declared it constitutional. Oregon brought back the death penalty in 1978. In 1995 New York became the thirty-eighth state to reinstate the death penalty, ending its eighteen-year ban on capital punishment.

After the nationwide moratorium ended in 1977, the number of executions began to rise. Executions hit the double digits in 1984, when twenty-one people were put to death in the United States, and peaked in 1999, when ninety-eight inmates were executed. (See Figure 1.2.) The number of criminals put to death then dipped to fifty-three in 2006—the lowest level in a decade. Overall, between 1976 and 2006, 1,057 people were put to death. Of course, these numbers were much smaller than the number of executions that occurred in the early part of the twentieth century. In 1938, for instance, 190 people were executed.

As shown in Figure 1.3, nearly five hundred people were on death row in 1977. The number climbed dramatically over the following decades, peaking at thirty-six hundred in 2000. It then began a downward trend, dropping to 3,250 in 2005. Figure 1.3 clearly shows the rarity

with which executions are carried out in the United States, compared to the large number of people under the sentence of death. Between 2000 and 2005 the United States executed an average of 68 people per year, whereas the number on death row averaged nearly 3,450 per year. This constitutes an execution rate of approximately 2% per year.

THE HOMICIDE RATE CONNECTION

The increase that began in the 1970s in the usage of capital punishment corresponded with rising homicide (murder) rates in the country. (See Figure 1.4.) According to data from the U.S. Department of Justice's Bureau of Justice Statistics, between 1964 and 1974 the homicide rate nearly doubled from 5.1 cases per 100,000 population to 10.1 cases per 100,000 population. In 1980 the rate peaked at its highest level in recorded history: 10.7 homicides per 100,000 population. After falling slightly in the early 1980s it surged again, reaching its penultimate (second-highest) level in 1991, when 10.5 homicides occurred for every 100,000 people. Since that time the rate has steadily declined. By 2000 it was 6.1 per 100,000 population.

The country also experienced a surge of homicides in the early 1930s, during the Prohibition Era. As mentioned earlier, this was a time when support for the death penalty strengthened around the country. As shown in Figure 1.2, the execution rate was historically high at that time—approximately 167 executions per year.

Figure 1.5 compares the homicide rate and the number of executions conducted each year between 1960 and 2005. The number of executions increased dramatically between 1980 and 2000, apparently a response to the unusually high homicide rates that persisted through the early 1990s. Both values began to drop after the turn of the twenty-first century and evened out in the early 2000s.

NEW RULES IN THE MODERN DEATH PENALTY ERA

Supreme Court decisions continued to redefine state death penalty laws well after the *Furman* opinion. In *Ford v. Wainwright* (477 U.S. 399, 1986), the Court ruled that executing an insane person constituted a cruel and unusual punishment and was thus in violation of the Eighth Amendment. Because a precedent did not exist in U.S. legal history about executing the insane, the justices looked to English common law to make this ruling. English law expressly forbade the execution of insane people. The English jurist Sir Edward Coke (1552–1634) observed that even though the execution of a criminal was to serve as an example, the execution of a madman was considered "of extreme inhumanity and cruelty, and can be no example to others."

FIGURE 1.3

Prisoners under sentence of death and executions, 1973–2005

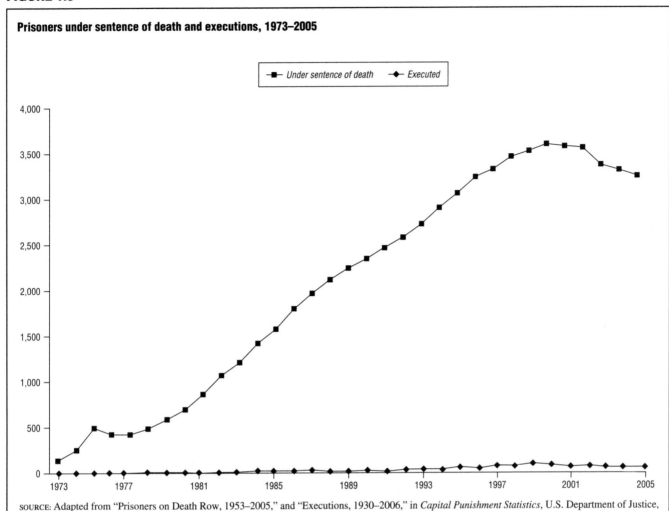

SOURCE: Adapted from "Prisoners on Death Row, 1953–2005," and "Executions, 1930–2006," in *Capital Punishment Statistics*, U.S. Department of Justice, Bureau of Justice Statistics, January 11, 2007, http://www.ojp.usdoj.gov/bjs/cp.htm (accessed July 23, 2007)

FIGURE 1.4

Homicide rate, 1900–2002

[Rate per 100,000 population]

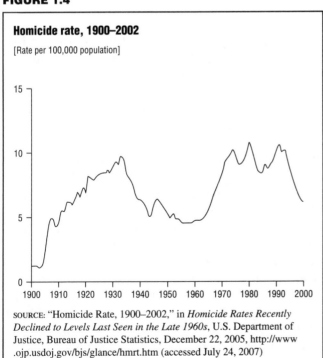

SOURCE: "Homicide Rate, 1900–2002," in *Homicide Rates Recently Declined to Levels Last Seen in the Late 1960s*, U.S. Department of Justice, Bureau of Justice Statistics, December 22, 2005, http://www.ojp.usdoj.gov/bjs/glance/hmrt.htm (accessed July 24, 2007)

In *Atkins v. Virginia* (536 U.S. 304, 2002), the Court held that executing mentally retarded people violates the Eighth Amendment's ban on a cruel and unusual punishment. The Court, however, did not define mental retardation but left it to each state to formulate its own definition. In *Roper v. Simmons* (543 U.S. 633, 2005), the Court decided that executing Donald Roper was cruel and unusual based on the fact that Roper was younger than eighteen when he committed murder. The majority reasoned that adolescents do not have the emotional maturity or understanding of lasting consequences that adults have and therefore should not be held to an adult standard or punished with a sentence of death.

In 1996 Congress passed and President Bill Clinton (1946–) signed the Antiterrorism and Effective Death Penalty Act (AEDPA). The law applied new restrictions and filing deadlines regarding appeals by death row inmates. In 2000 state court interpretations of the AEDPA were examined by the Supreme Court, which ruled that the law is valid unless lower courts upheld rulings contradictory to precedents established by the Court.

FIGURE 1.5

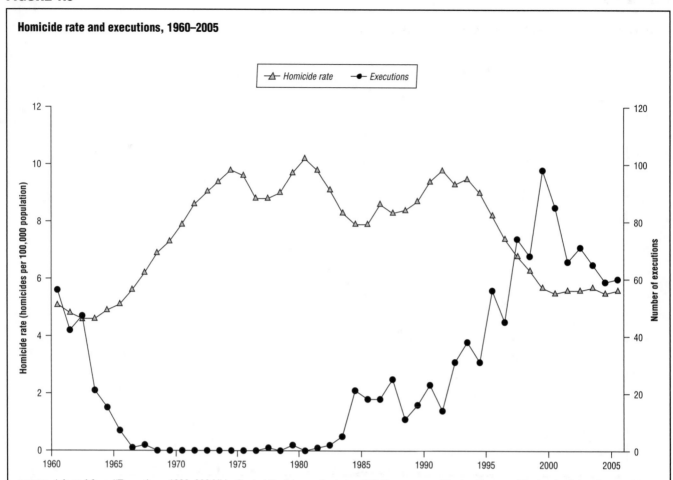

Homicide rate and executions, 1960–2005

SOURCE: Adapted from "Executions, 1930–2006," in *Capital Punishment Statistics*, U.S. Department of Justice, Bureau of Justice Statistics, January 11, 2007, http://www.ojp.usdoj.gov/bjs/cp.htm (accessed July 23, 2007) and James Alan Fox and Marianne W. Zawitz, "Homicide Victimization, 1950–2005," in *Homicide Trends in the United States*, U.S. Department of Justice, Bureau of Justice Statistics, January 17, 2007, http://www.ojp.usdoj .gov/bjs/pub/pdf/htius.pdf (accessed August 24, 2007)

DNA TAKES THE STAND

In the 1980s and 1990s deoxyribonucleic acid (DNA) testing procedures advanced to the point where such evidence could be used in criminal cases. Across the United States, police suddenly had the ability to identify a suspect and place him or her squarely at the scene of a crime with a small sample of hair, blood, or other biological material. Because of the accuracy of DNA testing, DNA evidence could hold as much sway in a courtroom as an eyewitness or camera footage. States started collecting biological samples, such as blood and saliva, from criminal offenders and storing these DNA profiles in databases.

In 1994 Virginia became the first state to execute a person who was convicted as a result of DNA evidence. The defendant, Timothy Spencer, was convicted in 1988 for several rapes and murders he committed starting in 1984. Virginia also became the first state to execute someone based on a DNA "cold hit" when it executed James Earl Patterson in March 2002. (A cold hit is when DNA

evidence collected at a crime scene matches a DNA sample already in a database.) In 1999 Patterson was in prison on a rape conviction when DNA from the 1987 rape and murder of Joyce Aldridge was found to match his DNA in the database. He confessed to the Aldridge crime in 2000 and was sentenced to death. Patterson waived his appeals to let his execution proceed as scheduled.

First Death Row Inmate Is Freed by DNA Testing

Not only has DNA evidence been useful in convicting felons but also it has been crucial in proving the innocence of falsely convicted criminals. Kirk Bloodsworth of Maryland was the nation's first death row inmate to be exonerated based on postconviction DNA testing. Bloodsworth was convicted for the rape and murder of a nine-year-old girl in 1984. He was sentenced to death in 1985. On retrial, Bloodsworth received two life terms. DNA testing in 1992 excluded him from the crime. In 1993 Bloodsworth was released from prison. In 1999 the state paid Bloodsworth $300,000 for wrongful conviction and imprisonment, including time on death row.

State and Federal Legislatures Enact Laws to Expand DNA Testing

The Innocence Protection Act of 2004 became law on October 30, 2004. The law laid down the conditions with which a federal prisoner who pleaded not guilty could receive postconviction DNA testing. If a trial defendant faced conviction, the act called for the preservation of the defendant's biological evidence. A five-year, $25 million grant program was also established to help eligible states pay for postconviction testing.

Many state legislatures have passed similar DNA testing legislation. The American Society of Law, Medicine, and Ethics (2006, http://www.aslme.org/dna_04/grid/index.php) maintains databases that list the relevant statutes and testing protocols on a state-by-state basis.

CAPITAL PUNISHMENT RECONSIDERED

During the 1980s and early 1990s public opinion polls showed strong support for capital punishment. According to the Gallup Corporation (2006, http://www.gallup.com/poll/1606/Death-Penalty.aspx), this support reached its highest level in 1994 when 80% of Americans favored use of the death penalty for murderers.

During the mid-1990s support for capital punishment began to wane for a variety of reasons. The advent of DNA testing resulted in highly publicized cases of inmates being released from prison, and even from death row. Abolitionists seized on these opportunities as proof that the U.S. capital punishment system was flawed. In addition, studies were released indicating that racial biases were occurring in death penalty cases and raising questions about the fairness of the system. By the turn of the twenty-first century capital punishment had been abolished in Canada and nearly all of Europe, leading to intense criticism in the international press of the United States' reliance on the death penalty. Pope John Paul II (1920–2005) also condemned capital punishment. Two popular movies—*Dead Man Walking* (1995) and *The Green Mile* (1999)—raised questions about the morality of the death penalty.

Two particular death penalty cases also aroused passion about the morality of capital punishment. Karla Faye Tucker became a born-again Christian while on death row in Texas for the brutal 1984 slayings of two people. In the months leading up to her execution in 1998, she received widespread media attention and garnered support nationally and internationally for commutation of her sentence to life in prison. Her supporters included some unlikely allies: a handful of conservative-minded religious and political figures who believed that Tucker's religious conversion merited clemency (an act of leniency by a convening authority to reduce a sentence). Nevertheless, the Texas governor George W. Bush (1946–) signed her death warrant. In 2005 the execution of Stanley "Tookie" Williams also garnered considerable public attention.

Williams received a death sentence for killing three people in 1981. At the time, he was a leading figure in the notorious and violent Crips gang in Los Angeles. During his decades on death row Williams became an outspoken critic of gangs and wrote books encouraging children to avoid gangs and violence. For his work he received nominations for the Nobel Peace Prize. His supporters included Hollywood celebrities who lobbied the California governor Arnold Schwarzenegger (1947–) for clemency, arguing that Williams had redeemed himself while in prison. The governor refused, noting that Williams had never expressed remorse for his crimes.

FEDERAL DEATH PENALTY

In modern times, capital punishment has generally fallen under the states' purview. Each year, the federal government pursues the death penalty in far fewer cases than most states with death penalty statutes. The reason for this is simple: most crimes are state crimes. Generally speaking, the federal government is only involved in prosecuting a relatively small number of crimes; crimes that cross state boundaries, are committed on federal property, or that affect federal officials or the working of the federal government. The federal government, however, has been executing criminals since it was formed. In 1790 Thomas Bird became the first inmate executed under the federal death penalty. He was hanged in Maine for murder. The Death Penalty Information Center (DPIC) states in "The Federal Death Penalty" (2007, http://www.deathpenaltyinfo.org/article.php?did=147&scid=) that between 1790 and 1963 the federal government put to death 336 men and 4 women. However, most of these executions took place early in U.S. history. Only thirty-four men and two women were executed between 1927 and 1963. On February 15, 1963, Victor Feguer was hanged in Iowa for kidnapping and murder. This was the last execution by the federal government until nearly forty years later.

Expansion of the Federal Death Penalty

In 1988 Congress enacted the first of several laws that broadened the scope of the federal death penalty. The Anti-Drug Abuse Act included a drug-kingpin provision, allowing the death penalty for murder resulting from large-scale illegal drug dealing. The act did not provide for the method of federal execution. In 1993 President George H. W. Bush (1924–) authorized the use of lethal injection under this law. As of June 30, 2005, three inmates were under sentence of death pursuant to this law.

In 1994 the Violent Crime Control and Law Enforcement Act (also known as the Federal Death Penalty Act) added more than fifty crimes punishable by death. Among these federal crimes are murder of certain government officials, kidnapping resulting in death, murder for hire, fatal drive-by shootings, sexual abuse crimes resulting in death, carjacking resulting in death, and other crimes not resulting in death, such as running a large-scale drug enterprise. The method of execution will be the same as that used in the state where the sentencing occurs. If the state does not allow the death penalty, the judge will choose a state with the death penalty.

Antiterrorism legislation came about in the wake of the Oklahoma City bombing in 1995 and the September 11, 2001, terrorist attacks. In 1996 Congress passed the AEDPA. The act, signed into law on April 24, 1996, just after the first anniversary of the Oklahoma City bombing by Timothy McVeigh (1968–2001), was intended "to deter terrorism, provide justice for victims, [and] provide for an effective death penalty." Another capital crime was added on June 25, 2002, as part of the Terrorist Bombings Convention Implementation Act of 2002. The law makes punishable by death the bombing of places of public use, government facilities, public transportation systems, and infrastructure facilities with the intent to cause death or serious physical injury or with intent to cause destruction resulting in major economic loss. The USA Patriot Act of 2001 and the USA Patriot Act Improvement and Reauthorization Act of 2005 expanded the list of terrorist acts deemed federal crimes that could be subject to the death penalty.

New Laws Lead to an Increase in Federal Capital Cases

In 1992 the Administrative Office of the United States Court established the Federal Death Penalty Resource Counsel Project (FDPRCP) to serve as a clearinghouse for information helpful to defense attorneys appointed in federal death penalty cases. According to Dick Burr, David Bruck, and Kevin McNally of the FDPRCP, in "An Overview of the Federal Death Penalty Process" (June 28, 2006, http://www.capdefnet.org/fdprc/contents/shared_files/docs/1_overview_of_fed_death_process.asp), between 1988, when the Anti-Drug Abuse Act was signed into law, to June 28, 2006, the U.S. attorney general authorized the government to seek the death penalty in 382 cases. One hundred ninety-two of the defendants were tried, of which three were executed. In 2006 sixty-two inmates were on trial or awaiting trial, and forty-four convicts were on death row in the federal penal system.

Federal Government Resumes Executions

McVeigh was sentenced to death for conspiracy and murder in 1997 for his bombing of the Alfred P. Murrah Federal Building in Oklahoma City, Oklahoma, on April 19, 1995, which killed 168 people. McVeigh received an execution date of May 16, 2001. The U.S. attorney general John D. Ashcroft (1942–), however, delayed the execution following the discovery that the Federal Bureau of Investigation (FBI) had failed to turn over more than three thousand documents to the defense and prosecution during the trial. McVeigh appealed for a second stay of execution, but the U.S. Court of Appeals for the Tenth Circuit denied his request, affirming a U.S. District Court's ruling that

there was no evidence that the federal government intentionally hid the FBI files from the defense. On June 11, 2001, the execution was carried out.

Eight days later, on June 19, 2001, the Texas drug boss Juan Raul Garza became the second federal prisoner to be executed since 1963. He was the first person to be executed under the Anti-Drug Abuse Act of 1988 for murders resulting from a drug enterprise. Garza received the death sentence in 1993 for the 1990 murders of three associates.

Garza was initially scheduled to be executed in August 2000. In July 2000 President Clinton granted a four-month reprieve (a stay of execution for a short time to resolve an issue) to allow the Department of Justice to establish clemency guidelines by which a death row inmate could plead for his or her life after exhausting all appeals. Some critics noted that the Clinton administration, which had been running the government for seven years, should have previously taken the time to put in place a clemency protocol for capital cases. Others claimed the government could have applied to capital cases the clemency guidelines that it uses for noncapital cases. It should be noted that, even with no formal guidelines in place, Garza could have pleaded for clemency.

On September 13, 2000, Garza asked President Clinton to commute his death sentence to life imprisonment without parole. Garza's lawyer argued that the Department of Justice study of the federal death penalty system, released the day before, showed the federal capital punishment is "plagued by systemic bias, disparity and arbitrariness." The defense counsel claimed that it would be unfair to put Garza to death because the federal death penalty discriminates against members of minorities and is administered unevenly geographically. (Of the eighteen men on federal death row at that time, sixteen were minorities, and six had been convicted in Texas.) Again, the president delayed the execution, this time to December 12, 2000. It took another six months for the U.S. government to carry out Garza's death penalty. The newly elected president George W. Bush, formerly the governor of Texas, refused to stay the execution, and Garza was executed June 19, 2001.

Louis Jones Jr., a retired soldier, was executed by the U.S. government on March 18, 2003. In 1995 Jones was convicted of killing a female soldier. He admitted kidnapping Tracie Joy McBride from an air force base in Texas. The federal government prosecuted Jones because his crime originally occurred at a U.S. military facility. As of November 2007, Jones was the last person to have been executed by the federal government.

THE U.S. MILITARY

The U.S. military has its own death penalty law: the Uniform Code of Military Justice (UCMJ) found under

U.S. Code, Title 10, Chapter 47. Lethal injection is the method of execution. For crimes that occurred on or after November 17, 1997, the UCMJ provides the alternative sentence of life without the possibility of parole. As commander in chief, the president of the United States can write regulations and procedures to implement the UCMJ provisions. The military needs the president's approval to implement a death sentence.

The first U.S. soldier to be executed since the Civil War was U.S. Army private Edward Slovik. In 1944 he was charged with desertion while assigned to the European theater during World War II (1939–1945). Even though Slovik was just one of hundreds of U.S. soldiers who were convicted of desertion and sentenced to death, he was the only one executed. It is believed that, among other reasons, the military wanted to use his case as a deterrent to future desertions. Slovik died by firing squad on January 31, 1945, in France. Since then no other soldier has been executed for desertion. The last military execution occurred on April 13, 1961, when U.S. Army private John A. Bennett was hanged for the 1955 rape and murder of an eleven-year-old girl.

In February 2006 the military officially recommended to the president that the death penalty be carried out against two prisoners: Ronald Gray and Dwight Loving. Gray was convicted in 1988 of rape, sodomy, and multiple murders committed while he was stationed at Fort Bragg in North Carolina. Loving was convicted in 1989 for murdering two taxi drivers while he was stationed at Fort Hood in Texas. As of November 2007, President Bush had not acted on the recommendations and was under no legal time limit to do so. According to the DPIC, in "The U.S. Military Death Penalty" (January 1, 2007, http://www.deathpenaltyinfo.org/article.php?did=180&), there were nine men on military death row in 2007: six African-Americans, two white, and one Asian. All were convicted of premeditated murder or felony murder (murder that occurs during the commission of another serious crime, such as arson). The military's death row is located at the U.S. Disciplinary Barracks at Fort Leavenworth, Kansas.

In July 2007 federal prosecutors announced their intention to seek the death penalty against a former soldier accused of committing atrocities against civilians in Iraq. Steven Green (1985–) and four of his comrades were charged in connection with the rape and murder of a teenage girl and the murder of three of her family members. Green, the alleged ringleader of the group, was the only one of the five defendants to face the death penalty. As of November 2007, the other four soldiers had been convicted in military court and sentenced to prison terms. Green's case was brought in federal (not military) court, because he had already been discharged from the army when he was arrested in 2006.

WORLDWIDE TREND

The de facto moratorium on the death penalty in the United States from 1967 to 1976 paralleled a general worldwide movement, especially among Western nations, toward the abolition of capital punishment. Even though the United States resumed executions in 1977, most of the Western world either formally or informally abolished capital punishment.

As of 2007, among the Western democratic nations (with which the United States traditionally compares itself), only the United States imposes the death penalty. There are technical exceptions: for example, Israel maintains the death penalty in its statute books for "crimes against mankind" but has executed only Adolf Eichmann (1906–1962). As a Schutzstaffel officer, Eichmann was responsible for the murder of millions of Jews in Nazi-occupied Europe during World War II. Some countries still maintain the death penalty for treason—although no Western democracy has actually imposed it. One of the first acts of the parliaments of many of the east European countries after the fall of communism was to abolish capital punishment.

According to Amnesty International (AI), in "Facts and Figures on the Death Penalty" (http://web.amnesty.org/pages/deathpenalty-facts-eng), as of October 2, 2007, sixty-four countries and territories around the world continued to maintain and use the death penalty for ordinary crimes (crimes committed during peacetime). However, some of these countries had not actually implemented a death sentence for many years. The AI reports that there were at least 1,591 executions carried out in twenty-five countries in 2006. The vast majority (1,010) were in China. China, Iran, Pakistan, Iraq, Sudan, and the United States accounted for 91% of all known executions. The AI estimates that more than twenty thousand prisoners worldwide were under the sentence of death at the end of 2006.

SUPREME COURT RULINGS: CONSTITUTIONALITY OF THE DEATH PENALTY, GUIDELINES FOR JUDGES AND JURIES, JURY SELECTION, AND SENTENCING PROCEDURES

In 1967 a coalition of anti-death penalty groups sued Florida and California, the states with the most inmates on death row at that time, challenging the constitutionality of state capital punishment laws. An unofficial moratorium (temporary suspension) of executions resulted, pending U.S. Supreme Court decisions on several cases on appeal. The defendants in these cases claimed that the death penalty is a cruel and unusual punishment in violation of the Eighth Amendment to the U.S. Constitution. Moreover, they alleged that the death penalty also violated the Fourteenth Amendment, which prevents states from denying anyone equal protection of the laws. This moratorium lasted until January 17, 1977, when convicted murderer Gary Gilmore, virtually at his own request, was executed by the state of Utah.

IS THE DEATH PENALTY CONSTITUTIONAL?

On June 29, 1972, a split 5–4 Supreme Court reached a landmark decision in *Furman v. Georgia* (408 U.S. 238, which included *Jackson v. Georgia* and *Branch v. Texas*), holding that "as the statutes before us are now administered.... [The] imposition and carrying out of death penalty in these cases held to constitute a cruel and unusual punishment in violation of Eighth and Fourteenth Amendments." In other words, the justices did not address whether capital punishment as a whole is unconstitutional. Rather, they considered capital punishment in the context of its application in state statutes (laws created by state legislatures). The justices, whether they were of the majority opinion or of the dissenting opinion, could not agree on the arguments explaining why they opposed or supported the death penalty. As a result, the decision consisted of nine separate opinions, the lengthiest ruling in Court history to date.

Majority Opinions in *Furman*

Justice William O. Douglas (1898–1980), in his concurring majority opinion, quoted the former U.S. attorney general Ramsey Clark's (1927–) observation in his book *Crime in America: Observations on Its Nature, Causes, Prevention, and Control* (1970): "It is the poor, the sick, the ignorant, the powerless, and the hated who are executed." Douglas added, "We deal with a system of law and of justice that leaves to the uncontrolled discretion of judges or juries the determination whether defendants committing these crimes should die or be imprisoned. Under these laws no standards govern the selection of the penalty. People live or die, dependent on the whim of one man or of 12.... Thus, these discretionary statutes are unconstitutional in their operation. They are pregnant with discrimination and discrimination is an ingredient not compatible with the idea of equal protection of the laws that is implicit in the ban on 'cruel and unusual' punishments."

Justice William J. Brennan (1906–1997) stated, "At bottom, then, the Cruel and Unusual Punishments Clause prohibits the infliction of uncivilized and inhuman punishments. The State, even as it punishes, must treat its members with respect for their intrinsic worth as human beings. A punishment is 'cruel and unusual,' therefore, if it does not comport with human dignity."

Justice Potter J. Stewart (1915–1985) stressed another point, saying, "These death sentences are cruel and unusual in the same way that being struck by lightning is cruel and unusual. For, of all the people convicted of rapes and murders in 1967 and 1968, many just as reprehensible as these, the petitioners are among a capriciously selected random handful upon whom the sentence of death has in fact been imposed."

This did not mean that Justice Stewart would rule out the death penalty. He believed that the death penalty was justified, but he wanted to see a more equitable system of determining who should be executed. He explained, "I cannot agree that retribution is a constitutionally impermissible ingredient in the imposition of punishment. The instinct for retribution is part of the nature of man, and channeling that instinct in the administration of criminal justice serves an important purpose in promoting the stability of a society governed by law. When people begin to believe that organized society is unwilling or unable to impose upon criminal offenders the punishment they 'deserve,' then there are sown the seeds of anarchy—of self-help, vigilante justice, and lynch law."

Justice Byron R. White (1917–2002), believing that the death penalty was so seldom imposed that executions were ineffective deterrents to crime, chose instead to address the role of juries and judges in imposing the death penalty. He concluded that the cases before the courts violated the Eighth Amendment because the state legislatures, having authorized the application of the death penalty, left it to the discretion of juries and judges whether or not to impose the punishment.

Justice Thurgood Marshall (1908–1993) thought that "the death penalty is an excessive and unnecessary punishment that violates the Eighth Amendment." He added that "even if capital punishment is not excessive, it nonetheless violates the Eighth Amendment because it is morally unacceptable to the people of the United States at this time in their history." Justice Marshall also noted that the death penalty was applied with discrimination against certain classes of people (the poor, the uneducated, and members of minority groups) and that innocent people had been executed before they could prove their innocence. He also believed that it hindered the reform of the treatment of criminals and that it promoted sensationalism during trials.

Dissenting Opinions

Chief Justice Warren Burger (1907–1995), disagreeing with the majority, observed that "the constitutional prohibition against 'cruel and unusual punishments' cannot be construed to bar the imposition of the punishment of death." Justice Harry A. Blackmun (1908–1999) was disturbed by Justices Stewart's and White's remarks that as long as capital punishment was mandated for specific crimes, it could not be considered unconstitutional. He feared "that statutes struck down today will be re-enacted by state legislatures to prescribe the death penalty for specified crimes without any alternative for the imposition of a lesser punishment in the discretion of the judge or jury, as the case may be."

Justice Lewis F. Powell Jr. (1907–1998) declared, "I find no support—in the language of the Constitution, in its history, or in the cases arising under it—for the view that this Court may invalidate a category of penalties because we deem less severe penalties adequate to serve the ends of penology.... This Court has long held that legislative decisions in this area, which lie within the special competency of that branch, are entitled to a presumption of validity."

In other words, the Court would not question the validity of a government entity properly doing its job unless its actions were way out of line.

Justice William H. Rehnquist (1924–2005) agreed with Justice Powell, adding, "How can government by the elected representatives of the people co-exist with the power of the federal judiciary, whose members are constitutionally insulated from responsiveness to the popular will, to declare invalid laws duly enacted by the popular branches of government?"

Summary of Court Decision

Only Justices Brennan and Marshall concluded that the Eighth Amendment prohibited the death penalty for all crimes and under all circumstances. Justice Douglas, while ruling that the death penalty statutes reviewed by the high court were unconstitutional, did not necessarily require the final abolition of the death penalty. Justices Stewart and White also did not rule on the validity of the death penalty, noting instead that, because of the capricious imposition of the sentence, the death penalty violated the Eighth Amendment. However, Justices Rehnquist, Burger, Powell, and Blackmun concluded that the Constitution allows capital punishment.

Consequently, most state legislatures went to work to revise their capital punishment laws. They strove to make these laws more equitable to swing the votes of Stewart and White (and later that of John Paul Stevens [1920–], who replaced the retired Justice Douglas).

PROPER IMPOSITION OF THE DEATH PENALTY

Four years later, on July 2, 1976, the Supreme Court ruled decisively on a series of cases. In *Gregg v. Georgia* (428 U.S. 153), perhaps the most significant of these cases, the justices concluded 7–2 that the death penalty was, indeed, constitutional as presented in some new state laws. With Justices Brennan and Marshall dissenting, the Court stressed (just in case *Furman* had been misunderstood) that "the death penalty is not a form of punishment that may never be imposed, regardless of the circumstances of the offense, regardless of the character of the offender, and regardless of the procedure followed in reaching the decision to impose it." Furthermore, "the infliction of death as a punishment for murder is not without justification and thus is not unconstitutionally severe."

The Court upheld death penalty statutes in Georgia (*Gregg v. Georgia*), Florida (*Proffitt v. Florida*, 428 U.S. 242, 1976), and Texas (*Jurek v. Texas*, 428 U.S. 262, 1976), but struck down laws in North Carolina (*Woodson v. North Carolina*, 428 U.S. 280, 1976) and Louisiana (*Roberts v. Louisiana*, 428 U.S. 40, 1976). It ruled that laws in the latter two states were too rigid in imposing mandatory death sentences for certain types of murder.

Citing the new Georgia laws in *Gregg*, Justice Stewart supported the bifurcated (two-part) trial system, in which the accused is first tried to determine his or her guilt. Then, in a separate trial, the jury considers whether the convicted person deserves the death penalty or whether mitigating factors (circumstances that may lessen or increase responsibility for a crime) warrant a lesser sentence, usually life imprisonment. This system meets the requirements demanded by *Furman*. Noting how the Georgia statutes fulfilled these demands, Justice Stewart observed:

> These procedures require the jury to consider the circumstances of the crime and the criminal before it recommends sentence. No longer can a Georgia jury do as Furman's jury did: reach a finding of the defendant's guilt and then, without guidance or direction, decide whether he should live or die. Instead, the jury's attention is directed to the specific circumstances of the crime: Was it committed in the course of another capital felony? Was it committed for money? Was it committed upon a peace officer or judicial officer? Was it committed in a particularly heinous way or in a manner that endangered the lives of many persons? In addition, the jury's attention is focused on the characteristics of the person who committed the crime: Does he have a record of prior convictions for capital offenses? Are there any special facts about this defendant that mitigate against imposing capital punishment (e.g., his youth, the extent of his cooperation with the police, his emotional state at the time of the crime). As a result, while some jury discretion still exists, "the discretion to be exercised is controlled by clear and objective standards so as to produce non-discriminatory application."

In addition, the Georgia law required that all death sentences be automatically appealed to the state supreme court, an "important additional safeguard against arbitrariness and caprice." The bifurcated trial system has since been adopted in the trials of all capital murder cases.

In *Proffitt v. Florida*, the high court upheld Florida's death penalty laws that had a bifurcated trial system similar to Georgia's. In Florida, however, the sentence was determined by the trial judge rather than by the jury, who assumed an advisory role during the sentencing phase. The Court found Florida's sentencing guidelines adequate in preventing unfair imposition of the death sentence.

Predictability of Future Criminal Activity

In *Jurek v. Texas*, the issue centered on whether a jury can satisfactorily determine the future actions of a convicted murderer. The Texas statute required that during the sentencing phase of a trial, after the defendant had been found guilty, the jury would determine whether it is probable the defendant would commit future criminal acts of violence that would threaten society. Even though agreeing with Jurek's attorneys that predicting future behavior is not easy, Justice Stewart noted:

The fact that such a determination is difficult, however, does not mean that it cannot be made. Indeed, prediction of future criminal conduct is an essential element in many of the decisions rendered throughout our criminal justice system. The decision whether to admit a defendant to bail, for instance, must often turn on a judge's prediction of the defendant's future conduct. And any sentencing authority must predict a convicted person's probable future conduct when it engages in the process of determining what punishment to impose. For those sentenced to prison, these same predictions must be made by parole authorities. The task that a Texas jury must perform in answering the statutory question in issue is thus basically no different from the task performed countless times each day throughout the American system of criminal justice.

Flexible Guidelines for Judges and Jurors Are Required

In *Woodson v. North Carolina*, the Supreme Court addressed for the first time the question of whether the jury's handing down of a death sentence under North Carolina's mandatory death penalty for all first-degree murders constituted a cruel and unusual punishment within the meaning of the Eighth and Fourteenth Amendments. If a person was convicted of first-degree murder in North Carolina, he or she was automatically sentenced to death. The justices held that as a whole the American public rejected the idea of mandatory death sentences long ago. In addition, North Carolina's new statute provided "no standards to guide the jury in its inevitable exercise of the power to determine which first-degree murderers shall live and which shall die." Furthermore, the North Carolina law did not let the jury consider the convicted defendant's character, criminal record, or the circumstances of the crime before the imposition of the death sentence.

The Louisiana mandatory death sentence for first-degree murder suffered from similar inadequacies. It did, however, permit the jury to consider lesser offenses such as second-degree murder. In *Roberts v. Louisiana*, the Supreme Court rejected the Louisiana law because it forced the jury to find the defendant guilty of a lesser crime to avoid imposing the death penalty. In other words, if the crime was not heinous enough to warrant the death penalty, then the jury was forced to convict the defendant of second-degree murder or a lesser charge. The jury did not have the option of first determining if the accused was indeed guilty of first-degree murder for the crime he or she had actually committed and then recommending a lesser sentence if there were mitigating circumstances to support it.

As a result of either *Furman* or *Gregg* or both, virtually every state's capital punishment statute had to be rewritten. These statutes would provide flexible guidelines for judges and juries so that they might fairly decide capital cases and consider, then impose, if necessary, the death penalty.

JURY MAY CONSIDER A LESSER CHARGE

In 1977 Gilbert Beck was convicted of robbing and murdering eighty-year-old Roy Malone. According to Beck, he and an accomplice entered Malone's home and were tying up the victim to rob him when Beck's accomplice unexpectedly struck and killed Malone. Beck admitted to the robbery but claimed the murder was not part of the plan. Beck was tried under an Alabama statute for "robbery or attempts thereof when the victim is intentionally killed by the defendant."

Under Alabama law the judge was specifically prohibited from giving the jury the option of convicting the defendant of a lesser, included offense. Instead, the jury was given the choice of either convicting the defendant of the capital crime, in which case he possibly faced the death penalty, or acquitting him, thus allowing him to escape all penalties for his alleged participation in the crime. The judge could not have offered the jury the lesser alternative of felony murder, which did not deal with the accused's intentions at the time of the crime.

Beck appealed, claiming this law created a situation in which the jury was more likely to convict. The Supreme Court, in *Beck v. Alabama* (447 U.S. 625, 1980), agreed and reversed the lower court's ruling, thus vacating (annulling) his death sentence. The high court observed that, while not a matter of due process, it was virtually universally accepted in lesser offenses that a third alternative be offered. The Court noted, "That safeguard would seem to be especially important in a case such as this. For when the evidence unquestionably establishes that the defendant is guilty of a serious, violent offense—but leaves some doubt with respect to an element that would justify conviction of a capital offense—the failure to give the jury the 'third option' of convicting on a lesser included offense would seem inevitably to enhance the risk of an unwarranted conviction."

According to the ruling, such a risk could not be tolerated in a case where the defendant's life was at stake. *Beck*, however, did not require a jury to consider a lesser charge in every case, but only where the consideration would be justified.

EXCLUSION FROM JURIES OF THOSE AGAINST CAPITAL PUNISHMENT

In *Witherspoon v. Illinois* (391 U.S. 510, 1968), the Supreme Court held that a death sentence cannot be carried out if the jury that imposed or recommended such punishment was selected by excluding prospective jurors simply because they have qualms against the death penalty or reservations against its infliction. The Court found that the prosecution excluded those who opposed the death penalty without determining whether their beliefs would compel them to reject capital punishment out of hand. The defendant argued that this selective process

had resulted in a jury that was not representative of the community.

The justices could not definitively conclude that the exclusion of jurors opposed to the death penalty results in an unrepresentative jury. However, they believed that a person who opposes the death penalty can still abide by his or her duty as a juror and consider the facts presented at trial before making his or her decision about the defendant's punishment. The Court observed, "If the State had excluded only those prospective jurors who stated in advance of trial that they would not even consider returning a verdict of death, it could argue that the resulting jury was simply 'neutral' with respect to penalty. But when it swept from the jury all who expressed conscientious or religious scruples against capital punishment and all who opposed it in principle, the State crossed the line of neutrality. In its quest for a jury capable of imposing the death penalty, the State produced a jury uncommonly willing to condemn a man to die."

The Court specifically noted that its findings in *Witherspoon* did not prevent the infliction of the death sentence when the prospective jurors excluded had made it "unmistakably clear" that they would automatically vote against the death sentence without considering the evidence presented during the trial or that their attitudes toward capital punishment would keep them from making a fair decision about the defendant's guilt. Consequently, based on *Witherspoon*, it has become the practice in most states to exclude prospective jurors who indicate that they could not possibly in good conscience return a death penalty.

This ruling was reinforced in *Lockett v. Ohio* (438 U.S. 586, 1978). The defendant in Lockett contended, among several things, that the exclusion of four prospective jurors violated her Sixth Amendment right to trial by an impartial jury and Fourteenth Amendment rights under the principles established in *Witherspoon*. The Supreme Court upheld *Witherspoon* in this case because the prospective jurors told the prosecutor that they were so against the death penalty they could not be impartial about the case. They had also admitted that they would not take an oath saying they would consider the evidence before making a judgment of innocence or guilt.

A Special Selection Process Is Not Required When Selecting Jurors in Capital Cases

In *Wainwright v. Witt* (469 U.S. 412, 1985), a 7–2 Supreme Court decision eased the strict requirements of *Witherspoon*. Writing for the majority, Justice Rehnquist declared that the new capital punishment procedures left less discretion to jurors. Rehnquist indicated that potential jurors in capital cases should be excluded from jury duty in a manner similar to how they were excluded in noncapital cases. (In a noncapital case, the prospective jurors typically go through a selection process in which the prosecution and the defense question them about their attitudes toward the crime and the people and issues related to it to determine if they are too biased to be fair.)

No longer would a juror's "automatic" bias against imposing the death penalty have to be proved with "unmistakable clarity." A prosecutor could not be expected to ask all the questions necessary to determine if a juror would automatically rule against the death penalty or fail to convict a defendant if he or she were likely to face execution. Fundamentally, the question of exclusion from a jury should be determined by the interplay of the prosecutor and the defense lawyer and by the decision of the judge based on his or her initial observations of the prospective juror. Judges can see firsthand whether prospective jurors' beliefs would bias their ability to impose the death penalty.

In his dissent, Justice Brennan claimed that making it easier to eliminate those who opposed capital punishment from the jury created a jury not only more likely to impose the death sentence but also more likely to convict. He also attacked the majority interpretation that now treated exclusion from a capital case as being similar to exclusion from any other case.

It Does Not Matter If "Death-Qualified" Juries Are More Likely to Convict

In *Lockhart v. McCree* (476 U.S. 162, 1986), the Supreme Court firmly resolved the issue presented in *Witherspoon* regarding a fair trial with a death-qualified jury. (A death-qualified jury is another name for a jury that is willing to sentence a person to death after hearing the evidence of the case.)

Ardia McCree was convicted of murdering Evelyn Boughton while robbing her gift shop and service station in Camden, Arkansas, in February 1978. In accordance with Arkansas law, the trial judge removed eight prospective jurors because they indicated they could not, under any circumstances, vote for the imposition of the death sentence. The resulting jury then convicted McCree and, even though the state sought the death penalty, sentenced the defendant to life imprisonment without parole.

McCree appealed, claiming that the removal of the so-called *Witherspoon* excludables violated his right to a fair trial under the Sixth and Fourteenth Amendments. These amendments guaranteed that his innocence or guilt would be determined by an impartial jury selected from a representative cross-section of the community, which would include people strongly opposed to the death penalty. McCree cited several studies, revealing that death-qualified juries were more likely to convict. Both the federal district court and the federal court of appeals agreed with McCree, but in a 6–3 decision, the Supreme Court disagreed.

The high court majority did not accept the validity of the studies. Speaking for the majority, Justice Rehnquist

argued that, even if the justices did accept the validity of these studies, "the Constitution does not prohibit the States from 'death qualifying' juries in capital cases." Justice Rehnquist further observed:

> The exclusion from jury service of large groups of individuals not on the basis of their inability to serve as jurors, but on the basis of some immutable characteristic such as race, gender, or ethnic background, undeniably gave rise to an "appearance of unfairness."

> [Nevertheless], unlike blacks, women, and Mexican-Americans, "*Witherspoon*-excludables" are singled out for exclusion in capital cases on the basis of an attribute that is within the individual's control. It is important to remember that not all who oppose the death penalty are subject to removal for cause in capital cases; those who firmly believe that the death penalty is unjust may nevertheless serve as jurors in capital cases so long as they state clearly that they are willing to temporarily set aside their own beliefs in deference to the rule of law. Because the group of "*Witherspoon*-excludables" includes only those who cannot and will not conscientiously obey the law with respect to one of the issues in a capital case, "death qualification" hardly can be said to create an "appearance of unfairness."

Writing in dissent, Justice Marshall observed that if the high court thought in *Witherspoon* that excluding those who opposed the death penalty meant that a convicted murderer would not get a fair hearing during the sentencing part of the trial, it would also logically mean that he or she would not get a fair hearing during the initial trial part. The Court minority generally accepted the studies showing "that 'death qualification' in fact produces juries somewhat more 'conviction-prone' than 'non-death-qualified' juries."

DOES THE BUCK STOP WITH THE JURY?

During the course of a robbery Bobby Caldwell shot and killed the owner of a Mississippi grocery store in October 1980. He was tried and found guilty. During the sentencing phase of the trial Caldwell's attorney pleaded for mercy, concluding his summation by emphasizing to the jury, "I implore you to think deeply about this matter.... You are the judges and you will have to decide his fate. It is an awesome responsibility, I know—an awesome responsibility."

Responding to the defense attorney's plea, the prosecutor played down the responsibility of the jury, stressing that a life sentence would be reviewed by a higher court: "[The defense] would have you believe that you're going to kill this man and they know—they know that your decision is not the final decision.... Your job is reviewable.... They know, as I know, and as Judge Baker has told you, that the decision you render is automatically reviewable by the Supreme Court."

The jury sentenced Caldwell to death, and the case was automatically appealed. The Mississippi Supreme Court upheld the conviction, but split 4–4 on the validity of the death sentence, thereby upholding the death sentence by an equally divided court. Caldwell appealed to the Supreme Court.

In a 5–3 decision (Justice Powell took no part in the decision), the Supreme Court, in *Caldwell v. Mississippi* (472 U.S. 320, 1985), vacated (annulled) the death sentence. Writing for the majority, Justice Marshall noted, "It is constitutionally impermissible to rest a death sentence on a determination made by a sentencer who has been led to believe, as the jury was in this case, that the responsibility for determining the appropriateness of the defendant's death rests elsewhere.... [This Court] has taken as a given that capital sentencers would view their task as the serious one of determining whether a specific human being should die at the hands of the State."

Furthermore, the high court pointed out that the appeals court was not the place to make this life-or-death decision. Most appellate courts would presume that the sentencing was correctly done, which would leave the defendant at a distinct disadvantage. The jurors, expecting to be reversed by an appeals court, might choose to "send a message" of extreme disapproval of the defendant's acts and sentence him or her to death to show they will not tolerate such actions. Should the appeals court fail to reverse the decision, the defendant might be executed when the jury only intended to "send a message."

The three dissenting judges believed "the Court has overstated the seriousness of the prosecutor's comments" and that it was "highly unlikely that the jury's sense of responsibility was diminished."

KEEPING PAROLE INFORMATION FROM THE JURY

In 1990 Jonathan Dale Simmons beat an elderly woman to death in her home in Columbia, South Carolina. The week before his capital murder trial began, he pleaded guilty to first-degree burglary and two counts of criminal sexual conduct in connection with two prior assaults on elderly women. These guilty pleas resulted in convictions for violent offenses, which made him ineligible for parole if convicted of any other violent crime.

At the capital murder trial, over the defense counsel's objection, the court did not allow the defense to ask prospective jurors if they understood the meaning of a "life" sentence as it applied to the defendant. Under South Carolina law a defendant who was deemed a future threat to society and receiving a life sentence was ineligible for parole. The prosecution also asked the judge not to mention parole.

During deliberation, the jurors asked the judge if the imposition of a life sentence carried with it the possibility of parole. The judge told the jury, "You are instructed not to consider parole or parole eligibility in reaching your verdict.... The terms life imprisonment and death sentence are to be understood in their plan [*sic*] and ordinary meaning."

The jury convicted Simmons of murder, sentencing him to death. On appeal the South Carolina Supreme Court upheld the sentence. The case was brought before the U.S. Supreme Court. In *Simmons v. South Carolina* (512 U.S. 154, 1994), the high court overruled in the South Carolina Supreme Court in a 6–2 decision, concluding:

> Where a defendant's future dangerousness is at issue, and state law prohibits his release on parole, due process requires that the sentencing jury be informed that the defendant is parole ineligible. An individual cannot be executed on the basis of information which he had no opportunity to deny or explain. Petitioner's jury reasonably may have believed that he could be released on parole if he were not executed. To the extent that this misunderstanding pervaded its deliberations, it had the effect of creating a false choice between sentencing him to death and sentencing him to a limited period of incarceration. The trial court's refusal to apprise the jury of information so crucial to its determination, particularly when the State alluded to the defendant's future dangerousness in its argument, cannot be reconciled with this Court's well established precedents interpreting the Due Process Clause.

JUDGE SENTENCING
Florida

Under Florida's capital trial system the jury decides the innocence or guilt of the accused. If the jury finds the defendant guilty, it recommends an advisory sentence of either life imprisonment or death. The trial judge considers mitigating and aggravating circumstances, weighs them against the jury recommendation, and then sentences the convicted murderer to either life or death. (Mitigating circumstances may lessen the responsibility for a crime, whereas aggravating circumstances may increase the responsibility for a crime.)

In 1975 a Florida jury convicted Joseph Spaziano of torturing and murdering two women. The jury recommended that Spaziano be sentenced to life imprisonment, but the trial judge, after considering the mitigating and aggravating circumstances, sentenced the defendant to death. In his appeal, Spaziano claimed the judge's overriding of the jury's recommendation of life imprisonment violated the Eighth Amendment's prohibition against a cruel and unusual punishment. The Supreme Court, in a 5–3 decision in *Spaziano v. Florida* (468 U.S. 447, 1984), did not agree.

Spaziano's lawyers claimed juries, not judges, were better equipped to make reliable capital-sentencing decisions and that a jury's decision of life imprisonment should not be superseded. They reasoned that the death penalty was unlike any other sentence and required that the jury have the ultimate word. This belief had been upheld, Spaziano claimed, because thirty out of thirty-seven states with capital punishment had the jury decide the prisoner's fate. Furthermore, the primary justification for the death penalty was retribution and an expression of community outrage. The jury served as the voice of the community and knew best whether a particular crime was so terrible that the community's response must be the death sentence.

The high court indicated that even though Spaziano's argument had some appeal, it contained two fundamental flaws. First, retribution played a role in all sentences, not just death sentences. Second, a jury was not the only source of community input: "The community's voice is heard at least as clearly in the legislature when the death penalty is authorized and the particular circumstances in which death is appropriate are defined." That trial judges imposed sentences was a normal part of the judicial system. The Supreme Court continued, "In light of the facts that the Sixth Amendment does not require jury sentencing, that the demands of fairness and reliability in capital cases do not require it, and that neither the nature of, nor the purpose behind, the death penalty requires jury sentencing, we cannot conclude that placing responsibility on the trial judge to impose the sentence in a capital case is unconstitutional."

The Court added that just because thirty out of thirty-seven states let the jury make the sentencing decision did not mean states that let a judge decide were wrong. The Court pointed out that there is no one right way for a state to establish its method of capital sentencing.

Writing for the dissenters, Justice Stevens indicated, "Because of its severity and irrevocability, the death penalty is qualitatively different from any other punishment, and hence must be accompanied by unique safeguards to ensure that it is a justified response to a given offense. . . . I am convinced that the danger of an excessive response can only be avoided if the decision to impose the death penalty is made by a jury rather than by a single governmental official [because a jury] is best able to 'express the conscience of the community on the ultimate question of life or death.'"

Justice Stevens also gave weight to the fact that thirty out of thirty-seven states had the jury make the decision, attesting to the "high level of consensus" that communities strongly believe life-or-death decisions should remain with the people—as represented by the jury—rather than relegated to a single government official.

Alabama

In March 1988 Louise Harris asked a coworker, Lorenzo McCarter, with whom she was having an affair, to find someone to kill her husband. McCarter paid two accomplices $100, with a promise of more money after they killed the husband. McCarter testified against Harris in exchange for the prosecutor's promise that he would not seek the death penalty against McCarter. McCarter testified that Harris had asked him to kill her husband so they could share in his death benefits. An Alabama jury convicted Harris of capital murder. At the sentencing hearing witnesses testified to her good background and strong character. She was rearing seven children, held three jobs simultaneously, and was active in her church.

Alabama law gives capital sentencing authority to the trial judge, but requires the judge to "consider" an advisory jury verdict. The jury voted 7–5 to give Harris life imprisonment without parole. The trial judge then considered her sentence. He found one aggravating circumstance (the murder was committed for monetary gain), one statutory mitigating circumstance (Harris had no prior criminal record), and one nonstatutory mitigating circumstance (Harris was a hardworking, respected member of her church).

Noting that she had planned the crime, financed it, and stood to benefit from the murder, the judge felt that the aggravating circumstance outweighed the other mitigating circumstances and sentenced her to death. On appeal, the Alabama Supreme Court affirmed the conviction and sentence. It rejected Harris's arguments that the procedure was unconstitutional because Alabama state law did "not specify the weight the judge must give to the jury's recommendation and thus permits the arbitrary imposition of the death penalty."

On appeal, the U.S. Supreme Court upheld the Alabama court's decision (*Harris v. Alabama* [513 U.S. 504], 1995). Alabama's capital-sentencing process is similar to Florida's. Both require jury participation during sentencing but give the trial judge the ultimate sentencing authority. Nevertheless, even though the Florida statute requires that a trial judge must give "great weight" to the jury recommendation, the Alabama statute requires only that the judge "consider" the jury's recommendation.

As in the *Spaziano* case, the high court ruled that the Eighth Amendment does not require the state "to define the weight the sentencing judge must give to an advisory jury verdict." The Court stated, "Because the Constitution permits the trial judge, acting alone, to impose a capital sentence . . . it is not offended when a State further requires the judge to consider a jury recommendation and trusts the judge to give it the proper weight."

JURY SENTENCING

In 2002 the Supreme Court decided a case concerning death sentencing in Arizona involving the Sixth Amendment right to an impartial jury (as opposed to the Eighth Amendment, which bars a cruel and unusual punishment). Timothy Stuart Ring was convicted of murder in the armed robbery of an armored-car driver in 1994. According to Arizona law, Ring's offense was punishable by life imprisonment or death. He would only be eligible for the death penalty if the trial judge held a separate hearing and found that aggravating factors warranted the death penalty.

One of Ring's accomplices, who negotiated a plea bargain in return for a second-degree murder charge, testified against him at a separate sentencing hearing without a jury present. The same judge who had presided at Ring's trial concluded that Ring committed the murder and that the crime was committed "in an especially heinous, cruel or depraved manner." Weighing the two aggravating circumstances against the mitigating evidence of Ring's minimal criminal record, the judge sentenced Ring to death.

Ring appealed to the Arizona Supreme Court, claiming that the state's capital sentencing law violated his Sixth and Fourteenth Amendment rights because it allowed a judge, rather than a jury, to make the factual findings that made him eligible for a death sentence. The court put aside Ring's argument against the Arizona's judge-sentencing system in light of the U.S. Supreme Court's ruling in *Walton v. Arizona* (497 U.S. 639, 1990). The Court held in *Walton* that Arizona's sentencing procedure was constitutional because "the additional facts found by the judge qualified as sentencing considerations, not as 'elements of the offense of capital murder.'" Next, the Arizona Supreme Court threw out the trial judge's finding of the heinous nature of the crime but concluded that Ring's minimal criminal record was not enough to outweigh the aggravating evidence of "planned, ruthless robbery and killing." The court affirmed the death sentence.

Ring took his case to the U.S. Supreme Court. On June 24, 2002, by a 7–2 vote, the Court ruled in *Ring v. Arizona* (536 U.S. 584) that only juries and not judges can determine the presence of aggravating circumstances that warrant the death sentence. This case differs from the *Harris* and *Spaziano* cases in which the Court ruled simply that a judge could sentence a person to death after hearing a jury's recommendation. In the *Ring* opinion the Court included a discussion of *Apprendi v. New Jersey* (530 U.S. 466, 2000), in which it held that "the Sixth Amendment does not permit a defendant to be 'exposed ... to a penalty exceeding the maximum he would receive if punished according to the facts reflected in the jury verdict alone.'" *Apprendi* involved a defendant in a noncapital case who received a prison term beyond the maximum sentence. This occurred because New Jersey law allowed sentencing judges to increase the penalty if they found that a crime was racially motivated. In *Apprendi*, the Court held that any fact other than a prior conviction that increases the punishment for a crime beyond the maximum allowed by law must be found by a jury beyond a reasonable doubt. The Court found *Walton* and *Apprendi* irreconcilable. The Court overruled *Walton* "to the extent that it allows a sentencing judge, sitting without a jury, to find an aggravating circumstance necessary for imposition of the death penalty." Justice Ruth Bader Ginsburg (1933–), who delivered the opinion of the Court, wrote, "The right to trial by jury guaranteed by the Sixth Amendment would be senselessly diminished if it encompassed the factfinding necessary to increase a defendant's sentence by two years [referring to *Apprendi*], but not the factfinding necessary to put him to death. We hold that the Sixth Amendment applies to both."

However, Justice Antonin Scalia (1936–), joined by Justice Clarence Thomas (1948–), pointed out in a separate concurring opinion that under *Ring*, states that let judges impose the death sentence may continue to do so by requiring the finding of aggravating factors necessary to the imposition of the death penalty during the trial phase.

Justice Sandra Day O'Connor (1930–), in her dissenting opinion, joined by Chief Justice Rehnquist, claimed that just as the *Apprendi* decision has overburdened the appeals courts, the *Ring* decision will cause more federal appeals. O'Connor observed that *Ring v. Arizona* also invalidates the capital sentencing procedure of four other states. These included Idaho and Montana, where a judge had the sole sentencing authority, as well as Colorado and Nebraska, where a three-judge panel made the sentencing decisions. The Court ruling also potentially affected Alabama, Delaware, Florida, and Indiana, where the jury rendered an advisory verdict, but the judge had the ultimate sentencing authority.

Impact of the *Ring* Decision

As a result of the *Ring* decision, Arizona, Colorado, Delaware, Idaho, Nebraska, Indiana, and Montana passed legislation providing for jury sentencing. As of 2007, Florida and Alabama still allowed judges to override jury sentencing recommendations.

Some legal scholars suggest that states where judges previously made the life-or-death decisions would see fewer death sentences under the jury system. They note that judges are elected public officials who may be driven by political ambitions to issue death sentences and suggest that urban juries would be less likely to impose death sentences.

However, in "Jurors Dish out Death in Arizona; Sentencing Rate up since Judges Lost Say" (*Arizona Republic*, November 13, 2003), Jim Walsh calculates that after the state sentencing laws were revised per *Ring*, juries in that state handed down death sentences at a higher rate than judges had done under the previous system. According to Walsh, within a one-year period (November 2002 to November 2003), jurors in Maricopa County sentenced seven out of eight (87.5%) defendants to death. Statewide, jurors imposed a total of ten death sentences out of fifteen cases heard (66.7%). In comparison, between 1995 and 1999 Maricopa County judges imposed death sentences in eleven out of seventy-five (14.7%) cases. Statewide, within that four-year period, judges sentenced 29 out of 143 (20.3%) defendants to death.

The *Ring* Decision Does Not Retroactively Apply to Those Already Sentenced to Murder

The Arizona death row inmate Warren Summerlin was convicted of brutally crushing the skull of bill collector Brenna Bailey and then sexually assaulting her. Summerlin was convicted by a jury, and an Arizona trial judge sentenced him to death in 1982. After the *Ring* decision was handed down, the U.S. Court of Appeals for the Ninth Circuit ruled 8–3 in *Summerlin v. Stewart* (309 F.3d 1193 [9th Cir., 2003]) that in light of *Ring v. Arizona*, Summerlin's death sentence should be vacated. The appellate court held that the Supreme Court's ruling should apply retroactively, even to those inmates who have exhausted their appeals. The prosecution brought the case to the U.S. Supreme Court.

In *Schriro v. Summerlin* (No. 03-526, 2004), the Supreme Court reversed the appellate court's decision in a 5–4 vote. The nation's highest court concluded that the *Ring* ruling only changed the procedures involved in a sentencing trial for capital punishment cases and did not alter those fundamental legal guidelines judges and juries follow when sentencing a person to death. As such, the *Ring* ruling does not call into question the accuracy of past convictions and should not be retroactive. Speaking for the majority, Justice Scalia wrote, "[We] give retroactive effect to only a small set of 'watershed rules of criminal procedure' implicating the fundamental fairness and accuracy of the criminal proceeding. That a new procedural rule is 'fundamental' in some abstract sense is not enough; the rule must be one 'without which the likelihood of an accurate conviction is seriously diminished.'"

DOUBLE JEOPARDY

In 1991 David Sattazahn was convicted for the 1987 murder of a restaurant manager in Berks County, Pennsylvania. Sattazahn and an accomplice killed the manager in the process of robbing him of the day's receipts. The state sought the death sentence and included an aggravating circumstance—the commission of murder while perpetrating a felony. During the sentencing phase the jury could not reach a verdict as to life or death. The trial judge considered the jury as hung and imposed an automatic sentence of life imprisonment as mandated by state law.

On appeal to the Pennsylvania Superior Court, Sattazahn was granted a new trial. The court held that the trial judge had erred in jury instructions relating to his offenses and reversed his murder conviction. During the second trial the state again sought the death penalty, this time adding a second aggravating factor: the defendant's history of felony convictions involving using or threatening violence to the victim. The jury convicted Sattazahn of first-degree murder and sentenced him to death.

Next, the Pennsylvania Supreme Court heard Sattazahn's case. The death row inmate claimed, among other things, that the Pennsylvania Constitution prohibits the imposition of the death penalty in his case because it guarantees protection from double jeopardy. The Double Jeopardy Clause of the Fifth Amendment states that "no person shall . . . be subject for the same offense to be twice put in jeopardy of life or limb." In other words, no person can be tried or punished twice for the same crime.

Relying on its ruling in *Commonwealth v. Martorano* (634 A.2d 1063,1071 [Pa. 1993]), the Pennsylvania Supreme Court affirmed both Sattazahn's conviction and death sentence. In *Martorano*, the Court noted that the jury, as in Sattazahn's first trial, was deadlocked. The hung jury did not "acquit" the defendant of the death sentence. Therefore, there was no double jeopardy prohibition against the death penalty during the second trial.

In *Sattazahn v. Pennsylvania* (537 U.S. 101, 2003), the U.S. Supreme Court, by a 5–4 vote, agreed with the ruling of the Pennsylvania Supreme Court. Justice Scalia, writing the majority opinion, concluded that double jeopardy did not exist in this case. According to the Court, "The touchstone for double-jeopardy protection in capital-sentencing proceedings is whether there has been an 'acquittal.' Petitioner here cannot establish that the jury or the court 'acquitted' him during his first capital-sentencing proceeding. As to the jury: The verdict form returned by the foreman stated that the jury deadlocked 9-to-3 on whether to impose the death penalty; it made no findings with respect to the alleged aggravating circumstance. That result—or more appropriately, that non-result—cannot fairly be called an acquittal."

The Court added that the imposition of a life sentence by the judge did not "acquit" the defendant of the death penalty either because the judge was just following the state law. "A default judgment does not trigger a double jeopardy bar to the death penalty upon retrial."

Justice Ginsburg, writing for the dissent, was joined by Justices Stevens, David H. Souter (1939–), and Stephen G. Breyer (1938–). The dissenters argued that jeopardy terminated after the judge imposed a final judgment of life imprisonment when the jury was deadlocked. Therefore, he was "acquitted" of the death penalty the first time, which means that the state could not seek the death penalty the second time. Justice Ginsburg also pointed out that "the Court's holding confronts defendants with a perilous choice.... Under the Court's decision, if a defendant sentenced to life after a jury deadlock chooses to appeal her underlying conviction, she faces the possibility of death if she is successful on appeal but convicted on retrial. If, on the other hand, the defendant loses her appeal, or chooses to forgo an appeal, the final judgment for life stands. In other words, a defendant in Sattazahn's position must relinquish either her right to file a potentially meritorious appeal, or her state-granted entitlement to avoid the death penalty."

SENTENCING PROCEDURES
Comparative Proportionality Review: Comparing Similar Crimes and Sentences

On July 5, 1978, in Mira Mesa, California, Robert Harris and his brother decided to steal a car they would need for a getaway in a planned bank robbery. Harris approached two teenage boys eating hamburgers in a car. He forced them at gunpoint to drive to a nearby wooded area. The teenagers offered to delay telling the police of the car robbery and even to give the authorities misleading descriptions of the two robbers. When one of the boys appeared to be fleeing, Harris shot both of them. Harris and his brother later committed the robbery, were soon caught, and confessed to the robbery and murders.

Harris was found guilty. In California, a convicted murderer could be sentenced to death or life imprisonment without parole only if "special circumstances" existed and the murder had been "willful, deliberate, premeditated, and committed during the commission of kidnapping and robbery." This had to be proven during a separate sentencing hearing.

The state showed that Harris was convicted of manslaughter in 1975; he was found in possession of a makeshift knife and garrote (an instrument used for strangulation) while in prison; he and other inmates sodomized another inmate; and he threatened that inmate's life. Harris testified that he had an unhappy childhood, had little education, and his father had sexually molested his sisters. The jury sentenced Harris to death, and the judge concurred.

Harris claimed the U.S. Constitution, as interpreted in previous capital punishment rulings, required the state of California to give his case comparative proportionality review to determine if his death sentence was not out of line with that of others convicted of similar crimes. In comparative proportionality review, a court considers the seriousness of the offense, the severity of the penalty, the sentences imposed for other crimes, and the sentencing in other jurisdictions for the same crime. Courts have occasionally struck down punishments inherently disproportionate and, therefore, cruel and unusual. Georgia, by law, and Florida, by practice, had incorporated such

reviews in their procedures. Other states, such as Texas and California, had not.

When the case reached the U.S. Ninth Circuit Court of Appeals, the court agreed with Harris and ordered California to establish proportionality or lift the death sentence. In *Pulley v. Harris* (465 U.S. 37, 1984), the U.S. Supreme Court, in a 7–2 decision, did not agree. The Court noted that the California procedure contained enough safeguards to guarantee a defendant a fair trial and those convicted, a fair sentence. The high court added, "That some [state statutes] providing proportionality review are constitutional does not mean that such review is indispensable.... To endorse the statute as a whole is not to say that anything different is unacceptable.... Examination of our 1976 cases makes clear that they do not establish proportionality review as a constitutional requirement."

Justice Brennan, joined by Justice Marshall, dissented. He noted that the Supreme Court had thrown out the existing death penalty procedures during the 1970s because they were deemed arbitrary and capricious. He believed they still were, but the introduction of proportionality might "eliminate some, if only a small part, of the irrationality that currently surrounds the imposition of the death penalty."

Due Process and Advance Notice of Imposing the Death Penalty

Robert Bravence and Cheryl Bravence were beaten to death at their campsite near Santiam Creek, Idaho, in 1983. Two brothers, Bryan Lankford and Mark Lankford, were charged with two counts of first-degree murder. At the arraignment (a summoning before a court to hear and answer charges), the trial judge advised Bryan Lankford that, if convicted of either of the two charges (he was charged with both murders), the maximum punishment he might receive was either life imprisonment or death.

After the arraignment Bryan Lankford's attorney made a deal with the prosecutor. Bryan Lankford entered a plea bargain in which he agreed to take two lie-detector tests in exchange for a lesser sentence. Even though the results were somewhat unclear, they convinced the prosecutor that Lankford's older brother, Mark, was primarily responsible for the crimes and was the actual killer of both victims. Bryan Lankford's attorney and the prosecutor agreed on an indeterminate sentence with a ten-year minimum in exchange for a guilty plea, subject to commitment from the trial judge that he would impose that sentence. The judge refused to make such a commitment, and the case went to trial.

The judge also refused to instruct the jury that a specific intent to kill was required to support a conviction of first-degree murder. The jury found Bryan Lankford guilty on both counts. The sentencing hearing was postponed until after Mark Lankford's trial. He was also charged with both murders.

Before the sentencing trial, at Bryan Lankford's request, the trial judge ordered the prosecutor to notify the court and Lankford whether it would seek the death penalty and, if so, to file a statement of the aggravating circumstance on which the death penalty would be based. The prosecutor notified the judge that the state would not recommend the death penalty. Several proceedings followed, including Lankford's request for a new attorney, a motion for a new trial, and a motion for continuance of the sentencing hearing. At none of the proceedings was there any mention that Lankford might receive the death penalty.

At the sentencing hearing the prosecutor recommended a life sentence, with a minimum ranging between ten and twenty years. The trial judge indicated that he considered Lankford's testimony unbelievable and that the seriousness of the crime warranted more severe punishment than recommended by the state. He sentenced Lankford to death.

Lankford appealed, asserting that the trial judge violated the U.S. Constitution by failing to give notice that he intended to impose the death penalty in spite of the state's earlier notice that it would not seek the death penalty. The judge maintained that the Idaho Code provided Lankford with sufficient notice. The judge added that the fact the prosecutor said he would not seek the death penalty had "no bearing on the adequacy of notice to petitioner that the death penalty might be imposed." The Idaho Supreme Court agreed with the judge's decision.

In *Lankford v. Idaho* (500 U.S. 110, 1991), the U.S. Supreme Court reversed the state supreme court ruling and remanded the case for a new trial. Writing for the majority, Justice Stevens stated that the due process clause of the Fourteenth Amendment was violated. Stevens noted, "If defense counsel had been notified that the trial judge was contemplating a death sentence based on five specific aggravating circumstances, presumably she would have advanced arguments that addressed these circumstances; however, she did not make these arguments, because they were entirely inappropriate in a discussion about the length of petitioner's possible incarceration."

Stevens further indicated that the trial judge's silence, in effect, hid from Lankford and his attorney, as well as from the prosecutor, the principal issues to be decided.

In a dissenting opinion, Justice Scalia wrote that Lankford's due process rights were not violated because he knew that he had been convicted of first-degree murder, and the Idaho Code clearly states that "every person guilty of murder of the first degree shall be punished by death or by imprisonment for life." At the arraignment the trial judge told Lankford that he could receive either punishment. Scalia further noted that, in Idaho, the death penalty statute places full responsibility for determining the sentence on the judge.

SUPREME COURT RULINGS: CIRCUMSTANCES THAT DO AND DO NOT WARRANT THE DEATH PENALTY, RIGHT TO EFFECTIVE COUNSEL, APPEALS BASED ON NEW EVIDENCE, AND CONSTITUTIONALITY OF EXECUTION METHODS

CIRCUMSTANCES FOUND NOT TO WARRANT THE DEATH PENALTY

Rape and Kidnapping

On June 29, 1977, a 5–4 divided U.S. Supreme Court ruled in *Coker v. Georgia* (433 U.S. 584) and in *Eberheart v. Georgia* (433 U.S. 917) that the death penalty may not be imposed for the crime of raping an adult woman that does not result in death. The Court stated:

> Rape is without doubt deserving of serious punishment; but in terms of moral depravity and of the injury to the person and to the public, it does not compare with murder, which does involve the unjustified taking of human life. Although it may be accompanied by another crime, rape by definition does not include the death of or even the serious injury to another person. The murderer kills; the rapist, if no more than that, does not. Life is over for the victim of the murderer; for the rape victim, life may not be nearly so happy as it was, but it is not over and normally is not beyond repair. We have the abiding conviction that the death penalty, which "is unique in its severity and irrevocability," is an excessive penalty for the rapist who, as such, does not take human life.

Chief Justice Warren Burger (1907–1995), joined by Justice William H. Rehnquist (1924–2005), dissented. The justices stated:

> A rapist not only violates a victim's privacy and personal integrity, but inevitably causes serious psychological as well as physical harm in the process .... Rape is not a mere physical attack—it is destructive of the human personality. The remainder of the victim's life may be gravely affected, and this in turn may have a serious detrimental effect upon her husband and any children she may have .... Victims may recover from the physical damage of knife or bullet wounds, or a beating with fists or a club, but recovery from such a gross assault on the human personality is not healed by medicine or surgery. To speak blandly, as the plurality does, of rape victims who are "unharmed," or to classify the human outrage of

rape, as does Mr. Justice Powell, in terms of "excessively brutal," versus "moderately brutal," takes too little account of the profound suffering the crime imposes upon the victims and their loved ones.

The Court also held that kidnapping did not warrant the death penalty. Even though the victims usually suffered tremendously, they had not lost their lives. (If the kidnapped victim was killed, then the kidnapper would be tried for murder.)

An Unconstitutionally Vague Statute

During a heated dispute with his wife of twenty-eight years, Robert Godfrey threatened her with a knife. Mrs. Godfrey, saying she was leaving her husband, went to stay with relatives. That same day she went to court to file for aggravated assault. Several days later she initiated divorce proceedings and moved in with her mother. During subsequent telephone conversations, the couple argued over the wife's determination to leave Godfrey permanently.

About two weeks later Godfrey killed his wife and mother-in-law. Godfrey told police that his wife phoned him, telling him she expected all the money from the planned sale of their home. She also told Godfrey she was never reconciling with him. Godfrey confessed that he went to his mother-in-law's nearby trailer and shot his wife through a window, killing her instantly. He then entered the trailer, struck his fleeing eleven-year-old daughter on the head with the gun, and shot his mother-in-law in the head, killing her. Godfrey believed his mother-in-law was responsible for his wife's reluctance to reconcile with him.

Godfrey was convicted of killing his wife and mother-in-law and of the aggravated assault of his daughter. The Georgia Code permits the imposition of the death penalty in the case of a murder that "was outrageously or wantonly vile, horrible, or inhuman in that it involved torture, depravity of mind, or an aggravated brutality to the victim." Aware of this law, the jury sentenced Godfrey to die. He appealed, claiming that the statute was unconstitutionally vague. After the Georgia Supreme Court upheld the lower court decision, the case was appealed to the U.S. Supreme Court.

The Supreme Court, in *Godfrey v. Georgia* (446 U.S. 420, 1980), noted that the victims were killed instantly (i.e., there was no torture), the victims had been "causing [Godfrey] extreme emotional trauma," and he acknowledged his responsibility. The high court concluded that, in this case, the Georgia law was unconstitutionally vague. Moreover, the Georgia Supreme Court did not attempt to narrow the definition of "outrageously and wantonly vile." In a concurring opinion, Justice Thurgood Marshall (1908–1993), joined by Justice William J. Brennan (1906–1997), found this an example of the inherently arbitrary (subject to individual judgment) and capricious (unpredictable) nature of capital punishment, because even the prosecutor in Godfrey's case observed many times that there was no torture or abuse involved.

CRIMINAL INTENT

On April 1, 1975, Sampson Armstrong and Jeanette Armstrong, on the pretext of requesting water for their overheated car, tried to rob Thomas Kersey at home. Earl Enmund waited in the getaway car. Kersey called for his wife, who tried to shoot Jeanette Armstrong. The Armstrongs killed the Kerseys. Enmund was tried for aiding and abetting in the robbery-murder and sentenced to death.

In *Enmund v. Florida* (458 U.S. 782, 1982), the Supreme Court ruled 5–4 that, in this case, the death penalty violated the Eighth and Fourteenth Amendments to the U.S. Constitution. The majority noted that only nine of the thirty-six states with capital punishment permitted its use on a criminal who was not actually present at the scene of the crime. The exception was the case where someone paid a hit man to murder the victim.

Furthermore, over the years juries had tended not to sentence to death criminals who had not actually been at the scene of the crime. Certainly, Enmund was guilty of planning and participating in a robbery, but murder had not been part of the plan. Statistically, because someone is killed in one out of two hundred robberies, Enmund could not have expected that the Kerseys would be murdered during the robbery attempt. The Court concluded that, because Enmund did not kill or plan to kill, he should be tried only for his participation in the robbery. The Court observed:

> We have no doubt that robbery is a serious crime deserving serious punishment. It is not, however, a crime "so grievous an affront to humanity that the only adequate response may be the penalty of death" [from *Gregg v. Georgia*, 428 U.S. 153, 1976]. It does not

compare with murder, which does involve the unjustified taking of human life.... The murderer kills; the [robber], if no more than that, does not. Life is over for the victim of the murderer; for the [robbery] victim, life ... is not over and normally is not beyond repair.

Writing for the minority, Justice Sandra Day O'Connor (1930–) concluded that intent is a complex issue. It should be left to the judge and jury trying the accused to decide intent, not a federal court far removed from the actual trial.

Enmund Revisited

However, just because a person had no intent to kill does not mean that he or she cannot be sentenced to death. In the early morning of September 22, 1978, Crawford Bullock and his friend Ricky Tucker had been drinking at a bar in Jackson, Mississippi, and were offered a ride home by Mark Dickson, an acquaintance.

During the drive an argument ensued over money that Dickson owed Tucker, and Dickson stopped the car. The argument escalated into a fistfight, and, outside the car, Bullock held Dickson while Tucker punched Dickson and hit him in the face with a whiskey bottle. When Dickson fell, Tucker smashed his head with a concrete block, killing him. Tucker and Bullock disposed of the body. The next day police spotted Bullock driving the victim's car. After his arrest Bullock confessed.

Under Mississippi law a person involved in a robbery that results in murder may be convicted of capital murder regardless of "the defendant's own lack of intent that any killing take place." The jury was never asked to consider whether Bullock in fact killed, attempted to kill, or intended to kill. He was convicted and sentenced to death as an accomplice to the crime. During the appeals process the Mississippi Supreme Court confirmed that Bullock was indeed a participant in the murder.

In January 1986 a divided U.S. Supreme Court modified the *Enmund* decision with a 5–4 ruling in *Cabana v. Bullock* (474 U.S. 376). The Court indicated that even though *Enmund* had to be considered at some point during the judicial process, the initial jury trying the accused did not necessarily have to consider the *Enmund* ruling. The high court ruled that even though the jury had not been made aware of the issue of intent, the Mississippi Supreme Court had considered this question. Because *Enmund* did not require that intent be presented at the initial jury trial, only that it be considered at some time during the judicial process, the state of Mississippi had met that requirement.

The four dissenting justices claimed that it was difficult for any appeals court to determine intent from reading a typed transcript of a trial. Seeing the accused and others involved was important in helping determine who was telling the truth and who was not. This was why *Enmund* must be raised to the jury so it could consider the question of intent in light of what it had seen and heard directly.

"Reckless Indifference to the Value of Human Life"

Gary Tison was a convicted criminal who had been sentenced to life imprisonment for murdering a prison guard during an escape from the Arizona State Prison in Florence, Arizona. Tison's three sons, his wife, his brother, and other relatives planned a prison escape involving Tison and a fellow prisoner, Randy Greenawalt, also a convicted murderer.

On the day of the planned escape in July 1978, Tison's sons smuggled guns into the prison's visitation area. After locking up the guards and visitors, the five men fled in a car. They later transferred to another car and waited in an abandoned house for a plane to take them to Mexico. When the plane did not come, the men got back on the road. The car soon had flat tires. One son flagged down a passing car. The motorist who stopped to help was driving with his wife, their two-year-old son, and a fifteen-year-old niece.

Gary Tison then told his sons to go get some water from the motorists' car, presumably to be left with the family they planned to abandon in the desert. While the sons were gone, Gary Tison and Randy Greenawalt shot and killed the family. Several days later two of Tison's sons and Greenawalt were captured. The third son was killed, and Tison escaped into the desert, where he later died of exposure.

The surviving Tisons and Greenawalt were found guilty and sentenced to death. The sons, citing *Enmund*, appealed, claiming that they had neither pulled the triggers nor intended the deaths of the family who had stopped to help them. In *Tison v. Arizona* (481 U.S. 137, 1987), the Supreme Court ruled 5–4 to uphold the death sentence, indicating that the Tison sons had shown a "reckless indifference to the value of human life [which] may be every bit as shocking to the moral sense as an 'intent to kill.'"

The Tisons may not have pulled the triggers (and the Court fully accepted the premise that they did not do the shootings or directly intend them to happen), but they released and then assisted two convicted murderers. They should have realized that freeing two killers and giving them guns could very well put innocent people in great danger. Moreover, they continued to help the escapees even after the family was killed.

"These facts," concluded Justice O'Connor for the majority, "not only indicate that the Tison brothers' participation in the crime was anything but minor; they also would clearly support a finding that they both subjectively appreciated that their acts were likely to result in the taking of innocent life." Unlike the situation in the *Enmund* case, they were not sitting in a car far from the murder scene. They were direct participants in the whole event. The death sentence would stand.

Writing for the minority, Justice Brennan observed that had a prison guard been murdered (Gary Tison had murdered a prison guard in a previous escape attempt), then the Court's argument would have made sense. The murder of the family, however, made no sense and was not even necessary for the escape. The Tison sons were away from the murder scene getting water for the victims and could have done nothing to save them. Even though they were guilty of planning and carrying out an escape, the murder of the family who stopped to help them was an unexpected outcome of the escape.

Furthermore, the father had promised his sons that he would not kill during the escape, a promise he had kept despite several opportunities to kill during the actual prison escape. Therefore, it was not unreasonable for the sons to believe that their father would not kill in a situation that did not appear to warrant it. Justice Brennan concluded that "like Enmund, the Tisons neither killed nor attempted or intended to kill anyone. Like Enmund, the Tisons have been sentenced to death for the intentional acts of others which the Tisons did not expect, which were not essential to the felony, and over which they had no control."

In 1992 the Arizona Supreme Court overturned the death penalty sentences for the Tison sons. They were subsequently sentenced to life in prison.

RIGHT TO EFFECTIVE COUNSEL

In 1989 Kevin Eugene Wiggins received a death sentence for the 1988 drowning of an elderly Maryland woman in her home. The Maryland Court of Appeals affirmed his sentence in 1991. With the help of new counsel, Wiggins sought postconviction relief, challenging the quality of his initial lawyers. Wiggins claimed his lawyers failed to investigate and present mitigating evidence (evidence that may lessen responsibility for a crime) of his horrendous physical and sexual abuse as a child. The sentencing jury never heard that he was starved, that his mother punished him by burning his hand on the stove, and that after the state put him in foster care at age six, he suffered more physical and sexual abuse.

In 2001 a federal district court concluded that Wiggins's first lawyers should have conducted a more thorough investigation into his childhood abuse, which would have kept the jury from imposing a death sentence. However, the U.S. Court of Appeals for the Fourth Circuit reversed the district court decision, ruling that the original attorneys had made a "reasonable strategic decision" to concentrate their defense on raising doubts about Wiggins's guilt instead.

On June 26, 2003, the U.S. Supreme Court threw out the death sentence. In *Wiggins v. Smith* (No. 02-311), the Court ruled 7–2 that Wiggins's lawyers violated his Sixth

Amendment right to effective assistance of counsel. The Court noted, "Counsel's investigation into Wiggins' background did not reflect reasonable professional judgment.... Given the nature and extent of the abuse, there is a reasonable probability that a competent attorney, aware of this history, would have introduced it at sentencing, and that a jury confronted with such mitigating evidence would have returned with a different sentence."

When Does the Right to Counsel End?

Joseph Giarratano was a Virginia death row prisoner. He received full counsel for his trial and for his initial appeal. Afterward, Virginia would no longer provide him with his own lawyer. He went to court, complaining that because he was poor the state of Virginia should provide him with counsel to help prepare postconviction appeals. Virginia permitted the condemned prisoner the right to use the prison libraries to prepare an appeal, but it did not provide the condemned with his own personal attorney.

Virginia had unit attorneys, who were assigned to help prisoners with prison-related legal matters. A unit attorney could give guidance to death row inmates but could not act as the personal attorney for any one particular inmate. This case became a class action in which the federal district court certified a class comprising "all current and future Virginia inmates awaiting execution who do not have and cannot afford counsel to pursue postconviction proceedings."

The federal district court and the federal court of appeals agreed with Giarratano, but the Supreme Court, in *Murray v. Giarratano* (492 U.S. 1, 1989), disagreed. Writing for the majority, Chief Justice Rehnquist concluded that even though the Sixth and Fourteenth Amendments to the Constitution ensure an impoverished defendant the right to counsel at the trial stage of a criminal proceeding, they do not provide for counsel for postconviction proceedings, as the Court ruled in *Pennsylvania v. Finley* (481 U.S. 551, 1987). Because *Finley* had not specifically considered prisoners on death row, but all prisoners in general, the majority did not believe the decision needed to be reconsidered just because death row prisoners had more at stake.

Chief Justice Rehnquist agreed that those facing the death penalty have a right to counsel for the trial and during the initial appeal. During these periods the defendant needs a heightened measure of protection because the death penalty is involved. Later appeals, however, involve more procedural matters that "serve a different and more limited purpose than either the trial or appeal."

In dissent, Justice John Paul Stevens (1920–), who was joined by Justices Brennan, Marshall, and Harry A. Blackmun (1908–1999), indicated that he thought condemned prisoners in Virginia faced three critical differences from those considered in *Finley*. First, the Virginia prisoners had been sentenced to death, which made their condition differ-

ent from a sentence of life imprisonment. Second, Virginia's particular judicial decision forbids certain issues to be raised during the direct review or appeal process and forces them to be considered only during later postconviction appeals. This means that important issues may be considered without the benefit of counsel. Finally, "unlike the ordinary inmate, who presumably has ample time to use and reuse the prison library and to seek guidance from other prisoners experienced in preparing ... petitions ... a grim deadline imposes a finite limit on the condemned person's capacity for useful research."

He continued, quoting from the district court's decision on the matter, an "inmate preparing himself and his family for impending death is incapable of performing the mental functions necessary to adequately pursue his claims."

Federal Judges Can Delay Executions to Allow Habeus Corpus Reviews

In 1988 Congress passed the Anti-Drug Abuse Act, which guaranteed qualified legal representation for poor death row defendants wanting to file for habeas corpus (a prisoner's petition to be heard in federal court) so that the counsel could assist in the preparation of the appeal. In 1994 this law was brought to question before the Supreme Court by death row inmate Frank McFarland.

In November 1989 a Texas jury found McFarland guilty of stabbing to death a woman he had met in a bar. The state appellate court upheld his conviction, and two lower federal courts refused his request for a stay (postponement) of execution. The federal courts ruled that they did not have jurisdiction to stop the execution until McFarland filed a habeas corpus. The inmate argued that without the stay, he would be executed before he could obtain a lawyer to prepare the petition.

The Supreme Court granted a stay of execution. In *McFarland v. Scott* (512 U.S. 849, 1994), the Court ruled 5–4 to uphold the 1988 federal law. Once a defendant requested counsel, the federal court could postpone execution so the lawyer would have time to prepare an appeal. Justice Blackmun stated that "by providing indigent [poor] capital defendants with a mandatory right to qualified legal counsel in these proceedings, Congress has recognized that Federal habeas corpus has a particularly important role to play in promoting fundamental fairness in the imposition of the death penalty."

Does the Right to Counsel Extend to Crimes That Have Not Been Charged?

In 1994 Raymond Levi Cobb confessed to burglarizing the home of Lindsey Owings the previous year. He claimed no knowledge, however, of the disappearances of Owings's wife and infant at the time of the burglary. The court subsequently assigned Cobb a lawyer to represent him in the burglary offense. With the permission of Cobb's lawyer, investigators twice questioned Cobb regarding the disappearance of the Owings family. Both times Cobb denied any knowledge of the missing pair.

In 1995, while free on bond for the burglary and living with his father, Cobb told his father that he killed Margaret Owing and buried her baby, while still alive, with her. The father reported his son's confession to the police. When brought in, Cobb confessed to the police and waived his Miranda rights, which include the right to counsel. Cobb was convicted of the murders and sentenced to death. On appeal, Cobb claimed that his confession, obtained in violation of his Sixth Amendment right to counsel, should have been suppressed. He argued that his right to counsel attached (went into full effect) when he was reported for the burglary case, and despite his open confession to the police, he never officially gave up this right to counsel.

The Texas Court of Criminal Appeals reversed Cobb's conviction, ordering a new trial. The court considered Cobb's confession to the murders inadmissible, holding that "once the right to counsel attaches to the offense charged [burglary], it also attaches to any other offense [in this case, murder] that is very closely related factually to the offense charged."

The state appealed to the U.S. Supreme Court. In *Texas v. Cobb* (532 U.S. 162, 2001), the Court, in a 5–4 decision, stated, "The Sixth Amendment right [to counsel] is … offense specific. It cannot be invoked once for all future prosecutions, for it does not attach until a prosecution is commenced, that is, at or after the initiation of adversary judicial criminal proceedings—whether by way of formal charge, preliminary hearing, indictment, information, or arraignment" (citing *McNeil v. Wisconsin*, 501 U.S. 171, 1991).

This means that Cobb's right to counsel did not extend to crimes with which he had not been charged. Because this right did not prohibit investigators from questioning him about the murders without first notifying his lawyer, Cobb's confession was admissible.

CASES INVOLVING ERROR BY THE PROSECUTION

Coerced Confessions

Oreste C. Fulminante called the Mesa, Arizona, police to report the disappearance of his eleven-year-old step-daughter, Jeneane Michelle Hunt. Fulminante was caring for the child while his wife, Jeneane's mother, was in the hospital. Several days later Jeneane's body was found in the desert east of Mesa with two shots to the head, fired at close range by a large-caliber weapon. There was a ligature (a cord used in tying or binding) around her neck. Because of the decomposed state of her body, it was

not possible to determine whether she had been sexually assaulted.

Fulminante's statements about the child's disappearance and his relationship to her included inconsistencies that made him a suspect in her death. He was not, however, charged with the murder. Fulminante left Arizona for New Jersey, where he was eventually convicted on federal charges of unlawful possession of a firearm by a felon.

Even though incarcerated, he became friendly with Anthony Sarivola, a former police officer. Sarivola had been involved in loan-sharking for organized crime, but then became a paid informant for the Federal Bureau of Investigation (FBI). In prison he masqueraded as an organized crime figure. When Fulminante was getting some tough treatment from the other inmates, Sarivola offered him protection, but only on the condition that Fulminante tell him everything.

Fulminante was later indicted in Arizona for the first-degree murder of Jeneane. In a hearing before the trial, Fulminante moved to suppress the statement he had made to Sarivola in prison and then later to Sarivola's wife, Donna, following his release from prison. He maintained that the confession to Sarivola was coerced and that the second confession was the "fruit" of the first one.

The trial court denied the motion to remove the statements from the record, finding that, based on the specified facts, the confessions were voluntary. Fulminante was convicted of Jeneane's murder and subsequently sentenced to death.

In his appeal Fulminante argued, among other things, that his confession to Sarivola was coerced and that its use at the trial violated his rights of due process under the Fifth and Fourteenth Amendments to the Constitution. The Arizona Supreme Court ruled that the confession was coerced, but initially determined that the admission of the confession at the trial was a harmless error because of the overpowering evidence against Fulminante. In legal terms, harmless error refers to an error committed during the trial that has no bearing on the outcome of the trial, and as such, is not harmful enough to reverse the outcome of the trial on appeal.

After Fulminante motioned for reconsideration, however, the Arizona Supreme Court ruled that the U.S. Supreme Court had set a precedent that prevented the use of harmless error in the case of a coerced confession. The harmless-error standard, as stated in *Chapman v. California* (386 U.S. 18, 1967), held that an error is harmless if it appears "beyond a reasonable doubt that the error complained of did not contribute to the verdict obtained." The Arizona Supreme Court reversed the conviction and ordered that Fulminante be retried without the use of his confession to Sarivola. Because of differences in the state and federal courts over the admission of a coerced confession with regard to harmless-error analysis, the U.S. Supreme Court agreed to hear the case.

In *Arizona v. Fulminante* (499 U.S. 279, 1991), Justice Byron R. White (1917–2002), writing for the majority, stated that even though the question was a close one, the Arizona Supreme Court was right in concluding that Fulminante's confession had been coerced. He further noted, "The Arizona Supreme Court found a credible threat of physical violence unless Fulminante confessed. Our cases have made clear that a finding of coercion need not depend upon actual violence by a government agent; a credible threat is sufficient. As we have said, 'coercion can be mental as well as physical, and ... the blood of the accused is not the only hallmark of an unconstitutional inquisition.'"

Justice White further argued that the state of Arizona had failed to meet its burden of establishing, beyond a reasonable doubt, that the admission of Fulminante's confession to Sarivola was harmless. He added, "A confession is like no other evidence. Indeed, 'the defendant's own confession is probably the most probative [providing evidence] that can be admitted against him.... The admissions of a defendant come from the actor himself, the most knowledgeable and unimpeachable source of information about his past conduct. Certainly, confessions have profound impact on the jury, so much so that we may justifiably doubt its ability to put them out of mind even if told to do so'" (from *Bruton v. United States*, 391 U.S. 123, 1968).

Presumption of Malice

Dale Robert Yates and Henry Davis planned to rob a country store in Greenville County, South Carolina, in February 1981. When they entered the store, only the owner, Willie Wood, was present. Yates and Davis showed their weapons and ordered Wood to give them money from the cash register. Davis handed Yates $3,000 and ordered Wood to lie across the counter. Wood, who had a pistol beneath his jacket, refused.

Meanwhile, Yates was backing out of the store with his gun pointed at the owner. After being told to do so by Davis, Yates fired two shots. The first bullet wounded Wood; the second missed. Yates then jumped into the car and waited for Davis. When Davis did not appear, Yates drove off. Inside the store, although wounded, Wood pursued Davis. As the two struggled, Wood's mother, Helen, came in and ran to help her son. During the struggle Helen Wood was stabbed once in the chest and died at the scene. Wood then shot Davis five times, killing him.

After Yates was arrested and charged with murder, his primary defense was that Helen Wood's death was not the probable natural consequence of the robbery he had planned with Davis. He claimed that he had brought the weapon only to induce the owner to give him the cash and that neither he nor Davis intended to kill anyone during the robbery.

The prosecutor's case for murder hinged on the agreement between Yates and Davis to commit an armed robbery. He argued that they planned to kill any witness, thereby making homicide a probable or natural result of the robbery. The prosecutor concluded, "It makes no difference who actually struck the fatal blow, the hand of one is the hand of all."

The judge told the jury that under South Carolina law murder is defined as "the unlawful killing of any human being with malice aforethought either express or implied." In his instructions to the jury, the judge said, "Malice is implied or presumed by the law from the willful, deliberate, and intentional doing of an unlawful act without any just cause or excuse. In its general signification, malice means the doing of a wrongful act, intentionally, without justification or excuse.... I tell you, also, that malice is implied or presumed from the use of a deadly weapon."

The judge continued to instruct the jury on the theory of accomplice liability. The jury returned guilty verdicts on the murder charge and on all other counts in the indictment. Yates was sentenced to death.

Yates petitioned the South Carolina Supreme Court, asserting that the jury charge that "malice is implied or presumed from the use of a deadly weapon" was an unconstitutional burden-shifting instruction. The case was twice reviewed by the South Carolina Supreme Court, which agreed that the jury instructions were unconstitutional, but that allowing the jury to presume malice was a harmless error, one that had no bearing on the outcome of the trial. The South Carolina court found that the jury did not have to rely on presumptions of malice because Davis's "lunging" at Helen Wood and stabbing her were acts of malice.

The U.S. Supreme Court, in *Yates v. Evatt* (500 U.S. 391, 1991), reversed the decisions of the South Carolina Supreme Court and remanded the case (sent it back to the lower court for further proceedings). Justice David H. Souter (1939–), writing for the high court, ruled that the state supreme court failed to apply the proper harmless-error standard as stated in *Chapman*. "The issue under *Chapman* is whether the jury actually rested its verdict on evidence establishing the presumed fact beyond a reasonable doubt, independently of the presumption."

Justice Souter concluded by stating that there was clear evidence of Davis's attempt to kill Wood because he could have left the store with Yates but stayed to pursue Wood with a deadly weapon. The evidence that Davis intended to kill Helen Wood was not as clear. The record also showed that Yates heard a woman scream as he left the store but did not attempt to return and kill her.

The jury could have interpreted Yates's behavior to confirm his claim that he and Davis had not originally intended to kill anyone. Even the prosecutor, in summation, conceded that Helen Wood could have been killed inadvertently by Davis.

APPEALS BASED ON NEW EVIDENCE
Newly Discovered Evidence Does Not Stop Execution

On an evening in late September 1981 the body of Texas Department of Public Safety Officer David Rucker was found lying beside his patrol car. He had been shot in the head. At about the same time, Officer Enrique Carrisalez saw a vehicle speeding away from the area where Rucker's body had been found. Carrisalez and his partner chased the vehicle and pulled it over. Carrisalez walked to the car. The driver opened his door and exchanged a few words with the police officer before firing at least one shot into Carrisalez's chest. The officer died nine days later.

Leonel Torres Herrera was arrested a few days after the shootings and charged with capital murder. In January 1982 he was tried and found guilty of murdering Carrisalez. In July 1982 he pleaded guilty to Rucker's murder.

At the trial Officer Carrisalez's partner identified Herrera as the person who fired the gun. He also testified that there was only one person in the car. In a statement by Carrisalez before he died, he also identified Herrera. The speeding car belonged to Herrera's girlfriend, and Herrera had the car keys in his pocket when he was arrested. Splatters of blood on the car and on Herrera's clothes were the same type as Rucker's. Strands of hair found in the car also belonged to Rucker. Finally, a handwritten letter, which strongly implied that he had killed Rucker, was found on Herrera when he was arrested.

In 1992, ten years after the initial trial, Herrera appealed to the federal courts, alleging that he was innocent of the murders of Rucker and Carrisalez and that his execution would violate the Eighth and Fourteenth Amendments. He presented affidavits (sworn statements) claiming that he had not killed the officers, but that his now dead brother had. The brother's attorney, one of Herrera's cellmates, and a school friend all swore that the brother had killed the police officers. The dead brother's son also said that he had witnessed his father killing the police officers.

In *Herrera v. Collins* (506 U.S. 390, 1993), the U.S. Supreme Court ruled 6–3 that executing Herrera would not violate the Eighth and Fourteenth Amendments. The high court said that the trial—not the appeals process—judges a defendant's innocence or guilt. Appeals courts determine only the fairness of the proceedings.

Writing for the majority, Chief Justice Rehnquist stated:

> A person when first charged with a crime is entitled to a presumption of innocence, and may insist that his guilt be established beyond a reasonable doubt.... Once a

defendant has been afforded a fair trial and convicted of the offense for which he was charged, the presumption of innocence disappears.... Here, it is not disputed that the State met its burden of proving at trial that petitioner was guilty of the capital murder of Officer Carrisalez beyond a reasonable doubt. Thus, in the eyes of the law, petitioner does not come before the Court as one who is "innocent," but on the contrary as one who has been convicted by due process of two brutal murders.

> Based on affidavits here filed, petitioner claims that evidence never presented to the trial court proves him innocent....

> Claims of actual innocence based on newly discovered evidence have never been held to state a ground for [court] relief absent an independent constitutional violation occurring in the course of the underlying state criminal proceedings....

> This rule is grounded in the principle that [appeals] courts sit to ensure that individuals are not imprisoned in violation of the Constitution—not to correct errors of fact.

Rehnquist continued that states all allow the introduction of new evidence. Texas was one of seventeen states that require a new trial motion based on new evidence within sixty days. Herrera's appeal came ten years later. The chief justice, however, emphasized that Herrera still had options, saying, "For under Texas law, petitioner may file a request for executive clemency.... Executive clemency has provided the 'fail safe' in our criminal justice system.... It is an unalterable fact that our judicial system, like the human beings who administer it, is fallible. But history is replete with examples of wrongfully convicted persons who have been pardoned in the wake of after-discovered evidence establishing their innocence."

The majority opinion found the information presented in the affidavits inconsistent with the other evidence. The justices questioned why the affidavits were produced at the very last minute. The justices also wondered why Herrera had pleaded guilty to Rucker's murder if he had been innocent. They did note that some of the information in the affidavits might have been important to the jury, "but coming 10 years after petitioner's trial, this showing of innocence falls far short of that which would have to be made in order to trigger the sort of constitutional claim [to decide for a retrial]."

Speaking for the minority, Justice Blackmun wrote:

> We really are being asked to decide whether the Constitution forbids the execution of a person who has been validly convicted and sentenced but who, nonetheless, can prove his innocence with newly discovered evidence. Despite the State of Texas' astonishing protestation to the contrary.... I do not see how the answer can be anything but "yes."

> The Eighth Amendment prohibits "cruel and unusual punishments." This proscription is not static but rather

reflects evolving standards of decency. I think it is crystal clear that the execution of an innocent person is "at odds with contemporary standards of fairness and decency." ... The protection of the Eighth Amendment does not end once a defendant has been validly convicted and sentenced.

Claim of Miscarriage of Justice

Lloyd Schlup, a Missouri prisoner, was convicted of participating in the murder of a fellow inmate in 1984 and sentenced to death. He had filed one petition for habeas corpus, arguing that he had inadequate counsel. He claimed the counsel did not call fellow inmates and other witnesses to testify that could prove his innocence. He filed a second petition, alleging that constitutional error at his trial deprived the jury of crucial evidence that would again have established his innocence.

Using a previous U.S. Supreme Court ruling (*Sawyer v. Whitley*, 505 U.S. 333, 1992), the district court claimed that Schlup had not shown "by clear and convincing evidence that but for a constitutional error no reasonable jury would have found him guilty." Schlup's lawyers argued that the district court should have used another ruling (*Murray v. Carrier*, 477 U.S. 478, 1986), in which a petitioner need only to show that "a constitutional violation has probably resulted in the conviction of one who is actually innocent." The appellate court affirmed the district court's ruling, noting that Schlup's guilt, which had been proven at the trial, barred any consideration of his constitutional claim.

The U.S. Supreme Court, on appeal, reviewed the case to determine whether the *Sawyer* standard provides enough protection from a miscarriage of justice that would result from the execution of an innocent person. In *Schlup v. Delo* (513 U.S. 298, 1995), the Court observed, "If a petitioner such as Schlup presents evidence of innocence so strong that a court cannot have confidence in the outcome of the trial ... the petitioner should be allowed to ... argue the merits of his underlying claims."

The justices concluded that the less stringent *Carrier* standard, as opposed to the rigid *Sawyer* standard, focuses the investigation on the actual innocence, allowing the Court to review relevant evidence that might have been excluded or unavailable during the trial.

Schlup v. Delo Revisited in *House v. Bell*

In 2006 the Supreme Court heard a case involving Tennessee prisoner Paul House, who had been convicted in 1985 of murdering Carolyn Muncey. The prosecution alleged that House, a paroled sex offender, murdered Muncey during an attempted rape. He was convicted based on circumstantial evidence and forensics tests that showed semen stains on Muncey's clothing were of House's blood type. More incriminating were small blood stains found on House's blue jeans that matched Muncey's blood type.

In 1996 House's lawyers filed a habeas corpus petition in U.S. District Court and presented new evidence, including deoxyribonucleic acid tests showing the semen on Muncey's clothing was from her husband, not House. Several witnesses testified that Hubert Muncey Jr. had since confessed while drunk to committing the murder and had a history of beating his wife. In addition, the original blood evidence came into question, due to allegations of the mishandling of blood collected during the autopsy. The defense attorneys argued that some of the autopsy blood spilled on House's pants before they were tested at the FBI laboratory in Washington, D.C. The state admitted that the autopsy blood was improperly sealed and transported and spilled, but argued that the spill occurred after the pants were tested. The district court ruled that the new evidence did not demonstrate actual innocence as required under *Schlup v. Delo* and failed to show that House was ineligible for the death penalty under *Sawyer v. Whitley*. The ruling was eventually upheld on appeal.

In *House v. Bell* (No. 04-8990, 2006), the U.S. Supreme Court ruled 5–3 that House's habeas petition should proceed, because the new evidence constituted a "stringent showing" under *Schlup v. Delo*. The Court concluded:

> This is not a case of conclusive exoneration. Some aspects of the State's evidence—Lora Muncey's memory of a deep voice, House's bizarre evening walk, his lie to law enforcement, his appearance near the body, and the blood on his pants—still support an inference of guilt. Yet the central forensic proof connecting House to the crime—the blood and the semen—has been called into question, and House has put forward substantial evidence pointing to a different suspect. Accordingly, and although the issue is close, we conclude that this is the rare case where—had the jury heard all the conflicting testimony—it is more likely than not that no reasonable juror viewing the record as a whole would lack reasonable doubt.

As of November 2007, House remained on Tennessee's death row. He has contracted multiple sclerosis and is confined to a wheel chair. Supporters of his innocence, including members of the state legislature, have petitioned the governor for a pardon.

Suppressed Evidence Means a New Trial

Curtis Lee Kyles was convicted by a Louisiana jury of the first-degree murder of a woman in a grocery store parking lot in 1984. He was sentenced to death. It was revealed on review that the prosecutor had never disclosed certain evidence favorable to the defendant. Among the evidence were conflicting statements by an informant who, the defense believed, wanted to get rid of Kyles to get his girlfriend. The state supreme court, the federal district court, and the Fifth Circuit Court denied Kyles's appeals. The U.S. Supreme Court, in *Kyles v. Whitley* (514 U.S. 419, 1995), reversed the lower courts' decisions. The high court ruled, "Favorable evidence is material, and constitutional error results from its suppression by the government, if there is a 'reasonable probability' that, had the evidence been disclosed to the defense, the result of the proceeding would have been different.... [The] the net effect of the state-suppressed evidence favoring Kyles raises a reasonable probability that its disclosure would have produced a different result at trial."

The conviction was overturned. Four mistrials followed. On February 18, 1998, after his fifth and final trial ended with a hung jury, Kyles was released from prison. He had spent fourteen years on death row.

CHALLENGING THE ANTITERRORISM AND EFFECTIVE DEATH PENALTY ACT OF 1996

The Antiterrorism and Effective Death Penalty Act (AEDPA) became law in April 1996, shortly after the first anniversary of the Oklahoma City bombing. The AEDPA aims in part to "provide for an effective death penalty." After passage of the law the lower courts differed in their interpretations of certain core provisions. For the first time, on April 18, 2000, the U.S. Supreme Court addressed these problems.

Federal Habeas Corpus Relief and the AEDPA

The AEDPA restricts the power of federal courts to grant habeas corpus relief to state inmates who have exhausted their state appeals. Through the writ of habeas corpus, an inmate could have a court review his or her conviction or sentencing. The AEDPA bars a federal court from granting an application for a writ of habeas corpus unless the state court's decision "was contrary to, or involved an unreasonable application of, clearly established federal law, as determined by the Supreme Court of the United States." The idea was to curtail the amount of habeas reviews filed by convicts and thus save the overbooked federal courts time and money.

In 1986 Terry Williams, while incarcerated in a Danville, Virginia, city jail, wrote to police that he had killed two people and that he was sorry for his acts. He also confessed to stealing money from one of the victims. He was subsequently convicted of robbery and capital murder.

During the sentencing hearing the prosecutor presented many crimes Williams had committed besides the murder for which he was convicted. Two state witnesses also testified to the defendant's future dangerousness.

Williams's lawyer, however, called on his mother to testify to his being a nonviolent person. The defense also played a taped portion of a psychiatrist's statement, who said that Williams admitted to him of removing bullets from a gun used during robbery so as not to harm anyone. During his closing statement, however, the lawyer noted that the jury would probably find it hard to give his client

mercy because he did not show mercy to his victims. The jury sentenced Williams to death, and the trial judge imposed the sentence.

In 1988 Williams filed a state habeas corpus petition. The Danville Circuit Court found Williams's conviction valid. The court found, however, that the defense lawyer's failure to present several mitigating factors at the sentencing phase violated Williams's right to effective assistance of counsel as prescribed by *Strickland v. Washington* (466 U.S. 668, 1984). The mitigating circumstances included early childhood abuse and borderline mental retardation. The habeas corpus hearing further revealed that the state expert witnesses had testified that if Williams were kept in a "structured environment," he would not be a threat to society. The circuit court recommended a new sentencing hearing.

In 1997 the Virginia Supreme Court rejected the district court's recommendation for a new sentencing hearing, concluding that the omitted evidence would not have affected the sentence. In making their ruling, the state supreme court relied on what it considered to be an established U.S. Supreme Court precedent.

Next, Williams filed a federal habeas corpus petition. The federal trial judge ruled not only that the death sentence was "constitutionally infirm" but also that defense counsel was ineffective. However, the Fourth Circuit Court of Appeals reversed the federal trial judge's decision, holding that the AEDPA prohibits a federal court from granting habeas corpus relief unless the state court's decision "was contrary to, or involved an unreasonable application of, clearly established federal law, as determined by the Supreme Court of the United States."

On April 18, 2000, the U.S. Supreme Court, in *Williams v. Taylor* (529 U.S. 362, 2000), reversed the Fourth Circuit Court's ruling by a 6–3 decision. The Court concluded that the Virginia Supreme Court's decision rejecting Williams's claim of ineffective assistance was contrary to a Supreme Court–established precedent (*Strickland v. Washington*), as well as an unreasonable application of that precedent. This was the first time the Supreme Court had granted relief on such a claim.

On November 14, 2000, during a court hearing Williams accepted a plea agreement of a life sentence without parole after prosecutors agreed not to seek the death penalty.

Federal Evidentiary Hearings for Constitutional Claims

Under an AEDPA provision, if the petitioner has failed to develop the facts of his or her challenges of a constitutional claim in state court proceedings, the federal court shall not hold a hearing on the claim unless the facts involve an exception listed by the AEDPA.

In 1993, after robbing the home of Morris Keller Jr. and his wife, Mary Elizabeth, Michael Wayne Williams and his friend Jeffrey Alan Cruse raped the woman and then killed the couple. In exchange for the state's promise not to seek capital punishment, Cruse described details of the crimes. Williams received the death sentence for the capital murders. The prosecution told the jury about the plea agreement with Cruse. The state later revoked the plea agreement after discovering that Cruse had also raped the wife and failed to disclose it. After Cruse's court testimony against Williams, however, the state gave Cruse a life sentence, which Williams alleged amounted to a second, informal plea agreement.

Williams filed a habeas petition in state court, claiming he was not told of the second plea agreement between the state and his codefendant. The Virginia Supreme Court dismissed the petition (1994), and the U.S. Supreme Court refused to review the case (1995).

In 1996, on appeal, a federal district court agreed to an evidentiary hearing of Williams's claims of the undisclosed second plea agreement. The defendant had also claimed that a psychiatric report about Cruse, which was not revealed by the prosecution, could have shown that Cruse was not credible. Moreover, a certain juror might have had possible bias, which the prosecution failed to disclose. Before the hearing could be held, the state concluded that the AEDPA prohibited such a hearing. Consequently, the federal district court dismissed Williams's petition.

When the case was brought before the U.S. Court of Appeals for the Fourth Circuit, the court, interpreting the AEDPA, concluded that the defendant had failed to develop the facts of his claims. On April 18, 2000, in *Williams v. Taylor* (529 U.S. 420), a unanimous U.S. Supreme Court did not address Williams's claim of the undisclosed plea agreement between Cruse and the state. Instead, the high court held that the defendant was entitled to a federal district court evidentiary hearing regarding his other claims. According to the Court, "Under the [AEDPA], a failure to develop the factual basis of a claim is not established unless there is lack of diligence, or some greater fault, attributable to the prisoner or the prisoner's counsel.... We conclude petitioner has met the burden of showing he was diligent in efforts to develop the facts supporting his juror bias and prosecutorial misconduct claims in collateral proceedings before the Virginia Supreme Court."

High Court Upholds Restriction on Federal Appeals

Even though the Supreme Court ruled in favor of new resentencing hearings for Terry Williams and Michael Williams, it stressed that the AEDPA places a new restriction on federal courts with respect to granting habeas relief to state inmates. The Court noted in *Williams v. Taylor* (529 U.S. 362) that under the AEDPA:

> The writ may issue only if one of the following two conditions is satisfied—the state-court adjudication resulted in a decision that (1) "was contrary to... clearly established Federal law, as determined by the Supreme Court of the United States," or (2) "involved an unreasonable application of... clearly established Federal law, as determined by the Supreme Court of the United States." Under the "contrary to" clause, a federal habeas court may grant the writ if the state court arrives at a conclusion opposite to that reached by this Court on a question of law or if the state court decides a case differently than this Court has on a set of materially indistinguishable facts. Under the "unreasonable application" clause, a federal habeas court may grant the writ if the state court identifies the correct governing legal principle from this Court's decisions but unreasonably applies that principle to the facts of the prisoner's case.

METHODS OF EXECUTION
The Role of the U.S. Food and Drug Administration

The injection of a deadly combination of drugs has become the method of execution in most states permitting capital punishment. Condemned prisoners from Texas and Oklahoma, two of the first states to introduce this method, brought suit claiming that even though the drugs used had been approved by the U.S. Food and Drug Administration (FDA) for medical purposes, they had never been approved for use in nor tested for human executions.

The FDA commissioner refused to act, claiming serious questions whether the agency had jurisdiction in the area. The U.S. District Court for the District of Columbia disagreed with the condemned prisoners that the FDA had a responsibility to determine if the lethal mixture used during execution was safe and effective. The court noted that decisions by a federal agency not to take action were not reviewable in court.

A divided Court of Appeals for the District of Columbia reversed the lower court ruling. A generally irritated U.S. Supreme Court agreed to hear the case "to review the implausible result that the FDA is required to exercise its enforcement power to ensure that States only use drugs that are 'safe and effective' for human execution."

In *Heckler v. Chaney* (470 U.S. 821, 1985), the unanimous Court agreed that, in this case, the FDA did not have jurisdiction.

Is Execution by Hanging Constitutional?

Washington state law imposes capital punishment either by "hanging by the neck" or, if the condemned chooses, by lethal injection. Charles Rodham Campbell was convicted of three counts of murder in 1982 and sentenced to death. Campbell, in challenging the constitutionality of hanging under the Washington statute, claimed that execution by hanging violated his Eighth Amendment right because it was a cruel and unusual punishment. Furthermore, the direction that he be hanged unless he chose lethal injection was a cruel and unusual punishment. He claimed that such instruction further violated his First Amendment right by forcing him to participate in his own execution to avoid hanging.

In *Campbell v. Wood* (18 F.3d. 662, 9th Cir. 1994), the U.S. Court of Appeals for the Ninth Circuit noted, "We do not consider hanging to be cruel and unusual simply because it causes death, or because there may be some pain associated with death.... As used in the Constitution, 'cruel' implies 'something inhuman and barbarous, something more than the mere extinguishment of life.' ... Campbell is entitled to an execution free only of 'the unnecessary and wanton infliction of pain.'"

According to the court, just because the defendant was given a choice of a method of execution did not mean that he was being subjected to a cruel and unusual punishment: "We believe that benefits to prisoners who may choose to exercise the option and who may feel relieved that they can elect lethal injection outweigh the emotional costs to those who find the mere existence of an option objectionable."

Campbell argued that the state was infringing on his First Amendment right of free exercise of his religion. He claimed that it was against his religion to participate in his own execution by being allowed to elect lethal injection over hanging.

The court contended that Campbell did not have to choose an execution method or participate in his own execution. "He may remain absolutely silent and refuse to participate in any election." The death penalty statute does not require him to choose the method of execution; it simply offers a choice. On appeal (*Campbell v. Wood*, 511 U.S. 1119, 1994), the U.S. Supreme Court decided not to hear the case. In 1994 Campbell was executed by hanging. He refused to cooperate during the execution and had to be pepper sprayed and strapped to a board to carry out the hanging.

Is Execution by Lethal Gas Constitutional?

On April 17, 1992, three California death row inmates—David Fierro, Alejandro Gilbert Ruiz, and Robert Alton Harris—filed a suit on behalf of themselves and all others under sentence of execution by lethal gas. In *Fierro v. Gomez* (790 F. Supp. 966 [N.D. Cal. 1992]), the inmates alleged that California's method of execution by lethal gas violated the Eighth and Fourteenth Amendments. Harris was scheduled to be executed four days later, on April 21, 1992—an execution that was carried out.

The district court prohibited James Gomez, the director of the California Department of Corrections, and Arthur Calderon, the warden of San Quentin Prison, from executing any inmate until a hearing was held. On appeal from Gomez and Calderon, the U.S. Court of Appeals for the Ninth Circuit vacated (annulled) the district court's ruling. On his execution day Harris had filed a habeas corpus petition with the California Supreme Court, challenging the constitutionality of the gas chamber. The court declined to review the case, and Harris was put to death that day. In the aftermath of Harris's execution, the California legislature amended in 1993 its death penalty statute, providing that, if lethal gas "is held invalid, the punishment of death shall be imposed by the alternative means," lethal injection.

In October 1994 a federal district judge, Marilyn Hall Patel (1938–), ruled that execution by lethal gas "is inhumane and has no place in civilized society" (865 F. Supp. at 1415). She then ordered California's gas chamber closed and that lethal injection be used instead. This was the first time a federal judge had ruled that any method of execution violated the Eighth and Fourteenth Amendments. Even though the state of California maintained that cyanide gas caused almost instant unconsciousness, the judge referred to doctors' reports and witnesses' accounts of gas chamber executions, which indicated that the dying inmates stayed conscious for fifteen seconds to a minute or longer and suffered "intense physical pain."

Gomez and Calderon appealed Judge Patel's ruling on the unconstitutionality of the gas chamber before the U.S. Court of Appeals for the Ninth Circuit. The court also appealed the permanent injunction against the use of lethal gas as a method of execution. In February 1996, in *Fierro v. Gomez* (77 F.3d. 301, 9th Cir.), the appellate court affirmed Judge Patel's ruling.

Gomez and Calderon appealed the case to the U.S. Supreme Court. In October 1996 a 7–2 Supreme Court, in *Gomez v. Fierro* (519 U.S. 918), vacated the appellate court's ruling and returned the case to the appellate court for additional proceedings, citing the death penalty statute amended in 1993 (lethal injection as an alternative to lethal gas). As of November 2007, Fierro remained on death row. Ruiz died of natural causes in early 2007.

Does Electrocution Constitute a Cruel and Unusual Punishment?

In the 1990s, even though Florida had three botched executions using the electric chair, the state supreme court ruled each time that electrocution does not constitute a cruel and unusual punishment. In 1990 and 1997 flames shot out from the headpiece worn by the condemned man. On July 8, 1999, Allen Lee Davis developed a nosebleed during his execution in the electric chair.

Thomas Provenzano, who was scheduled to be electrocuted after Davis, challenged the use of the electric chair as Florida's sole method of execution. In *Provenzano v. Moore* (No. 95973, 1999), the Florida Supreme Court ruled 4–3 that the electric chair was not a cruel and unusual punishment. The court further reported that Davis's nosebleed occurred before the execution and did not result from the electrocution.

Subsequently, the court, as it routinely does with all its rulings, posted the *Provenzano* decision on the Internet. Three photographs of Davis covered with blood were posted as part of Justice Leander J. Shaw Jr.'s (1930–) dissenting opinion. The photographs brought public outcry worldwide. Justice Shaw claimed that Davis was "brutally tortured to death."

In October 1999, for the first time, the U.S. Supreme Court agreed to consider the constitutionality of electrocution. The death row inmate Anthony Braden Bryan asked the Court to review his case, based on the unreliability of the electric chair. Before the high court could hear the case, however, the Florida legislature voted in a special session to replace electrocution with lethal injection as the primary method of execution, but allowed a condemned person to choose the electric chair as an alternative.

On January 24, 2000, the Supreme Court dismissed *Bryan v. Moore* (No. 99-6723) as moot (irrelevant), based on Florida's new legislation. Governor Jeb Bush (1953–) agreed to sign the bill in conjunction with a second bill that limits, in most cases, death row inmates to two appeals in state courts, with the second appeal to be filed within six months of the first. This provision cut in half the time limit for the second appeal.

In 2001 the Georgia Supreme Court became the first appellate court to rule a method of execution unconstitutional. On October 5 the court held that electrocution was a cruel and unusual punishment in violation of the state constitution. In 2000 the Georgia legislature had passed a law making lethal injection the sole method of execution. Before the state supreme court ruling in October 2001, that law applied only to those sentenced after May 1, 2000.

Challenging the Form of Execution

In April 2006 the Supreme Court considered a case in which the Florida inmate Clarence E. Hill challenged the state's form of lethal injection as unnecessarily painful and thus a violation of his Eighth Amendment rights. Hill was convicted in 1983 for the capital murder of Officer Stephen Taylor and sentenced to death. After exhausting his state appeals, he filed for a federal writ of habeas corpus, which was denied. As Hill's execution loomed in January 2006, his lawyers filed a new challenge, this time against the lethal injection procedure itself. A trial court dismissed the claim, because Hill had already exhausted his federal habeas corpus appeals. Federal law prohibits multiple appeals of this type. The ruling was upheld by the Florida Supreme Court.

In *Hill v. McDonough* (No. 05-8794, 2006), the U.S. Supreme Court issued a unanimous 9–0 opinion that Hill's challenge of the form of execution did not constitute a second habeas corpus appeal, but was a new action of a different type. The decision came only minutes before Hill was to be executed. He was already strapped to a gurney and hooked up to intravenous lines. However, the reprieve proved to be temporary. Florida courts refused to hear Hill's challenge, arguing that it was presented too late. His execution date was reset and the Supreme Court denied a second appeal. In September 2006 Hill was executed by lethal injection.

DOES EXTENDED STAY ON DEATH ROW CONSTITUTE A CRUEL AND UNUSUAL PUNISHMENT?

In 2002 Charles Kenneth Foster, a Florida inmate, asked the U.S. Supreme Court to consider whether his long wait for execution constitutes a cruel and unusual punishment prohibited by the Eighth Amendment. Foster had been on death row since 1975 for a murder conviction. In 1981 and again in 1984 the defendant was granted a stay of execution to allow his federal habeas corpus petition.

Justice Stephen G. Breyer (1938–) dissented from the Court's refusal to hear the case (*Foster v. Florida*, No. 01-10868, 2002). Justice Breyer pointed out that the defendant's long wait on death row resulted partly from Florida's repeated errors in proceedings. The justice added, "Death row's inevitable anxieties and uncertainties have been sharpened by the issuance of two death warrants and three judicial reprieves. If executed, Foster, now 55, will have been punished both by death and also by more than a generation spent in death row's twilight. It is fairly asked whether such punishment is both unusual and cruel."

Concurring with the Court opinion not to hear Foster's case, Justice Clarence Thomas (1948–) observed that the defendant could have ended the "anxieties and uncertainties" of death row had he submitted to execution, which the people of Florida believe he deserves. As of November 2007, Foster remained in Florida prison on death row.

CHAPTER 4
SUPREME COURT RULINGS: MITIGATING CIRCUMSTANCES, YOUTH, INSANITY, MENTAL RETARDATION, THE ADMISSIBILITY OF VICTIM IMPACT STATEMENTS, AND THE INFLUENCE OF RACE IN CAPITAL CASES

MITIGATING CIRCUMSTANCES

Mitigating circumstances may lessen the responsibility for a crime, whereas aggravating circumstances may add to the responsibility for a crime. In 1978 an Ohio case highlighted the issue of mitigating circumstances before the U.S. Supreme Court after Sandra Lockett was convicted of capital murder for her role in a pawnshop robbery that resulted in the shooting death of the storeowner. Locket helped plan the robbery, drove the getaway car, and hid her accomplices in her home, but was not present in the store at the time the storeowner was shot. According to the Ohio death penalty statute, capital punishment had to be imposed on Lockett unless "(1) the victim induced or facilitated the offense; (2) it is unlikely that the offense would have been committed but for the fact that the offender was under duress, coercion, or strong provocation; or (3) the offense was primarily the product of the offender's psychosis or mental deficiency." Lockett was found guilty and sentenced to die.

Lockett appealed, claiming that the Ohio law did not give the sentencing judge the chance to consider the circumstances of the crime, the defendant's criminal record, and the defendant's character as mitigating factors, lessening her responsibility for the crime. In July 1978 the Supreme Court, in *Lockett v. Ohio* (438 U.S. 586), upheld Lockett's contention. Chief Justice Warren Burger (1907–1995) observed, "A statute that prevents the sentencer in capital cases from giving independent mitigating weight to aspects of the defendant's character and record and to the circumstances of the offense proffered in mitigation creates the risk that the death penalty will be imposed in spite of factors that may call for a less severe penalty, and when the choice is between life and death, such risk is unacceptable and incompatible with the commands of the Eighth and Fourteenth Amendments."

Mitigating Circumstances Must Always Be Considered

In *Hitchcock v. Dugger* (481 U.S. 393, 1987), a unanimous Supreme Court further emphasized that all mitigating circumstances had to be considered before the convicted murderer could be sentenced. A Florida judge had instructed the jury not to consider evidence of mitigating factors that were not specifically indicated in the Florida death penalty law. Writing for the Court, Justice Antonin Scalia (1936–) stressed that a convicted person had the right "to present any and all relevant mitigating evidence that is available."

CAN A MINOR BE SENTENCED TO DEATH?

On April 4, 1977, sixteen-year-old Monty Lee Eddings and several friends were pulled over by a police officer as they traveled in a car in Oklahoma. Eddings had several guns in the car, which he had taken from his father. When the police officer approached the car, Eddings shot and killed him. Eddings was tried as an adult even though he was sixteen at the time of the murder. He was convicted of first-degree murder for killing a police officer and was sentenced to death.

At the sentencing hearing following the conviction, Eddings's lawyer presented substantial evidence of a turbulent family history, beatings by a harsh father, and serious emotional disturbance. The judge refused, as a matter of law, to consider the mitigating circumstances of Eddings's unhappy upbringing and emotional problems. He ruled that the only mitigating circumstance was the petitioner's youth, which was insufficient to outweigh the aggravating circumstances.

In *Eddings v. Oklahoma* (455 U.S. 104, 1982), the Supreme Court, in a 5–4 opinion, ordered the case remanded (sent back to the lower courts for further proceedings). The justices based their ruling on *Lockett v. Ohio*, which required the trial court to consider and weigh all the mitigating evidence concerning the petitioner's family background and personal history.

By implication, because the majority did not reverse the case on the issue of age, the decision let stand

Oklahoma's decision to try Eddings as an adult. Meanwhile, Chief Justice Burger, who filed the dissenting opinion in which Justices Byron R. White (1917–2002), Harry A. Blackmun (1908–1999), and William H. Rehnquist (1924–2005) joined, observed, "the Constitution does not authorize us to determine whether sentences imposed by state courts are sentences we consider 'appropriate'; our only authority is to decide whether they are constitutional under the Eighth Amendment. The Court stops far short of suggesting that there is any constitutional proscription against imposition of the death penalty on a person who was under age 18 when the murder was committed."

Hence, even though the high court did not directly rule on the question of minors being sentenced to death, the sense of the Court would appear to be that it would uphold such a sentencing. Eddings's sentence was subsequently changed to life in prison.

Not at Fifteen Years Old

With three adults, William Thompson brutally murdered a former brother-in-law in Oklahoma. Thompson was fifteen at the time of the murder, but the state determined that Thompson, who had a long history of violent assault, had "virtually no reasonable prospects for rehabilitation … within the juvenile system and … should be held accountable for his acts as if he were an adult and should be certified to stand trial as an adult." Thompson was tried as an adult and found guilty. As in *Eddings*, Thompson's age was considered a mitigating circumstance, but the jury still sentenced him to death.

Thompson appealed, and even though the Court of Criminal Appeals of Oklahoma upheld the decision, the U.S. Supreme Court, in *Thompson v. Oklahoma* (487 U.S. 815, 1988), did not. In a 5–3 majority vote, with Justice Sandra Day O'Connor (1930–) agreeing to vacate (annul) the sentence but not agreeing with the majority reasoning, the case was reversed. (Justice Anthony M. Kennedy [1936–] took no part in the decision.)

Writing for the majority, Justice John Paul Stevens (1920–) observed that "inexperience, less education, and less intelligence make the teenager less able to evaluate the consequences of his or her conduct while at the same time he or she is much more apt to be motivated by mere emotion or peer pressure than is an adult. The reasons why juveniles are not trusted with the privileges and responsibilities of an adult also explain why their irresponsible conduct is not as morally reprehensible as that of an adult."

Justice Stevens noted that eighteen states required the age of at least sixteen years before the death penalty could be considered. Counting the fourteen states prohibiting capital punishment, a total of thirty-two states did not execute people under sixteen.

Justice O'Connor agreed with the judgment of the Court that the appellate court's ruling should be reversed. O'Connor pointed out, however, that even though most fifteen-year-old criminals are generally less blameworthy than adults who commit the same crimes, some may fully understand the horrible deeds they have done. Individuals, after all, have different characteristics, including their capability to distinguish right from wrong.

Writing for the minority, Justice Scalia found no national consensus forbidding the execution of a person who was sixteen at the commission of the murder. The justice could not understand the majority's calculations establishing a "contemporary standard" that forbade the execution of young minors. He reasoned that abolitionist states (states with no death penalty) should not be considered in the issue of executing minors because they did not have executions in the first place. Rather, the eighteen states that prohibited the execution of offenders who were younger than sixteen when they murdered should be compared to the nineteen states that applied the death penalty to young offenders.

For a Number of Years Minors Could Be Sentenced to Death at Sixteen or Seventeen

In 1989 a majority of the Court, with Justice O'Connor straddling the fence, found the death penalty unacceptable for an offender who was less than sixteen when he or she committed murder. A majority of the Court, however, found the death sentence acceptable for a minor who was sixteen or seventeen during the commission of murder. The Supreme Court, in two jointly considered cases, *Stanford v. Kentucky* and *Wilkins v. Missouri* (492 U.S. 361, 1989), ruled that inmates who committed their crimes at ages sixteen or seventeen could be executed for murder.

In January 1981 seventeen-year-old Kevin Stanford and an accomplice raped Barbel Poore, an attendant at a Kentucky gas station they were robbing. They then took the woman to a secluded area near the station, where Stanford shot her in the face and in the back of the head. Stressing the seriousness of the offense and Stanford's long history of criminal behavior, the court certified him as an adult. He was tried, found guilty, and sentenced to death.

In July 1985 sixteen-year-old Heath Wilkins stabbed Nancy Allen to death while he was robbing the convenience store where she worked. Wilkins indicated he murdered Allen because "a dead person can't talk." Based on his long history of juvenile delinquency, a Missouri court ordered Wilkins to be tried as an adult. He was found guilty and sentenced to death.

Writing for the majority, Justice Scalia could find no national consensus that executing minors aged sixteen and seventeen constituted a cruel and unusual punishment. Scalia observed that of the thirty-seven states whose statutes allowed the death penalty, just twelve refused to impose it on seventeen-year-old offenders, and besides those twelve, only three more states refused to impose it on sixteen-year-old offenders.

Furthermore, Justice Scalia saw no connection between the defendant's argument that those under eighteen were denied the right to drive, drink, or vote because they were not considered mature enough to do so responsibly and whether this standard of maturity should be applied to a minor's understanding that murder is terribly wrong. Scalia added, "Even if the requisite degrees of maturity were comparable, the age statutes in question would still not be relevant .... These laws set the appropriate ages for the operation of a system that makes its determinations in gross, and that does not conduct individualized maturity tests for each driver, drinker, or voter .... In the realm of capital punishment in particular, 'individualized consideration [is] a constitutional requirement,' and one of the individualized mitigating factors that sentencers must be permitted to consider is the defendant's age."

Writing for the minority, Justice William J. Brennan (1906–1997) found a national consensus among thirty states when he added the twelve states forbidding the execution of a person who was sixteen years during the commission of the crime to those with no capital punishment, and the states that, in practice if not in law, did not execute minors. Justice Brennan, taking serious exception to the majority's observation that they had to find a national consensus in the laws passed by the state legislatures, stated, "Our judgment about the constitutionality of a punishment under the Eighth Amendment is informed, though not determined ... by an examination of contemporary attitudes toward the punishment, as evidenced in the actions of legislatures and of juries. The views of organizations with expertise in relevant fields and the choices of governments elsewhere in the world also merit our attention as indicators whether a punishment is acceptable in a civilized society."

In 1996 Wilkins was retried in Missouri and sentenced to three life terms. Stanford remained on Kentucky's death row until 2003, when his sentence was commuted to life without parole by Governor Paul E. Patton (1937–).

The Supreme Court Reverses Its Decision Regarding Minors

For fifteen years the nation's highest court held fast on its decision to allow for the execution of minors who committed capital crimes. The Supreme Court even rejected another appeal by Stanford in 2002. In *Roper v. Simmons* (543 U.S. 633, 2005), however, the Court reversed its earlier opinion when it ruled that executing Christopher Simmons was cruel and unusual based on the fact that Simmons was a minor when he committed murder.

In 1993 seventeen-year-old Simmons and two friends, John Tessmer and Charles Benjamin, planned the elaborate burglary and murder of Shirley Cook, who lived in Fenton, Missouri. The three teenagers wanted to experience the thrill of the crime, reasoning that they would not be held accountable because they were under the age of eighteen. On the night of the murder, Tessmer and Simmons broke into Cook's house. (Benjamin backed out.) When Cook identified who the boys were, they covered her eyes and mouth with duct tape and bound her hands. The teenagers drove Cook to a state park, wrapped more duct tape over her entire face, tied her hands and feet with electrical wire, and threw her off a railroad trestle into a river.

The next day Simmons began bragging about the murder at school and was picked up by the police along with the two other teenagers. Simmons confessed on videotape and was tried and sentenced to death. He made a number of unsuccessful appeals and pleas for habeas corpus (a petition to be heard in federal court). Just weeks before he was scheduled to die, the Missouri Supreme Court called off the execution and reopened the debate in light of the U.S. Supreme Court's *Atkins* decision. (In *Atkins v. Virginia* [536 U.S. 304], the Court ruled that executing mentally retarded criminals was a violation of the Eighth Amendment because the mentally retarded do not have as strong a sense of lasting consequences or of right and wrong as normal adults.) The state court overturned Simmons's death sentence 6–3, stating that a national consensus had developed against executing minors since *Stanford* and *Wilkins* were decided. Simmons was resentenced to life without parole.

The U.S. Supreme Court upheld the Missouri court's decision in a 5–4 vote, reversing *Stanford*. The majority reasoned that adolescents do not have the emotional maturity and understanding of lasting consequences that adults have. As such, they cannot be held to as high of a standard and should not be sentenced to death. The majority also agreed with the Missouri court in that a national and international consensus had changed over the past fifteen years. The Court noted, "To implement this framework we have established the propriety and affirmed the necessity of referring to 'the evolving standards of decency that mark the progress of a maturing society.'"

Justices O'Connor, Scalia, Rehnquist, and Clarence Thomas (1948–) dissented, claiming that the guidelines for executing minors should not be inflexible and that a great many U.S. citizens still favor the death penalty for teenagers who commit especially heinous crimes. Scalia stated that the majority was bowing to international pressures. In his dissent, he wrote, "Though the views of our own citizens are essentially irrelevant to the Court's decision today, the views of other countries and the so-called international community take center stage."

Youth: A Mitigating Circumstance Even for Those over Eighteen

On March 23, 1986, Dorsie Lee Johnson Jr. and an accomplice staked out a convenience store in Snyder, Texas, with the intention of robbing it. They learned that only one employee worked during the predawn hours. Agreeing to leave no witnesses to the crime, the nineteen-year-old Johnson shot and killed the clerk, Jack Huddleston. They then emptied the cash register and stole some cigarettes.

The following month Johnson was arrested and subsequently confessed to the robbery and murder. During jury selection the defense attorneys asked potential jurors whether they believed that people were capable of change and whether they, the potential jurors, had ever done things in their youth that they would not now do.

The only witness the defense called was Johnson's father, who told of his son's drug use, grief over the death of his mother two years before the crime, and the murder of his sister the following year. He spoke of his son's youth and the fact that, at age nineteen, he did not evaluate things the way a person of thirty or thirty-five would.

Johnson was tried and convicted of capital murder. Under Texas law the homicide qualified as a capital offense because Johnson intentionally or knowingly caused Huddleston's death. Moreover, the murder was carried out in the course of committing a robbery.

In the sentencing phase of the trial, the judge instructed the jury to answer two questions: (1) whether Johnson's actions were deliberate and intended to kill, and (2) whether there was a possibility that he would continue to commit violent crimes and be a threat to society. If the jury answered "yes" to both questions, Johnson would be sentenced to death. If the jury returned a "no" answer to either question, the defendant would be sentenced to life in prison. The jury was not to consider or discuss the possibility of parole.

Of equal importance was the instruction that the jury could consider all the evidence, both aggravating and mitigating, in either phase of the trial. The jury unanimously answered yes to both questions, and Johnson was sentenced to death.

Five days after the state appellate court denied Johnson's motions for a rehearing, the U.S. Supreme Court issued its opinion in *Penry v. Lynaugh* (492 U.S. 302, 1989), in which it held that the jury should have been instructed that it could consider mental retardation as a mitigating factor during the penalty phase. Based on the *Penry* ruling, Johnson appealed once more, claiming that a separate instruction should have been given to the jurors that would have allowed them to consider his youth. Again, the appellate court rejected his petition.

Affirming the Texas appellate court decision, Justice Kennedy delivered the opinion of the Supreme Court in *Johnson v. Texas* (509 U.S. 350, 1993). He was joined by Justices Rehnquist, White, Scalia, and Thomas. Kennedy noted that the Texas special-issues system (two questions asked of the jury and instruction to consider all evidence) allowed for adequate consideration of Johnson's youth. Justice Kennedy stated:

> Even on a cold record, one cannot be unmoved by the testimony of petitioner's father urging that his son's actions were due in large part to his youth. It strains credulity to suppose that the jury would have viewed the evidence of petitioner's youth as outside its effective reach in answering the second special issue. The relevance of youth as a mitigating factor derives from the fact that the signature qualities of youth are transient; as individuals mature, the impetuousness and recklessness that may dominate in younger years can subside .... As long as the mitigating evidence is within "the effective reach of the sentencer," the requirements of the Eighth Amendment are satisfied.

Justice O'Connor, in a dissenting opinion joined by Justices Blackmun, Stevens, and David H. Souter (1939–), stated that the jurors were not allowed to give full effect to his strongest mitigating circumstance: his youth. Hearing of his less than exemplary youth, a jury might easily conclude, as Johnson's did, that he would continue to be a threat to society.

In 1997 Johnson was executed by lethal injection in the state of Texas.

ROLE OF PSYCHIATRISTS

Validity of a Psychiatrist's Testimony

In 1978 Thomas Barefoot was convicted of murdering a police officer in Bell County, Texas. During the sentencing phase of his trial the prosecution put two psychiatrists on the stand. Neither psychiatrist had actually interviewed Barefoot, nor did either ask to do so. Both psychiatrists agreed that an individual with Barefoot's background and who had acted as Barefoot had in murdering the policeman represented a future threat to society. Partially based on their testimony, the jury sentenced Barefoot to death.

Barefoot's conviction and sentence were appealed many times, and in 1983 his case was argued before the U.S. Supreme Court. Among the issues debated was the validity of the testimony of psychiatrists. Barefoot's lawyers questioned whether it was necessary for the psychiatrists to have interviewed Barefoot or if it was enough for them to answer hypothetical questions that pertained to a hypothetical individual who acted like Barefoot.

Barefoot's attorneys claimed that psychiatrists could not reliably predict that a particular offender would commit other crimes in the future and be a threat to society. They further argued that psychiatrists should also not be allowed to testify about an offender's future dangerousness in response to hypothetical situations presented by the prosecutor and without having first examined the offender.

In *Barefoot v. Estelle* (463 U.S. 880, 1983), the Supreme Court ruled 6–3 that local juries were in the best position to decide guilt and impose a sentence. The Court referred to *Jurek v. Texas* (428 U.S. 262, 1976), an earlier case that, among other things, upheld the testimony of laypeople concerning a defendant's possible future actions. Therefore, the Court looked on psychiatrists as just another group of people presenting testimony to the jury for consideration. The Court claimed that like all evidence presented to the jury, a psychiatric observation "should be admitted and its weight left to the factfinder, who would have the benefit of cross-examination and contrary evidence by the opposing party. Psychiatric testimony predicting dangerousness may be countered not only as erroneous in a particular case but also as generally so unreliable that it should be ignored. If the jury may make up its mind about future dangerousness unaided by psychiatric testimony, jurors should not be barred from hearing the views of the State's psychiatrists along with opposing views of the defendant's doctors."

The high court dismissed the amicus curiae brief (a friend-of-the-court brief prepared to enlighten the court) presented by the American Psychiatric Association (APA), indicating that psychiatric testimony was "almost entirely unreliable" in determining future actions. The Court countered that such testimony had been traditionally accepted. The high court also observed that arguments, such as the APA brief, were founded "on the premise that a jury will not be able to separate the wheat from the chaff," a sentiment with which the Court did not agree.

The high court also dismissed Barefoot's contention that the psychiatrists should have personally interviewed him. Such methods of observation and conclusion were quite normal in courtroom procedures, and the psychiatric observations had been based on established facts. Barefoot's appeal was denied.

Justice Blackmun strongly dissented from the majority decision. He declared, "In the present state of psychiatric knowledge, this is too much for me. One may accept this in a routine lawsuit for money damages, but when a person's life is at stake—no matter how heinous his offense—a requirement of greater reliability should prevail. In a capital case, the specious testimony of a psychiatrist, colored in the eyes of an impressionable jury by the inevitable untouchability of a medical specialist's words, equates with death itself."

The state of Texas executed Barefoot by lethal injection in 1984.

A Prisoner Maintains Rights during Psychiatric Examination

During the commission of a robbery in 1973 Ernest Smith's accomplice fatally shot a grocery clerk (Smith had tried to shoot the clerk, but his weapon had jammed). The state of Texas sought the death penalty against Smith based on the Texas law governing premeditated murder.

Thereafter, the judge ordered a psychiatric examination of Smith by James P. Grigson to determine if Smith was competent to stand trial. Without permission from Smith's lawyer, Grigson interviewed Smith in jail for about ninety minutes and found him competent. Grigson then discussed his conclusions and diagnosis with the state attorney. Smith was eventually found guilty. During the sentencing phase of the trial, over the protests of the defendant's lawyers, Grigson testified that Smith was a "very severe sociopath," who would continue his previous behavior, which would get worse. The jury sentenced Smith to death.

Smith appealed his sentence, claiming he was not informed of his rights. Both the federal district court and the appeals court agreed. So did a unanimous Supreme Court. In *Estelle v. Smith* (451 U.S. 454, 1981), the Court ruled that the trial court had the right to determine if Smith was capable of standing trial. It had no right, however, to use the information gathered without first advising him of his Fifth Amendment right against self-incrimination. According to the Court, the psychiatrist was "an agent of the state" about whom the defendant had not been warned, but who was reporting about the defendant. Noting *Miranda v. Arizona* (384 U.S. 436, 1966), the Court continued, "The Fifth Amendment privilege is available outside of criminal court proceedings and serves to protect persons in all settings in which their freedom of action is curtailed in any significant way from being compelled to incriminate themselves."

The Court reiterated that the prosecution may not use any statements made by a suspect under arrest "unless it demonstrates the use of procedural safeguards effective to secure the privilege against self-incrimination."

In 1981 Smith was convicted of a lesser charge and sentenced to life in prison.

Needing a Psychiatrist to Prove Insanity

In 1979 Glen Burton Ake and Steven Hatch shot and killed the Reverend Richard Douglass and Marilyn Douglass and wounded their children, Brooks and Leslie, in Canadian County, Oklahoma. Before the trial, because of Ake's bizarre behavior, the trial judge ordered him examined by a psychiatrist to determine if he should be put under observation. The psychiatrist diagnosed Ake as a probable paranoid schizophrenic and reported that his client claimed "to be the 'sword of vengeance' of the Lord." The physician recommended a long-term psychiatric examination to determine Ake's competency to stand trial.

Ake's psychiatric evaluation confirmed his paranoid schizophrenia. Consequently, the court pronounced him incompetent to stand trial and ordered him committed to the state mental hospital.

Six weeks later the hospital psychiatrist informed the court that Ake had become competent to stand trial. Under daily treatment with an antipsychotic drug, he could stand trial. The state of Oklahoma resumed proceedings against the accused murderer.

Before the trial Ake's lawyer told the court of his client's insanity defense. He also informed the court that for him to defend Ake adequately, he needed to have Ake examined by a psychiatrist to determine his mental condition at the time he committed murder. During his stay at the mental hospital, Ake was evaluated as to his "present sanity" to stand trial but not his mental state during the murder. Because Ake could not afford a psychiatrist, his counsel asked the court to provide a psychiatrist or the money to hire one. The trial judge refused his request, claiming the state is not obligated to provide a psychiatrist, even to poor defendants in capital cases.

Ake was tried for two counts of first-degree murder and for two counts of shooting with intent to kill. During the trial Ake's only defense was insanity; however, none of the psychiatrists at the state mental hospital could testify to his mental state at the time of the crime.

The judge instructed the jurors that Ake could be found not guilty by reason of insanity if he could not distinguish right from wrong when he committed murder. The jurors were told they could presume Ake sane at the time of the crime unless he presented sufficient evidence to raise a reasonable doubt about his sanity during the crime. The jury found him guilty on all counts. The jury sentenced Ake to death based on the earlier testimony of the psychiatrist, who concluded that Ake was a threat to society. On appeal, the Oklahoma Court of Appeals agreed with the trial court that the state did not have the responsibility to provide an impoverished defendant with a psychiatrist to help with his defense.

The U.S. Supreme Court disagreed. In *Ake v. Oklahoma* (470 U.S. 68, 1985), the Court ruled 8–1 to reverse the lower court's ruling, finding that "there was no expert testimony for either side on Ake's sanity at the time of the offense." The high court further observed, "This Court has long recognized that when a State brings its judicial power to bear on an indigent [poor] defendant in a criminal proceeding, it must take steps to assure that the defendant has a fair opportunity to present his defense. This elementary principle, grounded in significant part on the Fourteenth Amendment's due process guarantee of fundamental fairness, derives from the belief that justice cannot be equal where, simply as a result of his poverty, a defendant is denied the opportunity to participate

meaningfully in a judicial proceeding in which his liberty is at stake."

In 1986 Ake was retried, found guilty, and sentenced to life in prison.

INSANITY AND EXECUTION
Can an Insane Person Be Executed?

In 1974 Alvin Ford was convicted of murder and sentenced to death in Florida. There was no question that he was completely sane at the time of his crime, at the trial, and at the sentencing. Eight years later, Ford began to show signs of delusion—from thinking that people were conspiring to force him to commit suicide to believing that family members were being held hostage in prison.

Ford's lawyers had a psychiatrist examine their client. After fourteen months of evaluation and investigation, the doctor concluded that Ford suffered from a severe mental disorder that would preclude him from assisting in the defense of his life. A second psychiatrist concluded that Ford did not understand why he was on death row.

Florida law required the governor to appoint a panel of three psychiatrists to determine whether Ford was mentally capable of understanding the death penalty and the reasons he was being sentenced to death. The three state-appointed doctors met with Ford once for about thirty minutes and then filed separate reports. Ford's lawyers were present but were ordered by the judge not to participate in the examination "in any adversarial manner."

The three psychiatrists submitted different diagnoses, but all agreed that Ford was sane enough to be executed. Ford's lawyers attempted to submit to the governor the reports of the first two psychiatrists along with other materials. However, the governor refused to inform the lawyers whether he would consider these reports. He eventually signed Ford's death warrant.

Ford's appeals were denied in state and federal courts, but a 7–2 Supreme Court, in *Ford v. Wainwright* (477 U.S. 399, 1986), reversed the earlier judgments. In light of the fact that there had been no precedent formed for such a case in U.S. history, the justices turned to English law. Writing for the majority, Justice Thurgood Marshall (1908–1993) observed that even though the reasons appear unclear, English common law forbade the execution of the insane. The English jurist Sir William Blackstone (1723–1780) had labeled such a practice "savage and inhuman." Likewise, the other noted English judicial resource, Sir Edward Coke (1552–1634), observed that even though the execution of a criminal was to serve as an example, the execution of a madman was considered "of extreme inhumanity and cruelty, and can be no example to others." Consequently, because the Eighth Amendment forbidding a cruel and unusual punishment was prepared by men who accepted

English common law, there could be no question that the Eighth Amendment prohibited the execution of the insane.

The issue then became the method the state used to determine Ford's insanity. The high court noted that Florida did not allow the submission of materials that might be relevant to the decision whether or not to execute the condemned man. In addition, Ford's lawyers were not given the chance to question the state-appointed psychiatrists about the basis for finding their client competent. Questions the defense could have asked included the possibility of personal bias on the doctors' part toward the death penalty, any history of error in their judgment, and their degree of certainty in reaching their conclusions. Finally, the justices pointed out that the greatest defect in Florida's practice is its entrusting the ultimate decision about the execution entirely to the executive branch. The high court observed, "Under this procedure, the person who appoints the experts and ultimately decides whether the State will be able to carry out the sentence that it has long sought is the Governor, whose subordinates have been responsible for initiating every stage of the prosecution of the condemned from arrest through sentencing. The commander of the State's corps of prosecutors cannot be said to have the neutrality that is necessary for reliability in the factfinding proceeding."

The high court further observed that even though a prisoner has been sentenced to death, he is still protected by the Constitution. Therefore, ascertaining his sanity as a basis for a legal execution is as important as other proceedings in a capital case.

In dissent, Justice Rehnquist, joined by Chief Justice Burger, thought the Florida procedure consistent with English common law, which had left the decision to the executive branch. Rehnquist warned, "A claim of insanity may be made at any time before sentence and, once rejected, may be raised again; a prisoner found sane two days before execution might claim to have lost his sanity the next day, thus necessitating another judicial determination of his sanity and presumably another stay of his execution."

Ford remained on Florida's death row until 1991, when he died of natural causes.

Can an Insane Person Stabilized by Drugs Be Executed?

In 1979 Charles Singleton stabbed Mary Lou York twice in the neck after robbing her grocery store in Hamburg, Arkansas. He was tried, convicted, and sentenced to death. He was sane during the murder and throughout the trial.

However, Singleton developed schizophrenia while in prison. At one point during his incarceration, Singleton claimed his prison cell was possessed by demons. When given antipsychotic medication, however, Singleton regained his sanity. Fearing a psychotic outburst from Singleton, the prison forced medication on him when he refused to take it. Singleton filed several habeas corpus petitions in state and federal courts, claiming that in light of *Ford*, he was not competent enough to be executed. He also argued that the forcible administration of antipsychotic medication was a violation of the Eighth Amendment, which forbids a cruel and unusual punishment.

The case was taken up by the U.S. Court of Appeals for the Eighth Circuit. In *Singleton v. Norris* (319 F.3d 1018 [8th Cir., 2003]), the appellate court upheld the death penalty for Singleton in a 5–4 decision. The majority felt that as long as Singleton was on medication and in full control of his faculties, his execution was not a violation of the Eighth Amendment. Singleton appealed to the U.S. Supreme Court, but the high court turned the case down, effectively endorsing the decision of the appellate court. Singleton was executed by the state of Arkansas on January 6, 2004.

CAN A MENTALLY RETARDED PERSON BE EXECUTED?

Penry I

In 1979 Pamela Carpenter was brutally raped, beaten, and stabbed with a pair of scissors in Livingston, Texas. Before she died, she was able to describe her attacker, and as a result, Johnny Paul Penry was arrested for, and later confessed to, the crime. At the time of the crime, Penry was out on parole for another rape. He was found guilty for the murder of Carpenter and sentenced to death.

Among the issues considered in his appeal was whether the state of Texas could execute a mentally retarded person. At Penry's competency hearing a psychiatrist testified that the defendant had an intelligence quotient (IQ) of fifty-four. Penry had been tested in the past as having an IQ between fifty and sixty-three, indicating mild to moderate retardation. According to the psychiatrist, during the commission of the crime the twenty-two-year-old Penry had the mental age of a child six-and-a-half years old and the social maturity of someone who was nine to ten years old. Penry's attorneys argued, "Because of their mental disabilities, mentally retarded people do not possess the level of moral culpability to justify imposing the death sentence .... There is an emerging national consensus against executing the mentally retarded."

Writing for the majority regarding the execution of mentally retarded people, Justice O'Connor, in *Penry v. Lynaugh* (492 U.S. 302, 1989), found no emerging national consensus against such executions. Furthermore, even though profoundly retarded people had not been executed for murder historically, Penry did not fall into this group.

Justice O'Connor noted that Penry was found competent to stand trial. He was able to consult rationally with his lawyer and understood the proceedings against him. She thought that the defense was guilty of lumping all mentally retarded people together, ascribing, among other things, a lack of moral capacity to be culpable for actions that call for the death punishment. O'Connor wrote:

> Mentally retarded persons are individuals whose abilities and experiences can vary greatly. [If the mentally retarded were not treated as individuals, but as an undifferentiated group,] a mildly mentally retarded person could be denied the opportunity to enter into contracts or to marry by virtue of the fact that he had a "mental age" of a young child .... In light of the diverse capacities and life experiences of mentally retarded persons, it cannot be said on the record before us today that all mentally retarded people, by definition, can never act with the level of culpability associated with the death penalty.

Furthermore, the majority could find no national movement toward any type of consensus on this issue. Even though *Penry* produced several public opinion polls that indicated strong public opposition to executing the retarded, almost none of this public opinion was reflected in death penalty legislation. Only the federal Anti-Drug Abuse Act of 1988 and the states of Georgia and Maryland at the time banned the execution of retarded people found guilty of a capital crime.

Justice Brennan disagreed. Even though he agreed that lumping mentally retarded people together might result in stereotyping and discrimination, he believed there are characteristics that fall under the clinical definition of mental retardation. Citing the amicus curiae brief prepared by the American Association on Mental Retardation, he noted, "Every individual who has mental retardation—irrespective of his or her precise capacities or experiences—has 'a substantial disability in cognitive ability and adaptive behavior.' ... Though individuals, particularly those who are mildly retarded, may be quite capable of overcoming these limitations to the extent of being able to 'maintain themselves independently or semi-independently in the community,' nevertheless, the mentally retarded by definition 'have a reduced ability to cope with and function in the everyday world.'"

Justice Brennan did not believe that executing a person not fully responsible for his or her actions would serve the "penal goals of deterrence or retribution." What is the point of executing someone who did not fully recognize the terrible evil that he or she had done? Furthermore, he argued, executing a mentally retarded person would not deter nonretarded people, those who would be aware of the possibility of an execution.

Even though the Supreme Court held that executing people with mental retardation was not a violation of the Eighth Amendment, it ruled that Penry's Eighth Amendment right was violated because the jury was not instructed that it could consider mental retardation as a mitigating factor during sentencing. The case was sent back to the lower court. In 1990 Texas retried Penry, and he was again found guilty of capital murder. During the sentencing phase the prosecution used a specific portion of a psychiatric report to point out the doctor's opinion that, if released from custody, Penry would be a threat to society. Penry appealed his case all the way to the Supreme Court. Ten years later, in November 2000, with Penry less than three hours from being put to death, the Supreme Court granted a stay of execution to hear Penry's claims.

Penry II

Penry once again appealed to the Supreme Court after his case was retried. In his appeal to the Supreme Court, Penry argued that the use of a portion of an old psychiatric report at his 1990 retrial violated his Fifth Amendment right against self-incrimination. In 1977 Penry was arrested in connection with another rape. During this rape case the state of Texas provided Penry with a psychiatrist at the request of his lawyer. The psychiatrist was to determine the defendant's competency to stand trial. In 2000 Penry argued that the psychiatrist was an "agent of the state" and that the prosecution's use of his report in the 1990 retrial for murder violated Penry's right against self-incrimination. Penry also claimed jury instructions were inadequate.

On June 4, 2001, the Supreme Court ruled 6–3 in *Penry v. Johnson* (532 U.S. 782) that the admission of the psychiatrist's report did not violate Penry's Fifth Amendment right. The Court held that this case was different from *Estelle v. Smith*, discussed earlier, in which the justices found that the psychiatrist's testimony about the defendant's future dangerousness based on the defendant's statements without his lawyer present violated his Fifth Amendment right. The justices emphasized that *Estelle* was restricted to that particular case.

The justices, however, sent the case back to the trial court for resentencing because, as in the original *Penry* case, the state did not give the sentencing jury adequate instructions about how to weigh mental retardation as a mitigating factor.

The Court Revisits Mental Retardation

Daryl Renard Atkins was convicted and sentenced to death for a 1996 abduction, armed robbery, and capital murder. On appeal to the Virginia Supreme Court, Atkins argued that he could not be executed because he was mentally retarded. Relying on *Penry v. Lynaugh*, the court affirmed the conviction. The court ordered a sentencing retrial because the trial court had used the wrong verdict form. As with the first penalty trial, a psychologist testified that Atkins was "mildly mentally retarded," having an IQ of fifty-nine. The jury sentenced Atkins to death for a second time. Atkins again appealed to the Virginia Supreme Court, which upheld the trial court ruling.

The U.S. Supreme Court unanimously agreed to hear Atkins's case. Thirteen years after ruling that executing the mentally retarded does not violate the Constitution, the Supreme Court, in a 6–3 decision, reversed its 1989 *Penry* decision. On June 20, 2002, in *Atkins v. Virginia* (536 U.S. 304), most of the Court held that "executions of mentally retarded criminals are 'cruel and unusual punishments' prohibited by the Eighth Amendment."

Justice Stevens delivered the opinion of the Court. Justices O'Connor, Kennedy, Souter, Ruth Bader Ginsburg (1933–), and Stephen G. Breyer (1938–) joined the opinion. According to the Court, since *Penry*, many states had concluded that death is not a suitable punishment for mentally retarded offenders, reflecting society's sentiments that these individuals are less culpable than average offenders. The Court observed, "Mentally retarded persons ... have diminished capacities to understand and process information, to communicate, to abstract from mistakes and learn from experience, to engage in logical reasoning, to control impulses, and to understand the reactions of others .... Their deficiencies do not warrant an exemption from criminal sanctions, but they do diminish their personal culpability."

The justices also noted that even though the theory is that capital punishment would serve as deterrence to those contemplating murder, this theory does not apply to the mentally retarded because their diminished mental capacities prevent them from appreciating the possibility of execution as punishment. Moreover, the lesser culpability of mentally retarded criminals does not warrant the severe punishment of death.

Justice Scalia disagreed with the ruling that a person who is slightly mentally retarded does not possess the culpability to be sentenced to death. He claimed that the ruling finds "no support in the text or history of the Eighth Amendment." The justice also noted that current social attitudes do not support the majority decision. He pointed out that the state laws that the majority claimed reflect society's attitudes against executing the mentally retarded are still in their infancy and have not undergone the test of time.

On the relationship between a criminal's culpability and the deserved punishment, Justice Scalia stated:

> Surely culpability, and deservedness of the most severe retribution, depends not merely (if at all) upon the mental capacity of the criminal (above the level where he is able to distinguish right from wrong) but also upon the depravity of the crime—which is precisely why this sort of question has traditionally been thought answerable not by a categorical rule of the sort the Court today imposes upon all trials, but rather by the sentencer's weighing of the circumstances (both degree

of retardation and depravity of crime) in the particular case. The fact that juries continue to sentence mentally retarded offenders to death for extreme crimes shows that society's moral outrage sometimes demands execution of retarded offenders. By what principle of law, science, or logic can the Court pronounce that this is wrong? There is none. Once the Court admits (as it does) that mental retardation does not render the offender morally *blameless* ... there is no basis for saying that the death penalty is *never* appropriate retribution, no matter *how* heinous the crime.

Penry's Sentence Revisited

On July 3, 2002, about two weeks after the Supreme Court ruled that it is unconstitutional to execute a mentally retarded person, a Texas jury concluded that Penry is not mentally retarded. He was resentenced to death. Three years later the Texas Court of Criminal Appeals ruled that the jury had not fully considered Penry's claim of mental retardation and ordered a new sentencing hearing. The Texas attorney general appealed the decision. As of November 2007, Penry remained on death row in Texas awaiting his fourth sentencing hearing.

COMPETENCY STANDARD

In Las Vegas, Nevada, on August 2, 1984, Richard Allen Moran fatally shot a bartender and a patron four times each. Several days later he went to the home of his former wife and fatally shot her, then turned the gun on himself. However, his suicide attempt failed, and Moran confessed to his crimes. Later, the defendant pleaded not guilty to three counts of first-degree murder. Two psychiatrists examined Moran and concluded that he was competent to stand trial. Approximately ten weeks after the evaluations, the defendant decided to dismiss his attorneys and change his plea to guilty. After review of the psychiatric reports, the trial court accepted the waiver for counsel and the guilty plea. The defendant was later sentenced to death.

Seven months later Moran appealed his case, claiming that he had been "mentally incompetent to represent himself." The appellate court reversed the conviction, ruling that "competency to waive constitutional rights requires a higher level of mental functioning than that required to stand trial." A defendant is considered competent to stand trial if he can understand the proceedings and help in his defense. Yet, for a defendant to be considered competent to waive counsel or to plead guilty, he has to be capable of "'reasoned choice' among the alternatives available to him." The appellate court found Moran mentally incapable of the reasoned choice needed to be in a position to waive his constitutional rights.

The Supreme Court ruled 7–2 in *Godinez v. Moran* (509 U.S. 389, 1993) to reverse the judgment of the court of appeals, holding that the standard for measuring a criminal defendant's competency to plead guilty or to waive his right to counsel is not higher than the standard for standing trial. The high court then sent the case back to the lower courts for further proceedings. Moran was executed in March 1996.

VICTIM IMPACT STATEMENTS

First, They Are Not Constitutional

John Booth and Willie Reid stole money from elderly neighbors to buy heroin in 1983. Booth, knowing his neighbors could identify him, tied up the elderly couple and then repeatedly stabbed them in the chest with a kitchen knife. The couple's son found their bodies two days later. Booth and Reid were found guilty.

The state of Maryland permitted a victim impact statement to be read to the jury during the sentencing phase of the trial. The victim impact statement prepared in this case explained the tremendous pain caused by the murder of the parents and grandparents to the family. A 5–4 Supreme Court, in *Booth v. Maryland* (482 U.S. 496, 1987), while recognizing the agony caused to the victim's family, ruled that victim impact statements, as required by Maryland's statute, were unconstitutional and could not be used during the sentencing phase of a capital murder trial.

Writing for the majority, Justice Lewis F. Powell Jr. (1907–1998) indicated that a jury must determine whether the defendant should be executed, based on the circumstances of the crime and the character of the offender. These factors had nothing to do with the victim. The high court noted that it is the crime and the criminal that are at issue. Had Booth and Reid viciously murdered a drunken bum, the crime would have been just as horrible. Furthermore, some families could express the pain and disruption they suffered as a result of the murder better than other families, and a sentencing should not depend on how well a family could express its grief.

Willie Reid's sentence was later converted to two life terms. As of November 2007 Booth remained on Maryland's death row.

... And Then They Are

Pervis Tyrone Payne of Tennessee spent the morning and early afternoon of June 27, 1987, injecting cocaine and drinking beer. Later, he drove around the town with a friend, each of them taking turns reading a pornographic magazine. In midafternoon, Payne went to his girlfriend's apartment, who was away visiting her mother in Arkansas. Charisse Christopher lived across the hall from the apartment. Payne entered Christopher's apartment and made sexual advances toward Christopher, who resisted. Payne became violent.

When the police arrived, they found Christopher on the floor with forty-two direct knife wounds and forty-two defensive wounds on her arms and hands. Her two-year-old daughter had suffered stab wounds to the chest, abdomen, back, and head. The murder weapon, a butcher knife, was found at her feet. Christopher's three-year-old son, despite several stab wounds that went completely through his body, was still alive. Payne was arrested, and a Tennessee jury convicted him of the first-degree murders of Christopher and her daughter and of the first-degree assault, with intent to murder, of Christopher's son, Nicholas.

During the sentencing phase of the trial, Payne called his parents, his girlfriend, and a clinical psychologist to testify about the mitigating aspects of his background and character. The prosecutor, however, called Nicholas's grandmother, who testified how much the child missed his mother and baby sister. In arguing for the death penalty, the prosecutor commented on the continuing effects the crime was having on Nicholas and his family. The jury sentenced Payne to death on each of the murder counts. The state supreme court agreed, rejecting Payne's claim that the admission of the grandmother's testimony and the state's closing argument violated his Eighth Amendment rights under *Booth v. Maryland*.

On hearing the appeal, the U.S. Supreme Court ruled 6–3 in *Payne v. Tennessee* (501 U.S. 808, 1991) to uphold the death penalty and overturned *Booth v. Maryland*. In *Payne*, the Court ruled that the Eighth Amendment does not prohibit a jury from considering, at the sentencing phase of a capital trial, victim impact evidence relating to a victim's personal characteristics and the emotional impact of the murder on the victim's family. The Eighth Amendment also does not bar a prosecutor from arguing such evidence at the sentencing phase.

The Court reasoned that the assessment of harm caused by a defendant as a result of a crime has long been an important concern of criminal law in determining both the elements of the offense and the appropriate punishment. Victim impact evidence is simply another form or method of informing the sentencing jury or judge about the specific harm caused by the crime in question.

The *Booth* case unfairly weighted the scales in a capital trial. No limits were placed on the mitigating evidence the defendant introduced relating to his own circumstances. The state, however, was potentially barred from offering a glimpse of the life of the victim or from showing the loss to the victim's family or to society. *Booth* was decided by narrow margins, the Court continued, and had been questioned by members of the Supreme Court as well as by the lower courts.

Dissenting, Justice Stevens stated that a victim impact statement "sheds no light on the defendant's guilt or moral culpability, and thus serves no purpose other than to encourage jurors to decide in favor of death rather than life on the basis of their emotions rather than their reason."

As of November 2007, Payne remained on Tennessee's death row.

THE ISSUE OF RACE IN CAPITAL CASES

In 1978 Willie Lloyd Turner, an African-American, robbed a jewelry store in Franklin, Virginia. Angered because the owner had set off a silent alarm, Turner first shot the owner in the head, wounding him, and then shot him twice in the chest, killing him for "snitching." Turner's lawyer submitted to the judge the following question for the jurors: "The defendant, Willie Lloyd Turner, is a member of the Negro race. The victim, W. Jack Smith, Jr., was a white Caucasian. Will these facts prejudice you against Willie Lloyd Turner or affect your ability to render a fair and impartial verdict based solely on the evidence?"

The judge refused to allow this question to be asked. A jury of eight whites and four African-Americans convicted Turner and then, in a separate sentencing hearing, recommended the death sentence, which the judge imposed.

Turner appealed his conviction, claiming that the judge's refusal to ask prospective jurors about their racial attitudes deprived him of his right to a fair trial. Even though his argument failed to convince state and federal appeals courts, the U.S. Supreme Court heard his case. The high court ruled 7–2 in *Turner v. Murray* (476 U.S. 28, 1986) to overturn Turner's death sentence, but not his conviction.

Writing for the majority, Justice White noted that, in considering a death sentence, the jury makes a subjective decision that is uniquely his or her own regarding what punishment should be meted out to the offender. White further stated:

> Because of the range of discretion entrusted to a jury in a capital sentencing hearing, there is a unique opportunity for racial prejudice to operate but remain undetected. On the facts of this case, a juror who believes that blacks are violence prone or morally inferior might well be influenced by that belief in deciding whether petitioner's crime involved the aggravating factors specified under Virginia law. Such a juror might also be less favorably inclined toward petitioner's evidence of mental disturbance as a mitigating circumstance. More subtle, less consciously held racial attitudes could also influence a juror's decision in this case. Fear of blacks, which could easily be stirred up by the violent facts of petitioner's crime, might incline a juror to favor the death penalty.

The high court recognized that the death sentence differs from all other punishments and, therefore, requires a more comprehensive examination of how it is imposed. The lower court judge, by not asking prospective jurors about their racial attitudes, had not exercised this thorough examination. Consequently, the Supreme Court reversed

Turner's death sentence. Justice Powell, in his dissent, observed that the Court ruling seemed to be "based on what amounts to a constitutional presumption that jurors in capital cases are racially biased. Such presumption unjustifiably suggests that criminal justice in our courts of law is meted out on racial grounds."

In 1995 Turner was executed by the state of Virginia.

Limits to Consideration of Racial Attitudes

On May 13, 1978, Warren McCleskey and three armed men robbed a furniture store in Fulton County, Georgia. A police officer, responding to a silent alarm, entered the store, was shot twice, and died. McCleskey was African-American; the officer was white. McCleskey admitted taking part in the robbery but denied shooting the police officer. The state proved that at least one shot came from the weapon McCleskey was carrying and produced two witnesses who had heard McCleskey admit to the shooting. A jury found him guilty, and McCleskey, offering no mitigating circumstances during the sentencing phase, received the death penalty.

McCleskey eventually appealed his case all the way to the U.S. Supreme Court. Part of his appeal was based on two major statistical studies of more than two thousand Georgia murder cases that occurred during the 1970s. Prepared by David C. Baldus, Charles A. Pulanski Jr., and George Woodworth, the statistical analyses were referred to as the Baldus study. (The two studies were "Comparative Review of Death Sentences: An Empirical Study of the Georgia Experience" [*Journal of Criminal Law and Criminology*, vol. 74, no. 3, 1983] and "Monitoring and Evaluating Contemporary Death Sentencing Systems: Lessons from Georgia" [*University of California Davis Law Review*, vol. 18, no. 1375, 1985].)

The Baldus study found that defendants charged with killing white people received the death penalty in 11% of cases, but defendants charged with killing African-Americans received the death penalty in only 1% of the cases. The study also found a reverse racial difference, based on the defendant's race—4% of the African-American defendants received the death penalty, as opposed to 7% of the white defendants.

Furthermore, the Baldus study reported on the cases based on the combination of the defendant's race and that of the victim. The death penalty was imposed in 22% of the cases involving African-American defendants and white victims, in 8% of the cases involving white defendants and white victims, in 3% of the cases involving white defendants and African-American victims, and in 1% of the cases involving African-American defendants and African-American victims.

The Baldus study also found that prosecutors sought the death penalty in 70% of the cases involving African-American defendants and white victims, in 32% of the cases involving white defendants and white victims, in 19% of the cases involving white defendants and African-American victims, and in 15% of the cases involving African-American defendants and African-American victims.

Finally, after taking account of variables that could have explained the differences on nonracial grounds, the study concluded that defendants charged with killing white victims were 4.3 times as likely to receive the death penalty as defendants charged with killing African-Americans. In addition, African-American defendants were 1.1 times as likely to get a death sentence as other defendants were. Therefore, McCleskey, who was African-American and killed a white victim, had the greatest likelihood of being sentenced to death.

In court testimony Baldus testified that, in really brutal cases where there is no question the death penalty should be imposed, racial discrimination on the part of the jurors tends to disappear. The racial factors usually come into play in midrange cases, such as McCleskey's, where the jurors were faced with choices.

Even though the federal district court did not accept the Baldus study, both the court of appeals and the U.S. Supreme Court accepted the study as valid. However, a 5–4 Supreme Court, in *McCleskey v. Kemp* (481 U.S. 279, 1987), rejected McCleskey's appeal. McCleskey had to show that the state of Georgia had acted in a discriminatory manner in his case, and the Baldus study was not enough to support the defendant's claim that any of the jurors had acted with discrimination.

Justice Powell noted that statistics, at most, may show that a certain factor might likely enter some decision-making processes. The Court recognized that a jury's decision could be influenced by racial prejudice, but the majority believed previous rulings had built in enough safeguards to guarantee equal protection for every defendant. The Court declared, "At most, the Baldus study indicates a discrepancy that appears to correlate with race. Apparent disparities in sentencing are an inevitable part of our criminal justice system.... We hold that the Baldus study does not demonstrate a constitutionally significant risk of racial bias affecting the Georgia capital sentencing process."

The Court expressed concern that if it ruled that Baldus's findings did represent a risk, the findings might well be applied to lesser cases. It further noted that it is the job of the legislative branch to consider these findings and incorporate them into the laws to guarantee equal protection in courts of law.

Justice Brennan, who, along with Justice Marshall, believed capital punishment constitutes a cruel and unusual punishment and, therefore, is unconstitutional, thought the Baldus study powerfully demonstrated that it is impossible to eliminate arbitrariness in the imposition of the death penalty. Therefore, he argued, the death penalty must be abolished altogether because the Court cannot rely on legal safeguards to guarantee an African-American defendant a fair sentencing. Even though the Baldus study did not show that racism necessarily led to McCleskey's death sentence, it had surely shown that McCleskey faced a considerably greater likelihood of being sentenced to death because he was an African-American man convicted of killing a white man.

Also writing in dissent, Justice Blackmun thought the Court majority had concentrated too much on the potential racial attitudes of the jury. As important, he thought, were the racial attitudes of the prosecutor's office, which the Baldus study found to be much more likely to seek the death penalty for an African-American person who had killed a white person than for other categories.

The district attorney for Fulton County had testified that no county policy existed on how to prosecute capital cases. Decisions to seek the death penalty were left to the judgment of the assistant district attorneys who handled the cases. Blackmun thought that such a system was certainly open to abuse. Without guidelines, the prosecutors could let their racial prejudices influence their decisions.

Blackmun also noted that the Court majority had totally dismissed Georgia's history of racial prejudice as past history. Even though it should not be the overriding factor, this bias should be considered in any case presented to the high court, he thought. Justice Blackmun found most disturbing the Court's concern that, if the Baldus findings were upheld, they might be applied to other cases, leading to constitutional challenges. Blackmun thought that a closer scrutiny of the effects of racial discrimination would benefit the criminal justice system and, ultimately, society.

In 1991 McCleskey was executed in the electric chair by the state of Georgia.

Prosecutor's Racially Based Use of Peremptory Challenges in Jury Selection

James Ford, an African-American, was charged with the kidnapping, rape, and murder of a white woman on February 29, 1984. The state of Georgia informed Ford that it planned to seek the death penalty. Before the trial, Ford filed a "Motion to Restrict Racial Use of Peremptory Challenges," claiming that the prosecutor had consistently excluded African-Americans from juries where the victims were white.

At a hearing on the defendant's motion, Ford's lawyer noted that it had been his experience that the district attorney and his assistants had used their peremptory challenges (the right to reject a juror without giving a reason) to excuse potential African-American jurors. Ford's lawyer asked the trial judge to prevent this from happening by ordering the district attorney to justify on the record his reasons for excusing potential African-American jurors.

The prosecutor denied any discrimination on his part. He referred to the U.S. Supreme Court decision in *Swain v. Alabama* (380 U.S. 202, 1965), which said, in part, "It would be an unreasonable burden to require an attorney for either side to justify his use of peremptory challenges." The judge denied the defense attorney's motion because he had previously seen the district attorney passing over prospective white jurors in favor of potential African-American jurors.

During jury selection the prosecutor used nine of his ten peremptory challenges to dismiss prospective African-American jurors, leaving only one African-American member seated on the jury. In closed sessions, the judge allowed Ford's attorney's observation, for the record, that nine of the ten African-American prospective members had been dismissed on peremptory challenges by the prosecutor. The judge, however, told the prosecutor that he did not have to offer any reasons for his peremptory actions.

Ford was convicted on all counts and sentenced to death. His attorney, believing that the jury did not represent a fair cross-section of the community, called for a new trial and claimed that Ford's "right to an impartial jury as guaranteed by Sixth Amendment to the United States Constitution was violated by the prosecutor's exercise of his peremptory challenges on a racial basis." On appeal, the Georgia Supreme Court affirmed the conviction.

Ford appealed to the U.S. Supreme Court. In *Ford v. Georgia* (498 U.S. 411, 1991), the high court reversed the decision of the Georgia Supreme Court. The Court vacated Ford's conviction and ruled that its decision in *Batson v. Kentucky* (476 U.S. 79, 1986) could be applied retroactively to Ford's case, which had been tried in 1984. In 1986 the high court had superseded *Swain* when it ruled in *Batson* that a defendant could make a case claiming the denial of equal protection of the laws solely on evidence that the prosecutor had used peremptory challenges to exclude members of the defendant's race from the jury.

Delivering the opinion for a unanimous Court, Justice Souter held that the Georgia Supreme Court had erred when it ruled that Ford had failed to present a proper equal protection claim. Even though Ford's pretrial motion did not mention the Equal Protection Clause (of the Fourteenth Amendment), and his new trial motion had cited the Sixth Amendment rather than the Fourteenth, the motion referring to a pattern of excluding African-American members "'over a long period of time' constitutes the assertion of an equal protection claim." As of November 2007 Ford was in the Georgia State Prison serving a sentence of life without the possibility of parole.

Using Race/Ethnicity to Obtain a Death Sentence

On June 5, 2000, the Supreme Court, in a summary disposition, ordered the Texas Court of Criminal Appeals to hold a new sentencing hearing for Victor Saldano, an Argentine national on death row. In a summary disposition, the Court decides a case in a simple proceeding without a jury. Generally, a summary disposition is rare in criminal cases. In this instance, the crime was committed by a foreign national and thus fell outside of a trial jury's mandate. In *Saldano v. Texas* (No. 99-8119), the Court cited the confession of error by the Texas attorney general John Cornyn (1952–) regarding the use of race as a factor in sentencing the defendant.

Texas death penalty statutes require that the jury consider a defendant's future dangerousness to determine whether or not to impose the death penalty. At the sentencing hearing Walter Quijano, the court-appointed psychologist, testified that Saldano was "a continuing threat to society" because he is Hispanic. Quijano told the jury that because Hispanics are "over-represented" in prisons they are more likely to be dangerous. Following this decision, other death row inmates whose cases reflected similar circumstances were granted new sentencing hearings. Saldano's own case continued in the courts; in March 2004 the Fifth U.S. Circuit Court of Appeals refused to reinstate Saldano's death sentence. As of November 2007, Saldano remained on Texas's death row.

CHAPTER 5

DEATH PENALTY LAWS: OFFENSES, SENTENCES, APPEALS, AND EXECUTION METHODS

CAPITAL OFFENSES

Before the late 1960s U.S. death penalty laws varied considerably from state to state and from region to region. Few national standards existed on how a murder trial should be conducted or which types of crimes deserved the death penalty. In South Carolina, for instance, a person could be executed for rape or robbery. In Georgia and in a number of other states, juries were given complete discretion in delivering a sentence along with the conviction. Though verdicts were swift, the punishments such juries meted out were frequently arbitrary and at times discriminatory.

In the late 1960s and early 1970s the U.S. Supreme Court undertook a series of cases that questioned the constitutionality of state capital punishment laws. In *Furman v. Georgia* (408 U.S. 238, 1972), the Court ruled that the death penalty, as it was then being administered, constituted a cruel and unusual punishment in violation of the Eighth and Fourteenth Amendments to the U.S. Constitution. According to the Court, the state laws that were then in effect led to arbitrary sentencing of the death penalty. As a result, many states changed their laws to conform to standards set by the *Furman* decision. Since *Furman*, review of individual state statutes has continued as appeals of capital sentences reach state courts or the U.S. Supreme Court.

Under revised laws most states now use a bifurcated (two-part) trial system, where the first trial is used to determine a defendant's guilt, and the second trial determines the sentence of a guilty defendant. In most trials jurors are usually only given the option of either sentencing a convicted felon to life in prison or to death. During a sentencing hearing juries must consider all the aggravating circumstances presented by the prosecution and the mitigating circumstances presented by the defense. Mitigating circumstances may lessen responsibility for a crime, whereas aggravating circumstances may add to responsibility for a crime.

Different types of capital murder have been specifically defined as well. Even though varying somewhat from one jurisdiction to another, the types of homicide most commonly specified are murder carried out during the commission of a felony (serious offense such as rape, robbery, or arson); murder of a peace officer, corrections employee, or firefighter engaged in the performance of official duties; murder by an inmate serving a life sentence; and murder for hire (contract murder). Different statutory terminology may be used in different states to designate essentially similar crimes. Terms such as *capital murder, first-degree murder, capital felony,* or *murder Class 1 felony* may indicate the same offense in different states. Table 5.1 and Table 5.2 show capital offenses by state and federal laws providing for the death penalty in 2005.

The U.S. Supreme Court ruled in *Eberheart v. Georgia* (433 U.S. 917, 1977) that kidnapping that does not result in homicide is not a capital crime. Even though other offenses (most notably treason and air piracy or hijacking) do carry the death penalty, most have not yet had their constitutionality tested.

Terrorism

As in the past, states with the death penalty have continued to revise their statutory provisions relating to the death penalty. In the aftermath of the September 11, 2001, attacks on the World Trade Center and the Pentagon, several states expanded their laws, including both death penalty and non-death penalty states. According to Donna Lyons of the National Conference of State Legislatures, in "States Enact New Terrorism Crimes and Penalties" (*State Legislative Report*, vol. 27, no. 19, November 2002), New York, Florida, and North Carolina amended their death penalty statutes in 2001, making murder committed in furtherance of a terrorist act a capital crime. In 2002 ten more states—Georgia, Idaho, New Jersey, Ohio, Oklahoma, South Carolina, South Dakota, Tennessee, Utah, and

TABLE 5.1

Capital offenses, by state, 2005

Alabama. Intentional murder with 18 aggravating factors (Ala. Stat. Ann. 13A-5-40(a)(1)-(18)).

Arizona*. First-degree murder accompanied by at least 1 of 14 aggravating factors (A.R.S. § 13-703(F)).

Arkansas*. Capital murder (Ark. Code Ann. 5-10-101) with a finding of at least 1 of 10 aggravating circumstances; treason.

California*. First-degree murder with special circumstances; train wrecking; treason; perjury causing execution.

Colorado*. First-degree murder with at least 1 of 17 aggravating factors; treason.

Connecticut*. Capital felony with 8 forms of aggravated homicide (C.G.S. 53a-54b).

Delaware*. First-degree murder with aggravating circumstances.

Florida*. First-degree murder; felony murder; capital drug trafficking; capital sexual battery.

Georgia*. Murder; kidnapping with bodily injury or ransom when the victim dies; aircraft hijacking; treason.

Idaho*. First-degree murder with aggravating factors; aggravated kidnapping; perjury resulting in death.

Illinois*. First-degree murder with 1 of 21 aggravating circumstances.

Indiana*. Murder with 16 aggravating circumstances (IC 35-50-2-9).

Kansas*. Capital murder with 8 aggravating circumstances (KSA 21-3439).

Kentucky*. Murder with aggravating factors; kidnapping with aggravating factors (KRS 32.025).

Louisiana*. First-degree murder; aggravated rape of victim under age 12; treason (La. R.S. 14:30, 14:42, and 14:113).

Maryland*. First-degree murder, either premeditated or during the commission of a felony, provided that certain death eligibility requirements are satisfied.

Mississippi. Capital murder (97-3-19(2) MCA); aircraft piracy (97-25-55(1) MCA).

Missouri*. First-degree murder (565.020 RSMO 2000).

Montana. Capital murder with 1 of 9 aggravating circumstances (46–18–303 MCA); capital sexual assault (45-5-503 MCA).

Nebraska*. First-degree murder with a finding of at least 1 statutorily-defined aggravating circumstance.

Nevada*. First-degree murder with at least 1of 15 aggravating circumstances (NRS 200.030, 200.033, 200.035).

New Hampshire. Six categories of capital murder (RSA 630:1, RSA 630:5).

New Jersey. Murder by one's own conduct, by solicitation, committed in furtherance of a narcotics conspiracy, or during commission of a crime of terrorism (NJSA 2C:11-3c).

New Mexico*. First-degree murder with at least 1 of 7 statutorily-defined aggravating circumstances (Section 30-2-1 A, NMSA).

New York*. First-degree murder with 1 of 13 aggravating factors (NY Penal Law §125.27).

North Carolina*. First-degree murder (NCGS §14–17).

Ohio*. Aggravated murder with at least 1 of 10 aggravating circumstances (O.R.C. secs. 2903.01, 2929.02, and 2929.04).

Oklahoma. First-degree murder in conjunction with a finding of at least 1 of 8 statutorily-defined aggravating circumstances.

Oregon. Aggravated murder (ORS 163.095).

Pennsylvania. First-degree murder with 18 aggravating circumstances.

South Carolina*. Murder with 1 of 11 aggravating circumstances (§ 16-3-20(C)(a)).

South Dakota*. First-degree murder with 1 of 10 aggravating circumstances; aggravated kidnapping.

Tennessee*. First-degree murder with 1 of 15 aggravating circumstances (Tenn. Code Ann. § 39-13-204).

Texas. Criminal homicide with 1 of 9 aggravating circumstances (TX Penal Code 19.03).

Utah*. Aggravated murder (76-5-202, Utah Code Annotated).

Virginia*. First-degree murder with 1 of 13 aggravating circumstances (VA Code § 18.2-31).

Washington*. Aggravated first-degree murder.

Wyoming. First-degree murder.

*As of December 31, 2005, 27 states excluded mentally retarded persons from capital sentencing: Arizona, Arkansas, California, Colorado, Connecticut, Delaware, Florida, Georgia, Idaho, Illinois, Indiana, Kansas, Kentucky, Louisiana, Maryland, Missouri, Nebraska, Nevada, New Mexico, New York, North Carolina, Ohio, South Dakota, Tennessee, Utah, Virginia, and Washington. Mental retardation is a mitigating factor in South Carolina.

SOURCE: Tracy L. Snell, "Table 1. Capital Offenses, by State, 2005," in *Capital Punishment, 2005*, U.S. Department of Justice, Bureau of Justice Statistics, December 2006, http://www.ojp.usdoj.gov/bjs/pub/pdf/cp05.pdf (accessed July 23, 2007)

Virginia—added murder committed in the perpetration of terrorism punishable by death.

Arkansas and Texas expanded their definitions of criminal homicide to include terrorism in 2003, the same year in which Colorado authorized the death penalty for anyone who used chemical, biological, or radiological weapons to kill more than one person.

Sexual Crimes

The U.S. Supreme Court has held, in *Coker v. Georgia* (433 U.S. 584, 1977), that rape of an adult woman in which the victim survives does not warrant the death penalty.

As of November 2007, several state statutes allowed for the death penalty when sexual assault is committed against a child. They included Florida, Montana, Georgia, South Carolina, Oklahoma, Texas, and Louisiana.

Since 1974 a Florida law has been on the books that allows the death penalty for sexual battery committed against children. The upper limit of the age range was originally eleven, but was changed to twelve in 1984. However, that same year the Florida Supreme Court ruled that the death sentence for sexual battery was a cruel and unusual punishment. Even though the law has never been changed, in practice, those convicted of capital sexual battery in Florida receive a mandatory life sentence. A similar situation existed in Georgia law that listed, as of 2007, the death penalty as a possible sentence for rape.

Montana law provides for the death penalty as a possible sentence for repeat sexual offenders who cause "serious bodily injury" to victims less than sixteen years of age. However, as of November 2007 no Montana defendants had received the death penalty for this crime.

Oklahoma (2006), South Carolina (2006), and Texas (2007) have all recently changed their laws to allow for the death penalty for repeat offenders who commit rape or sodomy against a child. The upper age limit of the child victim is fourteen in Oklahoma and Texas and eleven in South Carolina. These new laws are generally referred to as "Jessica's Laws," in memory of Jessica Lunsford, a nine-year-old Florida girl who was brutally raped and murdered in 2005 by a paroled sex offender.

LOUISIANA. In August 1995 Louisiana enacted a law allowing the death penalty for rape when the victims are under age twelve. In December 1995 Anthony Wilson was

TABLE 5.2

Federal laws providing for the death penalty, 2005

8 U.S.C. 1342—Murder related to the smuggling of aliens.	18 U.S.C. 1111—First-degree murder.	18 U.S.C. 1958—Murder for hire.
18 U.S.C. 32–34—Destruction of aircraft, motor vehicles, or related facilities resulting in death.	18 U.S.C. 1114—Murder of a federal judge or law enforcement official.	18 U.S.C. 1959—Murder involved in a racketeering offense.
18 U.S.C. 36—Murder committed during a drug-related drive-by shooting.	18 U.S.C. 1116—Murder of a foreign official.	18 U.S.C. 1992—Willful wrecking of a train resulting in death.
18 U.S.C. 37—Murder committed at an airport serving international civil aviation.	18 U.S.C. 1118—Murder by a federal prisoner.	18 U.S.C. 2113—Bank-robbery-related murder or kidnapping.
18 U.S.C. 115(b)(3) [by cross-reference to 18 U.S.C. 1111]—Retaliatory murder of a member of the immediate family of law enforcement officials.	18 U.S.C. 1119—Murder of a U.S. national in a foreign country.	18 U.S.C. 2119—Murder related to a carjacking.
18 U.S.C. 241, 242, 245, 247—Civil rights offenses resulting in death.	18 U.S.C. 1120—Murder by an escaped federal prisoner already sentenced to life imprisonment.	18 U.S.C. 2245—Murder related to rape or child molestation.
18 U.S.C. 351 [by cross-reference to 18 U.S.C. 1111]—Murder of a member of Congress, an important executive official, or a Supreme Court Justice.	18 U.S.C. 1121—Murder of a state or local law enforcement official or other person aiding in a federal investigation; murder of a state correctional officer.	18 U.S.C. 2251—Murder related to sexual exploitation of children.
18 U.S.C. 794—Espionage.	18 U.S.C. 1201—Murder during a kidnapping.	18 U.S.C. 2280—Murder committed during an offense against maritime navigation.
18 U.S.C. 844(d), (f), (i)—Death resulting from offenses involving transportation of explosives, destruction of government property, or destruction of property related to foreign or interstate commerce.	18 U.S.C. 1203—Murder during a hostage taking.	18 U.S.C. 2281—Murder committed during an offense against a maritime fixed platform.
	18 U.S.C. 1503—Murder of a court officer or juror.	18 U.S.C. 2332—Terrorist murder of a U.S. national in another country.
18 U.S.C. 924(i)—Murder committed by the use of a firearm during a crime of violence or a drug-trafficking crime.	18 U.S.C. 1512—Murder with the intent of preventing testimony by a witness, victim, or informant.	18 U.S.C. 2332a—Murder by the use of a weapon of mass destruction.
18 U.S.C. 930—Murder committed in a federal government facility.	18 U.S.C. 1513—Retaliatory murder of a witness, victim, or informant.	18 U.S.C. 2340—Murder involving torture.
18 U.S.C. 1091—Genocide.	18 U.S.C. 1716—Mailing of injurious articles with intent to kill or resulting in death.	18 U.S.C. 2381—Treason.
	18 U.S.C. 1751 [by cross-reference to 18 U.S.C. 1111]—Assassination or kidnapping resulting in the death of the President or Vice President.	21 U.S.C. 848(e)—Murder related to a continuing criminal enterprise or related murder of a federal, state, or local law enforcement officer.
		49 U.S.C. 1472–1473—Death resulting from aircraft hijacking.

Note: U.S.C. is United States code.

SOURCE: Tracy L. Snell, "Appendix Table 1. Federal Laws Providing for the Death Penalty, 2005," in *Capital Punishment, 2005*, U.S. Department of Justice, Bureau of Justice Statistics, December 2006, http://www.ojp.usdoj.gov/bjs/pub/pdf/cp05.pdf (accessed July 23, 2007)

charged by a grand jury with the aggravated rape of a five-year-old girl. (A grand jury differs from a regular jury in that the former, typically consisting of up to twenty-three jurors, determines whether the criminal complaint brought by the prosecutor warrants an indictment and a trial.) In April 1996 Patrick Dewayne Bethley pled innocent to raping three girls between December 1995 and January 1996. One of the girls was his daughter. At the time of the rapes, the girls were five, seven, and nine years old. The two defendants moved to quash their indictments. They claimed that the death penalty, when imposed for rape, constitutes a cruel and unusual punishment and, therefore, is unconstitutional under the Eighth Amendment and Article I, Section 20, of the Louisiana Constitution. On December 13, 1996, the Louisiana Supreme Court, in *State v. Wilson* (685 So.2d 1063), held by a 5–2 vote that the state death penalty statute was constitutional. The Louisiana Supreme Court concluded, "Given the appalling nature of the crime, the severity of the harm inflicted upon the victim, and the harm imposed on society, the death penalty is not an excessive penalty for the crime of rape when the victim is a child under the age of twelve years old."

In 1998 Bethley entered into a plea agreement with prosecutors in which he received a life sentence for rape. In turn, the state of Louisiana did not seek the death penalty

against him. In 1999, on appeal, Wilson was found mentally retarded and, therefore, unable to assist in his defense.

In 2003 Patrick Kennedy was convicted of the brutal 1998 rape of his eight-year-old stepdaughter. The child suffered extensive internal damage in the attack and required reconstructive surgery. Kennedy was sentenced to death, and a subsequent motion for a new trial was denied. In May 2007 the Louisiana Supreme Court upheld his conviction and death sentence. Legal scholars believe the constitutionality of the sentence will ultimately be decided by the U.S. Supreme Court.

LEGAL CONTROVERSY. Capital punishment for sexual crimes against children is highly controversial even among those who support the death penalty in general. For example, in "The Death Penalty for Child Rape: Why Texas May Help Louisiana" (May 2, 2007, http://jurist. law.pitt.edu/forumy/2007/05/death-penalty-for-child-rape-why-texas.php), Adam Gershowitz of the South Texas College of Law explains that many prosecutors fear that the new laws will discourage children from reporting sexual abuse committed by parents and relatives and could encourage child molesters to kill their victims.

The Texas "Law of Parties"

Under Texas law a person who is party to, but does not actually commit, a murder can receive the death penalty. Section 7.02 of the Texas Penal Code took effect in 1974 and allows prosecutors to charge an accomplice with capital murder if the accomplice should have anticipated that the murder was going to occur. This is known informally as "the law of parties" and is explained by Jordan Smith, in "Wrong Place, Wrong Time" (*Austin Chronicle*, February 11, 2005). The law of parties received national attention when it was used in 1997 to impose a death sentence against Kenneth Foster for his role as the get-away driver in a murder. Foster and three other men were arrested in 1996. They had been robbing people at gunpoint when they saw an attractive woman in a suburban neighborhood. One of the men, Mauriceo Brown, left the car to talk to the woman and wound up shooting and killing her boyfriend, Michael LaHood Jr. Allegedly, Brown was at least eighty feet away from the car when the shooting occurred. He fled back to the car containing the other three men and they sped from the scene. Brown was sentenced to death; he was executed in 2006. The other two men involved were not charged with capital murder.

Foster garnered the support of abolitionists who argued that a death sentence was too harsh a penalty for his crime. After exhausting all appeals Foster faced execution on August 31, 2007. Just hours before the scheduled execution the Texas governor Rick Perry (1950–) granted clemency—a very rare occurrence in the state. Foster's sentence was changed to life imprisonment with a possibility for parole.

Minimum Age for Execution

Under state laws, the term *juvenile* refers to people below the age of eighteen. Literature on the death penalty typically considers "juvenile offenders" as people younger than eighteen at the time of their crimes. According to Victor L. Streib of Ohio Northern University, in *The Juvenile Death Penalty Today: Death Sentences and Executions for Juvenile Crimes, January 1, 1973–December 31, 2004* (2005), the first execution of a juvenile in the United States took place in Plymouth Colony, Massachusetts, in 1642. Through 2004 an estimated 366 inmates who were juveniles during the commission of their crimes had been executed in the United States. Inmates spent from six years to more than twenty years on death row before execution.

Before 1999 the last execution of a person who was sixteen at the time of his crime occurred on April 10, 1959, when Maryland executed Leonard Shockley. After a forty-year respite in the United States, in February 1999 Oklahoma executed Sean Sellers, who was sixteen when he committed his crime and twenty-nine years old at the time of execution. He had been convicted for the murders of his mother, stepfather, and a convenience-store clerk. His supporters claimed Sellers suffered from multiple personality disorder, which was diagnosed after his conviction.

According to the Death Penalty Information Center (DPIC), since 1973 twenty-two inmates who were juveniles at the time of their crimes have been executed. (See Table 5.3.) Texas implemented the death penalty of thirteen juvenile offenders, followed by Virginia (three) and Oklahoma (two). Florida, Georgia, Missouri, and South Carolina each executed one juvenile offender.

On March 1, 2005, the Supreme Court ruled in *Roper v. Simmons* (543 U.S. 633) that the execution of a person

TABLE 5.3

Juveniles executed, January 1, 1973–August 24, 2007

Name	Date of execution	Place of execution	Race	Age at crime	Age at execution
Charles Rumbaugh	9/11/85	Texas	White	17	28
J. Terry Roach	1/10/86	South Carolina	White	17	25
Jay Pinkerton	5/15/86	Texas	White	17	24
Dalton Prejean	5/18/90	Louisiana	Black	17	30
Johnny Garrett	2/11/92	Texas	White	17	28
Curtis Harris	7/1/93	Texas	Black	17	31
Frederick Lashley	7/28/93	Missouri	Black	17	29
Ruben Cantu	8/24/93	Texas	Latino	17	26
Chris Burger	12/7/93	Georgia	White	17	33
Joseph Cannon	4/22/98	Texas	White	17	38
Robert Carter	5/18/98	Texas	Black	17	34
Dwayne Allen Wright	10/14/98	Virginia	Black	17	24
Sean Sellers	2/4/99	Oklahoma	White	16	29
Douglas Christopher Thomas	1/10/00	Virginia	White	17	26
Steven Roach	1/13/00	Virginia	White	17	23
Glen McGinnis	1/25/00	Texas	Black	17	27
Shaka Sankofa (Gary Graham)	6/22/00	Texas	Black	17	36
Gerald Mitchell	10/22/01	Texas	Black	17	33
Napoleon Beazley	5/28/02	Texas	Black	17	25
T.J. Jones	8/8/02	Texas	Black	17	25
Toronto Patterson	8/28/02	Texas	Black	17	24
Scott Allen Hain	4/3/03	Oklahoma	White	17	32

Note: No juveniles were executed between January 1, 1973 and September 10, 1985.

SOURCE: "Juveniles Executed in the United States in the Modern Era (Since January 1, 1973)," in *Execution of Juveniles in the U.S. and Other Countries*, Death Penalty Information Center, 2005, http://www.deathpenaltyinfo.org/article.php?scid=27did=203 (accessed August 24, 2007)

who committed a crime as a minor was unconstitutional. The Court reversed an opinion issued fifteen years earlier in *Stanford v. Kentucky* (492 U.S. 361, 1989), where it held that juvenile murderers below the age of eighteen could be executed. In light of *Roper*, states are required to amend their statutes regarding juvenile executions.

Executing Mentally Retarded People

In 1989 the Supreme Court held, in *Penry v. Lynaugh* (492 U.S. 302), that it was not unconstitutional to execute a mentally retarded person found guilty of a capital crime. According to the Court, there was no emerging national consensus against such execution. Just two death penalty states—Georgia and Maryland—banned putting mentally retarded people to death. In 1988 Georgia became the first state to prohibit the execution of murderers found "guilty but mentally retarded." The legislation resulted from the 1986 execution of Jerome Bowden, who had an intelligence quotient (IQ) of sixty-five. It is generally accepted that an IQ below seventy is evidence of mental retardation. (Normal IQ is considered ninety and above.) In 1988 Maryland passed similar legislation, which took effect in July 1989.

Between 1989 and 2001 eighteen states outlawed the execution of offenders with mental retardation. The federal government also forbids the execution of mentally retarded inmates. In the Anti-Drug Abuse Act of 1988, the government permits the death penalty for any person working "in furtherance of a continuing criminal enterprise or any person engaging in a drug-related felony offense, who intentionally kills or counsels, commands, or causes the intentional killing of an individual," but forbids the imposition of the death penalty against anyone who is mentally retarded who commits such a crime. In 1994, when Congress enacted the Federal Death Penalty Act, adding more than fifty crimes punishable by death, it also exempted people with mental retardation from the death sentence.

Even though the Supreme Court had agreed to review the case of the North Carolina death row inmate Ernest McCarver in 2001 to consider whether it is unconstitutional to execute inmates with mental retardation, the case was rendered moot when a state bill was passed that banned such executions. On June 20, 2002, the Supreme Court finally ruled on a case involving the execution of mentally retarded convicts. In *Atkins v. Virginia* (536 U.S. 304), the Court ruled 6–3 that executing the mentally retarded violates the Eighth Amendment ban against a cruel and unusual punishment. The Court did not say what mental retardation consists of, leaving it to the states to set their own definitions.

Federal Capital Punishment in Non-death Penalty States

According to U.S. Department of Justice policy, federal criminal law can be enacted in any state. Federal law can also be enacted in any U.S. territory. In 2000 federal prosecutors in Puerto Rico sought the death penalty against two men for kidnapping and murder. Puerto Rico had its last execution in 1927 and had banned the death penalty in 1929. In August 2003 a federal jury voted to acquit the defendants.

Massachusetts outlawed capital punishment in 1975, but in 2000 the federal government sought the death penalty in the case of Kristen Gilbert in Massachusetts. Gilbert was charged with killing four patients at the Veterans Affairs Medical Center in Northampton, a federal hospital. The jury found Gilbert guilty of first-degree murder but was deadlocked on the death sentence. As a result, Judge Michael A. Ponsor (1946–) sentenced the defendant to life imprisonment without the possibility of parole.

Michigan has not executed an inmate under state law since it joined the Union in 1837. In 1938 Anthony Cherboris was executed in the state under federal law for killing a bystander during a bank robbery. This was the last federal death sentence in Michigan until March 16, 2002, when Marvin Gabrion received the death penalty for killing Rachel Timmerman in 1997 on federal property in Manistee National Forest. No execution date had been set as of November 2007.

In September 2003 Massachusetts was once again the scene of a federal death penalty case. The Federal Death Penalty Act of 1994 allowed federal prosecutors to seek the death penalty in the case of Gary Lee Sampson, who killed two men in separate carjacking incidents in 2001. Before the trial phase began, Sampson pleaded guilty to the crimes. The case proceeded to the penalty phase, in which a federal jury sentenced him to death. As of November 2007, Sampson remained on death row.

According to the DPIC (http://www.deathpenalty info.org/article.php?scid=29&did=193#list), as of October 26, 2007, four additional federal death sentences had been handed down in non-death penalty states as follows—Iowa (2004), Vermont (2005), North Dakota (2006), and West Virginia (2007). The sentence in North Dakota was particularly notable, because it involved a crime that began in neighboring Minnesota, also a non-death penalty state. In 2003 Dru Sjodin, a student at the University of North Dakota, was kidnapped, raped, and murdered. Her body was found in Minnesota. Alfonso Rodriguez Jr. was convicted of the crime and sentenced to death. The judge ordered the execution to take place in South Dakota, which allows the death penalty by means of lethal injection.

Federal prisoners in death penalty cases used to be imprisoned in the state where the trial was held, but during the 1990s the U.S. Bureau of Prisons built a fifty-cell federal death house in Terre Haute, Indiana, to accommodate the condemned. It started housing death row inmates in 1999.

FIGURE 5.1

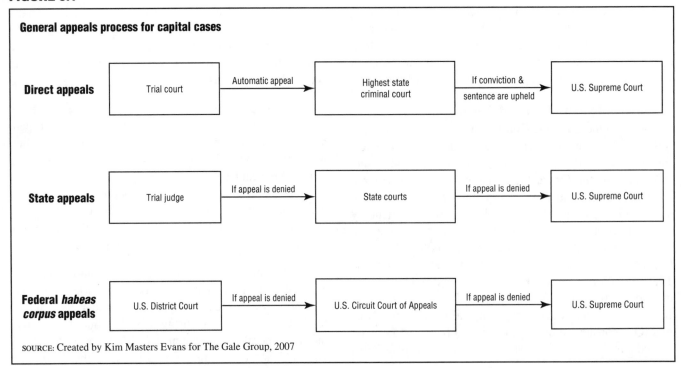

General appeals process for capital cases

Direct appeals	Trial court	Automatic appeal	Highest state criminal court	If conviction & sentence are upheld	U.S. Supreme Court	
State appeals	Trial judge	If appeal is denied	State courts	If appeal is denied	U.S. Supreme Court	
Federal *habeas corpus* appeals	U.S. District Court	If appeal is denied	U.S. Circuit Court of Appeals	If appeal is denied	U.S. Supreme Court	

SOURCE: Created by Kim Masters Evans for The Gale Group, 2007

THE APPEALS PROCESS IN CAPITAL CASES

The appeals process in capital cases varies slightly from state to state but generally includes the steps shown in Figure 5.1.

The appeals process begins with the direct appeal. In *Gregg v. Georgia* (428 U.S. 153, 1976), the U.S. Supreme Court ruled that any death sentence must be appealed from the trial court directly to the highest court in the state with criminal jurisdiction. The highest court of the state may be either the state supreme court or the highest court of criminal appeals. The state high court evaluates the trial court records for constitutional or legal errors. If the high court upholds the conviction and sentence, the defendant can appeal directly to the U.S. Supreme Court using a writ of certiorari. A writ of certiorari is a petition to the Supreme Court to review only the issues brought up in the direct appeal in the state's high court. If the Supreme Court denies certiorari, the trial court's ruling stands.

If the first round of direct appeals is denied, the inmate may then seek state habeas corpus appeals (federal appeals by which state and federal inmates request a federal court to determine whether they are being held in violation of their constitutional rights), starting with the trial judge. Habeas corpus review, which affords state and federal prisoners the chance to challenge the constitutionality of their convictions or sentences, has long been considered an important safeguard in all criminal trials, especially those involving the death penalty. If turned down by the trial judge, the convict may petition the first level of state appellate courts and finally the state's highest court. This second round of appeals differs from the direct appeal in that the condemned may raise issues that were not and could not have been raised during the direct appeal. These issues include the incompetence of the defense lawyer, jury bias, or the suppression of evidence by police or prosecution. If the state review is denied, the condemned can again appeal directly to the U.S. Supreme Court.

A death row inmate who has exhausted all state appeals can then file a petition for a federal habeas corpus review on grounds of violation of his or her constitutional rights. The right may involve a violation of the Sixth Amendment to the U.S. Constitution (the right to have the assistance of counsel for defense), the Eighth Amendment (the ban against a cruel and unusual punishment), or the Fourteenth Amendment (the right to due process). The inmate files the appeal with the district court in the state in which he or she was convicted. If the district court denies the appeal, the inmate can proceed to the U.S. Circuit Court of Appeals in the region. As of 2007 there were ninety-four federal judicial districts and twelve U.S. Circuit Courts of Appeal around the United States. (See Figure 5.2.) Finally, if the circuit court denies the appeal, the condemned can for a third time ask the U.S. Supreme Court for a certiorari review.

If a convict comes to the end of all appeals and is still on death row, the only way the sentence can be altered is through the power of clemency. The power of clemency may rest solely with a state's governor, with a clemency board, or with the governor and a board of advisers. In federal cases the president alone has clemency power. All

FIGURE 5.2

Geographic boundaries of United States Courts of Appeals and United States District Courts

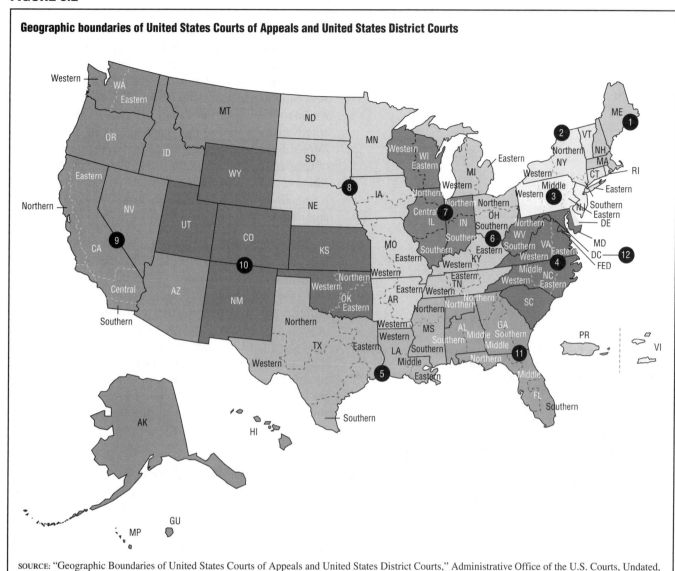

SOURCE: "Geographic Boundaries of United States Courts of Appeals and United States District Courts," Administrative Office of the U.S. Courts, Undated, http://www.uscourts.gov/images/CircuitMap.pdf (accessed July 30, 2007)

states provide for clemency, which may take the form of a reprieve, a commutation, or a pardon. A reprieve, which typically involves a stay of execution, is just a temporary measure to allow further investigation of a case. A commutation involves the reduction of a criminal sentence after a criminal conviction. In the context of capital punishment, a commutation typically means replacing the death sentence with a lesser sentence, such as life without parole. Neither a reprieve nor a commutation removes a person's responsibility for the crime. A pardon, however, frees from punishment a person convicted of a crime, as well as removes his or her criminal record as if the conviction never happened. Pardons are generally only given if investigators can prove beyond any doubt that a death row inmate did not commit the crime of which he or she was convicted.

According to the DPIC, 229 clemencies were granted by states and the federal government "for humanitarian reasons" between 1976 and 2005. (See Table 5.4.) The vast majority (172) occurred in Illinois. The DPIC (2007, http://www.deathpenaltyinfo.org/article.php?did=126) notes that in 2003 the Illinois governor George Ryan (1934–) commuted the death sentences of 167 prisoners to life in prison and pardoned 4 other inmates on death row. Despite this event, clemencies are rarely granted. As shown in Table 5.4, all other states (and the federal government) reported a small number of clemencies granted for humanitarian reasons between 1976 and 2005. Texas, a state with an active death penalty process, had only one clemency during this period.

State Variations in Appeals

In all states a death sentence is automatically reviewed by a state appellate court or supreme court for possible constitutional or legal errors that may have taken place in

TABLE 5.4

Clemencies granted, by state, 1976–2005

Clemencies granted by state since 1976	Number of clemencies
Illinois	172
Ohio	9
Virginia	7
Florida	6
Georgia	6
New Mexico	5
North Carolina	5
Indiana	3
Maryland	2
Missouri	2
Louisiana	2
Oklahoma	2
Alabama	1
Arkansas	1
Idaho	1
Kentucky	1
Montana	1
Nevada	1
Texas	1
Federal	1
Total	**229**

SOURCE: "Clemencies Granted by State Since 1976," in *Clemency*, Death Penalty Information Center, 2007, http://www.deathpenaltyinfo.org/article .php?did=126&scid=13 (accessed August 24, 2007)

the initial trial. Tracy L. Snell of the Bureau of Justice Statistics reports in *Capital Punishment, 2005* (December 2006, http://www.ojp.usdoj.gov/bjs/pub/pdf/cp05.pdf) that in 2005, among the thirty-eight states with capital punishment statutes, thirty-seven states provided for automatic review of all death sentences, regardless of the defendant's wishes. The remaining state, South Carolina, allowed the defendant to dispense with the sentence review if the court found him or her competent to decide for him- or herself (per the Supreme Court decision in *State v. Torrence*, 473 S.E.2d. 703 [S.C. 1996]). The federal death penalty procedures, however, do not provide for automatic review after a death sentence is imposed.

Even though most of the thirty-seven states authorized an automatic review of both conviction and sentence, Snell indicates that Idaho, Montana, Oklahoma, South Dakota, and Tennessee required review of the sentence only. In Idaho inmates who wanted their convictions reviewed had to file an appeal or lose the right to do so. In Indiana and Kentucky defendants were allowed to waive review of their convictions.

Generally, the state's highest court of appeals conducts the review regardless of whether the defendant requests it. If the appellate court vacates (annuls) the conviction or the sentence, the case could be returned to the trial court for additional proceedings or for retrial. Subsequent to the resentencing or retrial, the death sentence could be reinstated.

Limiting Federal Appeals

The Antiterrorism and Effective Death Penalty Act (AEDPA) of 1996 applied new restrictions and filing deadlines regarding appeals by death row inmates. It restricts death row inmates' use of habeas corpus petitions. The law requires death row inmates to file their habeas corpus petitions in the appropriate district courts within six months of the final state appeal. Before the enactment of this law, no filing deadline existed. Under the 1996 law, a defendant who fails to challenge his or her conviction or sentence within the time specified cannot file another petition unless approved by a three-judge appellate court. The AEDPA further dictates that federal judges must defer to the rulings of the state courts, unless the rulings violate the U.S. Constitution or U.S. laws or contradict "the Supreme Court's recognition of a new federal right that is made retroactively applicable."

Some opponents feared that the limitations on federal habeas corpus petitions required by the AEDPA would contribute to the execution of innocent people. In addition, they believed that the unclear language of the AEDPA allowed for varying interpretations in federal appeals courts. For the first time, in 2000, in *Williams v. Taylor* (529 U.S. 362) and *Williams v. Taylor* (529 U.S. 420), the U.S. Supreme Court addressed the lower courts' interpretation of the AEDPA, ultimately ruling that the AEDPA was valid as long as the state appellate courts did not uphold rulings contrary to the precedents laid down by the U.S. Supreme Court.

DEATH PENALTY METHODS

The Eighth Amendment of the U.S. Bill of Rights, using the language of the English Bill of Rights of 1689, prohibits the use of cruel and unusual punishment in carrying out an execution. For the most part, neither the colonies nor the United States ever used excessively brutal methods of execution, such as drawing and quartering, burying alive, boiling in oil, sawing in half, or crucifixion. Throughout most of the nineteenth century civilians sentenced to death were hanged, whereas the military usually shot spies, traitors, and deserters.

The federal government currently authorizes the method of execution under two different laws. Crimes prosecuted under 28 Code of Federal Regulations, Part 26, call for execution by lethal injection, whereas offenses covered by the Violent Crime Control and Law Enforcement Act of 1994 (also known as the Federal Death Penalty Act of 1994) are referred to the state where the conviction occurred.

Snell reports that thirty-seven states used lethal injection as the primary method of execution in 2005. (See Table 5.5.) Of these states, twenty used lethal injection as the sole means of execution. Seventeen states authorized more than one method of execution—lethal injection and an alternative method—generally letting the condemned prisoner choose the method. Of these seventeen states, Arizona, Arkansas, Delaware, Kentucky, and Tennessee

TABLE 5.5

Methods of execution, by state, 2005

Lethal injection			Electrocution	Lethal gas
Alabama[a]	Kentucky[a, b]	Ohio	Alabama[a]	Arizona[a, c]
Arizona[a, c]	Louisiana	Oklahoma[a]	Arkansas[a, d]	California[a]
Arkansas[a, d]	Maryland	Oregon	Florida[a]	Missouri[a]
California[a]	Mississippi	Pennsylvania	Kentucky[a, b]	Wyoming[a, e]
Colorado	Missouri[a]	South Carolina[a]	Nebraska	
Connecticut	Montana	South Dakota	Oklahoma[f]	**Firing squad**
Delaware[a, g]	Nevada	Tennessee[a, h]	South Carolina[a]	Idaho[a]
Florida[a]	New Hampshire[a]	Texas	Tennessee[a, h]	Oklahoma[f]
Georgia	New Jersey	Utah[a]	Virginia[a]	Utah[j]
Idaho[a]	New Mexico	Virginia[a]		
Illinois	New York	Washington[a]	**Hanging**	
Indiana	North Carolina	Wyoming[a]	Delaware[a, g]	
Kansas			New Hampshire[a, i]	
			Washington[a]	

[a]Authorizes 2 methods of execution.
[b]Authorizes lethal injection for persons sentenced on or after 3/31/98; inmates sentenced before that date may select lethal injection or electrocution.
[c]Authorizes lethal injection for persons sentenced after 11/15/92; inmates sentenced before that date may select lethal injection or gas.
[d]Authorizes lethal injection for those whose offense occurred on or after 7/4/83; inmates whose offense occurred before that data may select lethal injection or electrocution.
[e]Authorizes lethal gas if lethal injection is held to be unconstitutional.
[f]Authorizes electrocution if lethal injection is held to be unconstitutional and firing squad if both lethal injection and electrocution are held to be unconstitutional.
[g]Authorizes lethal injection for those whose capital offense occurred on or after 6/13/86; those who committed the offense before that date may select lethal injection or hanging.
[h]Authorizes lethal injection for those whose capital offense occurred after 12/31/98; those who committed the offense before that date may select electrocution by written waiver.
[i]Authorizes hanging only if lethal injection cannot be given.
[j]Authorizes firing squad if lethal injection is held unconstitutional. Inmates who selected execution by firing squad prior to May 3, 2004, may still be entitled to execution by that method.

SOURCE: Tracy L. Snell, "Table 2. Method of Execution, by State, 2005," in *Capital Punishment, 2005*, U.S. Department of Justice, Bureau of Justice Statistics, December 2006, http://www.ojp.usdoj.gov/bjs/pub/pdf/cp05.pdf (accessed July 23, 2007)

specified which method must be used, depending on the date of sentencing.

Lethal Injection

In 1977 Oklahoma became the first state to authorize lethal injection. It was not until 1982, however, that lethal injection was first used, when Texas executed Charles Brooks. Thomas P. Bonczar and Tracy L. Snell state in *Capital Punishment, 2003* (November 2004, http://www.ojp.usdoj.gov/bjs/pub/pdf/cp03.pdf) that by 1993 twenty-five of thirty-six states with capital punishment used lethal injection as the primary method of execution. Since then, most states with the death penalty have adopted lethal injection as a more humane alternative to other methods of execution. On February 18, 1993, the federal government adopted lethal injection as its sole means of execution.

Electrocution

At the end of the nineteenth century, alternating current electricity became one of the dominant symbols of progress. Many people thought this modern convenience would provide a more humane method of execution. In 1888 New York built the first electric chair and in 1890 it executed William Kemmler with the crude mechanism.

By 2001 just two states—Alabama and Nebraska—authorized electrocution as the sole method of execution. In 2002 Alabama amended its capital statute, authorizing

lethal injection as the primary means of execution, although an inmate may request electrocution. According to Snell, nine states continued to authorize electrocution as a method of execution in 2005. Except for Nebraska, which used electrocution as the sole method of execution, the other eight states gave the inmate the choice of lethal injection. (See Table 5.5.)

Lethal Gas

In 1921 Nevada became the first state to authorize the use of lethal gas for capital punishment. In 1924 Nevada executed Jon Gee using cyanide gas. This was the first time lethal gas was used for execution in the United States. The Nevada statute called for the condemned man to be executed in his cell, without warning, while asleep. Prison officials, unable to figure out a practical way to carry out the execution, ended up constructing a gas chamber. In 1994 a U.S. district judge in California ruled that lethal gas was an inhumane method of execution, a decision upheld by the U.S. Ninth Circuit Court of Appeals in 1995. The U.S. Supreme Court declined to rule on the case and remanded it back to the circuit court in 1996. In 2005 four states continued to authorize the use of lethal gas. (See Table 5.5.)

Hanging

Snell reports that in 2005 Delaware, New Hampshire, and Washington authorized hanging as a method of exe-

Death Penalty Laws: Offenses, Sentences, Appeals, and Execution Methods

cution. The state of Washington gave the condemned person the choice of death by lethal injection, whereas New Hampshire authorized hanging only if, for some reason, lethal injection could not be administered. (See Table 5.5.) On July 8, 2003, Delaware dismantled its gallows because it no longer had an inmate eligible to choose the option of hanging (only those whose capital offense had occurred before June 13, 1986, were eligible). For Delaware convicts whose offenses occurred on or after June 13, 1986, lethal injection is the sole method of execution.

WITNESSES TO EXECUTIONS

Death penalty states have statutes or policies (or both) that specify which witnesses may be present at an execution. Witnesses usually include prison officials, physicians, the condemned person's relatives, the victim's relatives, spiritual advisers, selected state citizens, and reporters. In celebrated cases, however, such as that of the Rosenbergs, who were convicted spies (1953), the notorious California killer Caryl Chessman (1960), and the convicted Oklahoma City bomber Timothy McVeigh (2001), the witnesses made up a larger group.

CHAPTER 6
STATISTICS: DEATH SENTENCES, CAPITAL CASE COSTS, AND EXECUTIONS

UNDER PENALTY OF DEATH

In *Capital Punishment, 2005* (December 2006, http://www.ojp.usdoj.gov/bjs/pub/pdf/cp05.pdf), Tracy L. Snell of the Bureau of Justice Statistics (BJS) reports that at year-end 2005 a total of 3,254 prisoners were held under the sentence of death in federal and state prisons. The vast majority (3,217) of the inmates were state prisoners held in thirty-six states. Two death penalty states—New Hampshire and Kansas—did not report any inmates under the sentence of death. The thirteen states with the most death row inmates are listed in Table 6.1. Three states accounted for more than 40% of death row prisoners: California (646), Texas (411), and Florida (372).

Figure 6.1 graphically shows the number of people under the sentence of death between 1955 and 2005. Between 1976, when the U.S. Supreme Court reinstated the death penalty, and 2000, the number of prisoners on death row increased each year. Since 2000 the total number of death row inmates has declined.

Snell notes that in 2005, 24 states reported their prisons received 122 people under the sentence of death. The federal Bureau of Prisons received six inmates. All the state and federal inmates were convicted of murder. The states receiving the most death row inmates were California (twenty-three), Florida (fifteen), Texas (fourteen), Alabama (twelve), and Arizona (eight). According to Snell, death row admissions declined fairly steadily between 1995 and 2005. (See Table 6.2.) In 1995 state and federal prisons received 325 inmates. The 2005 admission of 128 inmates was the lowest number since 1973, when 44 people entered death row.

Race

Snell indicates that at year-end 2005, 45% of all death row inmates were white and 42% were African-American. (See Figure 6.2.) Hispanic prisoners (who may be of any race) accounted for 11% of those under a death sentence. Other races represented 2% of death row inmates.

Gender

According to Snell, men comprised 98% of the total inmates on death row at year-end 2005. As shown in Table 6.3, only fifty-two women were under the sentence of death, most in California (fourteen), Texas (nine), and Pennsylvania (five).

Victor L. Streib of Ohio Northern University has been compiling information on female offenders and the death penalty in the United States since 1984. In *Death Penalty for Female Offenders: January 1, 1973, through June 30, 2007* (July 13, 2007, http://www.deathpenaltyinfo.org/FemDeathJune2007.pdf), Streib states that between 1973 and June 30, 2007, 160 females had been sentenced to death in the United States.

Characteristics of Prisoners

The BJS collects additional demographic information on death row inmates. Snell indicates that at year-end 2005 the median age of those under the sentence of death was forty-one years (this means that half of the inmates were younger than forty-one and half were older than that age). (See Table 6.4.) Nearly two-thirds (61%) were aged twenty-five to forty-four, and one-third (33%) were between thirty and thirty-nine years old. One inmate was under age twenty, and 110 inmates were sixty and older. The youngest inmate was twenty years old and was sentenced to death in October 2005. The oldest was ninety, having been sentenced in June 1983 at the age of sixty-eight. Half of all inmates under the sentence of death were aged twenty to twenty-nine when they were arrested for their capital offense.

Among those for whom information about education was available as of December 31, 2005, 39.6% had graduated from high school and only 9.2% had any college education. (See Table 6.5.) The median level of education was the eleventh grade. Most (54.4%) had never married, and about one-fifth (20.5%) were divorced or separated.

TABLE 6.1

Number of prisoners under sentence of death, December 31, 2005

California	646
Texas	411
Florida	372
Pennsylvania	218
Ohio	199
Alabama	189
North Carolina	174
Arizona	109
Georgia	107
Tennessee	103
Oklahoma	86
Louisiana	83
Nevada	82
24 other jurisdictions	475
Total	**3,254**

SOURCE: Adapted from Tracy L. Snell, "Highlights. Status of the Death Penalty, December 31, 2005," in *Capital Punishment, 2005*, U.S. Department of Justice, Bureau of Justice Statistics, December 2006, http://www.ojp.usdoj .gov/bjs/pub/pdf/cp05.pdf (accessed July 23, 2007)

Criminal History of Death Row Inmates

According to Snell, among prisoners on death row, nearly two-thirds (65%) had prior felony convictions.

TABLE 6.2

Inmates received under sentence of death, 1995–2005

Year	Inmates received
1995	325
1996	323
1997	281
1998	306
1999	283
2000	236
2001	166
2002	168
2003	153
2004	138
2005	128

SOURCE: Tracy L. Snell, "Number of Prisoners Sentenced to Death Decreased for Third Straight Year,"in *Capital Punishment,2005*,U.S. Department of Justice, Bureau of Justice Statistics, December 2006, http://www.ojp.usdoj .gov/bjs/pub/pdf/cp05.pdf (accessed July 23, 2007)

(See Table 6.6.) About one out of twelve (8.4%) had been previously convicted of murder or manslaughter. About two out of five (39.9%) had an active criminal justice record at the time of the murder for which they were condemned. Just over 16% of inmates were on parole at the time of their capital offense.

FIGURE 6.1

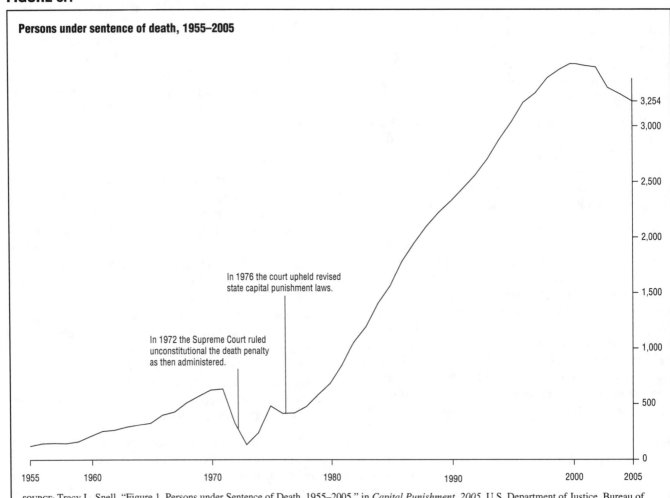

Persons under sentence of death, 1955–2005

In 1976 the court upheld revised state capital punishment laws.

In 1972 the Supreme Court ruled unconstitutional the death penalty as then administered.

SOURCE: Tracy L. Snell, "Figure 1. Persons under Sentence of Death, 1955–2005," in *Capital Punishment, 2005*, U.S. Department of Justice, Bureau of Justice Statistics, December 2006, http://www.ojp.usdoj.gov/bjs/pub/pdf/cp05.pdf (accessed July 23, 2007)

FIGURE 6.2

Persons under sentence of death, by race and Hispanic origin, December 31, 2005

[3,254 total]

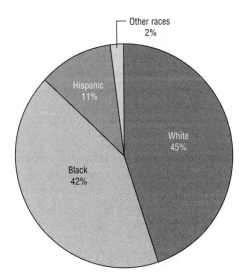

- Other races 2%
- Hispanic 11%
- White 45%
- Black 42%

SOURCE: Adapted from Tracy L. Snell, "Highlights. Persons under Sentence of Death," in *Capital Punishment, 2005*, U.S. Department of Justice, Bureau of Justice Statistics, December 2006, http://www.ojp.usdoj.gov/bjs/pub/pdf/cp05.pdf (accessed July 23, 2007)

TABLE 6.3

Women under sentence of death, by race, December 31, 2005

State	All races*	White	Black
Total	**52**	**35**	**14**
California	14	10	2
Texas	9	5	4
Pennsylvania	5	2	3
North Carolina	4	2	1
Alabama	3	1	2
Ohio	2	2	0
Tennessee	2	2	0
Arizona	2	2	0
Federal	1	1	0
Delaware	1	1	0
Florida	1	1	0
Georgia	1	1	0
Idaho	1	1	0
Kentucky	1	1	0
Mississippi	1	1	0
Oklahoma	1	1	0
Virginia	1	1	0
Indiana	1	0	1
Louisiana	1	0	1

*Includes races other than white and black.

SOURCE: Tracy L. Snell, "Women under Sentence of Death, 12/31/05," in *Capital Punishment, 2005*, U.S. Department of Justice, Bureau of Justice Statistics, December 2006, http://www.ojp.usdoj.gov/bjs/pub/pdf/cp05.pdf (accessed July 23, 2007)

Criminal history patterns varied slightly by race and Hispanic origin. African-Americans (70.3%) had somewhat more prior felony convictions than whites (61.6%) and Hispanics (61.3%). African-Americans (8.7%) and whites (8.4%) had a higher proportion of prior homicide convictions than Hispanics (7.3%). Hispanics (22.6%) and African-Americans (16.7%) were more likely than

TABLE 6.4

Age at time of arrest for capital offense and age of prisoners under sentence of death, December 31, 2005

	Prisoners under sentence of death			
	At time of arrest		On December 31, 2005	
Age	Number*	Percent	Number	Percent
Total number under sentence of death on 12/31/05	2,985	100%	3,254	100%
17 or younger	14	0.5	0	
18–19	328	11.0	0	
20–24	825	27.6	61	1.9
25–29	669	22.4	321	9.9
30–34	510	17.1	495	15.2
35–39	320	10.7	583	17.9
40–44	174	5.8	589	18.1
45–49	89	3.0	533	16.4
50–54	36	1.2	307	9.4
55–59	14	0.5	228	7.0
60–64	4	0.1	85	2.6
65 or older	2	0.1	52	1.6
Mean age	28 yrs.		42 yrs.	
Median age	27 yrs.		41 yrs.	

Note: The youngest person under sentence of death was a black male in Alabama, born in May 1985 and sentenced to death in October 2005. The oldest person under sentence of death was a white male in Arizona, born in September 1915 and sentenced to death in June 1983.
*Excludes 269 inmates for whom the date of arrest for capital offense was not available.

SOURCE: Tracy L. Snell, "Table 7. Age at Time of Arrest for Capital Offense and Age of Prisoners under Sentence of Death at Yearend 2005," in *Capital Punishment, 2005*, U.S. Department of Justice, Bureau of Justice Statistics, December 2006, http://www.ojp.usdoj.gov/bjs/pub/pdf/cp05.pdf (accessed July 23, 2007)

TABLE 6.5

Demographic characteristics of prisoners under sentence of death, 2005

Characteristic	Percent of prisoners under sentence of death, 2005		
	Yearend	Admissions	Removals
Total number under sentence of death	3,254	128	194
Gender			
Male	98.4%	96.1%	97.4%
Female	1.6	3.9	2.6
Race			
White	55.5%	54.7%	62.4%
Black	42.2	40.6	36.1
All other races*	2.4	4.7	1.5
Hispanic origin			
Hispanic	12.7%	15.5%	13.3%
Non-Hispanic	87.3	84.5	86.7
Education			
8th grade or less	14.3%	9.9%	24.1%
9th-11th grade	36.9	31.7	36.7
High school graduate/GED	39.6	48.5	29.5
Any college	9.2	9.9	9.6
Median	11th	12th	11th
Marital status			
Married	22.2%	17.6%	16.3%
Divorced/separated	20.5	19.6	22.5
Widowed	2.9	3.9	2.2
Never married	54.4	58.8	59.0

Note: Calculations are based on those cases for which data were reported. Detail may not add to total due to rounding. Missing data by category were as follows:

	Yearend	Admissions	Removals
Hispanic origin	410.0	18.0	21.0
Education	465.0	27.0	28.0
Marital status	337.0	26.0	16.0

*At yearend 2004, other races consisted of 28 American Indians, 32 Asians, and 14 self-identified Hispanics. During 2005, 3 American Indians and 3 Asians were admitted; and 1 Asian and 2 self-identified Hispanic inmates were removed.

SOURCE: Tracy L. Snell, "Table 5. Demographic Characteristics of Prisoners under Sentence of Death, 2005," in *Capital Punishment, 2005*, U.S. Department of Justice, Bureau of Justice Statistics, December 2006, http://www.ojp.usdoj.gov/bjs/pub/pdf/cp05.pdf (accessed July 23, 2007).

whites (14.1%) to be on parole when arrested for their capital crime. (See Table 6.6.)

A Long Wait

It can be a long wait on death row. Table 6.7 shows the average length of time prisoners spent under the sentence of death before they were executed between 1977 and 2005. The average time between the imposition of the death sentence and the execution was 125 months (10 years and 5 months). White prisoners waited an average of 123 months (10 years and 3 months) and African-American prisoners waited an average of 131 months (10 years and 11 months) before their execution. Snell indicates that of the 60 inmates executed in 2005, the average length of time they had been on death row was 128 months (10 years and 8 months).

Table 6.8 lists the average number of years inmates spent on death row in various states as of December 31, 2005. The longest time reported was in Idaho (13.7 years), followed by Nevada (13.2 years), Florida (12.7 years), Tennessee (12.5 years), and California (12 years). Snell reports that Idaho had eighteen prisoners under the sentence of death at the end of 2005. Of the three states with the highest death row populations at year-end 2005—California, Texas, and Florida—Texas reported the shortest average number of years under the sentence of death (8.8 years).

Getting off Death Row

A number of prisoners are removed from death row each year for reasons other than execution: resentencing, retrial, commutation (replacement of the death sentence with a lesser sentence), or death while awaiting execution (natural death, murder, or suicide). As Figure 6.3 shows, 7,662 people received a death sentence between 1973 and 2005. Of these, more than 35% had their sentence or conviction overturned, 13% were executed, 4% died of other causes, and 4% had their sentence commuted.

Table 6.9 provides a breakdown of death sentences and removals by state. California had the largest number (fifty) of death row inmates who died of causes other than execution, followed by Florida (forty-one), Texas (thirty-two), Alabama (twenty), and Ohio (nineteen). Of the 2,702 prisoners who had their sentence of conviction overturned, the highest numbers were in Florida (414), North Carolina (281), Oklahoma (153), Texas (144), and Georgia (141).

COSTS OF THE DEATH PENALTY

Many death penalty proponents believe that capital punishment costs the taxpayers less than a life sentence without parole. However, several studies indicate that the death penalty costs more than life imprisonment without parole. For example, Hugo Adam Bedau, in *The Case against the Death Penalty* (1997), finds that a "murder trial normally takes longer when the death penalty is at issue than when it is not. Litigation costs—including the time of judges, prosecutors, public defenders, and court reporters, and the high costs of briefs—are mostly borne by the taxpayer."

California

After combing through state and federal records, Rone Tempest notes in "Death Row Often Means a Long Life" (*Los Angeles Times*, March 6, 2005) that the death penalty system in California costs taxpayers more than $114 million each year. This amount is more than what it would cost to imprison California's 640 death row inmates for life without parole. Every year, the state spends approximately $57.5 million ($90,000 per prisoner) simply by housing these inmates on death row, where they live in a private cell and are surrounded by more guards than normal prisoners. Huge costs are also incurred during executions. Since

TABLE 6.6

Criminal history profile of prisoners under sentence of death, by race and Hispanic origin, 2005

	Number of prisoners under sentence of death				Percent of prisoners under sentence of death[a]			
	All[b]	White[c]	Black[c]	Hispanic	All[b]	White[c]	Black[c]	Hispanic
U.S. total	3,254	1,472	1,359	362	100%	100%	100%	100%
Prior felony convictions								
Yes	1,936	833	868	204	65.0%	61.6%	70.3%	61.3%
No	1,042	520	367	129	35.0	38.4	29.7	38.7
Not reported	276							
Prior homicide convictions								
Yes	269	121	116	26	8.4%	8.4%	8.7%	7.3%
No	2,926	1,327	1,214	331	91.6	91.6	91.3	92.7
Not reported	59							
Legal status at time of capital offense								
Charges pending	227	115	92	17	7.8%	8.7%	7.6%	5.2%
Probation	307	116	148	37	10.5	8.8	12.3	11.3
Parole	471	186	202	74	16.2	14.1	16.7	22.6
On escape	42	23	12	6	1.4	1.7	1.0	1.8
Incarcerated	102	53	39	8	3.5	4.0	3.2	2.4
Other status	14	5	7	1	0.5	0.4	0.6	0.3
None	1,752	825	707	184	60.1	62.4	58.6	56.3
Not reported	339							

[a]Percentages are based on those offenders for whom data were reported. Detail may not add to total because of rounding.
[b]Includes American Indians, Alaska Natives, Asians, Native Hawaiians, and other Pacific Islanders.
[c]White and black categories exclude Hispanics.

SOURCE: Tracy L. Snell, "Table 8. Criminal History Profile of Prisoners under Sentence of Death, by Race and Hispanic Origin, 2005," in *Capital Punishment, 2005*, U.S. Department of Justice, Bureau of Justice Statistics, December 2006, http://www.ojp.usdoj.gov/bjs/pub/pdf/cp05.pdf (accessed July 23, 2007)

California reinstated its death penalty in 1978, eleven people have been executed. Each of these executions cost taxpayers approximately $250 million. The death penalty has also burdened the courts. According to Ronald George, the chief justice of the California Supreme Court, the court spent 20% of its resources on capital cases. In the end, the state still did not have enough money to appoint lawyers to 115 death row inmates for their first direct appeal.

Washington

In *Washington's Death Penalty System: A Review of the Costs, Length, and Results of Capital Cases in Washington State* (November 2004, http://www.abolishdeathpenalty.org/PDF/WAStateDeathPenaltySystem.pdf), Mark A. Larranaga and Donna Mustard review costs incurred under Washington's capital punishment system between 1999 and 2003. Larranaga and Mustard find that on average a non-death penalty trial costs half as much as a death penalty trial. One estimate reveals that a death penalty trial cost about $432,000 and that a non-death penalty trial cost approximately $153,000. Capital punishment trials also take much longer than normal criminal trials. A typical death penalty trial lasts roughly twenty months, compared to fifteen months for a non-death penalty trial. A death penalty appellate review takes on average seven years, whereas a non-death penalty review takes about two years.

Despite the exorbitant costs of death penalty trials, few people sentenced to death in Washington have actually been executed. Between 1981—the year Wash-

ington reinstated capital punishment—and 2003 thirty-one death sentences were handed down in the state. Twenty-one convicts completed their appellate review by 2003, and nine were still awaiting their reviews. Of those convicts who received their review, seventeen had their death sentences reversed after an average of 6.9 years in the appeals process. Three of the remaining four offenders were executed after effectively waiving their appellate review. Only one person was executed after exhausting all options, which took eleven years.

Kansas

In *Performance Audit Report: Costs Incurred for Death Penalty Cases* (December 2003, http://www.kslegislature.org/postaudit/audits_perform/04pa03a.pdf), the state of Kansas finds that death penalty murder cases cost an average of $1.2 million from when the murder investigation begins to when the sentence is carried out. Murder cases where the death penalty is neither sought nor given cost $740,000.

The state itemizes these costs for each stage of a death penalty case. The cost of investigating a case in which the defendant is sentenced to death is $145,000, compared to $66,000 for a death penalty case in which the defendant receives a lesser sentence and $47,000 for a non-death penalty case. The average price tag for a trial that results in a death sentence is nearly sixteen times greater than for a non-death penalty trial ($508,000 as

TABLE 6.7

Time under sentence of death, by race, 1977–2005

Year of execution	Average elapsed time from sentence to execution for:		
	All races[a]	White[b]	Black[b]
Total	125 mo	123 mo	131 mo
1977–83	51 mo	49 mo	58 mo
1984	74	76	71
1985	71	65	80
1986	87	78	102
1987	86	78	96
1988	80	72	89
1989	95	78	112
1990	95	97	91
1991	116	124	107
1992	114	104	135
1993	113	112	121
1994	122	117	132
1995	134	128	144
1996	125	112	153
1997	133	126	147
1998	130	128	132
1999	143	143	141
2000	137	134	142
2001	142	134	166
2002	127	130	120
2003	131	135	120
2004	132	132	132
2005	147	144	155

Note: Average time was calculated from the most recent sentencing date.
[a]Includes American Indians, Alaska Natives, Asians, Native Hawaiians, and other Pacific Islanders.
[b]Includes Hispanics.

SOURCE: Adapted from Tracy L. Snell, "Table 11. Time under Sentence of Death and Execution, by Race, 1977–2005," in *Capital Punishment, 2005*, U.S. Department of Justice, Bureau of Justice Statistics, December 2006, http://www.ojp.usdoj.gov/bjs/pub/pdf/cp05.pdf (accessed July 23, 2007)

TABLE 6.8

Average number of years under sentence of death, December 31, 2005

State	Average number of years under sentence of death, 12/31/05
California	12.0
Florida	12.7
Texas	8.8
Tennessee	12.5
Alabama	9.9
Arizona	11.9
Pennsylvania	11.7
Nevada	13.2
Georgia	11.2
Mississippi	9.5
North Carolina	8.9
Idaho	13.7
Kentucky	11.9
Indiana	11.5
Missouri	9.5
Arkansas	8.9
Ohio	11.9
Oklahoma	7.5
South Carolina	8.4
Maryland	*
Montana	*
Nebraska	7.9
Louisiana	8.3
Utah	*
New Jersey	10.5
Connecticut	*
Oregon	7.7
Delaware	6.7
Washington	8.1
Federal system	4.1
South Dakota	*
New Mexico	*
Colorado	*
Virginia	4.3
Wyoming	*
Illinois	*
New York	*
Total	10.7

Note: For those persons sentenced to death more than once, the numbers are based on the most recent death sentence.
*Averages not calculated for fewer than 10 inmates.

SOURCE: Adapted from Tracy L. Snell, "Appendix Table 3. Prisoners under Sentence of Death on December 31, 2005, by State and Year of Sentencing," in *Capital Punishment, 2005*, U.S. Department of Justice, Bureau of Justice Statistics, December 2006, http://www.ojp.usdoj.gov/bjs/pub/pdf/cp05.pdf (accessed July 23, 2007)

opposed to $32,000), and the appeal is twenty-one times greater ($401,000 as opposed to $19,000). Keeping a convict on death row in Kansas costs roughly half as much as detaining a murderer for whom the death penalty is never sought ($350,000 versus $659,000). Kansas, however, did not have a large death row population at the time the study was performed. Only six inmates were on death row in December 2003. As of November 2007, that number had increased to nine, but no one had been executed in Kansas since the death penalty was reinstated in 1994.

Connecticut

In *Study Pursuant to Public Act No. 01-151 of the Imposition of the Death Penalty in Connecticut* (January 8, 2003, http://www.cga.ct.gov/olr/Death%20Penalty%20Commission%20Final%20Report.pdf), Connecticut's Commission on the Death Penalty addresses the cost of prosecuting capital cases. As of January 2002 Connecticut had seven death row inmates and had not executed any. The last execution occurred in 1960. Because Connecticut has not carried out an execution, the commission did not present any comparison between the cost of implementing the death penalty and keeping an inmate in prison without the possibility of parole. Nonetheless, the commission was

able to illustrate the defense costs for defendants sentenced to death (following trial and sentencing), compared to the defense costs incurred by defendants receiving life imprisonment without parole (also following trial and sentencing).

The commission reviewed the cases of the seven men on death row from 1973 to 2002. The defense costs ranged from nearly $102,000 to $1.1 million, with an average cost of about $380,000 per case. The prisoners serving life sentences without parole included those incarcerated from 1989 to 2001. Their defense costs ranged from $86,000 to $321,000, with an average cost of about $202,000 per inmate. Between 2005 and 2006 the Connecticut Division

FIGURE 6.3

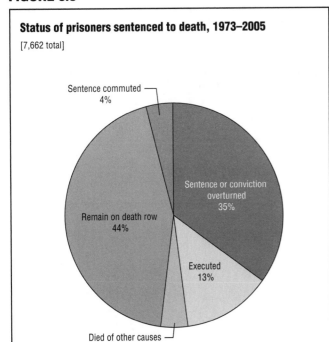

Status of prisoners sentenced to death, 1973–2005

[7,662 total]

- Sentence commuted 4%
- Sentence or conviction overturned 35%
- Remain on death row 44%
- Executed 13%
- Died of other causes 4%

Note: 0.4% were removed from under sentence of death for other reasons.

SOURCE: Adapted from Tracy L. Snell, "Appendix Table 4. Number Sentenced to Death and Number of Removals, by Jurisdiction and Reason for Removal, 1973–2005," in *Capital Punishment, 2005*, U.S. Department of Justice, Bureau of Justice Statistics, December 2006, http://www.ojp.usdoj.gov/bjs/pub/pdf/cp05.pdf (accessed July 23, 2007)

of Public Defender Services reports in "Cost of Public Defender Services: Cost Attributable to the Death Penalty" (February 16, 2007, http://www.ocpd.state.ct.us/Content/Annual2006/2006Chap4.htm) that it spent approximately $2.6 million for capital cases.

New York

In "Capital Punishment Proves to Be Expensive" (*New York Law Journal*, April 30, 2002), Daniel Wise investigates the costs of the death penalty in New York since its reinstatement in 1995. Between 1995 and 2001 defense costs had amounted to $68.4 million by that time. No national system is in place to track prosecution costs; however, the state Division of Criminal Justice Services paid counties that prosecuted capital cases $5.1 million between 1995 and 2001. Each year the allocation for the New York Court of Appeals increased by more than $533,000 to allow for the salary of an extra clerk for each of the seven judges. The New York Prosecutors Training Institute, which assists district lawyers in capital cases, costs $1.2 million annually to operate. The defense for Darrel Harris, the first person to be sentenced to death under New York's 1995 law, had spent about $1.7 million, and the Capital Defender Office spent $1.2 million just to prepare the brief. (Harris's conviction was subsequently ruled unconstitutional.) The Department of Correctional Services spent $1.3 million to construct a new death row, allocating another $300,000 annually to guard it.

Federal Death Penalty Costs

Since the passage of the Violent Crime Control and Law Enforcement Act of 1994 (also known as the Federal Death Penalty Act), the number of federal prosecutions, including crimes punishable by death, has risen. The Subcommittee on Federal Death Penalty Cases of the Judicial Conference Committee on Defender Services, in *Federal Death Penalty Cases: Recommendations Concerning the Cost and Quality of Defense Representation* (May 1998, http://www.uscourts.gov/dpenalty/2TABLE.htm), estimates that about 560 federal death penalty cases were filed between 1991 and 1997. The numbers increased each year. In 1991 there were 12 cases, rising nearly tenfold to 118 in 1995, and reaching 159 and 153 cases in 1996 and 1997, respectively.

Even though the decision to charge a crime punishable by death is made by the local federal prosecutor, the U.S. attorney general alone authorizes the seeking of the death penalty. Between 1988 and December 1997 the U.S. attorney general authorized seeking capital punishment in 111 cases. The attorney general's decision to authorize seeking the death penalty makes a substantial difference in the cost of representing a defendant. According to the Committee on Defender Services, from 1990 to 1997 the average total cost (for counsel and related services) per representation of a sample of cases in which the defendant was charged with noncapital homicide was $9,159. In contrast, in those cases in which the defendant was charged with an offense punishable by death and the attorney general authorized seeking the death penalty, the average cost was $218,113. This included cases resolved by a guilty plea as well as cases resolved by a trial. In contrast, the average total cost per representation in which the defendant was charged with an offense punishable by death where the attorney general did not authorize seeking the death penalty was $55,773. According to Ian F. Fergusson and Susan B. Epstein of the Congressional Research Service, in *Appropriations for FY2005: Commerce, Justice, State, the Judiciary, and Related Agencies* (January 12, 2005, http://digital.library.unt.edu/govdocs/crs/permalink/meta-crs-7885:1), the budget for Defender Services had risen from $624.1 million in 2004 to $676.4 million in 2005, an increase of 8.4%.

The decision whether to go to trial or to enter a guilty plea also affects the cost of representing the alleged offender. During the study period 1988 to 1997, of the 111 cases in which the attorney general sought the death sentence, 41 were tried for capital charges. Cases that ended in capital trials cost an average of $269,139, compared to $192,333 for cases resolved with a guilty plea.

Because a death penalty case differs from other cases in that a defendant's life is at stake, the defense generally devotes more time to the case. One time-consuming

TABLE 6.9

Number sentenced to death and number of removals, by jurisdiction and reason for removal, 1973–2005

State	Total sentenced to death, 1973–2005	Number of removals, 1973–2005					Under sentence of death, 12/31/05
		Executed	Died	Sentence or conviction overturned	Sentence commuted	Other removals	
U.S. total	7,662	1,004	327	2,702	341	34	3,254
Federal	47	3	0	6	1	0	37
Alabama	368	34	20	123	2	0	189
Arizona	261	22	12	111	6	1	109
Arkansas	105	27	3	35	2	0	38
California	851	12	50	128	15	0	646
Colorado	20	1	2	14	1	0	2
Connecticut	10	1	0	2	0	0	7
Delaware	52	14	0	22	0	0	16
Florida	907	60	41	414	18	2	372
Georgia	308	39	12	141	8	1	107
Idaho	42	1	3	17	3	0	18
Illinois	298	12	14	97	156	12	7
Indiana	99	16	2	53	6	2	20
Kansas	8	0	0	8	0	0	0
Kentucky	77	2	4	34	1	0	36
Louisiana	228	27	6	104	7	1	83
Maryland	53	5	2	35	4	0	7
Massachusetts	4	0	0	2	2	0	0
Mississippi	182	7	4	100	0	3	68
Missouri	174	66	9	51	2	0	46
Montana	15	2	2	6	1	0	4
Nebraska	30	3	3	12	2	0	10
Nevada	141	11	12	32	4	0	82
New Jersey	52	0	3	31	0	8	10
New Mexico	28	1	1	19	5	0	2
New York	10	0	0	9	0	0	1
North Carolina	517	39	15	281	8	0	174
Ohio	388	19	19	140	11	0	199
Oklahoma	332	79	12	153	2	0	86
Oregon	56	2	1	22	0	0	31
Pennsylvania	371	3	16	128	6	0	218
Rhode Island	2	0	0	2	0	0	0
South Carolina	190	35	4	80	3	0	68
South Dakota	5	0	1	0	0	0	4
Tennessee	216	1	13	94	3	2	103
Texas	994	355	32	144	51	1	411
Utah	26	6	1	9	1	0	9
Virginia	145	94	6	12	10	1	22
Washington	38	4	1	23	0	0	10
Wyoming	12	1	1	8	0	0	2
Percent	100%	13.1%	4.3%	35.3%	4.4%	0.4%	42.5%

Note: For those persons sentenced to death more than once, the numbers are based on the most recent death sentence.

SOURCE: Tracy L. Snell, "Appendix Table 4. Number Sentenced to Death and Number of Removals, by Jurisdiction and Reason for Removal, 1973–2005," in *Capital Punishment, 2005*, U.S. Department of Justice, Bureau of Justice Statistics, December 2006, http://www.ojp.usdoj.gov/bjs/pub/pdf/cp05.pdf (accessed July 23, 2007)

aspect of defense involves prolonged jury selection. Even though jury selection in noncapital cases may take several days, in capital cases it may take several months.

COSTS OF FEDERAL CASES IN NON-DEATH PENALTY STATES. Federal law can be enacted in any U.S. state or territory, even in a jurisdiction that does not have the death penalty. In March 2002 Michigan became the first non-death penalty state in which a federal jury sentenced a person to death. Marvin Gabrion had been convicted of the murder of nineteen-year-old Rachel Timmerman.

In 1997 Timmerman's body, which was tied with chains and handcuffs and secured to cinder blocks, was found in Oxford Lake in Michigan's Manistee National Forest. Authorities said she was thrown in the water while still alive. Timmerman was scheduled to testify against Gabrion for raping her in 1996. Authorities also believed Gabrion was involved in the disappearance of Timmerman's one-year-old daughter. Because Timmerman was found on federal property, the government authorized the death penalty.

The federal government's decision to pursue the death penalty meant that taxpayers nationwide had to foot the bill. Ed White notes in "Gabrion Defense Costs Taxpayers $730,168" (*Grand Rapids Press*, May 24, 2002) that the defense costs amounted to over $730,000. A major portion of the expenses (over $537,000) went toward attorney fees. According to Chief Justice Robert Holmes Bell of the U.S.

District Court of the Western District of Michigan, defending federal death penalty cases usually costs over $1 million. This price tag does not include the cost of prosecuting the case. However, prosecutors typically do not make an accounting of their expenses. White reports that even though the U.S. Attorney's Office disclosed it spent at least $316,201, it did not say what the total additional costs were. These included, among other things, staff salaries and Federal Bureau of Investigation expenses.

EXECUTIONS

Until 1930 the U.S. government did not keep any record of the number of people executed under the death penalty. Snell notes that from 1930 through 2003 a total of 4,863 executions were conducted under civil authority in the United States. (See Table 6.10.) Military authorities carried out an additional 160 executions between 1930 and 1961, the date of the last military execution.

From 1930 to 1939 a total of 1,667 inmates were executed, the highest number of people put to death in any decade. The number of executions generally declined between the 1930s and the 1960s. In 1930, 155 executions took place, reaching a high of 199 in 1935. By 1950 executions were down to eighty-two, further dropping to forty-nine each in 1958 and 1959, and then rising slightly to fifty-six in 1960. In 1967 a ten-year moratorium (temporary suspension) of the death penalty began as states waited for the U.S. Supreme Court to determine a constitutionally acceptable procedure for carrying out the death penalty. (See Figure 1.2 in Chapter 1.)

The moratorium ended in 1976, but no executions occurred that year. The first execution following the moratorium occurred in Utah in January 1977. In 1999 ninety-eight inmates were put to death, the most in the one year after the death penalty was reinstated. Between 1976 and the end of 2005, 1,004 people were put to death. Figure 6.4 shows the number of executions conducted by year between 1973 and 2005.

Locations of Executions

Table 6.10 shows the number of prisoners executed by state between 1930 and 2005 and between 1977 and 2005. Texas, by far, had the most executions during both time periods—652 executions between 1930 and 2005 and 355 executions between 1977 and 2005.

Overall, thirty-three states carried out executions between 1977 and 2005. The federal government executed three men. The largest number (355) of executions in a single state occurred in Texas, followed by Virginia (ninety-four), Oklahoma (seventy-nine), Missouri (sixty-six), Florida (sixty), Georgia (thirty-nine), and North Carolina (thirty-nine). Together, these seven states carried out nearly three-quarters of all executions during this twenty-eight-year period. (See Figure 6.5.)

TABLE 6.10

Number of persons executed, by jurisdiction, 1930–2005

State	Number executed	
	Since 1930	Since 1977
U.S. total	4,863	1,004
Texas	652	355
Georgia	405	39
New York	329	0
California	304	12
North Carolina	302	39
Florida	230	60
South Carolina	197	35
Ohio	191	19
Virginia	186	94
Alabama	169	34
Mississippi	161	7
Louisiana	160	27
Pennsylvania	155	3
Arkansas	145	27
Oklahoma	139	79
Missouri	128	66
Kentucky	105	2
Illinois	102	12
Tennessee	94	1
New Jersey	74	0
Maryland	73	5
Arizona	60	22
Indiana	57	16
Washington	51	4
Colorado	48	1
Nevada	40	11
District of Columbia	40	0
West Virginia	40	0
Federal system	36	3
Massachusetts	27	0
Delaware	26	14
Connecticut	22	1
Oregon	21	2
Utah	19	6
Iowa	18	0
Kansas	15	0
New Mexico	9	1
Montana	8	2
Wyoming	8	1
Nebraska	7	3
Idaho	4	1
Vermont	4	0
New Hampshire	1	0
South Dakota	1	0

SOURCE: Tracy L. Snell, "Table 9. Number of Persons Executed, by Jurisdiction, 1930–2005," in *Capital Punishment, 2005*, U.S. Department of Justice, Bureau of Justice Statistics, December 2006, http://www.ojp.usdoj.gov/bjs/pub/pdf/cp05.pdf (accessed July 23, 2007).

The breakdown by state for executions in 2005 is shown in Table 6.11. Texas led the nation with nineteen executions, followed by Indiana, Missouri, and North Carolina with five each.

Gender

The BJS does not provide state or yearly breakdowns of the number of women executed in the United States. However, Streib reports that between 1632 and June 30, 2007, 568 documented executions of women had been reported. Of this number, fifty women were put to death between 1900 and 2005.

Streib notes that in 1984 Margie Velma Barfield was executed in North Carolina for poisoning her boyfriend.

FIGURE 6.4

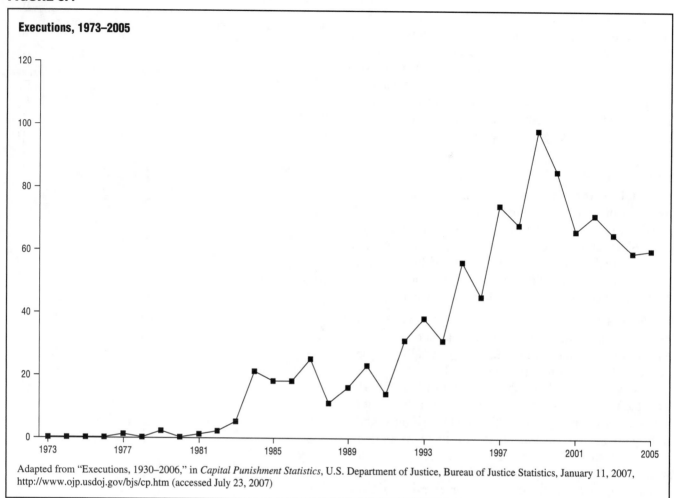

Executions, 1973–2005

Adapted from "Executions, 1930–2006," in *Capital Punishment Statistics*, U.S. Department of Justice, Bureau of Justice Statistics, January 11, 2007, http://www.ojp.usdoj.gov/bjs/cp.htm (accessed July 23, 2007)

FIGURE 6.5

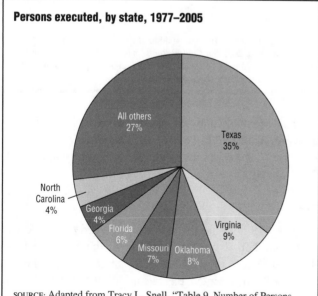

Persons executed, by state, 1977–2005

SOURCE: Adapted from Tracy L. Snell, "Table 9. Number of Persons Executed, by Jurisdiction, 1930–2005," in *Capital Punishment, 2005*, U.S. Department of Justice, Bureau of Justice Statistics, December 2006, http://www.ojp.usdoj.gov/bjs/pub/pdf/cp05.pdf (accessed July 23, 2007)

Karla Faye Tucker of Texas was convicted of beating two people to death with a pickax. In 1998 Tucker became the first woman to be executed in Texas since the Civil War (1861–1865). (In 1863 Chipita Rodriguez, the last woman to be executed in Texas, was put to death by hanging. She had been convicted of the ax murder of a horse trader.) In Florida Judias Buenoano was convicted of poisoning her husband with arsenic. She was also convicted of drowning her paraplegic son and of trying to kill her boyfriend. In 1998 Buenoano became the first woman to be executed in Florida since 1848, when a freed slave named Celia was hanged for killing her former owner.

In 2000 Betty Lou Beets was executed in Texas for killing her fifth husband. Christina Marie Riggs, convicted of killing her two children, was executed in Arkansas the same year. The last woman put to death in Arkansas before Riggs—Lavinia Burnett—was hanged in 1845 for being an accessory to murder.

In 2001 Oklahoma executed three female inmates: Wanda Jean Allen, Marilyn Kay Plantz, and Lois Nadean Smith. Allen was the first woman to be executed in Oklahoma since 1903. She was also the first African-American woman to be put to death in the United States

TABLE 6.11

Executions during 2005

Texas	19
Indiana	5
Missouri	5
North Carolina	5
Ohio	4
Alabama	4
Oklahoma	4
Georgia	3
South Carolina	3
California	2
Connecticut	1
Arkansas	1
Delaware	1
Florida	1
Maryland	1
Mississippi	1
Total	**60**

SOURCE: Adapted from Tracy L. Snell, "Highlights. Status of the Death Penalty, December 31, 2005," in *Capital Punishment, 2005*, U.S. Department of Justice, Bureau of Justice Statistics, December 2006, http://www.ojp.usdoj .gov/bjs/pub/pdf/cp05.pdf (accessed July 23, 2007)

FIGURE 6.6

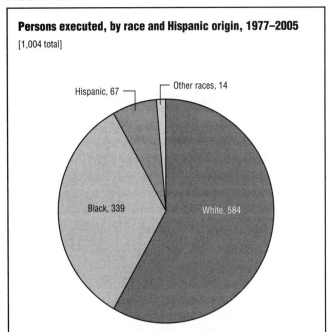

Persons executed, by race and Hispanic origin, 1977–2005

[1,004 total]

Hispanic, 67

Other races, 14

Black, 339

White, 584

SOURCE: Adapted from Tracy L. Snell, "Table 10. Executions and Other Dispositions of Inmates Sentenced to Death, by Race and Hispanic Origin, 1977–2005," in *Capital Punishment, 2005*, U.S. Department of Justice, Bureau of Justice Statistics, December 2006, http://www.ojp .usdoj.gov/bjs/pub/pdf/cp05.pdf (accessed July 23, 2007)

since 1954. She was convicted of murdering her gay lover in 1988. Plantz was executed for the 1988 murder of her husband. She had hired two men to kill her husband. One of the men, William Bryson, was executed in June 2000 for the murder, and the other, Clinton McKimble, received a life sentence in exchange for his testimony against Plantz and Bryson. Smith was convicted of killing

George Sibley 2002 Alabama man to be executed y was executed d of killing six hal injection in executed in the n of Texas, exed and their two

ic makeup of the 7 and 2005. The e white. Slightly -American, and a

Educational Fund USA, which tracks l executions in the stics not only on the their victims. These t cases to decide the The courts have to African-Americans

received lighter sentences than African-Americans who murdered whites and whether those sentences violated the equal protection rights of the Constitution.

The LDF notes in *Death Row USA: Winter 2007* (January 1, 2007, http://www.naacpldf.org/content/pdf/pubs/ drusa/DRUSA_Winter_2007.pdf) that from 1976 through 2006, 79.5% of the victims of executed inmates were white and 14% were African-American. Examination of the defendant-victim racial combinations reveals that 53.6% of white defendants murdered white victims, whereas only 1.4% murdered African-American victims. Among African-American defendants, 20.6% were executed for murdering white victims, whereas 10.9% had African-American victims.

CRIMES WARRANTING THE DEATH PENALTY

According to Kathleen Maguire and Ann L. Pastore, in the *Sourcebook of Criminal Justice Statistics 2003* (2004, http://www.albany.edu/sourcebook/), the vast majority of executions from 1930 through 1998 were for murder, followed by rape. The remaining executions included twenty-five cases for armed robbery, twenty for kidnapping, eleven for burglary, six for sabotage, six for aggravated assault, and two for espionage. Since 1965 all those executed have been convicted on murder charges. Figure 6.7 shows a breakdown by criminal offense of people executed from 1930 through 2005. Ninety percent

FIGURE 6.7

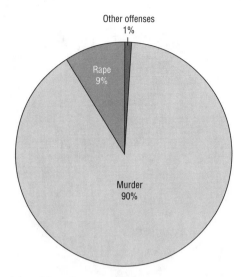

Prisoners executed, by offense, 1930–2005

Other offenses
1%

Rape
9%

Murder
90%

SOURCE: Adapted from "Execution, 1930–2006," in *Capital Punishment Statistics*, U.S. Department of Justice, Bureau of Justice Statistics, January 11, 2007, http://www.ojp.usdoj.gov/bjs/cp.htm (accessed July 23, 2007) and Kathleen Maguire and Ann L. Pastore, eds., "Table 6.86. Prisoners Executed under Civil Authority, by Race and Offense, United States, 1930–1998" in *Sourcebook of Criminal Justice Statistics 2003*, U.S. Department of Justice, Bureau of Justice Statistics, 2004, http://www.albany.edu/sourcebook/pdf/t686.pdf (accessed August 24, 2007)

of the executions were for murder, whereas 9% were for rape and 1% were for other offenses.

According to Maguire and Pastore, the last executions for rape occurred in 1964. Six executions for rape occurred in three states that year: Texas (three), Missouri (two), and Arkansas (one). The Supreme Court ruled in *Coker v. Georgia* (433 U.S. 584, 1977) that rape did not warrant the death penalty. The case concerned the rape of an adult woman. The Court did not address the rape of a child. In December 1996, however, the Louisiana Supreme Court ruled that death is a just and constitutional punishment for the rape of a child under twelve years of age. As of November 2007, no one had been executed under Louisiana's statute.

METHOD OF EXECUTION

According to Snell, among the 1,004 prisoners executed between 1977 and 2005, 836 (83%) received lethal injection, followed by electrocution (152, or 15%). (See Table 6.12.) Eleven executions were carried out by lethal gas, three by hanging, and two by firing squad. Texas, the state with the largest number of prisoners executed, used lethal injection in all 355 cases. Virginia executed sixty-seven inmates by lethal injection and twenty-seven inmates by electrocution. Oklahoma put to death seventy-nine prisoners, all by lethal injection.

TABLE 6.12

Executions, by state and method, 1977–2005

State	Number executed	Lethal injection	Electrocution	Lethal gas	Hanging	Firing squad
U.S. total	1,004	836	152	11	3	2
Federal	3	3	0	0	0	0
Alabama	34	10	24	0	0	0
Arizona	22	20	0	2	0	0
Arkansas	27	26	1	0	0	0
California	12	10	0	2	0	0
Colorado	1	1	0	0	0	0
Connecticut	1	1	0	0	0	0
Delaware	14	13	0	0	1	0
Florida	60	16	44	0	0	0
Georgia	39	16	23	0	0	0
Idaho	1	1	0	0	0	0
Illinois	12	12	0	0	0	0
Indiana	16	13	3	0	0	0
Kentucky	2	1	1	0	0	0
Louisiana	27	7	20	0	0	0
Maryland	5	5	0	0	0	0
Mississippi	7	3	0	4	0	0
Missouri	66	66	0	0	0	0
Montana	2	2	0	0	0	0
Nebraska	3	0	3	0	0	0
Nevada	11	10	0	1	0	0
New Mexico	1	1	0	0	0	0
North Carolina	39	37	0	2	0	0
Ohio	19	19	0	0	0	0
Oklahoma	79	79	0	0	0	0
Oregon	2	2	0	0	0	0
Pennsylvania	3	3	0	0	0	0
South Carolina	35	29	6	0	0	0
Tennessee	1	1	0	0	0	0
Texas	355	355	0	0	0	0
Utah	6	4	0	0	0	2
Virginia	94	67	27	0	0	0
Washington	4	2	0	0	2	0
Wyoming	1	1	0	0	0	0

SOURCE: Tracy L. Snell, "Appendix Table 5. Executions, by State and Method, 1977–2005," in *Capital Punishment, 2005*, U.S. Department of Justice, Bureau of Justice Statistics, December 2006, http://www.ojp.usdoj.gov/bjs/pub/pdf/cp05.pdf (accessed July 23, 2007)

CHAPTER 7

ISSUES OF FAIRNESS: RACIAL BIAS AND QUALITY OF LEGAL REPRESENTATION

Capital punishment opponents frequently raise issues about the fairness with which the death penalty is applied in the United States. These challenges avoid emotionally charged arguments about the moral rightness or wrongness of capital punishment to focus on more legally definable issues, such as discrimination and the denial of legal rights. An enduring idea of U.S. jurisprudence (the philosophy of law) is that "justice is blind." In other words the merits of a criminal case should be decided without regard to the race, ethnicity, or economic status of the accused. Death penalty opponents argue that death sentences are unfairly administered because of racial bias, political motivations, and—in the case of poor defendants—poor legal representation. These factors, they say, prove that the U.S. capital punishment system is flawed and should be eliminated. Death penalty advocates counter that the judicial process contains adequate safeguards to ensure that defendants receive fair trials. They believe that if any discrepancies do exist in capital convictions and sentences, they should be remedied by applying the death penalty more often, not less often.

RACIAL BIAS IN THE DEATH PENALTY?

One of the most contentious issues within the death penalty debate is race. Capital punishment opponents argue that racial bias on the behalf of prosecutors, judges, and juries results in disproportionately high numbers of convictions and death penalties for African-American defendants. Figure 7.1 shows the racial makeup of all prisoners under the sentence of death and those executed between 1977 and 2005. Nearly half (48%) of death row inmates were white, whereas 41% were African-American. Among people executed, 58% were white and 34% were African-American. According to U.S. Census data, African-Americans comprised 11% to 13% of the nation's population over this time period. Thus, the percentages of African-Americans comprising all death row and executed inmates far exceeded their relative presence in the U.S. population as a whole.

Race and Homicide Statistics

According to James Alan Fox and Marianne W. Zawitz of the Bureau of Justice Statistics, in *Homicide Trends in the United States* (July 11, 2007, http://www.ojp.usdoj.gov/bjs/pub/pdf/htius.pdf), African-Americans are disproportionately represented among homicide offenders and victims. Figure 7.2 shows the U.S. homicide rate per one hundred thousand population between 1976 and 2005 for African-American and white murderers. Fox and Zawitz note that more than half of the offenders (52.2%) were African-American, whereas 45.8% were white. Furthermore, they report that in 2005 the offending rate for African-Americans (36.9) was more than seven times higher than the rate for whites (4.8). Statistics also show that African-Americans make up a disproportionate percentage of homicide victims. (See Figure 7.3.) Of all homicide victims between 1976 and 2005, 46.9% were African-American. White victims comprised 50.9% of the total. In 2005 the homicide victimization rate for African-Americans (29.6) was six times higher than the rate for whites (4.7).

Fox and Zawitz indicate that the vast majority of homicides committed between 1976 and 2005 were intraracial: 86% of white victims were murdered by whites and 94% of African-American victims were murdered by African-Americans. Figure 7.4 graphically illustrates the percentage breakdown for homicides by the race of the murderer and the race of the victim. Cases of "black on white" and "white on black" homicide are relatively uncommon.

Table 7.1 provides details from Fox and Zawitz regarding the circumstances of homicides committed by different races between 1976 and 2005. The data indicate that white murderers were most often involved in workplace (70.5%), sex-related (54.7%), and gang-related (54.3%) killings. African-American murderers were more frequently associated with drug-related killings (65%), felony murders (59.3%), and homicides resulting from arguments (51.1%).

FIGURE 7.1

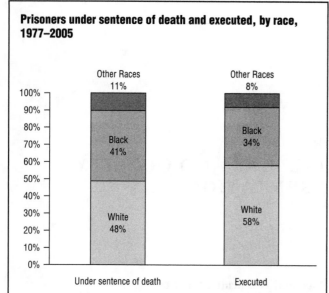

Prisoners under sentence of death and executed, by race, 1977–2005

SOURCE: Adapted from Tracy L. Snell, "Table 10. Executions and Other Dispositions of Inmates Sentenced to Death, by Race and Hispanic Origin, 1977–2005," in *Capital Punishment, 2005*, U.S. Department of Justice, Bureau of Justice Statistics, December 2006, http://www.ojp.usdoj.gov/bjs/pub/pdf/cp05.pdf (accessed July 23, 2007)

FIGURE 7.3

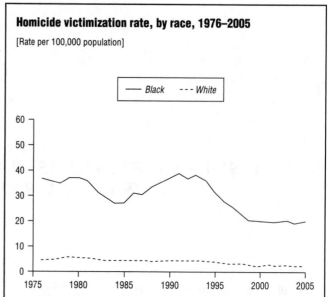

Homicide victimization rate, by race, 1976–2005

[Rate per 100,000 population]

SOURCE: James Alan Fox and Marianne W. Zawitz, "Homicide Victimization by Race, 1976–2005," in *Homicide Trends in the United States*, U.S. Department of Justice, Bureau of Justice Statistics, July 11, 2007, http://www.ojp.usdoj.gov/bjs/pub/pdf/htius.pdf (accessed July 24, 2007)

The Baldus Study

In 1986 lawyers appealing the case of Warren McCleskey, a convicted murderer, brought before the U.S. Supreme Court the Baldus study (by David C. Baldus, Charles A. Pulanski Jr., and George Woodworth. The study

FIGURE 7.2

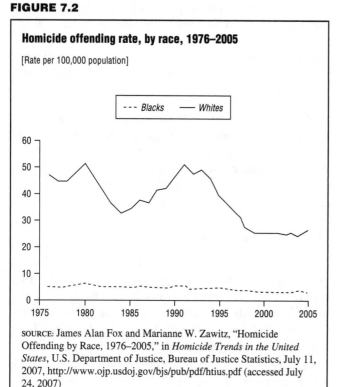

Homicide offending rate, by race, 1976–2005

[Rate per 100,000 population]

SOURCE: James Alan Fox and Marianne W. Zawitz, "Homicide Offending by Race, 1976–2005," in *Homicide Trends in the United States*, U.S. Department of Justice, Bureau of Justice Statistics, July 11, 2007, http://www.ojp.usdoj.gov/bjs/pub/pdf/htius.pdf (accessed July 24, 2007)

FIGURE 7.4

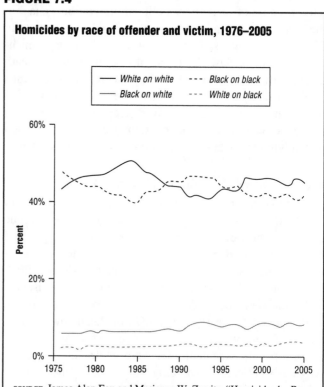

Homicides by race of offender and victim, 1976–2005

SOURCE: James Alan Fox and Marianne W. Zawitz, "Homicides by Race of Offender and Victim, 1976–2005," in *Homicide Trends in the United States*, U.S. Department of Justice, Bureau of Justice Statistics, July 11, 2007, http://www.ojp.usdoj.gov/bjs/pub/pdf/htius.pdf (accessed July 24, 2007)

TABLE 7.1

Circumstances of homicides committed, by race of offender, 1976–2005

| | Offenders | | |
	White	Black	Other
Circumstances			
Felony murder	39.1%	59.3%	1.6%
Sex-related	54.7%	43.4%	1.9%
Drug-related	33.9%	65.0%	1.1%
Gang-related	54.3%	41.2%	4.4%
Argument	46.8%	51.1%	2.2%
Workplace	70.5%	26.7%	2.8%

SOURCE: Adapted from James Alan Fox and Marianne W. Zawitz, "Homicide Type by Race, 1976–2005," in *Homicide Trends in the United States*, U.S. Department of Justice, Bureau of Justice Statistics, July 11, 2007, http://www.ojp.usdoj.gov/bjs/pub/pdf/htius.pdf (accessed July 24, 2007)

actually consisted of two studies: "Comparative Review of Death Sentences: An Empirical Study of the Georgia Experience" [*Journal of Criminal Law and Criminology*, vol. 74, no. 3, 1983] and "Monitoring and Evaluating Contemporary Death Sentencing Systems: Lessons from Georgia" [*University of California Davis Law Review*, vol. 18, no. 1375, 1985]), an analysis of two thousand cases in Georgia in the 1970s.

This study showed that African-American defendants who were convicted of killing whites were more likely to receive death sentences than white murderers or African-Americans who had killed African-Americans. The justices, in *McCleskey v. Kemp* (481 U.S. 279, 1987), rejected the study, declaring that "apparent disparities in sentencing are an inevitable part of our criminal justice system" and that there were enough safeguards built into the legal system to protect every defendant.

In "Racial Discrimination and the Death Penalty in the Post-*Furman* Era: An Empirical and Legal Analysis with Recent Findings from Philadelphia" (*Cornell Law Review*, vol. 83, 1998), David C. Baldus et al. find evidence of race-of-victim disparities in twenty-six out of twenty-nine death penalty states. The researchers note that the race of the victim was related to whether capital punishment was imposed. A defendant was more likely to receive the death penalty if the victim was white than if the victim was African-American.

The U.S. General Accounting Office Study

These studies were consistent with a February 1990 U.S. government study of capital punishment. The U.S. General Accounting Office (GAO; now the U.S. Government Accountability Office), in *Death Penalty Sentencing: Research Indicates Pattern of Racial Disparities* (http://archive.gao.gov/t2pbat11/140845.pdf), reviewed twenty-eight studies on race and the death penalty. The GAO reported that "in 82% of the studies, the race of the victim was found to influence the likelihood of being charged

with capital murder or receiving the death penalty." The GAO found that when the victim was white, the defendant, whether white or African-American, was more likely to get the death sentence.

GAO added that in the small number of horrendous murders, death sentences were more likely to be imposed, regardless of race. Nevertheless, when the offender killed a person while robbing him or when the murderer had a previous record, the race of the victim played a role. The GAO also explained that for crimes of passion, the convicted person (regardless of race) rarely received the death penalty.

Racial Justice Legislation

In 1998 Kentucky became the first state to enact a racial justice law (Racial Justice Act) that prohibited the execution of a convicted person when evidence shows racial discrimination in prosecution or sentencing. Other states that have considered similar legislation include Florida, Georgia, Indiana, Nebraska, New Mexico, North Carolina, Ohio, Oregon, and Texas. As of November 2007, however, no other state had passed such legislation.

First U.S. Department of Justice Study of Racial and Ethnic Bias

In July 2000 President Bill Clinton (1946–) ordered the U.S. Department of Justice to review the administration of the federal death penalty system. This order came in the aftermath of a request for clemency by Raul Juan Garza, who was granted a stay by President Clinton, but who was ultimately executed in June 2001. Garza's lawyer contended that it was unfair to execute his client because the federal death penalty discriminated against members of minorities.

In September 2000 the Justice Department released *The Federal Death Penalty System: A Statistical Survey (1988–2000)* (http://www.usdoj.gov/dag/pubdoc/dpsurvey.html), which provided information on the federal death penalty since the passage of the first federal capital punishment law in 1988 (the Anti-Drug Abuse Act). From 1988 to 1994 prosecutors in the ninety-four federal districts were required to submit to the U.S. attorney general for review and approval only those cases that the attorney general deemed worthy for the death penalty. During this period the prosecutors sought the death penalty in fifty-two cases and received authorization from the attorney general in forty-seven cases.

In 1995 the Justice Department adopted a new protocol that required U.S. attorneys to submit for review all cases in which a defendant was charged with a crime subject to the death penalty, regardless of whether they intended to seek authorization to pursue the death penalty. These cases were first reviewed by the attorney general's Review Committee on Capital Cases, a committee of senior Justice Department lawyers.

TABLE 7.2

Distribution of defendants within each stage of the federal death penalty process, 1995–2000

State	Total #	Total %	White #	White %	Black #	Black %	Hispanic #	Hispanic %	Other #	Other %
Submitted by U.S. attorneys	682	100.0%	134	19.6%	324	47.5%	195	28.6%	29	4.3%
No recommendation	5	100.0%	1	20.0%	1	20.0%	3	60.0%	0	0.0%
Recommendation not to seek death penalty (DP)	494	100.0%	85	17.2%	242	49.0%	153	31.0%	14	2.8%
Recommendation to seek DP	183	100.0%	48	26.2%	81	44.3%	39	21.3%	15	8.2%
Considered by review committee	618	100.0%	119	19.3%	301	48.7%	172	27.8%	26	4.2%
No recommendation	15	100.0%	4	26.7%	6	40.0%	4	26.7%	1	6.7%
Recommendation not to seek DP	420	100.0%	68	16.2%	215	51.2%	125	29.8%	12	2.9%
Recommendation to seek DP	183	100.0%	47	25.7%	80	43.7%	43	23.5%	13	7.1%
Considered by attorney general (AG)	588	100.0%	115	19.6%	287	48.8%	160	27.2%	26	4.4%
Decision deferred or pending	12	100.0%	3	25.0%	4	33.3%	4	33.3%	1	8.3%
Authorization not to seek DP	417	100.0%	68	16.3%	212	50.8%	124	29.7%	13	3.1%
Authorization to seek DP	159	100.0%	44	27.7%	71	44.7%	32	20.1%	12	7.5%
Authorized by AG to seek DP	159	100.0%	44	27.7%	71	44.7%	32	20.1%	12	7.5%
DP notice withdrawn—plea agreement	51	100.0%	21	41.2%	18	35.3%	9	17.6%	3	5.9%
DP notice withdrawn—subsequent AG decision	11	100.0%	1	9.1%	3	27.3%	5	45.5%	2	18.2%
DP notice dismissed or trial terminated	4	100.0%	0	0.0%	1	25.0%	3	75.0%	0	0.0%
Pending trial or completion of trial	51	100.0%	11	21.6%	23	45.1%	13	25.5%	4	7.8%
Not convicted of capital charge	1	100.0%	0	0.0%	1	100.0%	0	0.0%	0	0.0%
Convicted of capital charge	41	100.0%	11	26.8%	25	61.0%	2	4.9%	3	7.3%
Convicted of capital charge	41	100.0%	11	26.8%	25	61.0%	2	4.9%	3	7.3%
Jury verdict—DP not recommended	21	100.0%	7	33.3%	12	57.1%	0	0.0%	2	9.5%
Jury verdict—DP recommended	20	100.0%	4	20.0%	13	65.0%	2	10.0%	1	5.0%
Sentenced to death	20	100.0%	4	20.0%	13	65.0%	2	10.0%	1	5.0%
DP recommended by jury but not yet imposed	2	100.0%	0	0.0%	0	0.0%	2	100.0%	0	0.0%
DP vacated by court, further action pending	4	100.0%	1	25.0%	3	75.0%	0	0.0%	0	0.0%
Death sentence pending	14	100.0%	3	21.4%	10	71.4%	0	0.0%	1	7.1%

SOURCE: "Table 1A. Distribution of Defendants within Each Stage of the Federal Death Penalty Process (1995–2000)," in *The Federal Death Penalty System: A Statistical Survey (1988–2000)*, U.S. Department of Justice, September 12, 2000, http://www.usdoj.gov/dag/pubdoc/_table_set_i_corrected.pdf (accessed August 24, 2007)

The period 1995–2000, which provides a more extensive picture of the Justice Department's internal decision process as it pertains to the federal death penalty, showed that between January 27, 1995, and July 20, 2000, at every phase of the federal process, minority defendants were overrepresented. Of the 682 defendants whose cases were submitted for review by federal prosecutors, 47.5% were African-American, 28.6% were Hispanic, and 19.6% were white. (See Table 7.2.) The prosecutors recommended seeking the death penalty for 183 out of 682 cases submitted for review. Of these 183 cases, two-thirds (44.3% African-Americans and 21.3% Hispanics) were members of minorities. The attorney general reviewed 588 of the cases and authorized the U.S. attorneys to seek the death penalty in 159 cases. Of the 159 defendants, 44.7% were African-American and 20.1% were Hispanic. Only about 27.7% were white.

Racial Disparity in Plea Bargaining?

It should be noted that the attorney general's decision to seek the death penalty may be changed up until the jury has returned a sentencing verdict. This change may be sought by the defense lawyer, the U.S. attorney, the Review Committee, or by the attorney general. A plea agreement is one avenue that may result in the withdrawal of the death penalty. This means that the defendant enters into an agreement with the U.S. attorney resulting in a guilty plea, saving him or her from the death penalty. From 1995 to 2000, after the attorney general sought the death penalty for 159 defendants, 51 defendants entered into plea agreements. (See Table 7.2.) Almost twice as many white defendants (48%, or twenty-one out of forty-four) as African-Americans (25%, or eighteen out of seventy-one) received a plea agreement. About 28% (nine out of thirty-two) of Hispanics entered into a plea agreement.

GOVERNMENT DEFENDS DATA. The National Institute of Justice (NIJ) observes in the solicitation *Research into the Investigation and Prosecution of Homicide: Examining the Federal Death Penalty System* (July 20, 2001, http://www.ncjrs.gov/pdffiles1/nij/sl000490.pdf) that, "generally speaking, once submitted for review [to obtain a death penalty authorization], minorities proceeded to the next stages in the death penalty process at lower rates than whites." The NIJ claims that the attorney general authorized the death penalty for 38% (44 out of 115) of whites being considered, compared to 25% (71 out of 287) of African-American defendants and 20% (32 out of 160) of Hispanic defendants. (See Table 7.2.)

Second Justice Department Study of Racial and Ethnic Bias

On June 6, 2001, the Justice Department released a supplement to the September 2000 report—*The Federal Death Penalty System: Supplementary Data, Analysis, and Revised Protocols for Capital Case Review* (http://www.usdoj.gov/dag/pubdoc/deathpenaltystudy.htm). That same day U.S. attorney general John D. Ashcroft (1942–) told the Judiciary Committee of the U.S. House of Representatives that the report confirmed that the subsequent study of the administration of the federal death penalty showed no indication of racial or ethnic bias.

The follow-up study had been ordered by his predecessor, U.S. attorney general Janet Reno (1938–). Besides the 682 cases submitted by federal prosecutors for review in the first study of the federal death penalty, another 291 cases were analyzed, for a total of 973 cases. These included cases that should have been submitted for review for the first report but were not, those in which the defendant eventually entered into a plea agreement for a lesser sentence, and cases in which the death penalty could have been sought but was not. Among the 973 defendants, 408 (42%) were African-American, 350 (36%) were Hispanic, and 166 (17%) were white.

According to the supplement, from 1995 to 2000, of the 973 defendants eligible for capital charges, federal prosecutors requested authorization to pursue the death penalty against 81% of whites, 79% of African-Americans, and 56% of Hispanics. The attorney general ultimately authorized seeking the death penalty for 27% of the white defendants, 17% of the African-American defendants, and 9% of the Hispanic defendants.

Critics of the supplementary report pointed out that the second federal review failed to address many issues. Following the release of the September 2000 survey, Attorney General Reno ordered a study to find out how death penalty cases are taken into the federal system when there is joint state and federal jurisdiction. The June 2001 report did not cover this issue. Instead, the report described a January 10, 2001, NIJ meeting in which researchers and practitioners agreed that such a study "would entail a highly complex, multi-year research initiative" and that "even if such a study were carried out, it could not be expected to yield definitive answers concerning the reasons for disparities in federal death penalty."

Testifying before the Senate Judiciary Committee, David C. Baldus (June 11, 2001, http://www.deathpenaltyinfo.org/article.php?did=252&scid=) of the University of Iowa reported that he was one of the researchers at the January 2001 NIJ meeting. Baldus claimed that even though it was true he and others at the meeting agreed that the study ordered by Attorney General Reno would likely take two years to complete, the consensus was that "such a study would provide the best possible evidence

on the question." Baldus further pointed out that quite some time had elapsed since that meeting and the first report, and still the Justice Department had not taken any steps to initiate such a study.

On July 20, 2001, the NIJ published the above-mentioned solicitation for research of the federal death penalty, including the decision-making factors that determine whether a homicide case is prosecuted in the federal or state system, as well as issues of race/ethnicity and geography in the imposition of the death penalty. This allows researchers to apply for government grants to complete the requested research, but such research has yet to be undertaken.

In "Analysis of June 6 Department of Justice Report on the Federal Death Penalty" (June 14, 2001, http://www.aclu.org/capital/general/10574pub20010614.html), the American Civil Liberties Union (ACLU) notes that, unlike the September 2000 Justice Department report, the June 2001 report did not include information on whether the supplemental 291 cases were from all or just some districts and, therefore, whether or not they represented all the death penalty–eligible cases between 1995 and 2000. The ACLU also pointed out that even though the report found that federal prosecutors were less likely to submit cases of African-American and Hispanic defendants to the attorney general for death penalty authorizations and that the attorney general authorized capital punishment for a higher proportion of whites than African-Americans and Hispanics, there was no information about the decision-making process behind prosecuting on the federal level and of offering plea agreements.

A North Carolina Study

On April 16, 2001, Isaac Unah and John Charles Boger of the University of North Carolina released the most comprehensive study of North Carolina's death penalty system in the state's history: *Race and the Death Penalty in North Carolina, an Empirical Analysis: 1993–1997* (http://www.common-sense.org/pdfs/NCDeathPenaltyReport2001.pdf). The researchers studied all 3,990 homicide cases between 1993 and 1997, including defendants who received death sentences, as well as those sentenced to life imprisonment.

On first analysis of all homicide cases, Unah and Boger found that, overall, the death-sentencing rate for white victims (3.7%) was almost twice as high as the rate where the victims were nonwhite (1.9%). In addition, the death-sentencing rate for nonwhite defendants/white victims (6.4%) was over two times higher than the rate for white defendants/white victims (2.6%).

When Unah and Boger confined their investigation to death-eligible cases (those imposing the death penalty, such as a case involving the murder of a police officer), race determined whether the defendant received the death sentence. The death-sentencing rate in all death-eligible cases was much higher in white-victim cases (8%) than in cases in which the victims were nonwhite (4.7%). As with all cases, nonwhite defendants in white-victim homicides received the death sentence at a higher rate (11.6%) than white defendants who murdered whites (6.1%).

After the initial analysis, Unah and Boger performed a more comprehensive investigation involving 502 defendants, collecting 113 factors about each crime. These factors included the circumstances of the homicide, the evidence, the charges brought against the defendant, the character and background of the defendant and the victim, the presence or absence of aggravating or mitigating circumstances as specified under the law, as well as the presence or absence of aggravating or mitigating circumstances not specified under the law. The researchers also looked into other factors that might have influenced the imposition of the death penalty, such as the coming reelection of the district attorney prosecuting the crime. Unah and Boger found that race—specifically the race of the victim—played a role in the imposition of capital punishment in North Carolina from 1993 to 1997. On average, the odds of receiving the death penalty were increased by a factor of 3.5 times when the victim was white.

A Maryland Study

In January 2003 Raymond Paternoster et al. released *An Empirical Analysis of Maryland's Death Sentencing System with Respect to the Influence of Race and Legal Jurisdiction* (http://www.newsdesk.umd.edu/pdf/finalrep.pdf), a state-commissioned study of the use of the death penalty in the state. The researchers reviewed 1,311 death-eligible cases out of 6,000 murder cases prosecuted between 1978 and 1999. Of the 1,311 death-eligible cases, state attorneys filed a formal notice to seek the death penalty in 353 (27%) cases. Of the 353 cases, state attorneys dropped the death penalty notice in 140 (40%) cases. The death penalty notice was retained in 213 (60%) cases, out of which 180 (84.5%) cases proceeded to the penalty phase.

Paternoster et al. examined the four decision stages in the death penalty sentencing system: the prosecutor's decision to seek the death penalty, the prosecutor's decision to drop or stick with the death penalty notice, the case's proceeding to a penalty trial, and the court's decision to impose the death sentence. The researchers "found no evidence that the race of the defendant matter[ed] in the processing of capital cases in the state." However, the race of the victim had an impact on whether the prosecutor sought the death penalty. Prosecutors were more likely to seek the death penalty for killers of white victims and were more likely to stick with their death penalty notification when the victims were white.

The study also revealed that jurisdictions affected whether state attorneys sought the death penalty. A defendant in Baltimore County was twenty-six times more likely

to be sentenced to death than a defendant in Baltimore City. A defendant was fourteen times more likely to get the death penalty in Baltimore County than in Montgomery County and seven times more likely to get the death penalty in Prince George's County.

A California Study

Glenn Pierce and Michael Radelet, in "The Impact of Legally Inappropriate Factors on Death Sentencing for California Homicides, 1990–99" (*Santa Clara Law Review*, vol. 46, no. 1, 2005), reviewed data from all homicides committed in California from 1990 through 1999 and compared those that did and did not result in a death sentence. To examine any potential racial biases in conviction and sentencing, they excluded cases in which killers had multiple victims of different races.

Pierce and Radelet found that convicted murderers with non-Hispanic white victims were 4.7 times more likely to receive a death sentence than those who killed Latinos and 3.7 times more likely to receive a death sentence than those who killed African-Americans.

A 2004 National Study

In "Explaining Death Row's Population and Racial Composition" (*Journal of Empirical Legal Studies*, vol. 1, no. 1, March 2004), John Blume, Theodore Eisenberg, and Martin T. Wells compared twenty-three years of death row statistics to state murder rates. They found that between 1977 and 1999 the number of death row inmates in most states, including those with a reputation for sending a high number of defendants to death row, was nearly proportional to the number of murders in that state.

Overall, the number of inmates on death row in each state was between 0.4% (Colorado) and 6% (Nevada) of murders in that state, and the mean (average) "death sentencing rate" among all states was 2.2%. Despite having the highest number of executions per year, Texas came in below this average with a death row to murder ratio of 2%. Even though Texas juries sentenced 776 people to death row, a total of 37,879 murders had been committed during the study period. Florida, which had a total death row population of 735 inmates, had experienced 121,837 murders and a death sentencing rate of 3.4%. By contrast, Nevada had 124 death row inmates, but only 2,072 murders, giving the state a death sentencing rate three times that of Texas. California, Virginia, Washington, New Mexico, and Maryland all had death sentencing rates below 1.5%.

To explain the slight discrepancy between states, Blume, Eisenberg, and Wells looked at the states' statutes, politics, and other factors that might influence sentencing rates. They found that death sentencing rates were nearly twice as high in states where a judge handed out the sentence as opposed to a jury (4.1% versus 2.1%). State statutes also made a big difference. States with more open-ended statutes that allowed a jury to base their verdicts on subjective standards, such as the heinousness of the murder, had sentencing rates of 2.7%. Sentencing rates dropped to 1.9% in states where specific murders, such as the murder of a pregnant woman or police officer, warranted the death sentence.

Blume, Eisenberg, and Wells then compared the race of the death row inmates to the number of murders committed by race across the country. Nationwide, African-Americans committed 51.5% of murders between 1977 and 1999, but they only made up 41.3% of death row. The researchers analyzed data from seven states—Georgia, Indiana, Maryland, Nevada, Pennsylvania, South Carolina, and Virginia—to determine why these percentages did not match.

Generally, what Blume, Eisenberg, and Wells found was that juries give the death sentence to a far smaller percentage of African-American murderers when the victim was also African-American, rather than white. In South Carolina, for instance, only 0.3% of African-Americans who killed African-Americans received the death penalty, whereas 6.8% of African-Americans who murdered whites were sentenced to death. Because 94% of African-American homicide victims were killed by African-Americans, the percentage of African-Americans on death row tended to be lower than the percentage of African-American murderers. Even though the researchers speculated that racism may figure into these percentages, they also believed that African-American juries in communities with a great deal of African-American-on-African-American crime were less likely to hand out the death sentence.

An Ohio Study

The Ohio Associated Press (AP) published an extensive study on the Ohio death penalty system on May 7, 2005. The news organization reviewed 2,543 reported cases in which prisoners were brought up on capital charges between 1981 and 2002. This number was narrowed to 1,936 after analysts weeded out charges that were dismissed or erroneously reported. Roughly 270 of the indictments led to a death sentence. The AP analyzed the indictments to find any discrepancies in sentencing involving race, sex, or jurisdiction. The results were presented by Andrew Welsh-Huggins in the three-part series "Death Penalty Unequal" (*Cincinnati Enquirer*, May 7–9, 2005).

With respect to race, those indicted (formally accused) of capital murder in Ohio were much more likely to receive the death sentence if the victim was white. Some 17.9% of indictments led to a death sentence if the victim was white, as opposed to 8.5% if the victim was African-American. However, unlike the Baldus study, these percentages were not dependent on the race of the defendant. In cases where the offender and victim were both white, 18.3% of offenders received the death sentence. Roughly the same number of African-American offenders (17.9%) were sentenced to death if the victim was white. If the victim was African-American, 8.4% of African-American offenders were sentenced to death, compared to 8.7% for white offenders.

Jurisdiction had a bigger impact than race on who received the death sentence in Ohio. The AP looked at indictments by county and compared the numbers with those aspects of each county that might influence death penalty verdicts. The news organization found that the politics of a county played a significant role in determining the percentage of defendants who received the death penalty. Hamilton County (Cincinnati metropolitan area) and Cuyahoga County (Cleveland metropolitan area) are both large counties that paid their defense attorneys reasonably well. Yet, only 8% of all capital cases ended with a death sentence in Democratic Cuyahoga County, as opposed to 43% in the largely Republican Hamilton County.

The Ohio report also found that compensation for lawyers who represent poor defendants varied drastically from county to county. The limits ranged from $3,000 maximum per death penalty case in rural Coshocton County (east-central Ohio) up to $75,000 in the more affluent Montgomery County (Dayton metropolitan area). Generally, death penalty cases place an enormous strain on the resources of a small county court as opposed to a large county court. Rural judges reported having to dedicate all their resources for months on end when capital cases came through their courts.

Other Claims of Racial Bias

Some people claim that district attorneys, who decide which cases to try as death penalty cases, may be motivated by politics or racial prejudice to impose the death penalty on minority defendants. Jeffrey Pokorak of St. Mary's University, in "Probing the Capital Prosecutor's Perspective: Race of the Discretionary Actors" (*Cornell Law Review*, vol. 83, 1998), finds that 1,794 out of 1,838 prosecutors (97.5%) in the thirty-eight states with capital punishment were white. Only 1.2% were African-American or Hispanic.

Jennifer Eberhardt et al., in "Looking Deathworthy. Perceived Stereotypicality of Black Defendants Predicts Capital-Sentencing Outcomes" (*Psychological Science*, vol. 17, no. 5, May 2006), note a possible link between racial stereotyping and imposition of the death penalty against African-American defendants. In the study, forty-four head shot photographs of male African-American defendants in Pennsylvania capital murder cases from 1979 to 1999 were shown to evaluators (undergraduate students) unaware of the defendants' history. All the defendants had been convicted of murdering white victims. The evaluators were mostly white; no African-Americans were included.

Each defendant was rated by the evaluators in terms of darkness of skin color and stereotypical features that might be associated with African-American people (such as large lips and broad noses). Eberhardt et al. conducted a statistical analysis of the results taking into account six nonracial factors: aggravating and mitigating circumstances presented at trial, the severity of the murder, the socioeconomic status of the defendant and victim, and the attractiveness of the defendant (as rated by the evaluators). They find that more than half of the defendants rated as having extremely stereotypical African-American facial features had been sentenced to death. Less than a quarter of the defendants that appeared more stereotypically white had been sentenced to death. This disparity did not appear when a similar study was conducted using photographs of African-American defendants who had murdered African-American victims. The authors conclude that "defendants who were perceived to be more stereotypically Black were more likely to be sentenced to death only when their victims were White."

Death Penalty Advocates Speak about the Race Issue

On February 1, 2006, the U.S. Senate Judiciary Subcommittee on the Constitution, Civil Rights, and Property Rights conducted the hearing "An Examination of the Death Penalty in the United States." One of the scholars who testified was John McAdams (http://judiciary.sena te.gov/testimony.cfm?id=1745&wit_id=4989) of Marquette University. McAdams noted that death penalty opponents often "play the race card" in debates over capital punishment. He argued that statistical studies do not support the notion that African-American murderers suffer racial bias in capital punishment cases. However, he acknowledged that studies do show "a huge bias" against African-American victims of homicide. He testified, "This is clearly unjust, but it leaves open the question of whether the injustice should be remedied by executing nobody at all, or rather executing more offenders who have murdered black people."

In *Death Penalty and Sentencing Information in the United States* (October 1, 1997, http://www.prodeathpenal ty.com/DP.html), Dudley Sharp of Justice for All, a Texas-based organization that promotes reform of the justice system to better protect the rights of victims, disputes claims that racial discrimination plays a role in death sentencing. He complains that "the most vile strategy of death penalty opponents is their use of propaganda to nurture hatreds and mistrust between race and class." Sharp notes that most murderers on death row at that time were white, not African-American. He cites data from various studies conducted by government and private entities that support the position that African-Americans are not overrepresented on death row or among the executed.

The Criminal Justice Legal Foundation (CJLF) is a California-based group that supports capital punishment.

In March 2003 the CJLF collaborated with the California District Attorneys Association to publish *Prosecutors' Perspective on California's Death Penalty* (http:// www.cdaa.org/WhitePapers/DPPaper.pdf). The report includes a section that attacks claims of racial bias in California's capital punishment system. The report notes that the racial makeup of the state's death row at the end of 2001 was 41.4% white, 34.6% African-American, 18.8% Hispanic, and 5.2% other races. However, the relatively large percentage of African-Americans among the condemned is attributed primarily to Los Angeles County gang activity: "It is well known that Los Angeles County is 'home territory' to many Black street gangs, such as Crips, Bloods, and the like. And, by their very nature, gang-member activities and prior criminal records frequently bring gang-related homicides within California's capital-sentencing scheme." The report claims that California's death row racial composition changes dramatically if condemned inmates in Los Angeles County are removed from the dataset. This results in a death row comprised of 49.6% white, 28.8% African-American, 17.1% Hispanic, and 4.5% other.

Wesley Lowe (June 20, 2007, http://www.wesleylo we.com/cp.html#race), another vocal death penalty advocate, maintains that the solution to any perceived problems with racial bias in death sentencing is to eliminate the opportunity for discrimination. He states, "For capital punishment to be applied equally to every criminal, rich or poor, black or white, it must be mandatory for ALL capital cases."

LEGAL REPRESENTATION: QUESTIONS ABOUT QUALITY

The Sixth Amendment to the U.S. Constitution guarantees the "assistance of counsel for defense" in federal criminal prosecution. In *Gideon v. Wainwright* (372 U.S. 335, 1963), the U.S. Supreme Court extended the right to counsel to state criminal prosecution of indigent (poor) people charged with felonies. In *Argersinger v. Hamlin* (407 U.S. 25, 1972), the high court held that poor people charged with any crime that carries a sentence of imprisonment have the right to counsel.

The Court later ruled in *Strickland v. Washington* (466 U.S. 688, 1984) that the lawyers provided for poor defendants must abide by certain professional standards in criminal cases. Some of these standards include demonstrating loyalty to the client, avoiding conflicts of interest, keeping the defendant informed of important developments in the trial, and conducting reasonable factual and legal investigations that may aid the client's case.

Ineffective Counsel?

Death penalty opponents claim that some lawyers who have defended capital cases were inexperienced, ill trained, or incompetent. They point to cases where the defense lawyers fell asleep during trial, drank to excess the night before, or even showed up in the courtroom intoxicated. They also cite the well-publicized cases of inmates exonerated as a result of college students finding evidence that defense lawyers had failed to uncover.

Several studies reveal that attorneys who took on capital murder cases involving poor defendants were often incompetent. In the five-part series "The Failure of the Death Penalty in Illinois" (*Chicago Tribune*, November 14–18, 1999), Ken Armstrong and Steve Mills examine all 285 death penalty cases since Illinois reinstated the death penalty in 1977. The journalists report that at least thirty-three defendants sentenced to death in Illinois had lawyers who were later suspended or disbarred, "sanctions reserved for conduct so incompetent, unethical, or even criminal the lawyer's license [was] taken away." A similar three-part series by Lise Olsen, "Uncertain Justice" (*Seattle Post-Intelligencer*, August 6–8, 2001), reveals that one-fifth of the eighty-four people who faced possible execution in Washington state between 1981 and 2001 were represented by attorneys who had been disbarred, suspended, or arrested sometime before or after the murder trial. These lawyers were some of the worst in Washington state.

The American Bar Association (ABA), in "*Gideon*'s Broken Promise: America's Continuing Quest for Equal Justice" (December 2004, http://www.abanet.org/legalservices/sclaid/defender/brokenpromise/fullreport.pdf), provides some insight into why poor defendants received such inadequate counsel. The ABA analyzes the indigent defense system in twenty-two states and finds that lawyers who took on poor defendants received low pay and that judges tended to let legal protocols slide to clear overcrowded dockets. In noncapital cases involving lesser offenses, prosecutors and judges sometimes forced defendants to plead guilty before receiving counsel to move them through the system. In addition, the ABA notes that indigent defense systems lack the basic accountability and oversight needed to ensure decent legal representation or correct these problems.

States generally vary in fulfilling *Gideon*. Some states have undertaken the establishment and funding of an indigent defense system; others have passed the responsibility on to individual counties. Across the United States different jurisdictions use one or a combination of three systems to provide counsel to poor defendants. The first system used by some jurisdictions has public defenders that are usually government employees. Under the second system, the court-assigned counsel system, a judge appoints private lawyers to represent the poor. A third system involves contract lawyers who bid for the job of providing indigent defense.

Court-assigned lawyers belong to a list of private lawyers who accept clients on a case-by-case basis. In

jurisdictions that employ these lawyers, judges appoint lawyers from a list of private bar members and determine their pay. In most cases the pay is low. Beth A. Wilkinson (June 27, 2001, http://www.thejusticeproject.org/press/statements/testimony-of-beth-wilkinson.html), the co-chair of the Constitution Project's Death Penalty Initiative, testified before a U.S. Senate Judiciary Committee hearing that many jurisdictions pay their court-appointed lawyers low hourly rates for capital defense. For example, Alabama paid $20 to $40 an hour, with a limit of $2,000. This means that a lawyer spending six hundred hours preparing for a capital case earned $3.33 an hour. (The ACLU estimates in "The Death Penalty" [*Briefing Paper*, no. 14, 1999] that defending a capital case at the trial level takes about seven hundred to one thousand hours.) Wilkinson added that Tennessee paid $20 to $30 an hour and that Mississippi had a $1,000 limit. According to the ABA, in "*Gideon*'s Broken Promise," salaried defense attorneys did not fare much better. For example, in Massachusetts salaries started at $35,000 for public defenders and were increased to $50,000 after ten years. Moreover, courts often refused to authorize the needed funds for investigating cases and using expert testimony. In contrast, the prosecution usually had unlimited funds at its disposal.

Some states have no statewide public defender system and have taken few steps to put one in place. Other states have taken strides since the late 1990s to improve their systems. When New York brought back capital punishment in 1995, the death penalty statute required the establishment of a capital defender office: the New York Capital Defender Office (2007, http://www.nycdo.org/caseload_041231_answers.pdf). This office participated in the defense of nearly two hundred defendants charged with capital crimes. In 2004 New York's death penalty was declared unconstitutional by the state's supreme court. In October 2007 the capital defender office announced plans to close down, after the state's last death row inmate was resentenced to life without parole.

In June 2001 Texas passed the Texas Fair Defense Act requiring state funding for indigent defense. The act required that counties adopt indigent defense systems meeting basic minimum standards specified in the statute (http://www.equaljusticecenter.org/new_page_2.htm).

To remedy some of the problems inherent in death penalty trials, Congress passed and President George W. Bush (1946–) signed the Innocence Protection Act of 2004. This act launched a program in which state governments receive grants from the federal government to improve the quality of legal representation for poor defendants in state capital cases. To receive such a grant, a state's capital defense system has to meet a number of requirements, which include establishing minimum standards for defense attorneys and monitoring the performance of these attorneys.

In 2005 Georgia legislation went into effect requiring defender offices within each judicial circuit to give representation in felony cases. That same year a defendant named Brian Nichols escaped from the Atlanta courthouse during his rape trial and allegedly killed four people before being recaptured. Jenny Jarvie reports in "Georgia Public Defender System on Trial" (*Los Angeles Times*, March 30, 2007) that the Georgia indigent defense program was in dire economic straits mostly because of the enormous cost of Nichols's defense, which totaled $1.4 million at that time and had not yet proceeded to trial. Nichols had offered to plead guilty in exchange for a life sentence, but this offer was rejected by the district attorney. According to Jarvie, Nichols's trial had to be postponed after the public defender system ran out of money. Bill Rankin notes in "Public Defender Chief Quits, Says Courts Should Be 'Told the Truth'" (*Atlanta Journal and Constitution*, August 31, 2007) that Chris Adams, the head of the capital defender program, resigned in August 2007 after the program received a budget allotment of only $4.3 million for the next fiscal year, far less than the $10.5 million he had requested. Adams complained that the amount was not sufficient to allow the capital defender office to adequately represent clients facing a death sentence.

Counsel for Postconviction Review

Even though death row inmates have the right to seek review of their conviction and sentence, they do not have the right to counsel for postconviction proceedings per the Supreme Court ruling in *Murray v. Giarratano* (492

U.S. 1, 1989). Because most of those awaiting execution are poor, they must find lawyers willing to handle appeals for free. In 1995 Congress discontinued federal funding of private organizations (called resource centers) that represented death row inmates in postconviction proceedings. As a result, private organizations and law firms, both proponents and opponents of the death penalty, concerned with the increasing problems in capital cases, now volunteer their services. Some hold training seminars on the complex process of appellate review, whereas others provide research and investigation.

In "In Pursuit of the Public Good: Lawyers Who Care" (April 9, 2001, http://www.supremecourtus.gov/publicinfo/speeches/sp_04-09-01a.html), Justice Ruth Bader Ginsburg (1933–) of the Supreme Court expresses her concerns about proper representation in capital cases. She states, "I have yet to see a death case, among the dozens coming to the Supreme Court on eve of execution petitions, in which the defendant was well represented at trial.... Public funding for the legal representation of poor people in the United States is hardly generous. In capital cases, state systems for affording representation to indigent defendants vary from adequate to meager."

In July 2001 Justice Sandra Day O'Connor (1930–), a longtime supporter of the death penalty, expressed concern about capital punishment. In October 2001 she told the Nebraska Bar Association that unless qualified lawyers are willing to work for indigent defendants who cannot afford counsel, innocent people may be sentenced to death.

CHAPTER 8

EXONERATIONS, MORATORIUMS, AND REFORMS

Since the 1990s dozens of death row inmates have been exonerated, meaning that the original capital charges against them have been dropped. In some cases new evidence has come to light casting doubt on their guilt. In other cases legal challenges have changed the parameters used to determine who can be sentenced to capital punishment. Exonerations are heralded by death penalty opponents as proof that the U.S. capital punishment system is flawed and should be abandoned. Advocates of the death penalty argue that the importance of exonerations is exaggerated and their occurrence proves that the capital justice system protects the rights of defendants. Nevertheless, exonerations and other concerns about the capital punishment system have prompted reforms and spurred several states to temporarily cease conducting executions. These moratoriums allow officials time to reexamine their capital punishment systems and determine if there are systematic problems in their administration.

EXONERATIONS

The Death Penalty Information Center (DPIC) is opposed to capital punishment. In "Innocence: List of Those Freed from Death Row" (May 22, 2007, http://www.deathpenaltyinfo.org/article.php?scid=6&did=110), the DPIC lists the names of 124 people that it claims have been exonerated from death row since 1973. The so-called Innocence List is often touted by death penalty opponents as proof that the U.S. capital punishment system is broken. According to the DPIC, defendants are added to the list when one of two things occurs: their conviction is overturned and they are acquitted on retrial or all charges are dropped; or they receive a governor's pardon because of new evidence of innocence.

Figure 8.1 shows the number of exonerations per year as of July 2, 2007. Between 1973 and 1998 a total of seventy-six inmates were exonerated, an average of three inmates per year. This average rose to eight between 1999 and 2003, with the highest number of exonerations (twelve) occurring in 2003. Only six inmates were exonerated from death row in 2004, followed by two inmates each in 2005 and 2006. Only one inmate had been exonerated in 2007 as of the date of publication of the figure.

As shown in Figure 8.2, six states account for over half of the exonerations: Florida (twenty-two), Illinois (eighteen), Louisiana (eight), Texas (eight), Arizona (eight), and Oklahoma (eight). The DPIC reports in "Innocence: List of Those Freed from Death Row" that seventy-three of the exonerated had their charges dismissed, forty-four were acquitted, and seven were pardoned. Fifteen defendants were exonerated based on deoxyribonucleic acid (DNA) evidence. Overall, the average amount of time that passed between death sentence and exoneration was 9.2 years.

Of the inmates exonerated, sixty-two were African-American and forty-nine were white. Twelve were Latino or Hispanic and one was of "other" race. Figure 8.3 shows the racial breakdown in percentage form.

Anthony Porter

According to the DPIC, in "Innocence: List of Those Freed from Death Row," Anthony Porter of Illinois was convicted of two 1982 murders and sentenced to death in 1983. He was convicted based on the testimony of two eyewitnesses who separately claimed they saw Porter commit the crimes. By 1998 Porter had exhausted all his appeals. On September 21, 1998, two days before Porter's scheduled execution, his defense lawyer filed an emergency petition with the Illinois Supreme Court, arguing that the defendant was mentally retarded (he had an intelligence quotient of fifty-one) and did not understand what was about to happen to him. The court granted Porter a stay of execution to determine his mental competency.

FIGURE 8.1

Exonerations by year, 1973–July 2, 2007

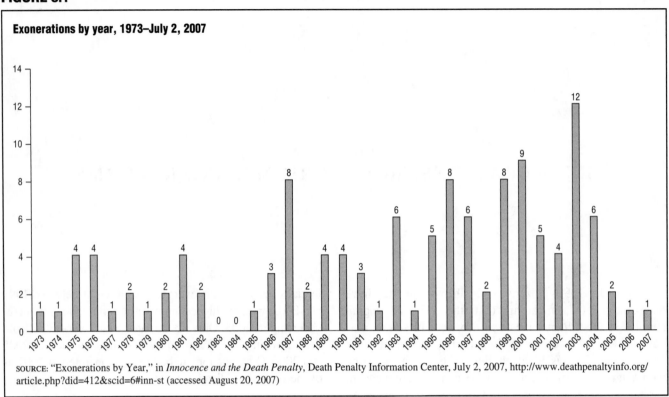

SOURCE: "Exonerations by Year," in *Innocence and the Death Penalty*, Death Penalty Information Center, July 2, 2007, http://www.deathpenaltyinfo.org/ article.php?did=412&scid=6#inn-st (accessed August 20, 2007)

FIGURE 8.2

Exonerations by state, 1973–July 2, 2007

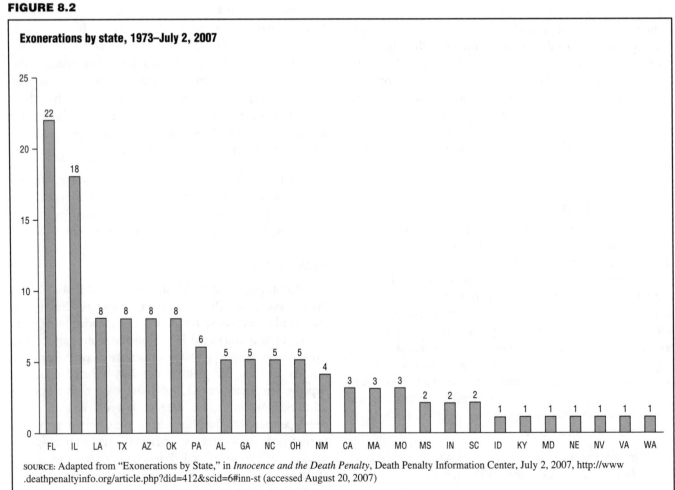

SOURCE: Adapted from "Exonerations by State," in *Innocence and the Death Penalty*, Death Penalty Information Center, July 2, 2007, http://www .deathpenaltyinfo.org/article.php?did=412&scid=6#inn-st (accessed August 20, 2007)

FIGURE 8.3

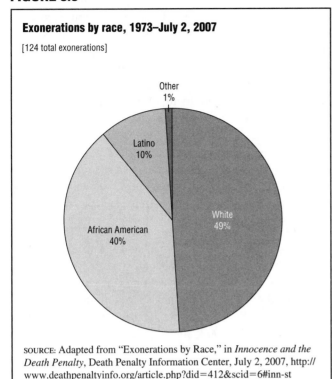

Exonerations by race, 1973–July 2, 2007

[124 total exonerations]

Other
1%

Latino
10%

White
49%

African American
40%

SOURCE: Adapted from "Exonerations by Race," in *Innocence and the Death Penalty*, Death Penalty Information Center, July 2, 2007, http://www.deathpenaltyinfo.org/article.php?did=412&scid=6#inn-st (accessed August 20, 2007)

In the meantime, an investigative journalism class taught by David Protess of Northwestern University had chosen Porter's case to review. The professor, his students, and Paul Ciolino, a private investigator, uncovered evidence of Porter's innocence. The first eyewitness (the second one had died) confessed to giving false testimony. The group tracked down the wife of the real murderer in Milwaukee (the couple had moved soon after Porter's arrest) and were able to convince her to confess to being present when her husband shot the victims. Next, the investigator succeeded in obtaining a videotaped confession from the murderer, Alstory Simon. On March 11, 1999, Porter's conviction was reversed; he had been on death row for seventeen years.

Curtis McCarty

Curtis McCarty of Oklahoma is the most recent death row exoneree. Cheryl Camp reports in "Convicted Murderer Is Freed in Wake of Tainted Evidence" (*New York Times*, May 22, 2007) that in 1986 he was convicted of killing Pamela Willis, who was found strangled and stabbed in 1982. There was much circumstantial evidence against McCarty including incriminating statements he made to friends and cell mates. Witnesses placed him at the scene on the day of the Willis murder. His conviction was also based on forensic evidence, primarily hairs, found on and in the victim's body.

In 1989 McCarty's verdict was overturned by a court of criminal appeals because of alleged misconduct by

prosecutors and the police chemist Joyce Gilchrist. Upon retrial McCarty was convicted and again sentenced to death. This sentence was reversed on appeal because the jury had not been properly informed about its options. At a 1996 resentencing hearing, McCarty received the death penalty for the third time. An appeal and a request for postconviction relief were denied. A second application for postconviction relief was filed in 2005 and granted based on allegations of evidence suppression and "bad faith" on the part of the state. In 2007 evidentiary hearings were held by the district court judge Twyla Mason Gray. The findings were presented to the state appeals court, which reversed McCarty's conviction, vacated (annulled) his death sentence, and remanded the case for a new trial.

Before a new trial could be held Judge Gray ordered McCarty released from prison. Her decision was based on a number of factors, including serious doubts about the reliability of Gilchrist's forensic work and testimony. Gilchrist was fired in 2001 after she was found to have committed misconduct in several criminal cases. She was accused of giving false and misleading testimony to help police and prosecutors convict suspects. She testified during McCarty's first two hearings that hairs found on and in the victim matched his hair type. In 2000, when McCarty's lawyers asked for DNA analysis of the hairs, Gilchrist reported they had been lost. The appeals court noted that "circumstantial evidence indicated Ms. Gilchrist had destroyed the evidence to prevent DNA testing." In addition, DNA testing in 2002 on semen found at the crime scene and in 2007 on scrapings from the fingernails of the victim did not match McCarty. Judge Gray ruled that she had no choice but to release McCarty despite misgivings about his role in the crime. She stated "I believe he was involved in some way in what is so horrific."

The Innocence List Disputed

Proponents of the death penalty are critical of the DPIC's Innocence List, claiming that it exaggerates the number of innocent people on death row. In 2000 the DPIC reported the one hundredth addition to the list, an event that was widely publicized in the media. In response, Ramesh Ponnuru attacked the list in "Bad List: A Suspect Roll of Death Row 'Innocents'" (*National Review*, September 16, 2002). Ponnuru claimed that most of the exonerations resulted from legal technicalities, rather than actual innocence. He recounted the violent criminal records of some of the exonerees and the formidable evidence introduced at trial against them. He described legal motions and maneuvers that ultimately resulted in the reversal of their sentences. He complained that "the list leads people to think that innocence has been proven when the most that can be said is that the legal system cannot establish guilt beyond a reasonable doubt."

Ponnuru argued that approximately 32 of the then 102 exonerees on the list could truly be regarded as innocent. He noted that more than seven thousand people have been on death row since 1973; thus, the percentage of actual innocence cases is extremely low.

In *Critique of DPIC List ("Innocence: Freed from Death Row")* (2002, http://www.prodeathpenalty.com/DPIC.htm), Ward A. Campbell, the supervising deputy attorney general in California, investigated the 102 cases of exonerated death row inmates on the DPIC list at that time. He concluded that at least 68 of the 102 inmates on the list should not have been included. Campbell found that "many defendants on the List were not 'actually innocent'"—that is, the prosecution found the defendant innocent of the crime. Some had pleaded guilty to lesser charges and had their sentences commuted. Campbell noted that "an acquittal because the prosecution has not proven guilt beyond a reasonable doubt does not mean that the defendant did not actually commit the crime."

On June 20, 2002, the Florida Commission on Capital Cases released *Case Histories: A Review of 24 Individuals Released from Death Row* (September 10, 2002, http://www.floridacapitalcases.state.fl.us/Publications/innocents project.pdf), which lists the results of its investigation into twenty-four cases on the DPIC list. The commission concluded:

> Of these 24 inmates, none were found "innocent," even when acquitted, because no such verdict exists. A defendant is found guilty or not guilty, never innocent. The guilt of only four defendants, however, was subsequently doubted by the prosecuting office or the Governor and Cabinet members.... An analysis of the remaining 20 inmates can be divided into three categories that account for their releases: (1) seven cases were remanded due to evidence issues, (2) an additional seven were remanded in light of witness issues, and (3) the remaining six were remanded as a result of issues involving court officials.

QUESTIONS ABOUT LEGAL ERRORS IN DEATH PENALTY CASES
Liebman Study

James S. Liebman, Jeffrey Fagan, and Valerie West conducted the first study of its kind—a statistical study of modern U.S. capital appeals—for the U.S. Senate Judiciary Committee. The study, called *A Broken System: Error Rates in Capital Cases, 1973–1995* (June 12, 2000, http://www2.law.columbia.edu/instructionalservices/liebman/liebman_final.pdf), examined all death penalty sentences (5,760) imposed in the United States over a twenty-three-year period.

On direct appeal, the state high courts reviewed 4,578 death sentences. Liebman, Fagan, and West found that 68% of the death sentences reviewed by courts across the country were found to have serious errors. For every

one hundred death sentences, forty-one were returned to the courts during state appeal because of serious errors. Of the fifty-nine death sentences that reached the second state appeal, another six went back to court because of errors. At the third level of appeal—with the federal courts—twenty-one more cases were remanded to the lower courts because of errors found. In all, of the original one hundred death penalty sentences, sixty-eight had serious errors that required retrial. Of the sixty-eight defendants who were retried, 82% (fifty-six) were found not deserving of the death penalty. Another five inmates were found not guilty of the capital crime for which they received the death sentence.

THE LIEBMAN STUDY IS ANALYZED. Critics challenged the results of the Liebman study. Appearing before the U.S. Senate Committee on the Judiciary hearing on "Reducing the Risk of Executing the Innocent: The Report of the Illinois Governor's Commission on Capital Punishment," Senator Strom Thurmond (R-SC, 1902–2003; June 12, 2002, http://judiciary.senate.gov/member_statement.cfm?id=256&wit_id&456) warned:

> A Columbia University report known as the Leibman [*sic*] study is often cited as proof that capital punishment in this country is deeply flawed. This study... alleged that from 1973 to 1995, 70% of death penalty convictions were reversed on appeal. The implication is that 70% of the time, innocent people were sentenced to death. This study should be viewed carefully because during the time period addressed by this study, the Supreme Court issued a series of retroactive rules that nullified a number of verdicts. These reversals were not based on the actual innocence of defendants, but rather were based on procedural rules.

The press release "Nevada's Death Penalty System Is Working!" (September 19, 2000, http://www.prodeathpenalty.com/Liebman/Nevada.htm) notes that Frankie Sue Del Papa, the Nevada attorney general, also took issue with the Liebman study. According to Del Papa, the Liebman study claimed that of the 108 death sentences in Nevada, 34 were reversed, accounting for an error rate of 38%. (The correct percentage is 31.5%.) The attorney general's researchers found 152 cases with 30 death sentence reversals for an error rate of 19%. The Liebman study also used a two-year period to determine the reversal rate of federal habeas appeals. It reached an overall error rate of 50% after finding two reversals out of four that underwent federal review. Del Papa's office found seventeen federal reviews with four reversals for a 23% error rate. According to Del Papa, the Liebman study "creates the impression that the reversals are due to innocence, but most are attorney or judge procedural errors. Some are cases where juries followed the existing law, but later the Supreme Court changed it, and constitutional changes are applied retroactively on death cases, to give the defendant every benefit. [The study] also failed to report that after a new trial or penalty hearing, in 12 of those 31 cases death sentences were imposed again. In 13 cases, inmates received 'life-in-prison' sentences. Those were not inmates found to be innocent of their murders!"

Latzer Study

In "Capital Appeals Revisited" (*Judicature*, vol. 84, no. 2, September–October 2000), Barry Latzer and James N. G. Cauthen noted that their reexamination of the Liebman study found that about one-fourth (27%)—and not two-thirds (68%)—of capital convictions were reversed between 1973 and 1995. Latzer and Cauthen stated that the Liebman study did not differentiate between reversals of convictions and reversals of death sentences.

Latzer and Cauthen conducted their own investigation, based on the theory that many of the appeals resulted in reversed sentences but not reversed convictions. The study covered the period 1990 to 1999, using reversal data in the same twenty-six states studied by Liebman and his colleagues. Latzer and Cauthen wanted more recent data of the death penalty system that would provide more complete reversal rate differences.

Latzer and Cauthen found that of the 837 death penalty reversals in state-level direct appeal or postconviction review, 61% were sentence reversals and 39% were conviction reversals (reversals addressing the guilt or innocence of the defendant). Using the Liebman study's conclusion that five out of ten capital judgments were reversed at either the direct-appeal phase or postconviction review phase, Latzer and Cauthen applied this finding to their study and concluded that, of the five reversals, three were sentence reversals and two were conviction reversals.

Latzer and Cauthen also investigated reversals at the federal level—the third stage of death penalty judgment review—using data from the Ninth Circuit Court of Appeals, the largest of the circuit courts. Of the twenty-nine capital cases reversed by the court during the ten-year period, twenty-one (72.4%) were sentence reversals and eight (27.7%) were conviction reversals. This was consistent with their findings regarding direct-appeal and postconviction sentence reversals at the state level. Using the Liebman study's finding that sixty-eight out of one hundred capital judgments were reversed, Latzer and Cauthen concluded, "If 68 of 100 capital decisions are reversed after direct, post-conviction, and federal habeas corpus review, and 39 percent of these are conviction reversals, then convictions in 26.52 (39 percent of 68) of 100 capital decisions are reversed."

DNA TESTING

Before DNA testing became available as proof of identity, the U.S. Supreme Court held the view that U.S. appellate courts could not reverse a murder conviction based on newly discovered post-trial evidence. The National Institute of Justice (NIJ) mentioned this in the report *Postconviction DNA Testing: Recommendations for Handling Requests* (September 1999, http://www.ncjrs.gov/pdffiles1/nij/177626.pdf). According to the commission, the nation's highest court ruled in *Herrera v. Collins* (506 U.S. 390, 1993) that newly discovered evidence does not constitute grounds for a federal habeas relief if there is no evidence of a constitutional violation occurring during state criminal proceedings. (In this case, Leonel Torres Herrera alleged ten years after his initial trial that he was innocent of a double murder, presenting "actual evidence" that his brother, who had since died, had committed the crime.) The commission, however, stated that with the availability of DNA testing, "the possibility of demonstrating actual innocence has moved from the realm of theory to the actual."

The science of DNA testing is improving rapidly. When DNA testing was first used in criminal trials starting in the mid-1980s, DNA samples had to be not only fresh but also contain thousands of cells. As DNA technology has become more sophisticated, scientists are able to test a single cell for DNA patterns that could link suspects to hair or semen found on a victim. In the twenty-first century a crime laboratory can identify unique DNA patterns in a tiny sample of less than fifty cells. DNA testing has played a substantial role in proving the innocence of a number of people wrongly convicted. The DPIC reports in "Innocence: List of Those Freed from Death Row" that as of May 2007, 15 of the 124 inmates released from death row since 1973 were exonerated by DNA evidence.

When biological material has been left at the scene of the crime, DNA testing can establish with near certainty a defendant's innocence or guilt. DNA, which stores the genetic code of the human body, is found in saliva, skin tissue, bones, blood, semen, and the root of hair. Biological samples that were difficult to test in the 1980s may yield more accurate information where previous results had proved inconclusive.

By the mid-1990s DNA evidence was being used to prove that certain prisoners on death row had been wrongly convicted. In 1996 David Protess and another group of students at Northwestern University's Medill School of Journalism helped uncover new evidence that proved the innocence of four African-American men who were convicted for a 1978 gang rape and double murder. Two received life imprisonment, whereas the other two were sentenced to death. DNA tests helped prove the men's innocence. In March 1999 the four men received a $36 million settlement from Cook County, Illinois, to resolve a lawsuit charging police misconduct. In a Florida case, Frank Lee Smith was sentenced to death in 1986 for the rape and murder of an eight-year-old girl. DNA testing performed in 2000 proved Smith's innocence. However, Smith had died of cancer the previous year while awaiting execution.

Backlog of DNA Testing

Given the high price of analyzing DNA samples (each test costs about $2,000 to perform), DNA evidence from crime scenes often goes untested. Such testing, however, could exonerate death row inmates who have been falsely accused. In December 2000 Congress authorized the U.S. Department of Justice to provide state crime laboratories more than $30 million to analyze the backlog of DNA samples that had been collected but never tested. Under the DNA Analysis Backlog Reduction Act of 2000, states would receive funding to conduct tests on about half a million samples collected from criminals and crime scenes that had never been analyzed. In August 2001 the U.S. attorney general John Ashcroft (1942–) announced that, besides the state initiative, the Justice Department had authorized the collection of DNA samples from about twenty thousand to thirty thousand federal, military, and District of Columbia offenders.

In *The Report to the Attorney General on Delays in Forensic DNA Analysis* (March 2003, http://www.ncjrs.gov/pdffiles1/nij/199425.pdf), the NIJ reveals that a task force assembled by the NIJ found a continuing backlog in the testing of DNA samples collected at crime scenes. Even though an estimated 350,000 rape and homicide DNA samples needed testing at that time, just 10% of the samples were in forensic crime laboratories. Most of the evidence samples were in the custody of law enforcement agencies because most laboratories lacked the proper storage facilities for preventing damage to the evidence.

Even if the laboratories had the proper storage facilities, the analysis of DNA samples could not take place because of the shortage of trained forensic scientists. Newly hired scientists need on-the-job training that requires an experienced scientist to spend time working one-on-one with new hires. The task force found that even when these problems were confronted, public crime laboratories could not retain their staff because of their lower compensation, compared to that paid by private companies.

Postconviction DNA Testing

The federal Innocence Protection Act became law on October 30, 2004. The law established the conditions under which a federal prisoner who pleads not guilty can receive postconviction DNA testing. If a trial defendant faces conviction, the act calls for the preservation of the defendant's biological evidence. A five-year, $25 million grant program was also established to help eligible states pay for postconviction testing.

MORATORIUMS AND REFORMS

Since the turn of the twenty-first century a number of moratoriums and reforms have been put in place in death penalty states in an attempt to remedy perceived problems in their capital punishment systems.

California

In 2004 the California Commission on the Fair Administration of Justice (CCFAJ) was created by the state's legislators to examine California's criminal justice system and make recommendations to remedy any problems. As of November 2007, the CCFAJ (http://www.ccfaj.org/reports.html) had released six reports:

- *Report and Recommendations Regarding Eye Witness Identification Procedures* (April 13, 2006)
- *Report and Recommendations Regarding False Confessions* (July 25, 2006)
- *Report and Recommendations Regarding Informant Testimony* (September 29, 2006)
- *Report and Recommendations Regarding Forensic Science Evidence* (May 8, 2007)
- *Emergency Report and Recommendations Regarding DNA Testing Backlogs* (February 20, 2007)
- *Report and Recommendations on Professional Responsibility and Accountability of Prosecutors and Defense Lawyers* (October 18, 2007)

California legislators acted on the recommendations provided in these reports by passing bills designed to reform the state's eyewitness identification procedures and require recording of suspect interrogations. In 2006 Governor Arnold Schwarzenegger (1947–) vetoed both bills citing procedural problems with them. Revamped versions of the bills passed the legislature in 2007, but were again vetoed by the governor.

In December 2006 a federal judge in California ruled in *Morales v. Tilton* (No. C 06 219 JF RS) the state's lethal injection protocol unconstitutional after hearing arguments from the lawyers for the death row inmate Michael Morales. The judge complained that the protocol "lacks both reliability and transparency" and results in "undue and unnecessary risk of an Eighth Amendment violation." The state began construction of a new execution chamber and development of new lethal injection protocols. As of November 2007, a de facto (in practice, as opposed to de jure, meaning in law) moratorium remained in effect in California.

Florida

In December 2006 the execution of Angel Diaz by the state of Florida attracted international attention after it took Diaz more than thirty minutes to die and required a second dosage of lethal injection chemicals. Public outcry led to revisions in the state's lethal injection protocols and a temporary moratorium on executions. In July 2007, with new protocols in place, the Florida governor

Charlie Crist (1956–) ended the moratorium by signing the death warrant for Mark Dean Schwab, a convicted murderer and child molester. Several days later a Florida circuit court judge reinstated the moratorium expressing concern that the new protocols are not adequate to address the problems that arose during the Diaz execution. On November 1, 2007, the Florida Supreme Court rejected challenges to the state's new lethal injection procedures and ruled that Schwab's execution could be carried out. On November 15, 2007, within hours of Schwab's execution, the U.S. Supreme Court issued a stay of execution and a de facto nationwide moratorium on executions until it considered a challenge to lethal injections in the spring of 2008.

Illinois

On January 31, 2000, Illinois became the first state to declare a moratorium on the death penalty. Governor George Ryan (1934–), a death penalty supporter, suspended all executions because he believed the state's death penalty system was "fraught with errors." The *Chicago Tribune* had issued a report showing that thirteen inmates in Illinois had been released from death row since 1976. The reasons for the exoneration of these inmates ranged from DNA evidence showing innocence, to false testimonies by jailhouse informants, to coercion of so-called witnesses by the prosecution and police.

Governor Ryan then established the Governor's Commission on Capital Punishment to investigate the thirteen cases, as well as all capital cases in Illinois. In April 2002 the *Report of the Governor's Commission on Capital Punishment* (http://www.idoc.state.il.us/ccp/ccp/reports/commission_report/summary_recommendations.pdf) was released. The commission issued eighty-five recommendations it thought would help reform the state's death penalty process. The recommended reforms included videotaping of capital suspects during interrogation at police facilities, banning the death penalty in cases where the conviction is based on a single-eyewitness testimony, and thorough examination of a jailhouse-informant testimony at a pretrial hearing to determine whether to use that testimony during trial.

John J. Kinsella (June 12, 2002, http://judiciary.senate.gov/testimony.cfm?id=256&wit_id=623), the first assistant state's attorney of DuPage County, Illinois, was asked to appear before the U.S. Senate Judiciary Committee to express his views as a prosecutor concerning Governor Ryan's moratorium and the Commission on Capital Punishment. Kinsella noted that the governor had only one active prosecutor among the fourteen commission members. Even though many of the commission recommendations involve how the police should perform their jobs, not one police officer was invited to be a part of the commission. No victim rights groups were also represented. Furthermore, most of the members were death penalty opponents.

According to the DPIC (2007, http://www.deathpenaltyinfo.org/article.php?did=126), on January 10, 2003, the day before leaving office, Governor Ryan pardoned four inmates who had been on death row in Illinois at least twelve years. The governor claimed the men were innocent of the murders for which they had been convicted. He found that the police had tortured the men into making false confessions. Three of the men had been released. The fourth inmate remained in prison because of a separate conviction. The following day Governor Ryan commuted 167 death sentences to life imprisonment without the possibility of parole, emptying death row.

Rod R. Blagojevich (1956–) entered office on January 12, 2003, and as of August 31, 2007, the Illinois moratorium had not been lifted. However, the Illinois death row has not remained empty. According to Tracy L. Snell of the Bureau of Justice Statistics, in *Capital Punishment, 2005* (December 2006, http://www.ojp.us doj.gov/bjs/pub/pdf/cp05.pdf), there were seven inmates on death row in Illinois at year-end 2005.

Maryland

In July 2001 a de facto moratorium occurred in Maryland pending the resolution by the state's high court of an appeal by inmate Steven Oken challenging the constitutionality of Maryland's capital punishment laws. Oken was sentenced to death in 1991 for the 1987 murder of Dawn Marie Garvin. He had also received life sentences for killing his sister-in-law and a motel desk clerk in Maine.

In May 2002 the Maryland governor Parris N. Glendening (1942–) imposed a moratorium to allow for the completion of a study on capital punishment. Robert L. Ehrlich Jr. (1957–), the newly elected governor, lifted the ban on executions in January 2003.

Maryland again imposed a moratorium in February 2003 after the state's highest court stayed the execution of Oken, who was scheduled to die the following month. The Maryland Court of Appeals granted the temporary reprieve to hear Oken's case at a future date. On May 1, 2003, during his fourth review by the state's appellate court, Oken argued that the state's death penalty is unconstitutional in light of the Supreme Court ruling in *Apprendi v. New Jersey* (530 U.S. 466, 2000), which held that jurors must use the higher standard of "beyond a reasonable doubt" in considering evidence during the sentencing phase of a trial.

In *Oken v. State* (No. 117, November 17, 2003), the Maryland Court of Appeals upheld Oken's death sentence. The court did not address Oken's *Apprendi* argument and ruled only on his claim that *Ring v. Arizona* (536 U.S. 584, 2002) implicated the state's death penalty law. The court rejected this claim. In 2003 Ehrlich signed Oken's death warrant, and Maryland's moratorium ended on July 17, 2004, with the execution of Oken by lethal injection.

In December 2006 another moratorium began after the Maryland Court of Appeals ordered a legislative review of the manual detailing lethal injection procedures for executions.

Nebraska

In May 1999 the Nebraska legislature became the first in the country to pass a bill proposing a two-year moratorium on executions. The bill also called for a study, during the moratorium, to determine the fairness of the administration of the death penalty. Governor Mike O. Johanns (1950–) vetoed the bill. The governor also vetoed the proposed study, but the legislature overrode his veto.

On July 25, 2001, David C. Baldus et al. released their findings concerning the state death penalty in *The Disposition of Nebraska Capital and Non-capital Homicide Cases (1973–1999): A Legal and Empirical Analysis* (http://www.ncc.state.ne.us/pdf/others/other_homicide/execsum.pdf), which was funded by the Nebraska Commission on Law Enforcement and Criminal Justice. Baldus et al. reviewed more than seven hundred homicide cases that resulted in a conviction. They then closely examined the decision-making process in 177 death-eligible cases, 27 of which received the death sentence. Baldus et al. did not find racial bias in the use of the death penalty. White defendants (15%) were just as likely as nonwhite defendants (16%) to receive the death penalty. Baldus et al. also concluded that there was no significant evidence of unfair treatment based on the victim's race—17% of defendants who murdered white victims and 11% of defendants who murdered minority victims were sentenced to death.

However, Baldus et al. found that death-eligible defendants who murdered victims of "high socioeconomic status" were nearly four times as likely to receive the death sentence than those who murdered poor victims, even when similar crimes had been committed. In addition, they found geographic disparities in seeking the death penalty. Prosecutors in rural capital trials were more likely to seek the death penalty than their urban counterparts (31% versus 20%).

New Hampshire

In May 2000 the New Hampshire legislature passed a bill abolishing the death penalty. However, Governor C. Jeanne Shaheen (1947–) vetoed the bill. A similar bill introduced in the New Hampshire House of Representatives in January 2001 was defeated three months later. Even though the death penalty is in the statute books, New Hampshire has not sentenced anyone to death since reinstating capital punishment in 1991. The state had not had an execution since 1939. As of November 2007, New Hampshire had no inmates on death row.

New Jersey

In 2006 the New Jersey legislature created the New Jersey Death Penalty Study Commission to assess the administration of capital punishment in the state. All death sentences were put on hold until at least sixty days after completion of the commission's report, *New Jersey Death Penalty Study Commission Report* (January 2007, http://www.njleg.state.nj.us/committees/dpsc_final.pdf). The report included eight major findings and recommendations:

- "No compelling evidence" was found to support the idea that the death penalty "serves a legitimate penological" purpose
- The costs of capital punishment were found to be higher than the costs of life in prison without parole
- Evidence indicated that the death penalty is "inconsistent with evolving standards of decency"
- Data did not support the idea that racial biases affect the application of capital punishment in New Jersey
- The abolishment of the death penalty would eliminate the "risk of disproportionality in capital sentencing"
- The penological benefit of capital punishment was deemed not worth the risk of possibly making an "irreversible mistake"
- Life sentences with no chance of parole were declared sufficient to ensure public safety and address other social and penological concerns
- State funds should be allocated to provide needed services to the families of murder victims

As of November 2007 a de facto moratorium on executions remained in place in New Jersey.

New York

GUILTY PLEAS. Until 1998 New York's death penalty statute prohibited the imposition of a death sentence when a defendant entered a guilty plea. The maximum penalty in such a case would be life imprisonment without parole. However, a defendant who pleaded not guilty would have to stand trial and face the possibility of a death sentence. The law provided two levels of penalty for the same offense, imposing the death penalty only on those who claimed innocence.

Defendants in two capital cases challenged the plea provisions of New York's death penalty statute, claiming these provisions violated their Fifth Amendment right against self-incrimination and Sixth Amendment right to a jury trial. This was the first major constitutional challenge to New York's death penalty law. On December 22, 1998, the New York Court of Appeals (New York's highest court), in *Hynes v. Tomei* (including *Relin v. Mateo*, 92 N.Y. 2d. 613, 706 N.E. 2d. 1201, 684 N.Y.S. 2d. 177), unanimously agreed, thereby striking down these plea-bargaining provisions as unconstitutional. The court, relying on the U.S. Supreme Court decision in *United States v. Jackson* (390

U.S. 570, 1968), observed that "the Supreme Court in *Jackson* prohibited statutes that 'needlessly' encourage guilty pleas, which are not constitutionally protected, by impermissibly burdening constitutional rights." The ruling left the death penalty intact, but the court could no longer give preference to those who entered a guilty plea.

JURY DEADLOCK INSTRUCTIONS. In 2004 the New York Court of Appeals agreed to hear another challenge to the constitutionality of New York's death penalty. Stephen LaValle was sentenced to death in 1999 by a New York jury for the murder and rape of Cynthia Quinn. Under New York law, a jury can sentence a defendant convicted of murder to life in prison without parole or to death. All jurors must vote unanimously. In the event of a hung jury, the court sentences a guilty defendant to life imprisonment with parole eligibility after serving a minimum of twenty to twenty-five years, leaving room for the convict to be released.

LaValle claimed that this "jury deadlock instruction" violated his constitutional rights because it would encourage members of the jury who do not favor the death penalty to vote for the death penalty if they are in the minority. LaValle even presented a study showing that most jurors would choose the death penalty if given the choice of the death penalty or imprisonment with a chance of parole. In *People v. LaValle* (783 NYS 2d, 485, 2004), the New York Court of Appeals agreed with LaValle and vacated his sentence. The state high court stated that this jury instruction was a cruel and unusual punishment in violation of the Eighth and Fourteenth Amendments, citing the U.S. Supreme Court's decision in *Woodson v. North Carolina* (428 U.S. 280, 1976). The Court held in *Woodson* that a mandatory death sentence for a capital offense was unconstitutional and forced jurors to charge the defendant with a lesser charge if they did not want to see the defendant sentenced to death.

This decision by the New York court effectively put a moratorium on the New York death penalty until the New York state legislature changed the death penalty statutes. Roughly a year later, the New York State Assembly Codes Committee (the state legislative committee in charge of changing death penalty statutes) defeated a bill to reinstate the death penalty, claiming that the system was riddled with flaws. As of November 2007, the unofficial moratorium on the death penalty remained in effect.

North Carolina

In August 2006 the North Carolina governor Mike F. Easley (1950–) signed a new law that created the North Carolina Innocence Inquiry Commission (NCIIC). The eight-member committee will review innocence claims and new evidence not previously presented at trial. After a majority recommendation by the committee, a disputed case will be reviewed by a panel of three North Carolina Superior

Court judges. A unanimous decision by the panel can overturn a conviction. The NCIIC is the first commission of its type in the United States. In "North Carolina Becomes First State with an Innocence Commission" (TalkLeft.com, August 3, 2003), Jeralyn Merritt reports that after signing the bill the governor remarked, "As a state that exacts the ultimate punishment, we should continue to ensure that we have the ultimate fairness in the review of our cases."

Tennessee

In February 2007 the Tennessee governor Phil N. Bredesen (1943–) ordered a ninety-day moratorium on executions until the state's lethal injection and electrocution procedures could be reviewed and revised. New lethal injection protocols were issued by May 2007, and the state ended the moratorium that month with the execution of Philip Workman. Workman had been convicted of killing a police officer in 1982. The state announced that a postexecution autopsy indicated the lethal injection procedure had proceeded properly.

Texas

In *Recommendations to Governor Rick Perry* (January 2006, http://www.governor.state.tx.us/divisions/general _counsel/files/CJAC-0106.doc), the Governor's Criminal Justice Advisory Council (CJAC) in Texas makes a number of recommendations to change the state's justice system to reduce the number of wrongful convictions. These include changes to allow greater postconviction DNA testing and grants for innocence projects at the state's law schools. In addition, the CJAC recommends greater funding for a public defenders office and increased compensation for prisoners who have been wrongfully convicted.

TEXAS FAIR DEFENSE ACT. On June 14, 2001, Governor Rick Perry (1950–) signed the Texas Fair Defense Act, providing, for the first time, state funding for indigent (poor) defense services. The $12 million yearly appropriation helps establish public defender offices. Two lawyers are provided in capital cases, unless the state indicates in writing that it will not seek the death penalty. The law also limits judges' powers by requiring appointments be made from a rotating list of qualified lawyers. Moreover, courts must pay reasonable fees, including necessary overhead reimbursements.

Under the law, death penalty lawyers have to attend annual training on capital defense to remain on the rotating list. In addition, the law established a Texas Task Force on Indigent Defense to be responsible for setting standards for lawyers. The task force also monitors the operation of the public defender programs in the counties. The task force and the county capital appointment committee review the list of lawyers who handle capital cases.

The Texas Fair Defense Act was passed as a result of findings by Texas Appleseed, a nonpartisan legal advocacy group. In December 2000 Texas Appleseed reported in *The*

Fair Defense Report: Analysis of Indigent Defense Practices in Texas (http://www.texasappleseed.net/pdf/projects_fairDefense_fairref.pdf) that, unlike other active death penalty states, Texas had been "virtually alone" in not having a statewide program to assist indigent defendants with legal representation. As of November 20, 2000, among states that most actively imposed the death penalty, Texas was one of two states that did not fund indigent defense representation (Arizona was the other state). Texas was also the only state that had no statewide oversight commission, public defender agencies, and capital trial unit.

Texas Appleseed pointed out that Texas did not have an oversight commission that could develop standards for appointment and compensation of lawyers in capital cases. In some states a similar commission also monitors the performance of the defense counsel and the judges' fee decisions.

Many death penalty states have a specialized statewide capital trial unit that assists court-appointed private defense lawyers. In addition, nine states—Colorado, Connecticut, Delaware, Maryland, Missouri, New Hampshire, New Jersey, New Mexico, and Wyoming—have a public defender program, most of which provide public defenders in every county statewide. Texas, however, used private lawyers appointed by judges on a case-by-case basis. These lawyers lacked the support of a public defender system that could make available the expertise of other lawyers more experienced in capital cases, as well as the training programs that such a system provides.

Washington

CONTROVERSY OVER GREEN RIVER KILLER PLEA BARGAIN. A plea agreement between a serial killer and Norm Maleng, the prosecutor for King County, Washington, caused controversy over the fair application of the death penalty. Gary Leon Ridgway escaped the death penalty by agreeing to provide information about the forty-eight women he had murdered. Ridgway, known as the Green River Killer because he dumped the bodies of his victims, many of them prostitutes and runaways, along the Green River near Seattle, Washington, committed his crimes between 1980 and 1998. Authorities say this is the largest number of murders ever committed by a serial killer. In November 2001 authorities linked Ridgway's DNA to samples found on some of the victims. In December 2003 Ridgway received forty-eight consecutive life terms without the possibility of parole. He was also ordered to pay $10,000 for each victim.

Both sides of the death penalty issue have used the Ridgway case to bolster their causes. Opponents of the death penalty argue that if a case involving the largest number of serial killings did not warrant the death penalty, then others involving fewer murders certainly do not deserve the ultimate punishment. Some note that if the criminal justice system did not sentence a white mass murderer to death, then it should think twice about impos-

ing the death penalty on an African-American who has killed just one person or a few. Proponents of capital punishment use the case as an example of how murderers can manipulate the system, and they call for shortening the time between death sentencing and execution. Still others think the prosecutor took the right course by not acting on his initial plan to seek the death sentence. He believed that victims' families could find closure through the information Ridgway could provide about their loved one's death.

In "The Ultimate Sacrificed" (*Seattle Times*, November 8, 2003), David A. Nichols, a Washington Superior Court judge, calls for the abolition of the death penalty in his state. He points out that it is a "mockery of all reasonable notions of justice" that a mass murderer is able to avoid the death penalty because he has something to offer in exchange for the deal, whereas another murderer gets the death sentence because he has nothing to offer. However, the case did not result in overturning the death penalty in Washington, which was still in effect in 2007.

The American Bar Association Advocates a Nationwide Moratorium

The American Bar Association (ABA) is a voluntary professional association for people in the legal profession. In 2001 the ABA began the Death Penalty Moratorium Implementation Project (DPMIP), an effort to secure a nationwide moratorium on the death penalty.

In 2004 the DPMIP began assessing state death penalty systems to determine their level of agreement with "minimum standards of fairness and due process." The project relies on the ABA publication *Death without Justice: A Guide for Examining the Administration of the Death Penalty in the United States* (June 2001, http://www.abanet.org/irr/finaljune28.pdf) to provide protocols (codes for correct conduct) against which it assesses each state's capital punishment laws and processes. As of November 2007, eight state assessments had been published:

- *Evaluating Fairness and Accuracy in State Death Penalty Systems: The Georgia Death Penalty Assessment Report* (January 2006, http://www.abanet.org/moratorium/assessmentproject/georgia/report.pdf)

- *Evaluating Fairness and Accuracy in State Death Penalty Systems: The Alabama Death Penalty Assessment Report* (June 2006, http://www.abanet.org/moratorium/assessmentproject/alabama/report.pdf)

- *Evaluating Fairness and Accuracy in State Death Penalty Systems: The Arizona Death Penalty Assessment Report* (July 2006, http://www.abanet.org/moratorium/assessmentproject/arizona/Report.pdf)

- *Evaluating Fairness and Accuracy in State Death Penalty Systems: The Florida Death Penalty Assessment Report* (September 2006, http://www.abanet.org/moratorium/assessmentproject/florida/report.pdf)

- *Evaluating Fairness and Accuracy in State Death Penalty Systems: The Tennessee Death Penalty Assessment Report* (March 2007, http://www.abanet.org/moratorium/assessmentproject/tennessee/finalreport.pdf)

- *Evaluating Fairness and Accuracy in State Death Penalty Systems: The Indiana Death Penalty Assessment Report* (February 2007, http://www.abanet.org/moratorium/assessmentproject/indiana/report.pdf)

- *Evaluating Fairness and Accuracy in State Death Penalty Systems: The Ohio Death Penalty Assessment Report* (September 2007, http://www.abanet.org/moratorium/assessmentproject/ohio/finalreport.pdf)

- *Evaluating Fairness and Accuracy in State Death Penalty Systems: The Pennsylvania Death Penalty Assessment Report* (October 2007, http://www.abanet.org/moratorium/assessmentproject/pennsylvania/finalreport.pdf)

ALABAMA. The DPMIP report for Alabama calls for reform of seven major problems it cites in the state's capital punishment system:

- Inadequate indigent defense services at trial and on direct appeal

- Lack of defense counsel for state postconviction proceedings

- Lack of a statute protecting people with mental retardation from execution

- Lack of a postconviction DNA testing statute

- Inadequate proportionality review by the Alabama Court of Criminal Appeals

- Lack of effective limitations on the interpretation of the "heinous, atrocious, or cruel" aggravating circumstance that could allow the circumstance to be used improperly as a "catchall provision"

- Capital juror confusion as evidenced by interviews with capital jurors indicating confusion about mitigating and aggravating factors and other legal issues arising during trial

ARIZONA. The DPMIP report for Arizona recommends reforms for four major problems identified in the state's capital punishment system:

- Decentralized defense services that lack adequate oversight and standards

- Insufficiently compensated appointed counsel

- Lack of a mechanism to ensure proportionality review to protect against arbitrariness in capital sentencing

- Lack of effective limitations on the "especially cruel, heinous, or depraved" aggravating circumstance to prevent ambiguity in its interpretation by capital juries

FLORIDA. The DPMIP report for Florida identifies eleven major problems requiring reform in the state's capital punishment system:

- Florida leads the nation in death-row exonerations

- Inadequate compensation for conflict trial counsel in death penalty cases

- Lack of qualified and properly monitored capital collateral registry counsel ("private lawyers who are appointed from the statewide registry to represent death-sentenced inmates during post-conviction proceedings")

- Inadequate compensation for capital collateral registry attorneys

- Significant capital juror confusion as evidenced by interviews with capital jurors

- Lack of unanimity in jury's sentencing decision in capital cases

- The practice of judicial override of jury recommendations of life imprisonment

- Lack of transparency in the clemency process

- Racial disparities in Florida's capital sentencing that make African-American defendants more likely to receive the death penalty if the victim is white, than if the victim is African-American

- Geographic disparities in Florida's capital punishment system

- Death sentences imposed on people with severe mental disability

GEORGIA. The DPMIP report for Georgia highlights seven major problems within the state's capital sentencing process:

- Inadequate defense counsel at trial

- Lack of defense counsel for state habeas corpus proceedings

- Inadequate proportionality review by the Georgia Supreme Court

- Inadequate jury instructions on mitigating factors as evidenced by interviews with capital jurors

- Racial disparities in capital sentencing in which both the race of the defendant and the race of the victim predict who is sentenced to death

- Inappropriate burden of proof for mentally retarded defendants

- Death penalty for felony murder (a killing in the commission of a felony irrespective of malice, meaning that a conviction of felony murder does not require a finding of an intent to kill or of a reckless indifference to life)

INDIANA. The DPMIP report for Indiana recommends reform of six problem areas identified in the state's capital punishment system:

- Inadequate qualification standards for defense counsel

- Lack of an independent appointing authority

- Lack of meaningful proportionality review of death sentences

- Significant capital juror confusion over roles and responsibilities when deciding whether to impose a death sentence

- Racial disparities that mean those convicted of killing white victims are sentenced more severely than those convicted of killing nonwhite victims.

- Death sentences imposed on people with severe mental disability

OHIO. The DPMIP report for Ohio notes ten major problems in the state's capital punishment system:

- Inadequate procedures to protect the innocent, specifically failure to require preservation of biological evidence for as long as the defendant remains incarcerated, failure to require that crime laboratories and law enforcement agencies be certified by nationally recognized certification organizations, failure to require the audio or videotaping of all interrogations in potential capital cases, and failure to implement lineup procedures that protect against incorrect eyewitness identifications

- Inadequate access to experts and investigators

- Inadequate qualification standards for defense counsel

- Insufficient compensation for defense counsel representing indigent capital defendants and death row inmates

- Inadequate appellate review of claims of error

- Lack of meaningful proportionality review of death sentences

- Virtually nonexistent discovery provisions in state postconviction

- Racial disparities in capital sentencing wherein perpetrators are more likely to end up on death row if the homicide victim is white rather than African-American

- Geographic disparities in capital sentencing within the state

- Death sentences imposed and carried out on people with severe mental disability

PENNSYLVANIA. The DPMIP report for Pennsylvania identifies eight major problems requiring reform in the state's capital punishment system:

- Inadequate procedures to protect the innocent, specifically failure to require preservation of biological evidence for as long as the defendant remains incarcerated, failure to require the audio or videotaping of all interrogations in potential capital cases, and failure to implement lineup procedures that protect against incorrect eyewitness identifications

- Inadequate safeguards against poor lawyering, specifically failure to guarantee the appointment of two attorneys at all stages of a capital case, inadequate compensation afforded capital attorneys, and lack of a statewide independent appointing authority responsible for training, selecting, and monitoring capital defense attorneys to ensure that competent representation is provided to each capital defendant

- No state funding of capital indigent defense services

- Inadequate access to experts and investigators

- Lack of data on death-eligible case means that Pennsylvania cannot ensure that its system ensures proportionality in charging or sentencing, or determine the extent of racial or geographic bias in its capital system

- Significant limitations on postconviction relief

- Significant capital juror confusion wherein capital jurors fail to understand their roles and responsibilities when deciding whether to impose a death sentence

- Racial and geographical disparities in the state's capital sentencing

TENNESSEE. The DPMIP report for Tennessee notes ten major problem areas in the state's capital punishment system:

- Inadequate procedures to address innocence claims and ensure they receive adequate judicial review

- Excessive caseloads for defense counsel in public defender offices representing capital defendants

- Inadequate access to experts and investigators by capital defendants

- Inadequate qualification and performance standards for defense counsel

- Lack of meaningful proportionality review by the Tennessee Supreme Court and the Tennessee Court of Criminal Appeals

- Lack of transparency in the clemency process

- Significant capital juror confusion as evidenced by capital juror interviews

- Racial disparities in the state's capital sentencing that favor the "majority" race or ethnicity

- Geographical disparities in the state's capital punishment system

- Death sentences imposed on people with severe mental disability

CHAPTER 9

PUBLIC ATTITUDES TOWARD CAPITAL PUNISHMENT

Like all statistics, those contained in public opinion polls should be viewed cautiously. The way a question is phrased can influence the respondents' answers. Many other factors may also influence a response in ways that are often difficult to determine. Respondents might never have thought of the issue until asked, or they might be giving the pollster the answer they think the pollster wants to hear. Organizations that survey opinions do not claim absolute accuracy. Their findings are approximate snapshots of the attitudes of the nation at a given time.

The surveys presented here have been selected from many polls taken on capital punishment. The Gallup Organization and Harris Interactive (formerly Louis Harris and Associates, Inc.), to name two such organizations, are well respected in their fields, and their surveys are accepted as representative of public opinions. A typical, well-conducted survey claims accuracy to about plus or minus three points.

THE MORALITY OF CAPITAL PUNISHMENT

Lydia Saad of the Gallup Organization, in "Americans Rate the Morality of 16 Social Issues" (June 4, 2007, http://www.gallup.com/poll/27757/Americans-Rate-Morality-Social-Issues.aspx), reports on a May 2007 values and beliefs poll regarding Americans' views about various moral issues. Respondents were asked about sixteen particular issues deemed important to society. Saad notes that eight of the issues elicited consensus responses (i.e., a majority of people shared a similar opinion). As shown in Table 9.1, the death penalty was rated the most morally acceptable of the eight consensus issues. Two-thirds (66%) of those asked said that the death penalty is morally acceptable, whereas more than a quarter (27%) said that it is morally wrong. These percentages are consistent with those obtained in previous years. Saad indicates that annual polling conducted from 2001 through 2006 found that moral acceptance for the death penalty ranged from 63%

to 71%, with the low value occurring in 2001 and the high value in 2006.

According to Saad, moral acceptance of the death penalty in the 2007 poll was "fairly uniform" across different age groups, genders, and political parties. Figure 9.1 provides a breakdown by self-described political philosophy. The morality of the death penalty was strongly supported by conservatives. Seventy-three percent of them deemed capital punishment morally acceptable, compared to 66% of moderates, and 54% of liberals.

SUPPORT FOR THE DEATH PENALTY

According to Gallup poll results from December 1936, about three out of five (59%) respondents favored the death penalty at that time. (See Figure 9.2.) This was the first time the Gallup Organization polled Americans regarding their attitudes toward the death penalty for murder. For the next three decades support for capital punishment fluctuated, dropping to its lowest point in 1966 (42%). Starting in early 1972 support for capital punishment steadily increased, peaking at 80% in 1994. (See Figure 9.3.) Between 1999 and 2006 support hovered at nearly 70%. In October 2006 Gallup found that 67% of Americans favored the death penalty for people convicted of murder.

The lowest proportion of Americans in support of capital punishment for murder was 42% in 1966, a period of civil rights and anti–Vietnam War marches and the peace movement. (See Figure 9.2.) It was also the only time in the period of record that those who opposed capital punishment (47%) outnumbered those who favored it.

According to the article "Death Penalty Poll Highlights" (April 26, 2007, http://abcnews.go.com/Politics/wireStory?id=3081914), an Associated Press/Ipsos poll conducted in February 2007, 69% of American respondents supported the death penalty for those convicted of

TABLE 9.1

Public opinion on the morality of social issues with a consensus opinion, May 2007

	Morally acceptable	Morally wrong
	%	%
The death penalty	66	27
Divorce	65	26
Medical research using stem cells obtained from human embryos	64	30
Gambling	63	32
Suicide	16	78
Cloning humans	11	86
Polygamy, when one husband has more than one wife at the same time	8	90
Married men and women having an affair	6	91

SOURCE: Adapted from Lydia Saad, "Consensus Issues: Large Majorities in Agreement, May 10–13, 2007," in *Americans Rate the Morality of 16 Social Issues*, The Gallup Organization, June 4, 2007, http://www.gallup.com/poll/27757/Americans-Rate-Morality-Social-Issues.aspx (accessed July 24, 2007). Copyright © 2007 by The Gallup Organization. Reproduced by permission of The Gallup Organization.

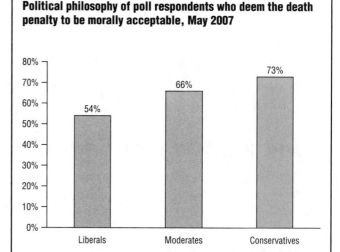

FIGURE 9.1

Political philosophy of poll respondents who deem the death penalty to be morally acceptable, May 2007

SOURCE: Adapted from Lydia Saad, "Percentage Calling Each 'Morally Acceptable," May 10–13, 2007," in *Americans Rate the Morality of 16 Social Issues*, The Gallup Organization, June 4, 2007, http://www.gallup.com/poll/27757/Americans-Rate-Morality-Social-Issues.aspx (accessed July 24, 2007). Copyright © 2007 by The Gallup Organization. Reproduced by permission of The Gallup Organization.

murder. In 2006 the *Washington Post* and ABC News (June 26, 2006, http://www.washingtonpost.com/wp-srv/politics/polls/postpoll_natsecurity_062606.htm) reported on a poll regarding the death penalty. The results showed that capital punishment was favored by 65% of Americans for convicted murderers. Thirty-two percent were opposed. According to the report *Trends in Political Values and Core Attitudes: 1987–2007* (March 22, 2007, http://people-press.org/reports/pdf/312.pdf), a poll performed between December 2006 and January 2007 for the Pew Research Center by Princeton Survey Research Associates, 64% of Americans supported capital punishment for those convicted of murder. Comparison to results from previous years shows that support has gradually declined since 1996, when it was at 78%.

The Higher Education Research Institute (HERI) of California conducts annual surveys on the opinions of college freshmen around the country. The latest results are published in *The American Freshman: Forty Year Trends* (2007, http://www.gseis.ucla.edu/heri/40yrtrends.php). HERI included a question about the death penalty in surveys conducted between 1969 and 1971 and between 1978 and 2006. The poll participants were asked to express their level of support for abolishing the death penalty. In 2006 more than one-third (34.5%) of college freshmen surveyed indicated they "agree strongly" or "agree somewhat" that the death penalty should be abolished. Support for abolishment was slightly stronger among women (37.6%) than among men (30.7%). Historically, the greatest discontent with capital punishment was reported between 1969 and 1971, when an average of 58% of respondents favored its abolishment. In 1978 support for abolishment was dramatically lower at 33.6%. It increased through the end of the decade and then

began to decline, reaching a low of 21.2% in 1994. Annual surveys conducted since that year have recorded steadily growing support for abolishment by college freshmen. A summarization of the polling data is provided by the Bureau of Justice Statistics (http://www.albany.edu/sourcebook/pdf/t2932006.pdf).

Demographic Differences

Some polling organizations provide detailed information on the demographic characteristics of poll respondents. According to the Pew Research Center, in *Trends in Political Values and Core Attitudes*, levels of support for the death penalty differed by gender, race, and political affiliation. Sixty-eight percent of men expressed support, compared to 60% of women. White respondents favored the death penalty much more than people of other races. Sixty-nine percent of whites expressed support for capital punishment, compared to 45% of Hispanics and 44% of African-Americans. More than three-fourths (78%) of Republicans and slightly over half (56%) of Democrats supported the death penalty.

Gallup conducted its annual minority rights and relations survey in June 2007. As shown in Figure 9.4, support for the death penalty for convicted murderers was voiced by 70% of whites, but only 40% of African-Americans. In fact, a majority (56%) of African-Americans were opposed to capital punishment. The difference of opinion on this issue is evident in Gallup polls dating back to 1972. (See Figure 9.5.) Historically, African-American respondents have expressed less support for the death penalty than have white respondents.

FIGURE 9.2

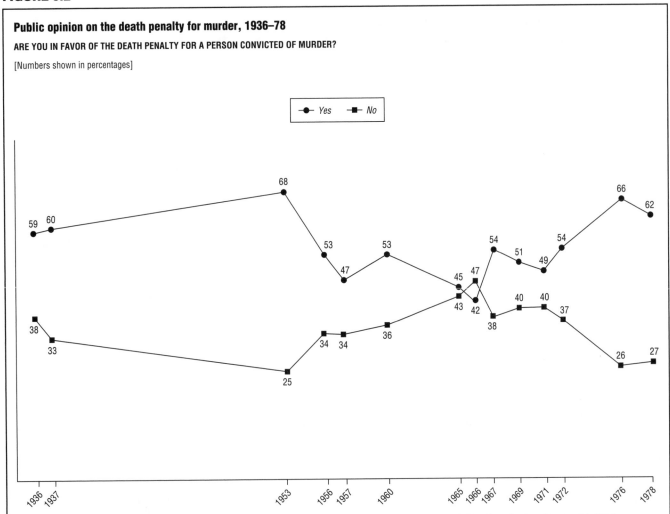

Public opinion on the death penalty for murder, 1936–78

ARE YOU IN FAVOR OF THE DEATH PENALTY FOR A PERSON CONVICTED OF MURDER?

[Numbers shown in percentages]

SOURCE: "Are you in favor of the death penalty for a person convicted of murder?" in *Death Penalty*, The Gallup Organization, October 24, 2006, http://www.gallup.com/poll/1606/Death-Penalty.aspx (accessed July 24, 2007). Copyright © 2006 by The Gallup Organization. Reproduced by permission of The Gallup Organization.

An October–December 2005 Gallup poll revealed differences between genders and age groups regarding the death penalty. (See Figure 9.6.) Seventy percent of male respondents supported capital punishment, compared to 59% of female respondents. Support by age group differed slightly. Respondents aged fifty to fifty-four were most likely to favor the death penalty. Sixty-nine percent of them expressed support for capital punishment, compared to 60% of young people aged eighteen to twenty-nine. Support among other age groups was between these two values. Figure 9.7 summarizes Gallup polling results from 2003 to 2005 for states with and without the death penalty at the time. More than two-thirds (68%) of respondents in the thirty-eight death penalty states favored capital punishment, whereas 28% were opposed to it. In the ten states without a death penalty on the books (Alaska and Hawaii were not included in this poll), only 58% of respondents supported capital punishment and 37% were opposed to it.

In *Religion and Politics: Contention and Consensus* (July 24, 2003, http://pewforum.org/publications/surveys/religion-politics.pdf), the Pew Research Center for the People and the Press examines polling data regarding various social issues. The results indicate a deep divide by race over the death penalty. Capital punishment was supported by 69% of whites, 50% of Hispanics, and only 39% of African-Americans. There were also distinct differences between religious persuasions among white respondents. The death penalty was supported by 76% of Evangelicals, compared to 70% of mainline Protestants and 69% of Catholics. Only 60% of white people classifying themselves as secular (nonreligious) favored capital punishment.

Kathleen Maguire and Ann L. Pastore report in the *Sourcebook of Criminal Justice Statistics 2003* (2004, http://www.albany.edu/sourcebook/) that in 2003 men (70%) were more likely than women (58%) to support capital punishment. Whites (67%) tended to favor the

FIGURE 9.3

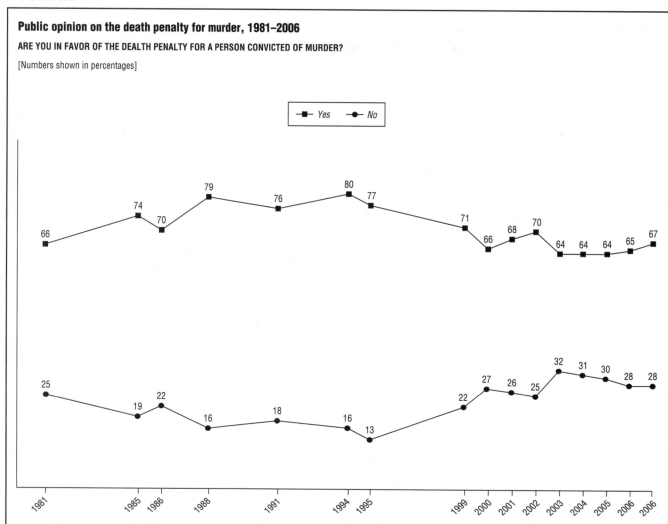

Public opinion on the death penalty for murder, 1981–2006

ARE YOU IN FAVOR OF THE DEATH PENALTY FOR A PERSON CONVICTED OF MURDER?

[Numbers shown in percentages]

SOURCE: "Are you in favor of the death penalty for a person convicted of murder?" in *Death Penalty*, The Gallup Organization, October 24, 2006, http://www.gallup.com/poll/1606/Death-Penalty.aspx (accessed July 24, 2007). Copyright © 2006 by The Gallup Organization. Reproduced by permission of The Gallup Organization.

death penalty more than African-Americans (39%) or non-whites (52%). Republicans (84%) were more likely than Independents (58%) and Democrats (51%) to believe in the death penalty. Maguire and Pastore find that the percentage of those supporting the death penalty varied with income. More than seven out of ten (72%) of people earning $30,000 to $49,999 favored the death penalty in 2003. Those with incomes under $20,000 demonstrated the least support (52%) for the death penalty. Views about the death penalty also varied somewhat with education levels, with those having a postgraduate degree (47%) favoring it the least. Regionally, people living in the South (71%) and West (69%) were more likely to favor the death penalty, compared to those in the Midwest (61%) and East (53%).

Recent State Polls

Mark DiCamillo and Mervin Field (March 3, 2006, http://www.field.com/fieldpollonline/subscribers/RLS2183 .pdf) of the Field Research Corporation, which conducts

polls in the state of California, report the results of a February 2006 poll regarding Californians' opinions about the death penalty. The pollsters found that 63% of respondents agreed that "the death sentence should be kept as a punishment for serious crimes." Another 32% favored "doing away with the death sentence." Angus Reid Global Monitor, in "Most in Kansas Support the Death Penalty" (February 21, 2007, February 21, 2007, http://www.angus reid.com/polls/index.cfm/fuseaction/viewItem/itemID/ 14807), reports that in 2007, 69% of state residents supported the death penalty, compared to 27% who opposed it.

REASONS FOR SUPPORTING AND OPPOSING THE DEATH PENALTY

The most recent nationwide Gallup poll (October 24, 2006, http://www.gallup.com/poll/1606/Death-Penalty .aspx) in which respondents were asked to give their reasons for supporting or opposing the death penalty was conducted in May 2003. At that time, 64% of respondents

FIGURE 9.4

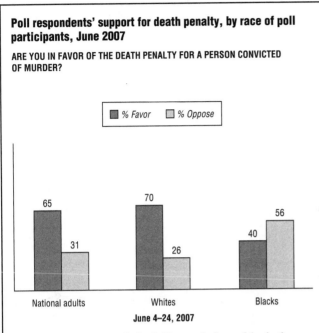

Poll respondents' support for death penalty, by race of poll participants, June 2007

ARE YOU IN FAVOR OF THE DEATH PENALTY FOR A PERSON CONVICTED OF MURDER?

SOURCE: Adapted from Lydia Saad, "Are you in favor of the death penalty for a person convicted of murder?" in *Racial Disagreement over Death Penalty Has Varied Historically*, The Gallup Organization, July 30, 2007, http://www.galluppoll.com/content/?ci=28243&pg=1 (accessed August 3, 2007). Copyright © 2007 by The Gallup Organization. Reproduced by permission of The Gallup Organization.

believed that the death penalty was the appropriate punishment for murder. These capital punishment supporters were asked why they favor the death penalty for convicted murderers. Most of the responses reflect a philosophical, moral, or religious basis of reasoning. Thirty-seven percent gave their reason as "an eye for an eye/they took a life/fits the crime." (See Table 9.2.) Another 13% said "they deserve it," whereas 5% cited biblical beliefs. Four percent stated that the death penalty will "serve justice," and 3% it is a "fair punishment." Together, these morality-based responses comprise 62% of all responses.

A minority of people who supported capital punishment in 2003 did so because of practical considerations. Eleven percent said the death penalty saves taxpayers' money. Another 11% thought that putting a murderer to death would set an example so that others would not commit similar crimes. Seven percent responded that the death penalty prevents murderers from killing again. Two percent each said that capital punishment helps the victims' families or believed that prisoners could not be rehabilitated. One percent each noted that prisoners given life sentences do not always spend life in prison or said that capital punishment relieves prison overcrowding. In total, just over a third (35%) of the reasons given for supporting the death penalty appear to be based on issues of practicality, rather than on morality.

Interestingly enough, death penalty opponents also rely heavily on moral reasoning to support their position.

In 2003 just 32% of respondents in the Gallup poll expressed opposition to capital punishment. Nearly half (46%) said that it is "wrong to take a life." (See Table 9.3.) A quarter feared that some innocent suspects may be "wrongly convicted." Another 13% cited their religious beliefs or noted that "punishment should be left to God." Five percent said that murderers "need to pay/suffer longer/think about their crime" (presumably by serving long prison sentences). By contrast, 5% said that there is a possibility of rehabilitation. Four percent opposed the death penalty because of "unfair application."

Obviously, moral values and ideas about justice and fairness have a tremendous influence on American attitudes about capital punishment.

DEATH PENALTY VERSUS LIFE IMPRISONMENT WITH NO PAROLE

Table 9.4 lists the states offering life without parole as a sentencing option in 2007. A sentence of life without parole is an option in all states except New Mexico (a death penalty state) and Alaska (a state without the death penalty).

Gary Langer, in *Capital Punishment, 30 Years On: Support, but Ambivalence as Well* (July 1, 2006, http://abcnews.go.com/images/Politics/1015a3DeathPenalty.pdf), analyses a June 2006 *Washington Post/ABC News* poll. Langer notes that 50% of respondents preferred a death penalty sentence versus 46% for life in prison with no chance of parole for people convicted of murder.

Gallup also finds that popular support for the death penalty decreases when poll participants are asked to choose between capital punishment and life imprisonment with "absolutely no possibility of parole" as the "better penalty" for murder. In a May 2006 poll 48% of respondents selected life imprisonment without parole, compared to 47% for the death penalty. As Table 9.5 shows, 2006 was the first time that life imprisonment without parole was preferred over capital punishment as the sentence for murder. For comparison, in 1985, 56% of poll respondents favored the death penalty versus only 34% for life imprisonment without parole.

Recent State Polls

The Quinnipiac University Polling Institute (February 1, 2007, http://www.quinnipiac.edu/x1322.xml?ReleaseID=1010) conducted a poll in January 2007 regarding Ohio residents' opinions about the death penalty. The results revealed that 48% of respondents preferred the death penalty for convicted murders, compared to 38% who favored a sentence of life in prison without parole. That same month the article "Death Penalty, Decline in Polls Reflects Less Faith in System" (*Lexington Herald Leader*, January 3, 2007) reported the results of a poll by the University of Kentucky Survey Research Center, which

FIGURE 9.5

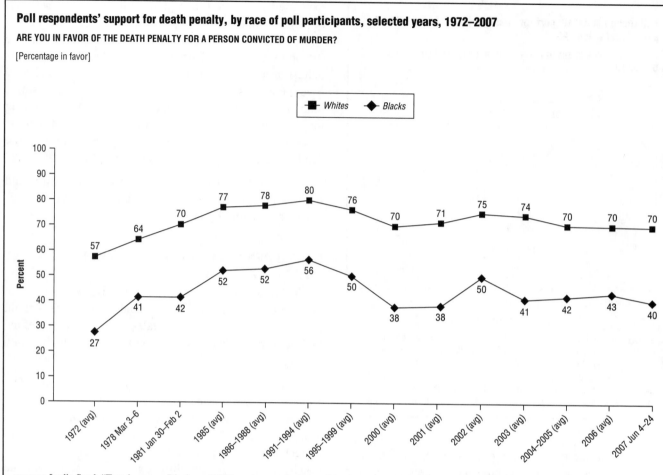

Poll respondents' support for death penalty, by race of poll participants, selected years, 1972–2007

ARE YOU IN FAVOR OF THE DEATH PENALTY FOR A PERSON CONVICTED OF MURDER?

[Percentage in favor]

SOURCE: Lydia Saad, "Trends among Blacks and Whites: Are you in favor of the death penalty for a person convicted of murder?" in *Racial Disagreement over Death Penalty Has Varied Historically*, The Gallup Organization, July 30, 2007, http://www.galluppoll.com/content/?ci=28243&pg=1 (accessed August 3, 2007). Copyright © 2007 by The Gallup Organization. Reproduced by permission of The Gallup Organization.

showed that only 30% of state residents favored the death penalty over a prison term for the crime of aggravated murder. More than a third (36%) of respondents preferred life in prison with no chance of parole. The remainder supported other prison sentencing options.

A September 2006 poll by the *New York Times* and CBS News (http://graphics8.nytimes.com/packages/pdf/nyregion/20060927_nys_poll.pdf) found that, given a choice of sentences, only 28% of New Yorkers supported the death penalty for people convicted of murder. Forty-eight percent felt that life without parole was the appropriate sentence, whereas 9% favored a "long" prison sentence with a chance of parole. Eleven percent of the respondents said that the sentence should depend on the circumstances.

IS THE DEATH PENALTY IMPOSED TOO OFTEN?

The May 2006 Gallup poll asked participants if the death penalty is imposed too often, about the right amount, or not often enough. Just over one-fifth (21%) of respondents believed the death penalty was imposed too often. (See

Figure 9.8.) A quarter felt it was imposed about the right amount. A majority (51%) said that it was not imposed enough. Comparison to results obtained in 2001 shows that the percentage of respondents believing that the death penalty is not imposed often enough increased from 38% in 2001 to 51% in 2006.

FAIRNESS OF THE DEATH PENALTY

The May 2006 Gallup poll questioned people about the fairness of the death penalty. As shown in Table 9.6, 60% of respondents believed that the death penalty is applied fairly in this country, compared to 35% who felt it is applied unfairly. The percentage of people expressing confidence in the fairness of the death penalty has hovered above 50% since the question was first asked in a 2000 poll.

THE DEATH PENALTY AND INNOCENCE

The May 2006 Gallup poll asked participants if they believed that an innocent person had been executed within the past five years. Nearly two-thirds (63%) of those asked

FIGURE 9.6

Gender and age breakdown of poll respondents who favor the death penalty, October–December 2005

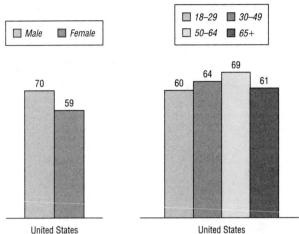

SOURCE: Adapted from David W. Moore, "Percentage Who Favor the Death Penalty Compared by Gender" and "Percentage Who Favor the Death Penalty Compared by Age" in *Death Penalty Gets Less Support from Britons, Canadians than Americans*, The Gallup Organization, February 20, 2006, http://www.galluppoll.com/content/?ci=21544& pg=1 (accessed July 24, 2007). Copyright ©2006 by The Gallup Organization. Reproduced by permission of The Gallup Organization.

FIGURE 9.7

Public opinion on the death penalty in states with and without the death penalty, 2003–05

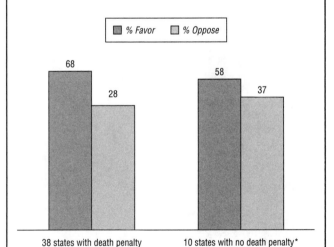

*Alaska and Hawaii not included.

SOURCE: Lydia Saad, "Support for Death Penalty According to State Law, 2003–2005," in *Support for the Death Penalty Steady at 64%*, The Gallup Organization, December 8, 2005, http://www.galluppoll .com/content/default.aspx?ci=20350&pg=1 (accessed August 23, 2007). Copyright © 2005 by The Gallup Organization. Reproduced by permission of The Gallup Organization.

TABLE 9.2

Poll respondents' reasons for supporting the death penalty, May 2003

WHY DO YOU FAVOR THE DEATH PENALTY FOR PERSONS CONVICTED OF MURDER? [OPEN-ENDED] (Based on 715 who favor the death penalty for persons convicted of murder)

	May 19–21, 2003
	%
An eye for an eye/they took a life/fits the crime	37
They deserve it	13
Save taxpayers money/cost associated with prison	11
Deterrent for potential crimes/set an example	11
They will repeat crime/keep them from repeating it	7
Biblical reasons	5
Depends on the type of crime they commit	4
Serve justice	4
Fair punishment	3
If there's no doubt the person committed the crime	3
Would help/benefit families of victims	2
Support/believe in death penalty	2
Don't believe they can be rehabilitated	2
Life sentences don't always mean life in prison	1
Relieves prison overcrowding	1
Other	4
No opinion	2

SOURCE: Adapted from "Why do you favor the death penalty for persons convicted of murder? [Open-ended], [Based on—715—who favor the death penalty for persons convicted of murder]," in *Death Penalty*, The Gallup Organization, October 24, 2006, http://www.gallup.com/poll/1606/Death-Penalty.aspx (accessed July 24, 2007). Copyright © 2006 by The Gallup Organization. Reproduced by permission of The Gallup Organization.

TABLE 9.3

Poll respondents' reasons for opposing the death penalty, May 2003

WHY DO YOU OPPOSE THE DEATH PENALTY FOR PERSONS CONVICTED OF MURDER? [OPEN-ENDED] (Based on 277 who oppose death penalty for persons convicted of murder)

	May 19–21, 2003
	%
Wrong to take a life	46
Persons may be wrongly convicted	25
Punishment should be left to God/religious belief	13
Need to pay/suffer longer/think about their crime	5
Possibility of rehabilitation	5
Depends on the circumstances	4
Unfair application of death penalty	4
Does not deter people from committing murder	4
Other	3
No opinion	4

SOURCE: Adapted from "Why do you oppose the death penalty for persons convicted of murder? [Open-ended], [Based on—277—who oppose the death penalty for persons convicted of murder]," in *Death Penalty*, The Gallup Organization, October 24, 2006, http://www.gallup.com/poll/1606/ Death-Penalty.aspx (accessed July 24, 2007). Copyright © 2006 by The Gallup Organization. Reproduced by permission of The Gallup Organization.

TABLE 9.4

States offering life without parole sentence, 2007

Death penalty states offering life without parole* (37/38 states)			Non-death penalty states offering life without parole (11/12 states)
Alabama	Louisiana	Oregon	Hawaii
Arizona	Maryland	Pennsylvania	Iowa
Arkansas	Mississippi	South Carolina	Maine
California	Missouri	South Dakota	Massachusetts
Colorado	Montana	Tennessee	Michigan
Connecticut	Nebraska	Texas	Minnesota
Delaware	Nevada	Utah	North Dakota
Florida	New Hampshire	Virginia	North Dakota
Georgia	New Jersey	Washington	Rhode Island
Idaho	New York	Wyoming	Vermont
Illinois	North Carolina	plus	West Virginia
Indiana	Ohio	Federal statute	Wisconsin
Kansas	Oklahoma	Military statute	plus District of
Kentucky			Columbia

Notes: The recent development of "three strikes" laws in some states may make life without parole available for at least some offenders in those states. New Mexico does not have life without parole.
Alaska does not have life without parole.

SOURCE: "Death Penalty States Offering Life Without Parole," and "Non-Death Penalty States Offering Life Without Parole," in *Life Without Parole*, Death Penalty Information Center, 2007, http://www.deathpenaltyinfo.org/article.php?did=555&scid=59 (accessed August 24, 2007)

TABLE 9.5

Public opinion on preferred sentence for murder, selected years 1985–2006

IF YOU COULD CHOOSE BETWEEN THE FOLLOWING TWO APPROACHES, WHICH DO YOU THINK IS THE BETTER PENALTY FOR MURDER—[ROTATED: THE DEATH PENALTY (OR) LIFE IMPRISONMENT, WITH ABSOLUTELY NO POSSIBILITY OF PAROLE]?

	The death penalty	Life imprisonment	No opinion
	%	%	%
2006 May 5–7*	47	48	5
2001 Feb 19–21*	54	42	4
2000 Aug 29–Sep 5*	49	47	4
2000 Feb 20–21	52	37	11
1999 Feb 8–9*	56	38	6
1997 Aug 12–13*	61	29	10
1993 Oct 13–18	59	29	12
1992 Mar 30–Apr 5	50	37	13
1991 Jun 13–16	53	35	11
1986 Jan 10–13	55	35	10
1985 Jan 11–14	56	34	10

*Asked of a half sample.

SOURCE: "If you could choose between the following two approaches, which do you think is the better penalty for murder—[ROTATED: the death penalty (or) life imprisonment, with absolutely no possibility of parole]?" in *Death Penalty*, The Gallup Organization, October 24, 2006, http://www.gallup.com/poll/1606/Death-Penalty.aspx (accessed July 24, 2007). Copyright © 2006 by The Gallup Organization. Reproduced by permission of The Gallup Organization.

FIGURE 9.8

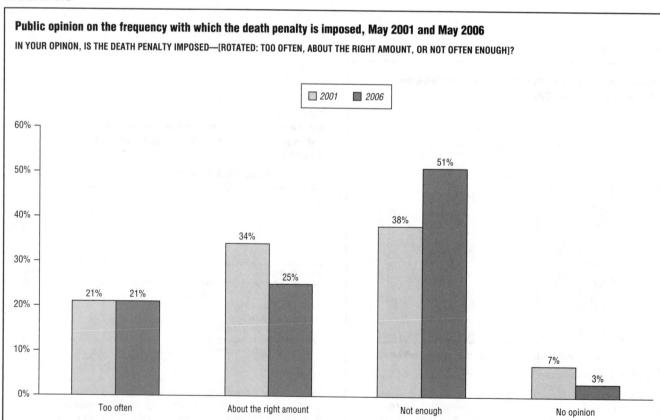

Public opinion on the frequency with which the death penalty is imposed, May 2001 and May 2006

IN YOUR OPINON, IS THE DEATH PENALTY IMPOSED—[ROTATED: TOO OFTEN, ABOUT THE RIGHT AMOUNT, OR NOT OFTEN ENOUGH]?

SOURCE: Adapted from "In your opinion, is the death penalty imposed—[ROTATED: too often, about the right amount, or not often enough]?" in *Death Penalty*, The Gallup Organization, October 24, 2006, http://www.gallup.com/poll/1606/Death-Penalty.aspx (accessed July 24, 2007). Copyright © 2006 by The Gallup Organization. Reproduced by permission of The Gallup Organization.

TABLE 9.6

Public opinion on the fairness of the death penalty, June 2000 and May 2002–May 2006

GENERALLY SPEAKING, DO YOU BELIEVE THE DEATH PENALTY IS APPLIED FAIRLY OR UNFAIRLY IN THIS COUNTRY TODAY?

	Fairly	Unfairly	No opinion
	%	%	%
2006 May 8–11	60	35	4
2005 May 2–5	61	35	4
2004 May 2–4	55	39	6
2003 May 5–7	60	37	3
2002 May 6–9	53	40	7
2000 Jun 23–25	51	41	8

SOURCE: "Generally speaking, do you believe the death penalty is applied fairly or unfairly in this country today?" in *Death Penalty*, The Gallup Organization, October 24, 2006, http://www.gallup.com/poll/1606/Death-Penalty.aspx (accessed July 24, 2007). Copyright © 2006 by The Gallup Organization. Reproduced by permission of The Gallup Organization.

FIGURE 9.9

Public opinion on whether an innocent person has been executed within the past five years, May 2006

HOW OFTEN DO YOU THINK THAT A PERSON HAS BEEN EXECUTED UNDER THE DEATH PENALTY WHO WAS, IN FACT, INNOCENT OF THE CRIME HE OR SHE WAS CHARGED WITH—DO YOU THINK THIS HAS HAPPENED IN THE PAST FIVE YEARS, OR NOT?

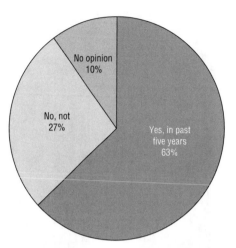

SOURCE: Adapted from "How often do you think that a person has been executed under the death penalty who was, in fact, innocent of the crime he or she was charged with—do you think this has happened in the past five years, or not?" in *Death Penalty*, The Gallup Organization, October 24, 2006, http://www.gallup.com/poll/1606/Death-Penalty.aspx (accessed July 24, 2007). Copyright © 2006 by The Gallup Organization. Reproduced by permission of The Gallup Organization.

agreed that this had occurred. (See Figure 9.9.) More than a quarter (27%) of respondents thought that an innocent person had not been executed within the last five years.

In "More Than Two-thirds of Americans Continue to Support the Death Penalty" (January 7, 2004, http://www.harrisinteractive.com/harris_poll/index.asp?PID=431), Humphrey Taylor of Harris Interactive notes that in December 2003 most Americans (95%) believed that, on average, for every one hundred people convicted of murder, approximately 11% were innocent. Women guessed that this occurred more often (estimated 13%) than men did (10%). African-Americans estimated that 23% of people convicted of murder were innocent, compared to estimates by Hispanics (16%) and whites (9%). Independents and those with a high school diploma or less were more likely to believe that a higher proportion of innocent people (13% and 13%, respectively) were convicted of murder, as opposed to Republicans and those with a four-year college degree (6% and 7%, respectively).

Though 95% of respondents indicated they believed that at least some of those charged with murder were innocent, the 11% error rate in executions did not seem to qualify as "substantial." When asked if they would still support the death penalty if a "substantial" number of innocent people were convicted of murder, only four out of ten (39%) said they would still support the death penalty. Over half (51%) would oppose it under these conditions. Nevertheless, the 39% who continued to support the death penalty were a larger proportion compared to their counterparts in 2001 and a smaller proportion than those in 2000 (36% and 53%, respectively).

MORATORIUM

On January 31, 2000, the Illinois governor George Ryan (1934–) declared a moratorium on executions in his state. Jeffrey M. Jones of the Gallup Organization notes in "Americans Closely Divided on Death Penalty Moratorium" (April 11, 2001, http://www.gallup.com/poll/1816/Americans-Closely-Divided-Death-Penalty-Moratorium.aspx) that in March 2001, 53% of poll respondents said they favored a moratorium on the death penalty in states with capital punishment. Such a moratorium was opposed by 40%. Gary Langer reports in "Poll: Public Ambivalent about Death Penalty" (ABCNews.com, May 2, 2001) that a poll conducted in April 2001 delivered similar results. This poll revealed that 51% of Americans favored a nationwide moratorium until a commission could study whether it was being administered fairly.

On January 11, 2003, Governor Ryan commuted 167 death sentences to life imprisonment without the possibility of parole. In "Poll: Lock the Doors on Death Row" (ABCNews.com, January 24, 2003), Dalia Sussman notes that a January 2003 ABC News/*Washington Post* poll surveyed people in the thirty-eight death penalty states. The respondents were told that Governor Ryan's action was a result of his belief that too many mistakes occurred in capital cases and were then asked if they would support or oppose a similar blanket commutation by their governor. Fifty-eight percent indicated they would oppose such an action.

FIGURE 9.10

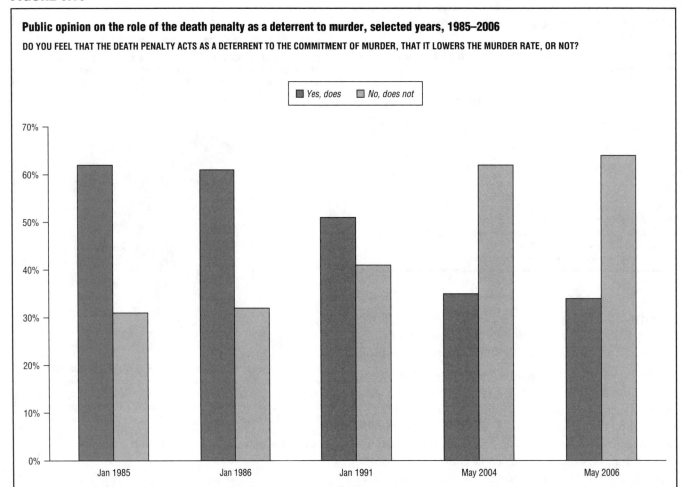

Public opinion on the role of the death penalty as a deterrent to murder, selected years, 1985–2006

DO YOU FEEL THAT THE DEATH PENALTY ACTS AS A DETERRENT TO THE COMMITMENT OF MURDER, THAT IT LOWERS THE MURDER RATE, OR NOT?

■ Yes, does   ■ No, does not

SOURCE: Adapted from "Do you feel that the death penalty acts as a deterrent to the commitment of murder, that it lowers the murder rate, or not?" in *Death Penalty*, The Gallup Organization, October 24, 2006, http://www.gallup.com/poll/1606/Death-Penalty.aspx (accessed July 24, 2007). Copyright © 2006 by The Gallup Organization. Reproduced by permission of The Gallup Organization.

In 2004 a New York appellate court declared that the state's death penalty was unconstitutional because of a flaw in a state statute. In 2005 the New York State Assembly refused to pass a bill that would effectively fix the statute and reinstate the death penalty. By doing so, the assembly ushered in an unofficial moratorium on the death penalty in New York. The Siena Research Institute (March 8, 2005, http://www.siena.edu/uploadedFiles/Home/Parents_and _Community/Community_Page/Siena_Research_Institute/ march%2005%20release.pdf) polled registered voters in the state between February and March 2005, asking them if they wanted the death penalty to be reinstated. Some 46% of New Yorkers replied that they did not, whereas 42% said they did. A May 2007 poll (http://www.siena.edu/ uploadedFiles/Home/Parents_and_Community/Community _Page/Siena_Research_Institute/07%20May%20SNYPoll% 20Release%20FINAL.pdf) by the same organization found that New Yorkers favored reinstating the death penalty for people convicted of killing law enforcement officers by a margin of 52% to 42%.

DETERRENT OR NOT?

Taylor notes that in December 2003 about four out of ten (41%) Americans believed that capital punishment deters (discourages) people from committing murders. However, 53% of Americans believed capital punishment does not have much effect. In 1976, when the death penalty was reinstated, 59% of Americans thought capital punishment was a deterrent, compared to 34% who thought it had little effect.

Just over one-third (34%) of respondents to the May 2006 Gallup poll thought that the death penalty acted as a deterrent to committing murder. (See Figure 9.10.) Nearly two-thirds (64%) maintained that the death penalty did not lower the murder rate. This represented a marked shift in sentiment from decades past. In January 1985 Gallup first asked Americans if they thought the death penalty lowered the murder rate, and two-thirds (62%) said it did, versus a mere one-third (31%) who responded that it did not.

CHAPTER 10
CAPITAL PUNISHMENT AROUND THE WORLD

UNITED NATIONS RESOLUTIONS

Capital punishment is controversial not only in the United States but also in many other countries. The ethical arguments that fuel the debate in the United States also characterize the discussions around the world. The United Nations' (UN) position on capital punishment is a compromise among those countries that want it completely abolished, those that want it limited to serious offenses, and those that want it left up to each country to decide. In 1946, just after the end of World War II (1939–1945), the UN General Assembly gathered to draft a bill of human rights for all UN member nations to follow. From the beginning, the death penalty was a topic of contention, and in 1948, when the assembly released the International Bill of Human Rights, there was no mention of the death penalty. After nine years of debate, the General Assembly included a statement on the death penalty in the International Covenant on Civil and Political Rights, which was later added to the International Bill of Human Rights. On December 16, 1966, the General Assembly adopted the covenant in Resolution 2200 (http://daccessdds.un.org/doc/RESOLUTION/GEN/NR0/005/03/IMG/NR000503.pdf?OpenElement). Article 6 of the covenant states:

1. Every human being has the inherent right to life. This right shall be protected by law. No one shall be arbitrarily deprived of his life.

2. In countries which have not abolished the death penalty, sentence of death may be imposed only for the most serious crimes in accordance with the law in force at the time of the commission of the crime and not contrary to the provisions of the present Covenant and to the Convention on the Prevention and Punishment of the Crime of Genocide [systematic killing of a racial, political, or cultural group]. This penalty can only be carried out pursuant to a final judgment rendered by a competent court.

3. When deprivation of life constitutes the crime of genocide, it is understood that nothing in this article shall authorize any State Party to the present Covenant to derogate [turn away] in any way from any obligation assumed under the provisions of the Convention on the Prevention and Punishment of the Crime of Genocide.

4. Anyone sentenced to death shall have the right to seek pardon or commutation of the sentence [replacement of the death sentence with a lesser sentence]. Amnesty, pardon or commutation of the sentence of death may be granted in all cases.

5. Sentence of death shall not be imposed for crimes committed by persons below eighteen years of age and shall not be carried out on pregnant women.

6. Nothing in this article shall be invoked to delay or to prevent the abolition of capital punishment by any State Party to the present Covenant.

The General Assembly has dealt with the death penalty in several other documents and meetings. Among them is Resolution 2393 (November 26, 1968, http://daccessdds.un.org/doc/RESOLUTION/GEN/NR0/243/53/IMG/NR024353.pdf?OpenElement), which specifies the following legal safeguards that should be offered to condemned prisoners by countries with capital punishment:

1. A person condemned to death shall not be deprived of the right to appeal to a higher judicial authority or, as the case may be, to petition for pardon or reprieve;

2. A death sentence shall not be carried out until the procedures of appeal or, as the case may be, of petition for pardon or reprieve have been terminated;

3. Special attention shall be given in the case of indigent [poor] persons by the provision of adequate legal assistance at all stages of the proceedings.

Since then the General Assembly has come out more strongly for eliminating capital punishment. Resolution

2857 (December 20, 1971, http://daccessdds.un.org/doc/RESOLUTION/GEN/NR0/328/73/IMG/NR032873.pdf?OpenElement) observes that "in order fully to guarantee the right to life, provided for in article 3 of the Universal Declaration of Human Rights [a section of the International Bill of Human Rights], the main objective to be pursued is that of progressively restricting the number of offences for which capital punishment may be imposed, with a view to the desirability of abolishing this punishment in all countries."

The UN Economic and Social Council Resolution 1574 of May 20, 1971, made a similar declaration. In 1984 the Economic and Social Council then adopted the *Safeguards Guaranteeing Protection of the Rights of Those Facing the Death Penalty*, including those of people younger than age eighteen at the time the crime was committed. Over the succeeding years General Assembly and Economic and Social Council resolutions have continued to call for the abolition of the death penalty.

On December 15, 1989, the General Assembly, under Resolution 44/128, adopted the Second Optional Protocol to the International Covenant on Civil and Political Rights, aimed at abolishing the death penalty. This international treaty allows countries to retain the death penalty in wartime as long as they reserve the right to do so at the time they become party to the treaty. As of October 19, 2007, thirty-five countries had signed the treaty (http://www.ohchr.info/english/bodies/ratification/12.htm), which indicated their intention to become parties to it at a later date. Signatories are not legally bound by the treaty but are obliged to avoid acts that would go against the treaty. Sixty-four countries had become parties to the protocol by ratification or accession, which means that they are legally bound by the terms of the treaty. Accession is similar to ratification, except that it occurs after the treaty has entered into force. In 1992 the United States ratified the International Covenant on Civil and Political Rights, but as of October 19, 2007, it had not signed the Second Optional Protocol to this treaty.

Push for a Moratorium

Since April 1997 the UN Human Rights Council (formerly the UN Commission on Human Rights) has adopted resolutions calling for a moratorium on executions and an eventual abolition of the death penalty. The United States has consistently voted against these resolutions. In a 2004 statement the U.S. delegation to the UN Commission on Human Rights (http://geneva.usmission.gov/humanrights/2004/statements/0421L-94.htm) noted "International law does not prohibit the death penalty when due process safeguards are respected and when capital punishment is applied only to the most serious crimes."

During its 2002 session the Human Rights Council, in Resolution 2002/77 (http://www.unhchr.ch/Huridocda/Huridoca.nsf/0/e93443efabf7a6c4c1256bab00500ef6?Opendocument), asked countries with the death penalty "to ensure that ... the death penalty is not imposed for non-violent acts such as financial crimes, non-violent religious practice or expression of conscience and sexual relations between consenting adults." The part of the resolution referring to sexual relations between consenting adults resulted from the potential execution of a Nigerian woman, who became pregnant while divorced. She was convicted of adultery and, in March 2002, was sentenced to die by stoning. The man who fathered the child claimed innocence, brought in three men to corroborate his claim as required by law, and was released. The woman was acquitted on September 25, 2003.

The Commission on Human Rights adopted Resolution 2003/67 on April 24, 2003. For the first time, the commission asked countries that retained capital punishment not to extend the application of the death penalty to offenses to which it does not currently apply. It also admonished those countries to inform the public of any scheduled execution and to abstain from holding public executions and inhuman forms of executions, such as stoning. The UN also called on death penalty countries not to impose the death sentence on mothers with dependent children.

On December 18, 2000, the UN secretary general Kofi Annan (1938–; http://www.unhchr.ch/huricane/huricane.nsf/view01/0CFC538C82EBB17FC12569BA002BE9A6?opendocument) announced that he received a petition signed by more than 3 million people from 130 countries appealing for an end to executions. Subsequently, the secretary general called for a worldwide moratorium on the death penalty, noting that the taking of life as punishment for crime is "too absolute [and] too irreversible."

In November 2007 a draft resolution was presented to a General Assembly panel calling for a moratorium on the death penalty by member states. The resolution was spearheaded by the Ministers of the European Union and cosponsored by seventy-two countries. In a vote of ninety-nine to fifty-two (with thirty-three abstentions) the resolution was passed. The United States was among the nations that voted against the resolution. The full 192-member General Assembly was expected to approve the decision within the next few months.

RETENTIONIST COUNTRIES

Amnesty International (AI), a human rights organization, maintains information on capital punishment throughout the world. The organization refers to countries that retain and use the death penalty as retentionist countries; those that no longer use the death penalty are called abolitionist countries.

As of August 8, 2007, sixty-seven countries and territories retained and used the death penalty as a possible

TABLE 10.1

Countries and territories which retain the death penalty for ordinary crimes, August 8, 2007

Afghanistan	Kuwait
Antigua and Barbuda	Laos
Bahamas	Lebanon
Bahrain	Lesotho
Bangladesh	Libya
Barbados	Malaysia
Belarus	Mongolia
Belize	Nigeria
Botswana	Oman
Burundi	Pakistan
Cameroon	Palestinian Authority
Chad	Qatar
China	Saint Christopher & Nevis
Comoros	Saint Lucia
Congo (Democratic Republic)	Saint Vincent & Grenadines
Cuba	Saudi Arabia
Dominica	Sierra Leone
Egypt	Singapore
Equatorial Guinea	Somalia
Eritrea	Sudan
Ethiopia	Syria
Guatemala	Taiwan
Guinea	Tajikistan
Guyana	Tanzania
India	Thailand
Indonesia	Trinidad and Tobago
Iran	Uganda
Iraq	United Arab Emirates
Jamaica	United States of America
Japan	Uzbekistan
Jordan	Vietnam
Kazakstan	Yemen
Korea (North)	Zimbabwe
Korea (South)	

SOURCE: Adapted from "Countries and Territories which Retain the Death Penalty for Ordinary Crimes," in *Abolitionist and Retentionist Countries*, Amnesty International, August 8, 2007, http://web.amnesty.org/web/web.nsf/print/714BB3479E3E999980256D51005D69BE (accessed August 20, 2007)

punishment for ordinary crimes. (See Table 10.1.) Ordinary crimes are crimes committed during peacetime. Ordinary crimes that could lead to the death penalty include murder, rape, and, in some countries, robbery or embezzlement of large sums of money. Exceptional crimes are military crimes committed during exceptional times, mainly wartime. Examples are treason, spying, or desertion (leaving the armed services without permission).

The AI notes in "Facts and Figures on the Death Penalty" (October 2, 2007, http://web.amnesty.org/pages/deathpenalty-facts-eng) that even though many of the retentionist countries had not executed anybody in many years, 25 countries performed at least 1,591 executions in 2006. In addition, at least 3,861 people were sentenced to death in 55 countries. The AI reports that 91% of the known executions occurred in only six countries: China (1,010), Iran (177), Pakistan (82), Iraq (65), Sudan (65), and the United States (53). China alone accounted for nearly two-thirds (63%) of all known executions, but the AI estimates that the actual number is larger, between seventy-five hundred to eight thousand. (Note: since 2004 the AI has relied on Internet-based reports instead of trial documents to

estimate the number of executions in China. Using the Internet has resulted in a much higher count than that provided by official sources.)

United States

The United States remains the only Western country that practices capital punishment. (As of 2007, the federal government, the U.S. military, and thirty-eight states approved the death penalty.) In September 1997 the UN monitor Bacre Waly Ndiaye, a lawyer from Senegal, investigated the use of the death penalty in the United States. This was the first time the UN had sent an investigator to report on the U.S. capital punishment system. In his report to the UN Commission on Human Rights, *Mission to the United States of America* (January 22, 1998, http://www.unhchr.ch/Huridocda/Huridoca.nsf/0/ce9d6cdd9353d632c125661300459b39?Opendocument), Ndiaye accuses the United States of unfair, arbitrary, and racist use of capital punishment. He claims that "allegations of racial discrimination in the imposition of death sentences are particularly serious in southern states, such as Alabama, Florida, Louisiana, Mississippi, Georgia and Texas, known as the 'death penalty belt.'"

FOREIGN NATIONALS. Under Article 36 of the Vienna Convention on Consular Relations (VCCR) local U.S. law enforcement officials are required to notify all detained foreigners "without delay" of their right to consult with the consulate of their home country. The United States ratified (formally approved and sanctioned) this international agreement and an Optional Protocol to the VCCR in 1969. The Optional Protocol provided that the International Court of Justice (ICJ; the UN's highest court) would have the authority to decide when VCCR rights have been violated. Capital punishment opponents claim that the United States has a poor record of informing foreign nationals under arrest of their rights under the VCCR.

Mark Warren of Human Rights Research (Ontario, Canada) provides information and expertise on human rights issues to government, nongovernmental organizations, consulates, and lawyers. According to Warren, as of October 4, 2006, the United States had executed twenty-two foreign nationals, and only one condemned prisoner (Angel Maturino Resendis) was informed of his VCCR right at the time of arrest. (See Table 10.2.) The Death Penalty Information Center (http://www.deathpenaltyinfo.org/article.php?did=198#Reported-DROW) reports that as of March 28, 2007, 124 foreign nationals were on death row in the United States. The largest number (fifty-four) were Mexican. The vast majority of foreign nationals under the sentence of death were in California (47), Texas (28), and Florida (21).

THE UNITED STATES DEFIES THE UN'S HIGHEST COURT. Angel Francisco Breard, a Paraguayan national, was arrested on charges of capital murder and attempted rape in 1992. In 1993 Breard was sentenced to death for

TABLE 10.2

Confirmed foreign nationals executed, 1976–October 4, 2006

Name	Vienna Convention on Consular Relations (VCCR) claim raised	Nationality	State	Date
Leslie Lowenfield		Guyana	Louisiana	13-Apr-88
Carlos Santana	#	Dominican Republic	Texas	23-Mar-93
Ramon Montoya	#	Mexico	Texas	25-Mar-93
Pedro Medina		Cuba	Florida	25-Mar-97
Irineo Tristan Montoya	#	Mexico	Texas	18-Jun-97
Mario Murphy	#(Fourth Circuit)	Mexico	Virginia	18-Sep-97
Angel Breard	#(US Supreme Court)	Paraguay	Virginia	14-Apr-98
Jose Villafuerte	#	Honduras	Arizona	22-Apr-98
Tuan Nguyen		Viet Nam	Oklahoma	10-Dec-98
Jaturun Siripongs	#	Thailand	California	9-Feb-99
Karl LaGrand	#(Ninth Circuit)	Germany	Arizona	24-Feb-99
Walter LaGrand	#(Ninth Circuit)	Germany	Arizona	3-Mar-99
Alvaro Calamvro	#	Philippines	Nevada	5-Apr-99
Joseph Stanley Faulder	#(Fifth Circuit)	Canada	Texas	17-Jun-99
Miguel Angel Flores	#(Fifth Circuit)	Mexico	Texas	9-Nov-00
Sebastian Bridges		South Africa	Nevada	21-Apr-01
Sahib al-Mosawi	#	Iraq	Oklahoma	6-Dec-01
Javier Suarez Medina	#	Mexico	Texas	14-Aug-02
Rigoberto Sanchez Velasco		Cuba	Florida	2-Oct-02
Mir Aimal Kasi	#	Pakistan	Virginia	14-Nov-02
Hung Thanh Le	#	Vietnam	Oklahoma	23-Mar-04
Angel Maturino Resendiz		Mexico	Texas	27-Jun-06

Notes: With the exception of Angel Maturino Resendiz, all indications are that none of these executed individuals were informed by U.S. authorities upon arrest of their right to have their consulate notified of their detention, as required under Article 36 of the Vienna Convention on Consular Relations. In several instances, prisoners on this list did not learn of their right to request consular assistance for more than a decade, by which time the treaty violation was considered by the appellate courts to be a procedurally defaulted claim. Cases indicated with (#) are those in which the consular notification issue was raised on appeal or in clemency proceedings (major appellate opinions on consular rights are in brackets).

SOURCE: Mark Warren, "Confirmed Foreign Nationals Executed since 1976," in *Foreign Nationals, Part II*, Death Penalty Information Center, October 4, 2006, http://www.deathpenaltyinfo.org/article.php?scid=31&did=582#executed (accessed August 20, 2007)

these crimes. Following the denial of his appeals before the Virginia Supreme Court and the U.S. Supreme Court, Breard invoked the provision of the VCCR. The U.S. District Court, in *Breard v. Netherland* (949 F. Supp. 1255, 1266 [ED Va. 1996]), rejected Breard's claim because he had "procedurally defaulted" the claim when he failed to raise it in state court during his state appeals. Without doing so, he could not raise the issue in his federal appeals. In addition, the district court concluded that Breard could not show cause and prejudice for this default.

Also in 1996 the Republic of Paraguay brought suit against Virginia officials for violation of the Vienna Convention because they failed to notify the Paraguayan consulate of Breard's arrest. The district court dismissed the suit, a decision that the appellate court affirmed. On April 3, 1998, the Republic of Paraguay brought the case before the ICJ, which ruled, on April 9, 1998, that the United States should stay (postpone) Breard's execution pending the ICJ's final decision. Paraguay had also petitioned the U.S. Supreme Court.

On April 14, 1998, the day of execution, the U.S. Supreme Court, voting 6–3, refused to intervene in the case despite requests for a stay of execution from the U.S. secretary of state Madeleine K. Albright (1937–). In *Breard v. Greene* (523 U.S. 371, 1998), the Court stated:

It is the rule in this country that assertions of error in criminal proceedings must first be raised in state court in order to form the basis for relief in habeas. . . . Claims not so raised are considered defaulted. By not asserting his Vienna Convention claim in state court, Breard failed to exercise his rights under the Vienna Convention in conformity with the laws of the United States and the Commonwealth of Virginia. Having failed to do so, he cannot raise a claim of violation of those rights now on federal habeas review. . . .

As for Paraguay's suits (both the original action and the case coming to us on petition for certiorari [a petition to the Supreme Court to review the issues brought up in the direct appeal]), neither the text nor the history of the Vienna Convention clearly provides a foreign nation a private right of action in United States courts to set aside a criminal conviction and sentence for violation of consular notification provisions. . . . Though Paraguay claims that its suit is within an exemption dealing with continuing consequences of past violations of federal rights, we do not agree. The failure to notify the Paraguayan Consul occurred long ago and has no continuing effect.

Breard was executed later that same day. In November 1998 the United States formally apologized to Paraguay for failing to inform Breard of his right to seek consular assistance. Paraguay withdrew its lawsuit following the apology.

GERMANY SUES THE UNITED STATES. In 1982 the German brothers Karl LaGrand and Walter LaGrand killed a bank employee during a robbery attempt in Tucson, Arizona. They were sentenced to death in 1984. In February 1999 Karl LaGrand was executed. On March 2, 1999, the day before Walter LaGrand's execution, Germany sued the United States at the ICJ. According to Germany, the United States violated Article 36 of the Vienna Convention by failing to inform the defendant after being arrested of his right to contact the German consulate for help. Germany also claimed that Arizona prosecutors violated Article 36 because they knowingly failed to inform Germany of the arrest and conviction until ten years after the murder. By that time it was too late, under "procedural default," for the defendant to raise the issue of the treaty violation. The U.S. rule of procedural default requires that claims challenging conviction and/or sentence have to be presented at the state appeals stage. Walter LaGrand had not argued for his Article 36 rights in previous court proceedings and, therefore, could not raise a violation of that right in later proceedings.

The ICJ ordered the United States to stay Walter LaGrand's execution, but Arizona let the execution take place. Despite the execution, Germany proceeded with the lawsuit. During a November 2000 hearing before the ICJ, the United States argued that Article 36 does not confer personal rights to individual nationals. In other words, the United States conceded that even though it violated its treaty obligations to Germany, it did not violate its obligations to the brothers. The United States added that even though German authorities knew of the LaGrand case in 1992, they waited until 1999 to intervene for the brothers.

On June 27, 2001, the ICJ, in *Germany v. United States of America*, ruled 14–1 that the United States had violated its obligations to Germany and to the LaGrand brothers under the VCCR. The ICJ also ruled that domestic law must not prevent the review of the conviction and sentencing when a defendant's right to consular notification has been violated. In addition, the United States must provide review and remedies should a similar case arise.

MEXICO SUES THE UNITED STATES. In 2003 the ICJ was asked to settle a case involving the United States and consular notification. On January 9, 2003, in *Avena and Other Mexican Nationals [Mexico v. United States of America]*, Mexico sued the United States for allegedly violating the VCCR with respect to fifty-four Mexican nationals on U.S. death row. Mexico also asked the court, pending final judgment of the case, to issue provisional measures ordering the United States to abstain from executing any Mexican national or schedule any such execution. The United States argued that Mexico's request for provisional measures should be rejected by the court because they were equivalent to "a sweeping prohibition on capital punishment for Mexican nationals in the United States, regardless of United States law."

On February 5, 2003, the ICJ unanimously issued an order directing the United States to take all necessary measures to ensure that three Mexican nationals, who faced possible execution in the coming months or even weeks, not be executed pending its final decision. Furthermore, the court noted that the other fifty-one death row inmates were not included in the provisional measures order because they were not in the same situation as the other three men.

Even though Judge Shigeru Oda (1924–) voted with the other fourteen court members regarding the order for provisional measures, he expressed his doubts about the court's definition of "disputes arising out of the interpretation or application" of the Vienna Convention. He had expressed the same doubts in the *Breard* and *LaGrand* cases. Judge Oda stated that because the United States had admitted its failure to abide by the Vienna Convention, no dispute concerning consular notification existed. He believed the current lawsuit "is in essence an attempt by Mexico to save the lives of its nationals sentenced to death by domestic courts in the United States." Judge Oda observed that the ICJ cannot act as a court of criminal appeal, adding that "if the rights of the accused as they relate to humanitarian issues are to be respected then, in parallel, the matter of the rights of victims of violent crime (a point which has often been overlooked) should be taken into consideration."

The ICJ handed down its decision on March 31, 2004. The court found that the United States had violated sections of the Vienna Convention by not informing the fifty-four Mexicans on death row of their right to notify their government about their detention. The court did not annul the convictions and sentences as Mexico had requested, but it did rule that the United States must review and reconsider the Mexican nationals' convictions and sentences.

THE MEDELLIN CASE. Jose Medellin was one of the fifty-four Mexicans on death row. Texas jurors sentenced him to death for participating in the rape and murder of two teenage girls in 1993. The Mexican consular did not learn of or have the opportunity to help Medellin with his legal defense until 1997, after Medellin had exhausted most of his appeals. When the ICJ decision regarding Mexican nationals was handed down, Medellin appealed once again to the U.S. Court of Appeals for the Fifth Circuit, claiming that he did not receive adequate counsel and that he was not allowed to contact the Mexican consulate after his indictment. The federal appellate court ruled against Medellin. The court cited *Breard v. Greene*, which stated that the issues addressed by the Vienna Convention had to be considered in the state courts before they could be addressed in federal court. Because Medellin had already gone through his appeals on the state level, he had no recourse. Medellin appealed to the U.S. Supreme Court and on December 10, 2004, the Court agreed to hear his case and to reassess its position on the Vienna Convention and ICJ rulings.

Just before the oral arguments in the Medellin case, President George W. Bush (1946–) signed an executive order on February 28, 2005, demanding that the appropriate U.S. state courts review the sentences and convictions of the fifty-four Mexicans on death row without applying the procedural default rule discussed in *Breard v. Greene*. By issuing this order, the president in essence forced the courts to comply to the ICJ ruling regarding the Mexicans. In light of the executive order, the U.S. Supreme Court dismissed Medellin's case, and it was sent back to the state courts for review.

According to Linda Greenhouse, in "Supreme Court to Hear Appeal of Mexican Death Row Inmate" (*New York Times*, May 1, 2007), the Texas Court of Criminal Appeals subsequently accused Bush of "intrusive" meddling in the state's court system and refused to comply with the president's order. In response, the Bush administration urged the U.S. Supreme Court to overturn the Texas court's decision. On October 10, 2007, the case was heard by the high court. As of November 2007, a decision had not been published.

THE U.S. WITHDRAWS FROM THE OPTIONAL PROTOCOL TO THE VCCR. On March 9, 2005, President Bush pulled the United States out of the Optional Protocol to the VCCR, which had been in place for thirty years. Charles Lane indicates in "U.S. Quits Pact Used in Capital Cases" (*Washington Post*, March 10, 2005) that the administration no longer wanted the U.S. court system to be influenced by the ICJ with regard to executing foreign nationals.

EXTRADITION AND CAPITAL PUNISHMENT. An increasing number of countries refuse to extradite (surrender for trial) criminals to the United States who might face the death penalty. In March 2000 French authorities arrested the fugitive James Charles Kopp, who was accused of murdering the abortion provider Barnett Slepian. It took months of negotiations before the French government agreed to send Kopp back to the United States for trial. The U.S. Department of Justice had to guarantee in writing that the United States would not charge Kopp with capital murder. In 2001 the supreme courts of Canada and South Africa ruled that both nations would not extradite any criminal to the United States or any country that advocates capital punishment. The governments of Mexico and many west European countries have made similar announcements.

In June 2007 the government of Cyprus agreed to extradite Yazeed Essa, a Palestinian, to the United States to stand trial in Ohio for murdering his wife in 2005. The agreement was reached after U.S. authorities promised that Essa would not face the death penalty.

Capital punishment has proven to be a sticking point in extraditions involving suspects in the U.S. wars on terror and on drugs. In 2005 the German government refused to extradite Mohammed Ali Hamadi to the United States out of fear that Hamadi would face the death penalty for his role in killing a U.S. Navy diver during a 1985 airplane hijacking. Hamadi served nineteen years of a life sentence in Germany for the hijacking before being paroled and deported to his native Lebanon. The Lebanese government has refused to turn him over to U.S. authorities. As of November 2007, Hamadi was on the Federal Bureau of Investigation's "Most Wanted Terrorists" list, and a $5 million reward was offered for information leading to his capture. In February 2007 U.S. authorities filed an extradition request for the accused drug-cartel leader Benjamin Arellano-Félix, who has been in custody in Mexico since 2002. His brother Francisco Javier Arellano-Félix was captured by the U.S. Coast Guard while in international waters in 2006. Both men are accused of operating a violent drug smuggling ring and committing multiple capital crimes subject to the death penalty under U.S. law. In November 2007 Francisco Javier Arellano-Félix received a life sentence without parole after a plea bargain deal was reached that eliminated the death penalty as an option in exchange for his guilty plea. It is considered unlikely that Mexico will extradite Benjamin Arellano-Félix without similar assurances that he will not face capital punishment.

China

Human rights groups find that China executes more people each year than all the other death penalty nations combined. In October 1999 the Chinese government passed a law allowing the imposition of the death sentence on leaders of the Falun Gong religious movement charged with murder and endangering national security. The government claimed the movement has caused the death of more than one thousand followers by dissuading them from seeking medical help.

According to the AI, in *Report 2002* (2002, http://web.amnesty.org/web/ar2002.nsf), a massive increase in executions occurred in 2001 as a result of a nationwide anticrime campaign called Strike Hard. Chinese officials had allegedly been inconsistent in determining which crimes warranted the death penalty. Law enforcement, under pressure to achieve results, sped up the criminal process by reportedly subjecting defendants to torture to extract confessions. In *Report 2005* (2005, http://web.amnesty.org/report2005/index-eng), the AI estimates that approximately thirty-four hundred people had been executed and six thousand had been sentenced to death in 2004. However, the organization reports that a Chinese government official had announced that the country executes about ten thousand people per year.

People convicted of nonviolent offenses, such as tax fraud, bribery, embezzlement, and counterfeiting, have been put to death in China. Joseph Kahn reports in "China Quick to Execute Drug Official" (*New York Times*, July 11, 2007) that in July 2007 Zheng Xiaoyu, the nation's former head of food and drug safety, was executed for taking bribes to approve medicines that had not been properly tested. He was sentenced in May 2007 and lost a subsequent appeal to China's Supreme Court. Zheng's execution was believed by many observers to be a political move to bolster international confidence in the quality of Chinese food and drugs after well-publicized problems surfaced with some products, including pet foods and toothpaste sold in the United States.

In "Chinese Try Mobile Death Vans" (*The Age*, March 13, 2003), Hamish McDonald notes that in 2003 eighteen mobile execution buses had been outfitted for use in Yunnan province in the southwest region of China. The buses were equipped with a bed and automatic syringe to facilitate lethal injections. Ivy Zhang, in "Death, Yunnan Style" (*Beijing Today*, March 3, 2007), states that four government officials participate in the executions: the executor, a court representative, a doctor, and an official from the procuratorate (legal supervisory organ of the state). Besides the vans being less costly for the government, McDonald indicates that one official told *Chinese Life Weekly* that the condemned prisoners prefer lethal injection to the former method, which was being shot in the head. The official said, "When they know they can't be pardoned, they accept this method calmly, and have less fear."

Japan

In *Report 2006* (2006, http://web.amnesty.org/report 2006/index-eng), the AI notes that one person was executed in Japan in 2005. According to the article "3 Executed, Bringing Total under Nagase's Watch to 10" (*Asahi Shimbun*, August 24, 2007), four convicts were hanged in December 2006, three in April 2007, and three in August 2007. The Japanese government typically reports only the number and locations of executions after they take place. It does not provide to the media the names of the executed or other information about them.

Death row inmates are forbidden from meeting with journalists and researchers collecting data on the death penalty. Any information gathered by these people usually results from significant investigations of their own. Families have limited access to the inmates, many of whom spend their days in solitary confinement.

Japan is also known for its drawn-out process of appeals. A case that drew worldwide attention involved a prisoner who, in 1997, after having been on death row for thirty years, was executed in secrecy. The inmate had committed multiple murders at age nineteen (a minor under Japanese law) but was convicted as an adult. The law requires the Ministry of Justice to carry out an execution within six months after appeals are finalized. However, according to human rights organizations, the ministry arbitrarily sets the execution date.

In "'Will This Day Be My Last?' The Death Penalty in Japan" (2007, http://asiapacific.amnesty.org/apro/APRO web.nsf/pages/appeals_japan_dp_okunishiMasaru), the AI indicates that the Japanese government does not announce impending executions or notify families and lawyers of death row inmates about scheduled executions. Even the inmate who is being put to death learns of his or her fate only about two hours before the execution. The government has been known to carry out executions when the Diet (parliament) is not in session or during holidays to avoid parliamentary debate, as reported by AI.

The AI states that many inmates have been on death row for more than thirty years, never knowing which day might be their last. According to the article "Sadamichi Hirasawa Is Dead; Was on Death Row 32 Years" (*New York Times*, May 11, 1987), the ninety-five-year-old Sadamichi Hirasawa died in 1987 while awaiting execution. He had been on death row for thirty-two years. The AI notes in "'Will This Day Be My Last?'" that in September 2003 the eighty-six-year-old Tomiyama Tsuneki died after having been on death row for thirty-nine years. The sixty-nine-year-old Hakamada Iwao had been on death row for thirty-seven years.

The South Asia Human Rights Documentation Center, in "Japan Hanging on to Death Penalty" (*Human Rights Features*, April 12, 2003), explains that Japanese law does not provide judges with the criteria needed to impose the death penalty. For example, homicide may be punishable by execution, life imprisonment, or a prison term of not less than three years.

Forum 90 is an abolitionist group that monitors capital punishment in Japan. In *The Hidden Death Penalty in Japan* (2001), which is edited by Sachiho Takahashi and Thomas Mariadason, Forum 90 reports that besides the other secret elements of the death penalty in Japan, the general public is not informed of the identities of those executed. Because Japan has no jury system, ordinary citizens find out about an execution only after the Ministry of Justice announces that it has occurred.

According to Charles Lane, in "Why Japan Still Has the Death Penalty" (*Washington Post*, January 16, 2005), the Japanese government claims that a large percentage of the public, as shown by a 1999 opinion poll, approves of the death penalty. However, experts point out that this percentage resulted from a problematic polling question. The people were asked whether they agreed that the death penalty system should be abolished in any case or whether the death penalty is necessary through unavoidable circumstances. A majority (79.3%) chose the second response. Lane notes that street crime had been on the rise in Japan and that this may have influenced support for the death penalty.

Initiatives toward abolishing the death penalty in Japan have not prevailed. In November 2002 the Japan Federation of Bar Associations called unsuccessfully for

TABLE 10.3

Countries that are abolitionist in practice, August 8, 2007

Country	Date (last execution)
Algeria	1993
Benin	1987
Brunei Darussalam	1957K
Burkina Faso	1988
Central African Republic	1981
Congo (Republic)	1982
Gabon	
Gambia	1981
Ghana	1993
Grenada	1978
Kenya	1987
Madagascar	1958K
Malawi	1992
Maldives	1952K
Mali	1980
Mauritania	1987
Morocco	1993
Myanmar	1980s
Nauru	Ind.
Niger	1976K
Papua New Guinea	1950
Russian Federation	1999
Sri Lanka	1976
Suriname	1982
Swaziland	1983
Togo	1978
Tongo	1982
Tunisia	1991
Zambia	1997

Notes: Countries that retain the death penalty for ordinary crimes such as murder but can be considered abolitionist in practice in that they have not executed anyone during the past 10 years and are believed to have a policy or established practice of not carrying out executions. The list also includes countries which have made an international commitment not to use the death penalty.
K=Date of last known execution.
Ind.=No executions since independence.

SOURCE: "Abolitionist and Retentionist Countries: Abolitionist in Practice," in *Abolitionist and Retentionist Countries*, Amnesty International, August 8, 2007, http://web.amnesty.org/web/web.nsf/print/714BB3479E3E999980256 D51005D69BE (accessed August 20, 2007)

a moratorium on the death penalty and a public debate on the issues of the death penalty system. In July 2003 the Japan Parliamentary League against the Death Penalty planned to introduce a bill to suspend executions while a commission was formed to discuss capital punishment. The opposition blocked this effort.

ABOLITIONISM IN PRACTICE

As of August 8, 2007, the AI considered twenty-nine countries as abolitionist in practice. (See Table 10.3.) These countries have death penalty laws for such crimes as murder but have not carried out an execution for the past ten years or more. Some of these nations have not executed anyone for the past fifty years or more. Others have made an international commitment not to impose the death sentence.

ABOLITIONIST COUNTRIES

In 1863 Venezuela became the first nation to outlaw the death penalty. Since that time many countries have abolished capital punishment. Several countries, however, including Argentina, Brazil, and Spain, restored it after previously rejecting it. Argentina revoked the death penalty in 1921 and in 1972 and then reinstated it in 1976 after a military takeover. Then, in 1984 it abolished capital punishment again for ordinary crimes. Brazil abolished the death penalty in 1882, restored it in 1969, and revoked it again in 1979 for ordinary crimes.

Similarly, Spain repealed the death penalty in 1932, brought it back for certain crimes in 1934, totally restored it in 1938, and then abolished it again in 1978 for ordinary crimes. In 1985 Spain outlawed the death penalty for all crimes. Such swings between banning and imposing capital punishment often reflect shifts in national government between democracy and dictatorship.

As of August 8, 2007, ninety countries had abolished the death penalty for all crimes. (See Table 10.4.) Since 1976, when the United States reinstated the death penalty after a nine-year moratorium, many countries have stopped imposing capital punishment. Belgium, the United Kingdom, and Greece, the last three west European democracies to have the death sentence, abolished it for all crimes in 1996, 1998, and 2004, respectively. In reality, Belgium has not executed any prisoner since 1950. The last two executions in the United Kingdom occurred in 1964. In 2002 Yugoslavia (now Serbia and Montenegro) and Cyprus abolished the death penalty for all crimes. Armenia shut down its death penalty system in 2003. The governments of Bhutan, Samoa, Senegal, and Turkey all announced that they abolished the death penalty for all crimes in 2004. Mexico and Liberia abolished the death penalty for all crimes in 2005. They were followed by the Philippines in 2006 and Albania and Rwanda in early 2007. (See Table 10.5 for a list of the countries that have abolished the death penalty since 1976.)

Abolitionist Countries for Ordinary Crimes Only

As of August 8, 2007, eleven countries did not impose the death penalty for ordinary crimes committed during peacetime, although they may impose it for exceptional crimes. (See Table 10.6.) Since 2000 two countries—Chile (2001) and Kyrgyzstan (2007)—have joined this group.

Capital Punishment Is Seldom Reintroduced

The AI notes in *Abolitionist and Retentionist Countries* (August 8, 2007, http://web.amnesty.org/pages/deathpenalty-countries-eng) that once a country abolishes capital punishment, it seldom brings it back. Between 1990 and August 8, 2007, just four abolitionist countries reimposed the death penalty: Nepal, the Philippines, Gambia, and Papua New Guinea. Nepal and the Philippines later reversed their positions and abolished the death penalty again. Gambia and Papua New Guinea were deemed by the AI to be abolitionist in practice, as neither had conducted an execution in over a decade.

TABLE 10.4

Countries that are abolitionist for all crimes, August 8, 2007

[Countries whose laws do not provide for the death penalty for any crime]

TABLE 10.4

Countries that are abolitionist for all crimes, August 8, 2007 [CONTINUED]

[Countries whose laws do not provide for the death penalty for any crime]

Country	Date (A)	Date (AO)	Date (last execution)
Albania	2007	2000	
Andorra	1990		1943
Angola	1992		
Armenia	2003		
Australia	1985	1984	1967
Austria	1968	1950	1950
Azerbaijan	1998		1993
Belgium	1996		1950
Bhutan	2004		1964K
Bosnia-Herzegovina	2001	1997	
Bulgaria	1998		1989
Cambodia	1989		
Canada	1998	1976	1962
Cape Verde	1981		1835
Colombia	1910		1909
Costa Rica	1877		
Cote d'Ivoire	2000		
Croatia	1990		
Cyprus	2002	1983	1962
Czech Republic	1990		
Denmark	1978	1933	1950
Djibouti	1995		Ind.
Dominican Republic	1966		
Ecuador	1906		
Estonia	1998		1991
Finland	1972	1949	1944
France	1981		1977
Georgia	1997		1994K
Germany	1987		
Greece	2004	1993	1972
Guinea-Bissau	1993		1986K
Haiti	1987		1972K
Honduras	1956		1940
Hungary	1990		1988
Iceland	1928		1830
Ireland	1990		1954
Italy	1994	1947	1947
Kiribati			Ind.
Kyrgzstan	2007		
Liberia	2005		
Liechtenstein	1987		1785
Lithuania	1998		1995
Luxembourg	1979		1949
Macedonia (Former Yug. Rep.)	1991		
Malta	2000	1971	1943
Marshall Islands			Ind.
Mauritius	1995		1987
Mexico	2005		1937
Micronesia (Federated States)			Ind.
Moldova	1995		
Monaco	1962		1847
Montenegro	2002		
Mozambique	1990		1986
Namibia	1990		1988K
Nepal	1997	1990	1979
Netherlands	1982	1870	1952
New zealand	1989	1961	1957
Nicaragua	1979		1930
Niue			
Norway	1979	1905	1948
Palau			
Panama	1922		1903K
Paraguay	1992		1928
Philippines	2006 (1987)		2000
Poland	1997		1988
Portugal	1976	1867	1849K
Romania	1989		1989
Rwanda	2007		1998
Samoa	2004		Ind.
San Marino	1865	1848	1468K
Sao Tome and Principe	1990		Ind.
Senegal	2004		1967
Serbia	2002		1992
Seychelles	1993		Ind.
Slovak Republic	1990		
Slovenia	1989		
Solomon Islands		1966	Ind.
South Africa	1997	1995	1991
Spain	1995	1978	1975
Sweden	1972	1921	1910
Switzerland	1992	1942	1944
Timor-Leste	1999		
Turkey	2004	2002	1984
Turkmenistan	1999		
Tuvalu			Ind.
Ukraine	1999		
United Kingdom	1998	1973	1964
Uruguay	1907		
Vanuatu			Ind.
Vatican City State	1969		
Venezuela	1863		

Notes: Date (A)=Date of abolition for all crimes.
Date (AO)=Date of abolition for ordinary crimes.
K=Date of last known execution.
Ind.=No executions since independence.

SOURCE: "Abolitionist and Retentionist Countries: Abolitionist for All Crimes," in *Abolitionist and Retentionist Countries*, Amnesty International, August 8, 2007, http://web.amnesty.org/web/web.nsf/print/deathpenalty-abolitionist1-eng (accessed August 20, 2007)

DEATH PENALTY AGAINST MINORS

The International Covenant on Civil and Political Rights, the UN Convention on the Rights of the Child, the African Charter on the Rights and Welfare of the Child, and the American Convention on Human Rights all ban the imposition of the death sentence on people who were less than eighteen years old at the time of their crime. In addition, the UN Convention on the Rights of the Child further prohibits the sentence of life without the possibility of parole for those younger than eighteen. Since 2000 most countries either had statutes prohibiting the execution of minors or abided by the provisions of one or another of the aforementioned treaties.

According to the AI, in "Facts and Figures on the Death Penalty," between 1990 and October 2, 2007, ten countries—Afghanistan, China, Congo (Democratic Republic), Iran, Nigeria, Pakistan, Saudi Arabia, Sudan, United States, and Yemen—executed fifty-eight offenders who were under the age of eighteen when they committed their crimes. Of these, nineteen executions occurred in the United States.

However, since 1990 several of the countries on the AI list, including the United States, have increased the age for imposition of the death penalty to eighteen. Pakistan raised the minimum age in 2000, and Yemen

TABLE 10.5

Countries that have abolished the death penalty, 1976–August 8, 2007

1976: **PORTUGAL** abolished the death penalty for all crimes.
1978: **DENMARK** abolished the death penalty for all crimes.
1979: **LUXEMBOURG, NICARAGUA** and **NORWAY** abolished the death penalty for all crimes. **BRAZIL, FIJI** and **PERU** abolished the death penalty for ordinary crimes.
1981: **FRANCE** and **CAPE VERDE** abolished the death penalty for all crimes.
1982: The **NETHERLANDS** abolished the death penalty for all crimes.
1983: **CYPRUS** and **EL SALVADOR** abolished the death penalty for ordinary crimes.
1984: **ARGENTINA** abolished the death penalty for ordinary crimes.
1985: **AUSTRALIA** abolished the death penalty for all crimes.
1987: **HAITI, LIECHTENSTEIN** and the **GERMAN DEMOCRATIC REPUBLIC**[a] abolished the death penalty for all crimes.
1989: **CAMBODIA, NEW ZEALAND, ROMANIA** and **SLOVENIA**[b] abolished the death penalty for all crimes.
1990: **ANDORRA, CROATIA**[b], the **CZECH AND SLOVAK FEDERAL REPUBLIC**[c], **HUNGARY, IRELAND, MOZAMBIQUE, NAMIBIA** and **SAO TOMÉ AND PRÍNCIPE** abolished the death penalty for all crimes.
1992: **ANGOLA, PARAGUAY** and **SWITZERLAND** abolished the death penalty for all crimes.
1993: **GUINEA-BISSAU, HONG KONG**[d] and **SEYCHELLES** abolished the death penalty for all crimes.
1994: **ITALY** abolished the death penalty for all crimes.
1995: **DJIBOUTI, MAURITIUS, MOLDOVA** and **SPAIN** abolished the death penalty for all crimes.
1996: **BELGIUM** abolished the death penalty for all crimes.
1997: **GEORGIA, NEPAL, POLAND** and **SOUTH AFRICA** abolished the death penalty for all crimes. **BOLIVIA** abolished the death penalty for ordinary crimes.
1998: **AZERBAIJAN, BULGARIA, CANADA, ESTONIA, LITHUANIA** and the **UNITED KINGDOM** abolished the death penalty for all crimes.
1999: **EAST TIMOR, TURKMENISTAN** and **UKRAINE** abolished the death penalty for all crimes. **LATVIA**[e] abolished the death penalty for ordinary crimes.
2000: **COTE D'IVOIRE** and **MALTA** abolished the death penalty for all crimes. **ALBANIA**[f] abolished the death penalty for ordinary crimes.
2001: **BOSNIA-HERZEGOVINA**[g] abolished the death penalty for all crimes. **CHILE** abolished the death penalty for ordinary crimes.
2002: **CYPRUS** and **YUGOSLAVIA** (now two states **SERBIA** and **MONTENEGRO**[h]) abolished the death penalty for all crimes.
2003: **ARMENIA** abolished the death penalty for all crimes.
2004: **BHUTAN, GREECE, SAMOA, SENEGAL** and **TURKEY** abolished the death penalty for all crimes.
2005: **LIBERIA**[i] and **MEXICO** abolished the death penalty for all crimes.
2006: **PHILIPPINES** abolished the death penalty for all crimes.
2007: **ALBANIA**[f], and **RWANDA** abolished the death penalty for all crimes. **KYRGYZSTAN** abolished the death penalty for ordinary crimes.

Notes:
[a]In 1990 the German Democratic Republic became unified with the Federal Republic of Germany, where the death penalty had been abolished in 1949.
[b]Slovenia and Croatia abolished the death penalty while they were still republics of the Socialist Federal Republic of Yugoslavia. The two republics became independent in 1991.
[c]In 1993 the Czech and Slovak Federal Republic divided into two states, the Czech Republic and Slovakia.
[d]In 1997 Hong Kong was returned to Chinese rule as a special administrative region of China. Since then Hong Kong has remained abolitionist.
[e]In 1999 the Latvian parliament voted to ratify Protocol No. 6 to the European Convention on Human Rights, abolishing the death penalty for peacetime offences.
[f]In 2007 Albania ratified Protocol No. 13 to the European Convention on Human Rights, abolishing the death penalty in all circumstances. In 2000 it had ratified Protocol No. 6 to the European Convention on Human Rights, abolishing the death penalty for peacetime offences.
[g]In 2001 Bosnia-Herzegovina ratified the Second Optional Protocol to the International Covenant on Civil and Political Rights, abolishing the death penalty for all crimes.
[h]Montenegro had already abolished the death penalty in 2002 when it was part of a state union with Serbia. It became an independent member state of the United Nations on 28 June 2006. Its ratification of Protocol No. 13 to the European Convention on Human Rights, abolishing the death penalty in all circumstances, came into effect on 6 June 2006.
[i]In 2005 Liberia ratified the Second Optional Protocol to the International Covenant on Civil and Political Rights, abolishing the death penalty for all crimes.

SOURCE: "Countries which Have Abolished the Death Penalty since 1976," in *Abolitionist and Retentionist Countries*, Amnesty International, August 8, 2007, http://web.amnesty.org/web/web.nsf/print/714BB3479E3E999980256D51005D69BE (accessed August 20, 2007)

TABLE 10.6

Countries that are abolitionist for ordinary crimes only, August 8, 2007

[Countries whose laws provide for the death penalty only for exceptional crimes such as crimes under military law or crimes committed in exceptional circumstances, such as wartime crimes]

Country	Date (AO)	Date (last execution)
Argentina	1984	
Bolivia	1997	1974
Brazil	1979	1855
Chile	2001	1985
Cook Islands		
El Salvador	1983	1973K
Fiji	1979	1964
Israel	1954	1962
Kyrgyzstan	2007	
Latvia	1999	1996
Peru	1979	1979

Notes: Date (AO)=Date of abolition for ordinary crimes.
K=Date of last known execution.

SOURCE: "Abolitionist and Retentionist Countries: Abolitionist for Ordinary Crimes Only," in *Abolitionist and Retentionist Countries*, Amnesty International, August 8, 2007, http://web.amnesty.org/pages/deathpenalty-abolitionist2-eng (accessed August 20, 2007)

followed suit in 2001. In March 2005 the U.S. Supreme Court ruled in *Roper v. Simmons* (543 U.S. 633) that executing people who committed their crimes under the age of eighteen constituted a cruel and unusual punishment. With this ruling, all states were required to stop executing minors. (See Chapter 4.)

INTERNATIONAL PUBLIC OPINION

As noted in Chapter 9, U.S. public opinion polls show that a majority of Americans favor the death penalty. Between October and December 2005 the Gallup Organization polled people in the United States, Great Britain, and Canada about capital punishment and compared the results. As shown in Figure 10.1, the highest support was reported in the United States, where 64% of respondents favored the death penalty. Surprisingly, almost half (49%) of respondents in Great Britain also expressed support for capital punishment. (Great Britain has been an abolitionist country since 1998.) Gallup found that 45% of British poll participants opposed the death penalty. Thus, supporters actually outnumbered opponents in Great Britain in 2005.

FIGURE 10.1

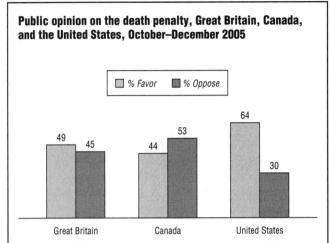

Public opinion on the death penalty, Great Britain, Canada, and the United States, October–December 2005

SOURCE: David W. Moore, "Attitudes toward Death Penalty Compared by Country," in *Death Penalty Gets Less Support from Britons, Canadians than Americans*, The Gallup Organization, February 20, 2006, http://www.galluppoll.com/content/?ci=21544&pg=1 (accessed July 24, 2007). Copyright © 2006 by The Gallup Organization. Reproduced by permission of The Gallup Organization.

FIGURE 10.2

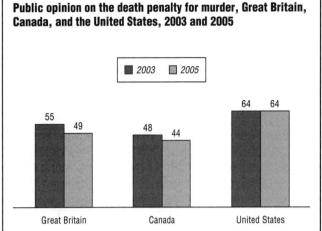

Public opinion on the death penalty for murder, Great Britain, Canada, and the United States, 2003 and 2005

SOURCE: David W. Moore, "Percentage Who Favor the Death Penalty for a Person Convicted of Murder," in *Death Penalty Gets Less Support from Britons, Canadians than Americans*, The Gallup Organization, February 20, 2006, http://www.galluppoll.com/content/?ci=21544&pg=1 (accessed July 24, 2007). Copyright © 2006 by The Gallup Organization. Reproduced by permission of The Gallup Organization.

The reverse was true in Canada. A slim majority (53%) of Canadians opposed the death penalty, compared to 44% who favored it.

Figure 10.2 compares the results from polls conducted in 2003 and 2005. Support for the death penalty declined slightly in Great Britain from 55% to 49% and in Canada from 48% to 44% between the two polls, but remained steady in the United States at 64% in both years.

The article "Death Penalty Poll Highlights" (April 26, 2007, http://abcnews.go.com/Politics/wireStory?id=3081914) reports on an Associated Press/Ipsos poll conducted in 2007 in Great Britain, Canada, France, Germany, Italy, Mexico, South Korea, Spain, and the United States. When asked whether they favored or opposed the death penalty for convicted murderers,

50% of British respondents, 45% of French respondents, 31% of Italian respondents, 28% of Spanish respondents, and 69% of American respondents voiced their support for capital punishment. However, only 34% in Great Britain, 21% in France, 16% in Italy, 12% in Spain, and 52% in the United States preferred the death penalty over prison when given a choice of sentences.

The results were much different in the non-European countries included in the survey. In Mexico 71% of those asked favored the death penalty for convicted murderers, and 46% preferred capital punishment over imprisonment. Nearly three-quarters (72%) of South Koreans expressed support for the death penalty for convicted murderers. When given a choice of sentences, only half as many favored capital punishment over imprisonment.

CHAPTER 11
THE DEBATE: CAPITAL PUNISHMENT SHOULD BE MAINTAINED

FROM TESTIMONY OF ANN SCOTT, TULSA, OKLAHOMA, BEFORE THE U.S. SENATE COMMITTEE ON THE JUDICIARY, SUBCOMMITTEE ON THE CONSTITUTION, CIVIL RIGHTS, AND PROPERTY RIGHTS, HEARING ON "AN EXAMINATION OF THE DEATH PENALTY IN THE UNITED STATES," FEBRUARY 1, 2006

Our daughter, Elaine Marie Scott, age 21, a fourth-year junior studying elementary education at the University of Oklahoma, was brutally beaten, tortured, sexually assaulted, and beaten to death by Alfred Brian Mitchell at the Pilot Recreation Center in Oklahoma City on January 7, 1991. Mitchell had just been released on his 18th birthday from Lloyd Rader Juvenile Detention Center in Sand Springs, Oklahoma. . . .

He had been locked up there for 3 years for raping a little 12-year-old girl that he dragged off from her bus stop early one morning. The Department of Human Services, DHS, could have kept him for another year, but chose not to because they couldn't help him. They needed his bed for someone that they thought that they could help, and so he came home.

Seventeen days after his release from Lloyd Rader, he beat, tortured, sexually assaulted, and beat our beautiful daughter to death using his fists and a golf club until it broke. He stabbed her in the neck five times with a compass that you would use to make circles with. And finally, he used a wooden coat tree that crushed her skull and sent shards of wood completely through her brain. She never had a chance. . . .

In June 1992, the trial finally started after preliminary hearings, many delays because of a lack of funds for expert defense witnesses, and several different dates for motion hearings. Again, and all through the trial, Mitchell smiled and laughed at the news reporters. Even when he was on the witness stand, he never admitted that he

and he alone had murdered Elaine. It took the jury one-and-a-half hours to find him guilty of murder, and 2 hours to give him the death penalty.

In 1999, there was an evidentiary hearing at the Federal court, where it was determined that the forensic chemist from the Oklahoma City Police Department had lied on the witness stand. Even though Judge Thompson from the Federal court threw out the rape charges, he upheld the death penalty because the murder itself was so heinous, atrocious, and cruel.

In July of 2000, at the Tenth Circuit Court, the judges overturned the sentence because it was felt by them that the jury might have given Mitchell a lesser punishment if the rape charge had never been presented, and so back to court we went in October of 2002 to redo the sentencing phase of the trial. After 2 weeks of listening to evidence, the case was given to the jury. It took them 5 hours, but they came back with a unanimous verdict and once again gave Mitchell the death penalty. Mitchell, true to form, stood at the elevator waiting to be taken back to prison, turned and gave our oldest son an ear-to-ear grin. He then got on the elevator and was once again taken away.

On October 11, 2005, we finally started the appeals process again with the State Court of Criminal Appeals. We have not as of this date had a decision from them, nor do we know when we will. But we will be ready to continue on and see this through to the end when it comes. . . .

Through all of this, Mitchell has never shown any remorse for his actions. If you ask if we seek retribution, yes, we do. Alfred Brian Mitchell was found guilty by two different juries of his peers. He was given the death penalty because of his crime and because it was felt that he would commit more crimes if he were ever, under any circumstances, released. I, me, I want this bully gone. I want him to disappear off the face of this earth. I want him to rot in hell for all of eternity. He is a bad seed that never should have been born. He is an animal, and when you have animals that attack people, you take them to the pound and you have them put away. What this animal has taken from us can never be returned. It has taken a lot of the love and the laughter from our home.

I have had my husband break down and sob in my arms, and I have watched his health, both mental and physical, deteriorate over the years. I have seen Elaine's two brothers struggle with life. David, the oldest, has gone through panic attacks and at times thought that he should be dead because he has outlived his sister and that is not the way it should be. I have watched Elaine's little brother clam up. To this day, Robert still cannot talk about his most favorite person in the whole wide world. His big sister is gone, taken violently from him, and he still can't deal with it. The rest of us, my husband and I, have closed ranks with our children. Even though they have grown and David is married now, we still have become more protective and we are frightened every time that they are out of sight or we don't hear from them.

Will we ever get over the murder of our daughter? Will there ever be any closure for us? I don't think so. Even after Mitchell has been executed, we will still be left with all of our wonderful memories of Elaine and all of the horror that was done to her. But perhaps once he is gone, we will be able to spend more time on the happy memories and less on thinking how her life ended. We will be at Alfred Brian Mitchell's execution. We will not rejoice, because it won't bring Elaine back. But we don't expect that it will. However, the process will finally be over and we will no longer have to spend any time or effort on pursuing justice for our daughter. Perhaps we will finally hear the remorse that so far has not been expressed. But for certain, what it will do is to ensure that he will never be able to hurt anyone ever again, and I hope and pray that you will never have to walk in our shoes.

FROM TESTIMONY OF JOHN MCADAMS, PROFESSOR OF POLITICAL SCIENCE, MARQUETTE UNIVERSITY, MILWAUKEE, WISCONSIN, BEFORE THE U.S. SENATE COMMITTEE ON THE JUDICIARY, SUBCOMMITTEE ON THE CONSTITUTION, CIVIL RIGHTS, AND PROPERTY RIGHTS, HEARING ON "AN EXAMINATION OF THE DEATH PENALTY IN THE UNITED STATES," FEBRUARY 1, 2006

One of the most compelling arguments against the death penalty, at least if one accepts the claims of the death penalty opponents at face value, is the claim that a great many innocent people have been convicted of murder and put on death row. Liberal Supreme Court Justice John Paul Stevens, just to pick one case out of hundreds, told the American Bar Association's Thurgood Marshall

Award dinner that "That evidence is profoundly significant, not only because of its relevance to the debate about the wisdom of continuing to administer capital punishment, but also because it indicates that there must be serious flaws in our administration of criminal justice."

The most widely publicized list of "innocents" is that of the Death Penalty Information Center (DPIC). As of January, 2003, it listed 122 people. That sounds like an appallingly large number, but even a casual examination of the list shows that many of the people on it got off for reasons entirely unrelated to being innocent. Back in 2001, I analyzed the list when it had ninety-five people on it. By the admission of the Death Penalty Information Center, thirty-five inmates on their list got off on procedural grounds. Another fourteen got off because a higher court believed the evidence against them was insufficient. If the higher court was right, this would be an excellent reason to release them, but it's far from proof of innocence.

Interestingly, prosecutors retried thirty-two of the inmates designated as "innocent." Apparently prosecutors believed these thirty-two were guilty. But many whom prosecutors felt to be guilty were not tried again for a variety of reasons, including the fact that key evidence had been suppressed, witnesses had died, a plea bargain was thought to be a better use of scarce resources, or the person in question had been convicted and imprisoned under another charge.

More detailed assessments of the "Innocents List" have shown that it radically overstates the number of innocent people who have been on death row. For example, the state of Florida had put on death row 24 inmates claimed, as of August 5, 2002, to be innocent by the DPIC. The resulting publicity led to a thorough examination of the twenty-four cases by the Florida Commission on Capital Crimes, which concluded that in only four of the twenty-four cases was the factual guilt of these inmates in doubt.

Examinations of the entire list have been no more favorable. For example, a liberal federal district judge in New York ruled, in *United States v. Quinones*, that the federal death penalty is unconstitutional. In this case, the court admitted that the DPIC list "may be over-inclusive" and, following its own analysis, asserted that for thirty-two of the people on the list there was evidence of "factual innocence." This hardly represents a ringing endorsement of the work of the Death Penalty Information Center. In academia, being right about a third of the time will seldom result in a passing grade.

Other assessments have been equally negative. Ward A. Campbell, Supervising Deputy Attorney General of the State of California, reviewed the list in detail, and concluded that: "... it is arguable that at least 68 of the 102 defendants on the List should not be on the list at all—leaving only 34 released defendants with claims of actual innocence—less than ½ of 1% of the 6,930 defendants sentenced to death between 1973 and 2000. . . ."

At this point, death penalty opponents will argue that it doesn't matter if their numbers are inflated. Even if only 20 or 30 innocent people have been put on death row, they will say, that is "too many" and calls for the abolition of the death penalty. If even one innocent person is executed, they claim, that would make the death penalty morally unacceptable.

This kind of rhetoric allows the speaker to feel very self-righteous, but it's not the sort of thinking that underlies sound policy analysis. Most policies have some negative consequences, and indeed often these involve the death of innocent people—something that can't be shown to have happened with the death penalty in the modern era. Just wars kill a certain number of innocent noncombatants. When the FDA approves a new drug, some people will quite likely be killed by arcane and infrequent reactions. Indeed, the FDA kills people with its laggard drug approval process. The magnitude of these consequences matters.

Death penalty opponents usually implicitly assume (but don't say so, since it would be patently absurd) that we have a choice between a flawed death penalty and a perfect system of punishment where other sanctions are concerned.

Death penalty opponents might be asked why it's acceptable to imprison people, when innocent people most certainly have been imprisoned. They will often respond that wrongfully imprisoned people can be released, but wrongfully executed people cannot be brought back to life. Unfortunately, wrongfully imprisoned people cannot be given back the years of their life that were taken from them, even though they may walk out of prison.

Perhaps more importantly, its cold comfort to say that wrongfully imprisoned people can be released, when there isn't much likelihood that that will happen. Wrongful imprisonment receives vastly less attention than wrongful death sentences, but Barry Scheck's book *Actual Innocence* lists 10 supposedly innocent defendants, of whom only 3 were sent to death row.

Currently, the Innocence Project website lists 174 persons who have been exonerated on the basis of hard DNA evidence. But the vast majority was not sentenced to death. In fact, only 15 death row inmates have been exonerated due to DNA evidence.

There is every reason to believe that the rate of error is much lower for the death penalty than for imprisonment. There is much more extensive review by higher courts, much more intensive media scrutiny, cadres of activists trying to prove innocence, and better quality

counsel at the appeals level (and increasingly at the trial level) if a case might result in execution. . . .

Death penalty opponents tend to inhabit sectors of society where claiming "racial disparity" is an effective tactic for getting what you want. In academia, the media, the ranks of activist organizations, etc. claiming "racial disparity" is an excellent strategy for getting anybody who has qualms about what you are proposing to shut up, cave in, and get out of the way.

Unfortunately, this has created a hot-house culture where arguments thrive that carry little weight elsewhere in society, and carry little weight for good reasons.

Consider the notion that, because there is racial disparity in the administration of the death penalty, it must be abolished. Applying this principle in a consistent way would be unthinkable. Suppose we find that black robbers are treated more harshly than white robbers?

Does it follow that we want to stop punishing robbers? Or does it follow that we want to properly punish white robbers also? Nobody would argue that racial inequity in punishing robbers means we have to stop punishing robbers. Nobody would claim that, if we find that white neighborhoods have better police protection than black neighborhoods that we address the inequity by withdrawing police protection from all neighborhoods. Or that racial disparity in mortgage lending requires that mortgage lending be ended. Yet people make arguments exactly like this where capital punishment is concerned. . . .

It cannot be stressed too strongly that we do not face the choice of a defective system on capital punishment and a pristine system of imprisonment. Rather, nothing about the criminal justice system works perfectly. Death penalty opponents give the impression that the death penalty is uniquely flawed by the simple expedient of dwelling on the defects of capital punishment (real and imagined) and largely ignoring the defects in the way lesser punishments are meted out.

The death penalty meets the expectations we can reasonably place on any public policy. But it can't meet the absurdly inflated standards imposed by those who are culturally hostile to it. But then, no other policy can either.

FROM TESTIMONY OF PAUL H. RUBIN, PROFESSOR OF ECONOMICS AND LAW, EMORY UNIVERSITY, ATLANTA, GEORGIA, BEFORE THE U.S. SENATE COMMITTEE ON THE JUDICIARY, SUBCOMMITTEE ON THE CONSTITUTION, CIVIL RIGHTS, AND PROPERTY RIGHTS, HEARING ON "AN EXAMINATION OF THE DEATH PENALTY IN THE UNITED STATES," FEBRUARY 1, 2006

Modern research on the economics of crime began with the work of the Nobel Prize winning economist Gary

Becker. One of Becker's arguments was that criminals should respond to incentives, where the major incentive in the criminal justice system is the probability and severity of punishment. Virtually all economists who study crime are now convinced that in the general case, this is true. An increased chance of punishment or a more severe sentence leads to reduced levels of crime. These reductions are not only due to incapacitation, but there is also a deterrent effect from increased severity and increased probability of punishment. When economists applied this argument to capital punishment, there was a political backlash, even though the theoretical grounds for believing it are the same as for any other class of punishments.

The debate in economics began with two papers by Isaac Ehrlich in the 1970s. Ehrlich, a student of Becker's, was the first to study capital punishment's deterrent effect using multi-variant regression analysis. This enabled Ehrlich to separate the effects on murder of many different factors, such as racial and age composition, the population, income, unemployment, and several other things. Ehrlich wrote two papers on capital punishment using different statistical techniques and data. Both of these found significant deterrent effects, about eight homicides deterred per execution, but the data available and the statistical methods meant that many people raised serious questions about his work and there were lots of papers using similar data and different methods and getting different results. Most of these studies suffer from flaws relative to what you can do now because of the data and the statistical methods available.

More recently, there have been 12 econometric or economic studies on capital punishment that have been conducted and published or accepted in refereed journals. Most of these studies used improved data and improved statistical techniques, various forms of multiple regression analysis, panel data analysis, and they look at things including demographics, economic factors, police effort, and so forth. They measured a marginal effect of execution. That is the effect of execution as it actually occurs given the alternatives that actually are available in the State and given that the person has already been convicted and usually sentenced. Virtually all 12 of these studies find a deterrent effect.

As I said, I was co-author of one of the studies which used 20 years of data from all U.S. counties to measure the effect of deterrent effect. Another study uses monthly data from all of the U.S. States to measure the short-term effect of capital punishment. Interestingly enough, this paper by my colleague, Joanna Shepherd, looks at different categories of murder to determine what kinds of murders are deterred by execution and she finds that all types of murders, including crimes of passion, are deterred, and she also finds that murders of both African-Americans and whites are deterred. So people raise racial questions

about the implementation of capital punishment. We don't address that, but her work does show that lives of African-Americans are saved by capital punishment.

Another study looks at the Supreme Court moratorium in the 1970s and finds that relaxing this moratorium led to fewer murders.

Other papers use different methods and data, but they all—virtually all—but all of them find a deterrent effect. Usually the numbers in the reported literature are between three and 18 homicides deterred per execution, again, depending on which kind of study you are looking at.

There is one paper that has recently been published in the *Stanford Law Review* that is critical of some of these studies. The authors find that it is possible to use various statistical manipulations to apparently eliminate some of the deterrent effect that some of the studies have found. Interestingly enough, this paper has not been subject to the scientific refereeing process. It was published in a law review, where the refereeing is done by students. It is in the process of being reexamined and it is hard to know what it will find, but even then, this paper only considers some of the empirical papers and some of the methods used. There are still many other papers that it does not consider that also find deterrent effect. So I think at this time, we have to say that the weight of the evidence is pretty clearly that there is deterrence. This is what economic theory would predict. It predicts that people respond to incentives. There is no stronger incentive than avoiding being executed. And the weight of the statistical evidence, as it exists now, is consistent with the deterrent effect.

FROM THE OPINION OF JUSTICE ANTONIN SCALIA, CONCURRING, IN *KANSAS V. MICHAEL LEE MARSH II* (548 U.S. ___), U.S. SUPREME COURT, JUNE 26, 2006

Since 1976 there have been approximately a half million murders in the United States. In that time, 7,000 murderers have been sentenced to death; about 950 of them have been executed; and about 3,700 inmates are currently on death row. As a consequence of the sensitivity of the criminal justice system to the due-process rights of defendants sentenced to death, almost two-thirds of all death sentences are overturned. "Virtually none" of these reversals, however, are attributable to a defendant's "'actual innocence.'" Most are based on legal errors that have little or nothing to do with guilt. The studies cited by the dissent demonstrate nothing more.

Like other human institutions, courts and juries are not perfect. One cannot have a system of criminal punishment without accepting the possibility that someone will be punished mistakenly. That is a truism, not a revelation. But with regard to the punishment of death in the current American system, that possibility has been reduced to an insignificant minimum. This explains why those ideologically driven to ferret out and proclaim a mistaken modern execution have not a single verifiable case to point to, whereas it is easy as pie to identify plainly guilty murderers who have been set free. The American people have determined that the good to be derived from capital punishment—in deterrence, and perhaps most of all in the meting out of condign justice for horrible crimes—outweighs the risk of error. It is no proper part of the business of this Court, or of its Justices, to second-guess that judgment, much less to impugn it before the world, and less still to frustrate it by imposing judicially invented obstacles to its execution.

FROM TESTIMONY OF WILLIAM G. OTIS, FORMER CHIEF OF THE APPELLATE DIVISION, U.S. ATTORNEY'S OFFICE, EASTERN DISTRICT OF VIRGINIA, FALLS CHURCH, VIRGINIA, BEFORE THE U.S. SENATE COMMITTEE ON THE JUDICIARY, SUBCOMMITTEE ON THE CONSTITUTION, CIVIL RIGHTS, AND PROPERTY RIGHTS, HEARING ON "OVERSIGHT OF THE FEDERAL DEATH PENALTY," JUNE 27, 2007

Today's discussion of the federal death penalty cannot be divorced from the broader national debate about capital punishment. Indeed, if anything, the federal government's death penalty procedures are widely recognized to be among the most careful and painstaking of any jurisdiction. So if the federal death penalty were to be abolished, it is difficult to see why capital punishment should exist anywhere in the country.

But it should, in federal law as elsewhere. The central reason for opposing abolition of the death penalty is that it is a one-size-fits-all proposition. It would intentionally turn a blind eye to the facts of any particular case, no matter how horrible the crime, how many victims, or how grotesque their fate. Yet more remarkably, it would refuse to consider the facts even where the typical objections to the death penalty, including those that inspire this hearing, have no application whatever. If the proposed legislation had been the law 10 years ago, for example, Timothy McVeigh would be with us today. Presumably he would still be seeking a national audience like the one he got on *Sixty Minutes* to explain why he was justified in murdering 168 of his fellow creatures, including 19 toddlers in the day care center at the Murrah Building.

It would be wrong to prohibit our juries—the conscience of our communities—from imposing the death penalty on a person like McVeigh. It would be especially wrong if it were the product of an a priori edict drafted in Washington. And to promulgate this edict on the basis of questions that might occur in some cases some of the time, but will often have nothing to do with the case at hand, would be incomprehensible. This was aptly explained by none other than Barry Scheck, the head of the Innocence

Project, who told the *Washington Post* (May 2, 2001, p. A3) that, "in McVeigh's case, 'there's no fairness issue.... There's no innocence issue. Millions of dollars were spent on his defense. You look at all the issues that normally raise concern about death penalty cases, and not one of them is present in this case, period.'" Mr. Scheck might have added explicitly what was implicit in his remarks, namely, that there was no racial issue either, a fact no serious person disputes. But today's proposed bill would have prevented McVeigh's execution, or the execution of others like him, notwithstanding the fact that the stated reasons for the bill, racial and otherwise, were entirely irrelevant to his case, and will be entire irrelevant to dozens if not hundreds of future cases.

Some will say it's unfair in the context of this hearing to use McVeigh as an example, but that is not so. There is nothing "unfair" in discussing at a hearing about the death penalty one compelling illustration of why we should keep it. Beyond that, McVeigh is fairly representative. Over the last 50 years, two-thirds of those executed by the federal government have been, like McVeigh, white. This largely mirrors the national experience: Since the death penalty was reinstated by the Supreme Court in 1976, nearly three-fifths of executed criminals have been white.

We understand all too well that al-Qaeda terrorists have butchered innocents across the globe, from Madrid to London to New York and Arlington. If today's proposed legislation becomes law, the federal government's ability even to ask a jury to consider the death penalty for terrorists will cease to exist, even if Osama bin Laden himself is in the dock. Millions of Americans would consider that an outrage, and a huge majority would consider it unjust. It is noteworthy that a majority of even those who in general oppose the death penalty thought it was appropriate for our domestic terrorist, Timothy McVeigh (*USA Today*/CNN/Gallup poll, published in *USA Today*, May 4, 2001, pp. A1–A2). All told, slightly more than 80% of the public thought the death penalty was right in that case. This bill would tell that 80% that, unbeknownst to them, their views are the stalking horse of racism. But that is not true, and it is not the American public I came to know in my years as a prosecutor. We are a fair-minded and conscientious people. When the moral compass of 80% of our fellow citizens says that the death penalty should be imposed, as it did for McVeigh and will for Osama and others, it is not for Congress to tell them—as this bill would—that their sense of justice doesn't count.

To preserve our country's heritage that justice must turn on the facts of each case individually considered, I respectfully submit that federal juries should continue to have discretion, acting out of conscience in egregious cases, to impose the death penalty.

FROM TESTIMONY OF DAVID B. MUHLHAUSEN, SENIOR POLICY ANALYST, CENTER FOR DATA ANALYSIS, HERITAGE FOUNDATION, WASHINGTON, D.C., BEFORE THE U.S. SENATE COMMITTEE ON THE JUDICIARY, SUBCOMMITTEE ON THE CONSTITUTION, CIVIL RIGHTS, AND PROPERTY RIGHTS, HEARING ON "OVERSIGHT OF THE FEDERAL DEATH PENALTY," JUNE 27, 2007

While opponents of capital punishment have been very vocal in their opposition, Gallup opinion polls consistently demonstrate that the American public overwhelmingly supports capital punishment. In Gallup's most recent poll, 67 percent of Americans favor the death penalty for those convicted of murder, while only 28 percent are opposed. From 2000 to the most recent poll in 2006, support for capital punishment consistently runs a 2:1 ratio in favor.

Despite strong public support for capital punishment, federal, state, and local officials must continually ensure that its implementation rigorously upholds constitutional protections, such as due process and equal protection of the law. However, the criminal process should not be abused to prevent the lawful imposition of the death penalty in appropriate capital cases.

As of December 2005, there were 37 prisoners under a sentence of death in the federal system. Of these prisoners, 43.2 percent were white, while 54.1 percent were African-American. The fact that African-Americans are a majority of federal prisoners on death row and a minority in the overall United States population may lead some to conclude that the federal system discriminates against African-Americans. However, there is little rigorous evidence that such disparities exist in the federal system.

Under a competitive grant process, the National Institute of Justice awarded the RAND Corporation a grant to determine whether racial disparities exist in the federal death penalty system. The resulting 2006 RAND study set out to determine what factors, including the defendant's race, victim's race, and crime characteristics, affect the decision to seek a death penalty case. Three independent teams of researchers were tasked with developing their own methodologies to analyze the data. Only after each team independently drew their own conclusions did they share their findings with each other.

When first looking at the raw data without controlling for case characteristics, RAND found that large race effects with the decision to seek the death penalty are more likely to occur when the defendants are white and when the victims are white. However, these disparities disappeared in each of the three studies when the heinousness of the crimes was taken into account. The RAND study concludes that the findings support the view that decisions to seek the death penalty are driven by

characteristics of crimes rather than by race. RAND's findings are very compelling because three independent research teams, using the same data but different methodologies, reached the same conclusions.

While there is little evidence that the federal capital punishment system treats minorities unfairly, some may argue that the death penalty systems in certain states may be discriminatory. One such state is Maryland. In May 2001, then-Governor Parris Glendening instituted a moratorium on the use of capital punishment in Maryland in light of concerns that it may be unevenly applied to minorities, especially African-Americans. In 2000, Governor Glendening commissioned University of Maryland Professor of Criminology Ray Paternoster to study the possibility of racial discrimination in the application of the death penalty in Maryland. The results of Professor Paternoster's study found that black defendants who murder white victims are substantially more likely to be charged with a capital crime and sentenced to death.

In 2003, Governor Robert L. Ehrlich wisely lifted the moratorium. His decision was justified. In 2005, a careful review of the study by Professor of Statistics and Sociology Richard Berk of the University of California, Los Angeles, and his coauthors found that the results of Professor Paternoster's study do not stand up to statistical scrutiny. According to Professor Berk's re-analysis, "For both capital charges and death sentences, race either played no role or a small role that is very difficult to specify. In short, it is very difficult to find convincing evidence for racial effects in the Maryland data and if there are any, they may not be additive." Further, race may have a small influence because "cases with a black defendant and white victim or 'other' racial combination are less likely to have a death sentence."

Federal, state, and local officials need to recognize that the death penalty saves lives. How capital punishment affects murder rates can be explained through general deterrence theory, which supposes that increasing the risk of apprehension and punishment for crime deters individuals from committing crime. Nobel laureate Gary S. Becker's seminal 1968 study of the economics of crime assumed that individuals respond to the costs and benefits of committing crime.

According to deterrence theory, criminals are no different from law-abiding people. Criminals "rationally maximize their own self-interest (utility) subject to constraints (prices, incomes) that they face in the marketplace and elsewhere." Individuals make their decisions based on the net costs and benefits of each alternative. Thus, deterrence theory provides a basis for analyzing how capital punishment should influence murder rates. Over the years, several studies have demonstrated a link between executions and decreases in murder rates. In fact, studies done in recent years, using sophisticated panel data methods, consistently demonstrate a strong link between executions and reduced murder incidents.

The rigorous examination of the deterrent effect of capital punishment began with research in the 1970s by Isaac Ehrlich, currently a University of Buffalo Distinguished Professor of Economics. Professor Ehrlich's research found that the death penalty had a strong deterrent effect. While his research was debated by other scholars, additional research by Professor Ehrlich reconfirmed his original findings. In addition, research by Professor Stephen K. Layson of the University of North Carolina at Greensboro strongly reconfirmed Ehrlich's previous findings.

Numerous studies published over the past few years, using panel data sets and sophisticated social science techniques, are demonstrating that the death penalty saves lives. Panel studies observe multiple units over several periods. The addition of multiple data collection points gives the results of capital punishment panel studies substantially more credibility than the results of studies that have only single before-and-after intervention measures. Further, the longitudinal nature of the panel data allows researchers to analyze the impact of the death penalty over time that cross-sectional data sets cannot address.

Using a panel data set of over 3,000 counties from 1977 to 1996, Professors Hashem Dezhbakhsh, Paul R. Rubin, and Joanna M. Shepherd of Emory University found that each execution, on average, results in 18 fewer murders. Using state-level panel data from 1960 to 2000, Professors Dezhbakhsh and Shepherd were able to compare the relationship between executions and murder incidents before, during, and after the U.S. Supreme Court's death penalty moratorium. They found that executions had a highly significant negative relationship with murder incidents. Additionally, the implementation of state moratoria is associated with the increased incidence of murders.

Separately, Professor Shepherd's analysis of monthly data from 1977 to 1999 found three important findings.

First, each execution, on average, is associated with three fewer murders. The deterred murders included both crimes of passion and murders by intimates.

Second, executions deter the murder of whites and African-Americans. Each execution prevents the murder of one white person, 1.5 African-Americans, and 0.5 persons of other races.

Third, shorter waits on death row are associated with increased deterrence. For each additional 2.75-year reduction in the death row wait until execution, one murder is deterred.

Professors H. Naci Mocan and R. Kaj Gittings of the University of Colorado at Denver have published two studies confirming the deterrent effect of capital punishment. The first study used state-level data from 1977 to 1997 to analyze the influence of executions, commutations, and removals from death row on the incidence of murder. For each additional execution, on average, about five murders were deterred. Alternatively, for each additional commutation, on average, five additional murders resulted. A removal from death row by either state courts or the U.S. Supreme Court is associated with an increase of one additional murder. Addressing criticism of their work, Professors Mocan and Gittings conducted additional analyses and found that their original findings provided robust support for the deterrent effect of capital punishment.

Two studies by Paul R. Zimmerman, a Federal Communications Commission economist, also support the deterrent effect of capital punishment. Using state-level data from 1978 to 1997, Zimmerman found that each additional execution, on average, results in 14 fewer murders. Zimmerman's second study, using similar data, found that executions conducted by electrocution are the most effective at providing deterrence.

Using a small state-level data set from 1995 to 1999, Professor Robert B. Ekelund of Auburn University and his colleagues analyzed the effect that executions have on single incidents of murder and multiple incidents of murder. They found that executions reduced single murder rates, while there was no effect on multiple murder rates.

In summary, the recent studies using panel data techniques have confirmed what we learned decades ago: Capital punishment does, in fact, save lives. Each additional execution appears to deter between three and 18 murders. While opponents of capital punishment allege that it is unfairly used against African-Americans, each additional execution deters the murder of 1.5 African-Americans. Further moratoria, commuted sentences, and death row removals appear to increase the incidence of murder.

CHAPTER 12
THE DEBATE: CAPITAL PUNISHMENT SHOULD BE ABOLISHED

FROM TESTIMONY OF VICKI A. SCHIEBER, CHEVY CHASE, MARYLAND, BEFORE THE U.S. SENATE COMMITTEE ON THE JUDICIARY, SUBCOMMITTEE ON THE CONSTITUTION, CIVIL RIGHTS, AND PROPERTY RIGHTS, HEARING ON "AN EXAMINATION OF THE DEATH PENALTY IN THE UNITED STATES," FEBRUARY 1, 2006

I am the mother of a murder victim and I serve on the board of directors of Murder Victims' Families for Human Rights (MVFHR), a national non-profit organization of people who have lost a family member to murder or state execution and who oppose the death penalty in all cases. There are MVFHR members in every state.

Discussions of the death penalty typically focus on the offender, the person convicted of murder. My focus, and the focus of those whom I am representing through this testimony, is on the victims of murder and their surviving families.

Losing a beloved family member to murder is a tragedy of unimaginable proportions. The effects on the family and even on the wider community extend well beyond the initial shock and trauma. The common assumption in this country is that families who have suffered this kind of loss will support the death penalty. That assumption is so widespread and so unquestioned that a prosecutor will say to a grieving family, "We will seek the death penalty in order to seek justice for your family." A lawmaker introduces a bill to expand the application of the death penalty and announces that he is doing this "to honor victims." A politician believes that she must run on a pro-death penalty platform or risk being labeled soft on crime and thus unconcerned about victims.

As a victim's family member who opposes the death penalty, I represent a growing and for the most part under-served segment of the crime victim population. Along with the other members of MVFHR, I have come to believe that the death penalty is not what will help me heal. Responding to one killing with another killing does not honor my daughter, nor does it help create the kind of society I want to live in, where human life and human rights are valued. I know that an execution creates another grieving family, and causing pain to another family does not lessen my own pain....

My husband and I were both raised in homes with a deep-seated religious faith. We were both raised in households where hatred was never condoned and where the ultimate form of hate was thought to be the deliberate taking of another person's life. The death penalty involves the deliberate, premeditated killing of another human being. In carrying forward the principles with which my husband and I were raised, and with which we raised our daughter, we cannot in good conscience support the killing of anyone, even the murderer of our own daughter, if such a person could be imprisoned without parole and thereby no longer a danger to society.

No one should infer from our opposition to the death penalty that we did not want Shannon's murderer caught, prosecuted, and put away for the remainder of his life. We believe he is where he belongs today, as he serves his prison sentence, and we rest assured that he will never again perpetrate his sort of crime on any other young women. But killing this man would not bring our daughter back. And it was very clear to us that killing him would have been partly dependent on our complicity in having it done. Had we bent to this natural inclination, however, it would have put us on essentially the same footing as the murderer himself: willing to take someone else's life to satisfy our own ends. That was a posture we were not willing to assume.

In my work with Murder Victims' Families for Human Rights, I have come to know several survivors of people who have been put to death by execution. Seeing the effects of an execution in the family, particularly the effects on children, raises questions for me about the short- and long-term social costs of the death penalty. What kind of message do we convey to young people when we tell them that killing another human being is wrong but then impose the death penalty on someone with whom they have some direct or indirect relationship? Isn't there the possibility that the imposition of the death penalty sends a conflicted message about our society's respect for life? Isn't it possible that the potentially biased application of the death penalty in certain racial contexts distorts the fundamental principles on which this nation was founded? Isn't it possible that the bitterness that arises out of this causes more social problems than it solves?

I remember when, back in 2001, then Attorney General John Ashcroft decided that family members of the Oklahoma City bombing victims should be allowed to witness the execution of Timothy McVeigh on closed-circuit television. His argument was that the experience would "meet their need for closure." The word closure is invoked so frequently in discussions of victims and the death penalty that victims' family members jokingly refer to it as "the c word." But I can tell you with all seriousness that there is no such thing as closure when a violent crime rips away the life of someone dear to you. As my husband and I wander through the normal things that we all do in our daily lives, we see constant reminders of Shannon and what we have lost. Killing Shannon's murderer would not stop the unfolding of the world around us with its constant reminders of unfulfilled hopes and dreams.

Indeed, linking closure for victims' families with the execution of the offender is problematic for two additional reasons: first, the death penalty is currently applied to only about one percent of convicted murderers in this country. If imposition of that penalty is really necessary for victims' families, then what of the 99% who are not offered it? Second, and even more critical from a policy perspective, a vague focus on executions as the potential source of closure for families too often shifts the focus away from other steps that could be taken to honor victims and to help victims' families in the aftermath of murder.

We have chosen to honor our daughter by setting up several memorials in her name—a scholarship at Duke University, and an endowment fund to replace roofs on inner city homes through the Rebuilding Together program in poor sections of our community, to name two. We also believe that we honor her by working to abolish the death penalty, because, for my husband and for me, working to oppose the death penalty is a way of working to create a world in which life is valued and in which our chief goal is to reduce violence rather than to perpetuate it.

FROM TESTIMONY OF STEPHEN B. BRIGHT, SOUTHERN CENTER FOR HUMAN RIGHTS, ATLANTA, GEORGIA, BEFORE THE U.S. SENATE COMMITTEE ON THE JUDICIARY, SUBCOMMITTEE ON THE CONSTITUTION, CIVIL RIGHTS, AND PROPERTY RIGHTS, HEARING ON "AN EXAMINATION OF THE DEATH PENALTY IN THE UNITED STATES," FEBRUARY 1, 2006

This is a most appropriate time to assess the costs and benefits of the death penalty. Thirty years ago, in 1976, the Supreme Court allowed the resumption of capital punishment after declaring it unconstitutional four years earlier in *Furman v. Georgia*. Laws passed in response to *Furman* were supposed to correct the constitutional defects identified in 1972.

However, 30 years of experience has demonstrated that those laws have failed to do so. The death penalty is still arbitrary. It's still discriminatory. It is still imposed almost exclusively upon poor people represented by court-appointed lawyers. In many cases the capabilities of the lawyer have more to do with whether the death penalty is imposed than the crime. The system is still fallible in deciding both guilt and punishment. In addition, the death penalty is costly and is not accomplishing anything. And it is beneath a society that has a reverence for life and recognizes that no human being is beyond redemption.

Many supporters of capital punishment, after years of struggling to make the system work, have had sober second thoughts it. Justice Sandra Day O'Connor, who leaves the Supreme Court after 25 years of distinguished service, has observed that "serious questions are being raised about whether the death penalty is being fairly administered in this country" and that "the system may well be allowing some innocent defendants to be executed."

Justices Lewis Powell and Harry Blackmun also voted to uphold death sentences as members of the court, but eventually came to the conclusion, as Justice Blackmun put it, that "the death penalty experiment has failed."

The *Birmingham News* announced in November that after years of supporting the death penalty it could no longer do so "[b]ecause we have come to believe Alabama's capital punishment system is broken. And because, first and foremost, this newspaper's editorial board is committed to a culture of life." The editorial is appended to this statement.

The death penalty is not imposed to avenge every murder and—as some contend—to bring "closure" to the family of every victim. There were over 20,000 murders in 14 of the last 30 years and 15,000 to 20,000 in the others. During that time, there have been just over 1,000 executions—an average of about 33 a year. Sixteen states carried out 60 executions last year. Twelve states carried out 59 executions in 2004, and 12 states put 65 people to death in 2003.

Moreover, the death penalty is not evenly distributed around the country. Most executions take place in the South, just as they did before *Furman*. Between 1935 and 1972, the South carried out 1,887 executions; no other region had as many as 500. Since 1976, the Southern states have carried out 822 of 1,000 executions; states in the Midwest have carried out 116; states in the west 64 and the Northeastern states have carried out only four. The federal government, which has had the death penalty since 1988, has executed three people. Only one state, Texas, has executed over 100 people since 1976. It has executed over 350.

Further experimentation with a lethal punishment after centuries of failure has no place in a conservative society that is wary of too much government power and skeptical of government's ability to do things well. We are paying an enormous cost in money and the credibility of the system in order to execute people who committed less than one percent of the murders that occur each year. The death penalty is not imposed for all murders, for most murders, or even for the most heinous murders. It is imposed upon a random handful of people convicted of murder—often because of factors such [as] the political interests and predilections of prosecutors, the quality of the lawyer appointed to defend the accused, and the race of the victim and the defendant. A fairer system would be to have a lottery of all people convicted of murder; draw 60 names and execute them.

Further experimentation might be justified if it served some purpose. But capital punishment is not needed to protect society or to punish offenders. We have not only maximum security prisons, but "super maximum" prisons where prisoners are completely isolated from guards and other inmates, as well as society....

Supreme Court Justice Arthur Goldberg said that the deliberate institutionalized taking of human life by the state is the greatest degradation of the human personality imaginable. It is not just degrading to the individual who is tied down and put down. It is degrading to the society that carries it out. It coarsens the society, takes risks with the lives of the poor, and diminishes its respect for life and its belief in the possible redemption of every person. It is a relic of another era. Careful examination will show that the death penalty is not serving any purpose in our society and is not worth the cost.

FROM TESTIMONY OF JEFFREY FAGAN, PROFESSOR OF LAW AND PUBLIC HEALTH, COLUMBIA UNIVERSITY, NEW YORK CITY, NEW YORK, BEFORE THE U.S. SENATE COMMITTEE ON THE JUDICIARY, SUBCOMMITTEE ON THE CONSTITUTION, CIVIL RIGHTS, AND PROPERTY RIGHTS, HEARING ON "AN EXAMINATION OF THE DEATH PENALTY IN THE UNITED STATES," FEBRUARY 1, 2006

Recent studies claiming that executions reduce murders have fueled the revival of deterrence as a rationale to expand the use of capital punishment. Such strong claims are not unusual in either the social or natural sciences, but like nearly all claims of strong causal effects from any social or legal intervention, the claims of a "new deterrence" fall apart under close scrutiny. These new studies are fraught with numerous technical and conceptual errors: inappropriate methods of statistical analysis, failures to consider all the relevant factors that drive murder rates, missing data on key variables in key states, the tyranny of a few outlier states and years, weak to nonexistent tests of concurrent effects of incarceration, statistical confounding of murder rates with death sentences, failure to consider the general performance of the criminal justice system, artifactual results from truncated time frames, and the absence of any direct test of deterrence. These studies fail to reach the demanding standards of social science to make such strong claims, standards such as replication, responding to counterfactual claims, and basic comparisons with other causal scenarios. Social scientists have failed to replicate several of these studies, and in some cases have produced contradictory results with the same data, suggesting that the original findings are unstable, unreliable and perhaps inaccurate. This evidence, together with some simple examples and contrasts including the experience in my state of New York, suggest extreme caution before concluding that there is new evidence that the death penalty deters murders.

The costs of capital punishment are extremely high. Even in states where prosecutors infrequently seek the death penalty, costs of obtaining convictions and executions in capital cases range from $2.5 to $5 million per case (in current dollars), compared to less than $1 million for each killer sentenced to life without parole. Local governments bear the burden of these costs, diverting $2 million per capital trial from local services—hospitals and health care, police and public safety, and education—or infrastructure repairs—roads and other capital expenditures—and causing counties to borrow money or raise local taxes. The costs are often transferred to state governments as "risk pools" or programs of local assistance to prosecute death penalty cases, diffusing death penalty costs to counties that choose not to use—or have no need for—the death penalty in capital cases.

The high costs of the death penalty, the unreliable evidence of its deterrent effects, and the fact that the states that execute the most people also have the highest error rates, create clear public policy choices for the nation. If a state is going to spend $500 million on law enforcement over the next two decades, is the best use of that money to buy two or three executions or, for example, to fund additional police detectives, prosecutors, and judges to arrest and incarcerate murderers and other criminals who currently escape any punishment because of insufficient law-enforcement resources?

Also, most states rarely use the death penalty, and both death sentences and executions have declined sharply over the past five years, even as murder rates have declined nationally. We cannot expect the rare use of the death penalty to have a deterrent effect on already declining rates of murder. Justice White noted long ago in *Furman v. Georgia* that when only a tiny proportion of the individuals who commit murder are executed, the penalty is unconstitutionally irrational: a death penalty that is almost never used serves no deterrent function, because no would-be murderer can expect to be executed.

Accordingly, a threshold question for state legislatures across the country is whether their necessary and admirable efforts to avoid error and the horror of the execution of the innocent won't—after many hundreds of millions of dollars of trying—burden the state with a death penalty that will be overturned again because of this additional constitutional problem?

FROM STATEMENT OF SENATOR RUSS FEINGOLD OF WISCONSIN ON INTRODUCTION OF S. 447, THE "FEDERAL DEATH PENALTY ABOLITION ACT OF 2007," ON JANUARY 31, 2007, IN THE U.S. SENATE, WASHINGTON, D.C.

Mr. President, today I am introducing the Federal Death Penalty Abolition Act of 2007. This bill would abolish the death penalty at the Federal level. It would put an immediate halt to executions and forbid the imposition of the death penalty as a sentence for violations of Federal law.

Since 1976, when the death penalty was reinstated by the Supreme Court, there have been 1,060 executions across the country, including three at the Federal level. During that same time period, 123 people on death row have been exonerated and released from death row. These people never should have been convicted in the first place.

Consider those numbers. One thousand and sixty executions, and 123 exonerations in the modern death penalty era. Had those exonerations not taken place, had those 123 people been executed, those executions would have represented an error rate of greater than 10 percent. That is more than an embarrassing statistic; it is a horrifying one, one that should have us all questioning the use of capital punishment in this country. In fact, since 1999 when I first introduced this bill, 46 death row inmates have been exonerated throughout the country.

In the face of these numbers, the national debate on the death penalty has intensified. For the second year in a row, the number of executions, the number of death sentences imposed, and the size of the death row population have decreased as a growing number of voices have joined to express doubt about the use of capital punishment in America. The voices of those questioning the fairness of the death penalty have been heard from college campuses and courtrooms and podiums across the Nation, to the Senate Judiciary Committee hearing room, to the United States Supreme Court. The American public understands that the death penalty raises serious and complex issues. The death penalty can no longer be exploited for political purposes. In fact, for the first time, a May 2006 Gallup Poll reported that more Americans prefer a sentence of life without parole over the death penalty when given a choice. If anything, the political consensus is that it is time for a change. We must not ignore these voices.

In the wake of the Supreme Court's decision in 1976 to allow capital punishment, the Federal Government first resumed death penalty prosecutions after enactment of a 1988 Federal law that provided for the death penalty for murder in the course of a drug-kingpin conspiracy. The Federal death penalty was then expanded significantly in 1994, when the omnibus crime bill expanded its use to a total of some 60 Federal offenses. And despite my best efforts to halt the expansion of the Federal death penalty, more and more provisions seem to be added every year. While the use of and confidence in the death penalty is decreasing overall, the Federal Government has been going in the opposite direction, making more defendants eligible for capital punishment and increasing the size of its Federal death row. Moreover, there are now six individuals on Federal death row from States that do not have capital punishment. The Federal Government is pulling in the wrong direction as the rest of the Nation moves toward a more just system.

… Years of study have shown that the death penalty does little to deter crime, and that defendants' likelihood of being sentenced to death depends heavily on illegitimate factors such as whether they are rich or poor. Since reinstatement of the modern death penalty, 80 percent of murder victims in cases where death sentences were handed down were white, even though only 50 percent of murder victims are white. Nationwide, more than half of the death row inmates are African Americans or Hispanic Americans. There is evidence of racial disparities, inadequate counsel, prosecutorial misconduct, and false scientific evidence in death penalty systems across the country.

At least Maryland, Illinois, North Carolina, and California have begun the process of investigating the flaws in their own systems. But there are 36 other States that have death penalty provisions in their laws, 36 other States with systems that are most likely plagued with the same flaws. And these systems come at great additional cost to the taxpayers. For example, a 2005 report found that California's death penalty system costs taxpayers $114 million in additional costs each year. Similar reports detailing the extraordinary financial costs of the death penalty have been generated for States across the Nation.

Moreover, there are growing concerns about the most common method of execution, lethal injection. These concerns are so grave that eight States and the Federal system all halted individual executions in 2006 to work through these problems. And these numbers are growing. Just this last week, executions in North Carolina were halted because of challenges to lethal injection. More and more research is emerging that suggests that lethal injections are unnecessarily painful and cruel, and that this method of capital punishment—however sanitary or humane it may appear—is no less barbaric than the more antiquated methods lethal injection was designed to replace, such as the noose or the firing squad, no less horrific than the electric chair or the gas chamber.

Nothing is more barbaric, of course, than the execution of an innocent person, and it is clearer than ever that the risk is very real. Already, information has surfaced that suggests that two men put to death in the 1990s may have been innocent. This is a chilling prospect, one that illustrates the very grave danger in imposing the death penalty. The loss of just one innocent life through capital punishment should be enough to force all of us to stop and reconsider this penalty.

And while we examine the flaws in our death penalty system, we cannot help but note that our use of the death penalty stands in stark contrast to the majority of nations, which have abolished the death penalty in law or practice. There are now 123 countries that have done so. In 2005, only China, Iran, and Saudi Arabia executed more people than we did. These countries, and others on the list of nations that actively use capital punishment, are countries that we often criticize for human rights abuses. The European Union denies membership in the alliance to those nations that use the death penalty. In fact, it passed a resolution calling for the immediate and unconditional global abolition of the death penalty, and it specifically called on all States within the United States to abolish the death penalty. This is significant because it reflects the unanimous view of a group of nations with which the United States enjoys close relationships and shares common values. We should join with them and with the over 100 other nations that have renounced this practice.

We are a Nation that prides itself on the fundamental principles of justice, liberty, equality and due process. We are a Nation that scrutinizes the human rights records of other nations. Historically, we are one of the first Nations to speak out against torture and killings by foreign governments. We should hold our own system of justice to the highest standard.

As a matter of justice, this is an issue that transcends political allegiances. A range of prominent voices in our country are raising serious questions about the death penalty, and they are not just voices of liberals, or of the faith community. They are the voices of former FBI Director William Sessions, former Justice Sandra Day O'Connor, Reverend Pat Robertson, George Will, former Mississippi warden Donald Cabana, the Republican former Governor of Illinois, George Ryan, and the Democratic former Governor of Maryland, Parris Glendening. The voices of those questioning our application of the death penalty are growing in number, they are growing louder, and they are reflected in some of the decisions of the highest court of the land. In recent years, the Supreme Court has held that the execution of juvenile offenders and the mentally retarded is unconstitutional.

As we begin a new year and a new Congress, I believe the continued use of the death penalty in the United States is beneath us. The death penalty is at odds with our best traditions. It is wrong and it is immoral. The adage "two wrongs do not make a right," applies here in the most fundamental way. Our Nation has long ago done away with other barbaric punishments like whipping and cutting off the ears of criminals. Just [as] we did away with these punishments as contrary to our humanity and ideals, it is time to abolish the death penalty as we seek to spread peace and justice both here and overseas. It is not just a matter of morality. The continued viability of our criminal justice system as a truly just system that deserves the respect of our own people and the world requires that we do so. Our Nation's goal to remain the world's leading defender of freedom, liberty and equality demands that we do so.

FROM TESTIMONY OF HILARY O. SHELTON, DIRECTOR OF THE NATIONAL ASSOCIATION FOR THE ADVANCEMENT OF COLORED PEOPLE, WASHINGTON BUREAU, WASHINGTON, D.C., BEFORE THE U.S. SENATE COMMITTEE ON THE JUDICIARY, SUBCOMMITTEE ON THE CONSTITUTION, CIVIL RIGHTS, AND PROPERTY RIGHTS, HEARING ON "OVERSIGHT OF THE FEDERAL DEATH PENALTY," JUNE 27, 2007

The NAACP remains resolutely opposed to the death penalty....

From the days of slavery, through years of lynchings and Jim Crow laws, and even today capital punishment has always been deeply affected by race. This is true among the states as well as at the federal level. Despite the fact that African Americans make up only 13% of our Nation's population, almost 50% of those who currently sit on the federal death row are African American.

Furthermore, across the Nation about 80% of the victims in the underlying murder in death penalty cases are white, while less than 50% of murder victims overall are white. This statistic implies that white lives are valued more than those of racial or ethnic minorities in our criminal justice system.

Finally, the NAACP is very concerned about the number of people who have been exonerated since being placed on death row. Since 1973, over 120 people have been released from death row with evidence of their innocence. The death penalty is the ultimate punishment, one that is impossible to reverse in light of new evidence.

The American criminal justice system has been historically, and remains today, deeply and disparately impacted by race. It is difficult for African Americans to have confidence in or be willing to work with an institution that is fraught with racism. And the fact that African Americans are so overrepresented on death row is alarming and disturbing, and certainly a critical element that leads to the distrust that exists in the African American community of our Nation's criminal justice system.

It bears repeating that 49% of all the people, or almost half of all those currently sitting on the federal death row, are African American. Perhaps more disturbing is the fact that nobody at the Department of Justice can conclusively say that race is not a factor in determining which defendants are to be tried in federal death penalty cases.

According to the DoJ's own figures, 48% of the defendants in federal cases in which the death penalty was sought between 2001 and 2006 were African Americans.

What we don't know, unfortunately, is whether or not this number is representative of the number of criminal defendants who are accused of crimes in which the death penalty may be sought. And, since there are several layers that must be examined to even begin to assess this number, including whether a crime is tried at the local or federal level, it is not an easy number to attain.

What is clear, though, is that at several different points in the process of determining who is tried in a federal death penalty case and who is not, a judgment is made by human beings in a process in which not everyone has similar views. And in a world in which 98% of the chief district attorneys in death penalty states are white and only 1% are black, it is this differential that gives us the most problem.

In addition to the factor of the race of the defendants, the NAACP is also deeply troubled by the role played in the race of the victim. Although at the federal level the weight of the victim's race appears to have changed over the last few years, at the state level the race of the victim still appears to play a big role. According to the Death Penalty Information Center, 79% of the murder victims in cases resulting in an execution were white, even though nationally only 50% of murder victims overall were white. A recent study in California found that those who killed whites were over 3 times more likely to be sentenced to death than those who killed African Americans and more than 4 times more likely than those who

killed Latinos. Another study in North Carolina found that the odds of receiving a death sentence rose by 3.5 times among defendants whose victims were white.

These studies, along with the fluctuations we see in all death penalty jurisdictions including the federal government, speak again to the varying factors involved in determining who is eligible for the death penalty and who is not. The overwhelming evidence that a defendant is more likely to be executed if the victim is white is also incredibly problematic; it sends a message that in our criminal justice system, white lives are more valuable than those of racial or ethnic minorities.

Obviously with race being so problematic and such an overwhelming factor in the application of the death penalty, the NAACP is also concerned that there be no room for error. Yet errors do occur, even today. Nationally, more than 120 people have been exonerated and freed from death row before they could be executed. Given the finality of the death sentence under which these people were living, they may in fact be considered the "lucky ones." Furthermore, considering the disparities in the number of African Americans on death row, it is likely that more African Americans are falsely executed, a fact that once again contributes to the mistrust that is endemic among the African American community of the American criminal justice system.

FROM TESTIMONY OF ANÍBAL ACEVEDO VILÁ, GOVERNOR OF THE COMMONWEALTH OF PUERTO RICO, BEFORE THE U.S. SENATE COMMITTEE ON THE JUDICIARY, SUBCOMMITTEE ON THE CONSTITUTION, CIVIL RIGHTS, AND PROPERTY RIGHTS, HEARING ON "OVERSIGHT OF THE FEDERAL DEATH PENALTY," JUNE 27, 2007

The Commonwealth favors the elimination of death as a form of punishment by the federal government.

At the outset, we would like to express our institutional rejection of the death penalty as a form of punishment for criminal activity. As a democratic and developed society, we should aspire to have laws and a criminal justice system premised on higher principles that demonstrate an absolute respect for human life, even for the life of a murderer. I believe that an overwhelming majority of Americans would strongly disapprove—and would most likely not even consider seriously debating the possibility of—implementing the state-sanctioned torture of a torturer or rape of a rapist as forms of punishment. I see no reason why the moral calculus should vary when considering the state-sanctioned killing of a killer. Taking the life of a murderer is a similarly disproportionate punishment.

In addition, the uniqueness of death as punishment, in that it is irrevocable, should give any government pause. Because no human system can be free of error, that system must provide reasonable reparation for the victims of mistakes. However, because of the irrevocability of death, victims of wrongful executions cannot obtain such reparation. Simply put, once an inmate is executed, nothing can be done to make amends if a mistake has been made.

Moreover, the possibility of mistakes in the application of the death penalty is not theoretical; in fact, the evidence suggests it is not even remote. There is considerable evidence that an alarming number of persons have been incorrectly sentenced to death by various jurisdictions within the United States. For example, a study conducted at the Columbia University School of Law found that the overall national rate of prejudicial error in capital cases was 68%. When the cases were retried, over 82% of the defendants were not sentenced to death and 7% were completely acquitted. See James S. Liebman et al., "A Broken System: Error Rates in Capital Cases 1973–1995," available at www.law.columbia.edu/instructionalservices/liebman/liebman_final.pdf.

DNA testing has also served to exonerate death row inmates. At least fourteen inmates exonerated by DNA testing were at one time sentenced to death or served time on death row. See Innocence Project, Benjamin N. Cardozo School of Law, "Facts on Post Conviction DNA Exonerations." Here, too, the justice system had concluded that these defendants were guilty and deserving of the death penalty. DNA testing became available only in the early 1990s, due to advancements in science. If this testing had not been discovered until ten years later, many of these inmates would have been executed. And if DNA testing had been applied to earlier cases where inmates were executed in the 1970s and 1980s, the odds are high that it would have proven that some of them were innocent as well.

In our view, whatever deterrent effect imposition of the death penalty might have is outweighed by moral considerations, the risk of wrongful executions and inequitable application of the penalty, and the additional cost involved. Moreover, the fact is that the value of the death penalty in decreasing criminal activity is highly questionable. In fact, some criminologists, such as William Bowers of Northeastern University, maintain that the death penalty has the opposite effect: that is, society is brutalized by the use of the death penalty, and this increases the likelihood of more murders. States within the union that do not employ the death penalty generally have lower murder rates than states that do. The same is true when the United States is compared to countries similar to it. The United States, with the death penalty, has a higher murder rate than Canada and the various European countries of Europe that have outlawed the death penalty. In our experience, the death penalty, in itself, is probably not an effective deterrent because most people who commit crimes (including those punishable by death) simply do not expect to get caught. The most effective deterrent, then, is to increase the perceived likelihood of being caught by increasing the government's effectiveness in apprehending and prosecuting criminals.

Finally, we have to consider that capital cases are notoriously protracted and expensive, and they constitute a significant drain on the resources of a prosecutor's office. At the trial level, death penalty cases are estimated to generate roughly $470,000 in additional costs to the prosecution and defense over the cost of trying the same case as an aggravated murder without the death penalty, as well as added costs of $47,000 to $70,000 for the courts. See http://www.deathpenaltyinfo.org; see also Katherine Baicker, National Bureau of Economic Research, "The Budgetary Repercussions of Capital Convictions," available at www.nber.org/papers/w8382. Elimination of this type of penalty would liberate a good part of our limited law-enforcement resources which could then be used to assure some form of punishment for more criminals who might otherwise escape justice altogether.

For all these reasons, I believe it is time to end capital punishment as part of the federal criminal justice system. Given the fact that the death penalty constitutes such a moral and economic burden on our legal system, I believe that we should all feel compelled to eliminate it.

IMPORTANT NAMES AND ADDRESSES

American Bar Association
Criminal Justice Section
740 Fifteenth St. NW, Tenth Fl.
Washington, DC 20005-1009
(202) 662-1500
FAX: (202) 662-1501
E-mail: crimjustice@abanet.org
URL: http://www.abanet.org/crimjust/
home.html

American Civil Liberties Union
125 Broad St., Eighteenth Fl.
New York, NY 10004
URL: http://www.aclu.org/

Amnesty International U.S.A.
5 Penn Plaza
New York, NY 10001
(212) 807-8400
FAX: (212) 627-1451
E-mail: aimember@aiusa.org
URL: http://www.amnestyusa.org/

Bureau of Justice Statistics
U.S. Department of Justice
810 Seventh St. NW
Washington, DC 20531
(202) 307-0765
E-mail: askbjs@ojp.usdoj.gov
URL: http://www.ojp.usdoj.gov/bjs

Criminal Justice Legal Foundation
PO Box 1199
Sacramento, CA 95812
(916) 446-0345
URL: http://www.cjlf.org/

Death Penalty Information Center
1101 Vermont Ave. NW, Ste. 701
Washington, DC 20005
(202) 289-2275
FAX: (202) 289-7336
URL: http://www.deathpen
altyinfo.org/

Federal Bureau of Investigation
J. Edgar Hoover Bldg.
935 Pennsylvania Ave. NW
Washington, DC 20535-0001
(202) 324-3000
URL: http://www.fbi.gov/

Federal Bureau of Prisons
320 First St. NW
Washington, DC 20534
(202) 307-3198
E-mail: info@bop.gov
URL: http://www.bop.gov/

Innocence Project
100 Fifth Ave., Third Fl.
New York, NY 10011
(212) 364-5340
E-mail: info@innocenceproject.org
URL: http://www.innocenceproject.org/

JURIST
c/o Professor Bernard Hibbitts
University of Pittsburgh School of Law
Pittsburgh, PA 15260
(412) 648-1400
E-mail: JURIST@pitt.edu
URL: http://jurist.law.pitt.edu/

Justice for All
9525 Katy Fwy.
Houston, TX 77024
(713) 935-9300
E-mail: info@jfa.net
URL: http://www.jfa.net/

Justice Research and Statistics
Association
777 N. Capitol St. NE, Ste. 801
Washington, DC 20002
(202) 842-9330
FAX: (202) 842-9329
E-mail: cjinfo@jrsa.org
URL: http://www.jrsa.org/

Moratorium Campaign
586 Harding Blvd.
Baton Rouge, LA 70807
E-mail: info@moratoriumcampaign.org
URL: http://www.moratoriumcampaign.org/

Murder Victims' Families for
Reconciliation
2100 M St. NW, Ste. 170-296
Washington, DC 20037
(877) 896-4702
E-mail: info@mvfr.org
URL: http://www.mvfr.org/

NAACP Legal Defense and Educational
Fund
99 Hudson St., Ste. 1600
New York, NY 10013
(212) 965-2200
URL: http://www.naacpldf.org/

National Association of Criminal Defense
Lawyers
1150 Eighteenth St. NW, Ste. 950
Washington, DC 20036
(202) 872-8600
FAX: (202) 872-8690
E-mail: assist@nacdl.com
URL: http://www.nacdl.org/

National Center for Victims of Crime
2000 M St. NW, Ste. 480
Washington, DC 20036
(202) 467-8700
FAX: (202) 467-8701
URL: http://www.ncvc.org/

National Coalition to Abolish the Death
Penalty
1705 DeSales St. NW, Fifth Fl.
Washington, DC 20036
(202) 331-4090
E-mail: info@ncadp.org
URL: http://www.ncadp.org/

National Criminal Justice Reference Service
PO Box 6000
Rockville, MD 20849-6000
(301) 519-5500
1-800-851-3420
FAX: (301) 519-5212
URL: http://www.ncjrs.org/

National District Attorneys Association
99 Canal Center Plaza, Ste. 510
Alexandria, VA 22314
(703) 549-9222
FAX: (703) 836-3195
URL: http://www.ndaa.org/

Office of the United Nations High Commissioner for Human Rights
1211 Geneva 10
Geneva, Switzerland
+41 22 917 9000
E-mail: InfoDesk@ohchr.org
URL: http://ohchr.org/english/

Sentencing Project
514 Tenth St. NW, Ste. 1000
Washington, DC 20004
(202) 628-0871
FAX: (202) 628-1091

E-mail: staff@sentencingproject.org
URL: http://www.sentencingproject.org/

U.S. Commission on Civil Rights
624 Ninth St. NW
Washington, DC 20425
(202) 376-7700
URL: http://www.usccr.gov/

U.S. Department of Justice
950 Pennsylvania Ave. NW
Washington, DC 20530-0001
(202) 514-2000
E-mail: askdoj@usdoj.gov
URL: http://www.usdoj.gov/

U.S. Government Accountability Office
441 G St. NW
Washington, DC 20548
(202) 512-3000
E-mail: contact@gao.gov
URL: http://www.gao.gov/

U.S. House Committee on the Judiciary
2138 Rayburn House Office Bldg.
Washington, DC 20515
(202) 225-3951
URL: http://judiciary.house.gov/

U.S. Senate Committee on the Judiciary
224 Dirksen Senate Office Bldg.
Washington, DC 20510
(202) 224-7703
FAX: (202) 224-9516
URL: http://judiciary.senate.gov/

U.S. Sentencing Commission Office of Public Affairs
1 Columbus Circle NE
Washington, DC 20002-8002
(202) 502-4500
E-mail: pubaffairs@ussc.gov
URL: http://www.ussc.gov/

U.S. Supreme Court
1 First St. NE
Washington, DC 20543
(202) 479-3000
URL: http://www.supremecourtus.gov/

World Coalition against the Death Penalty
197/199 Ave. Pierre Brossolette
Montrouge, France 92120
+33 1 57 21 22 73
FAX: +33 1 57 21 22 74
E-mail: coalition@abolition.fr
URL: http://www.worldcoalition.org/
modules/accueil/index.php?sel_
lang=english/

RESOURCES

The U.S. Department of Justice collects statistics on death row inmates as part of its National Prisoner Statistics (NPS) program. Based on voluntary reporting, the NPS program collects and interprets data on state and federal prisoners. Founded by the U.S. Census Bureau in 1926, the program was transferred to the Federal Bureau of Prisons in 1950, to the now-defunct Law Enforcement Assistance Administration (LEAA), and then to the Bureau of Justice Statistics (BJS) in 1979.

Since 1972 the Census Bureau, as the collecting agent for the LEAA and the BJS, has been responsible for compiling the relevant data. The BJS annually prepares the bulletin *Capital Punishment*, which provides an overview of capital punishment in the United States. The BJS's *Sourcebook of Criminal Justice Statistics 2003* (Kathleen Maguire and Ann L. Pastore, eds., 2004) is the most complete compilation of criminal justice statistics.

The Department of Justice released *Homicide Trends in the United States* (July 2007), *The Federal Death Penalty System: A Statistical Survey (1988–2000)* (September 2000), and *The Federal Death Penalty System: Supplementary Data, Analysis, and Revised Protocols for Capital Case Review* (June 2001). *The Report to the Attorney General on Delays in Forensic DNA Analysis* (March 2003) and *Postconviction DNA Testing: Recommendations for Handling Requests* (September 1999), both by the National Institute of Justice, were helpful in the preparation of this book. *Federal Death Penalty Cases: Recommendations Concerning the Cost and Quality of Defense Representation* (May 1998), prepared by the Subcommittee on Federal Death Penalty Cases of the Judicial Conference Committee on Defender Services, provides information on the cost of federal death penalty cases.

The NAACP Legal Defense and Educational Fund (LDF) maintains statistics on capital punishment and is strongly opposed to the death penalty. Despite its name, the LDF is not part of the National Association for the Advancement of Colored People, even though it was founded by this organization. Since 1957 the LDF has had a separate board of directors, program, staff, office, and budget. The LDF publishes *Death Row U.S.A.*, a periodic compilation of capital punishment statistics and information, including the names of all those currently on death row. Data from this quarterly were helpful in preparing this book.

The Death Penalty Information Center (DPIC) is a nonprofit organization that provides the media and the general public with information and analysis regarding capital punishment. The DPIC, which is against the death penalty, serves as a resource for those working on this issue. Its reports and charts on capital punishment were used in preparing this book. The National Coalition against the Death Penalty maintains an up-to-date list of news stories from the media regarding the death penalty.

Amnesty International is the Nobel Prize–winning human rights organization headquartered in London, England, and is strongly opposed to the death penalty. Amnesty International maintains information on the death penalty and torture throughout the world and periodically publishes its findings. Its publication *Abolitionist and Retentionist Countries* (August 2007) provided data on the status of capital punishment worldwide.

Charts and data from *Death Penalty for Female Offenders: January 1, 1973, through June 30, 2007* (July 2007) and *The Juvenile Death Penalty Today: Death Sentences and Executions for Juvenile Crimes, January 1, 1973–December 31, 2004* (2005) by Victor L. Streib of Ohio Northern University were used in the preparation of this book. *JURIST* is an online database of legal news and research maintained by the University of Pittsburgh, School of Law. It was an invaluable resource.

Other studies used in this book include *New Jersey Death Penalty Study Commission Report* (January 2007) by the New Jersey Death Penalty Study Commission; "Explaining Death Row's Population and Racial Composition" (*Journal of Empirical Legal Studies*, vol. 1, no. 1, March 2004) by John Blume, Theodore Eisenberg, and Martin T. Wells; *Performance Audit Report: Costs Incurred for Death Penalty Cases* (December 2003) by the state of Kansas; *Study Pursuant to Public Act No. 01-151 of the Imposition of the Death Penalty in Connecticut* (January 2003) by the Commission on the Death Penalty in Connecticut; *Critique of DPIC List ("Innocence: Freed from Death Row")* (2002) by Ward A. Campbell; *Case Histories: A Review of 24 Individuals Released from Death Row* (September 2002) by the Florida Commission on Capital Cases; "Capital Punishment Proves to Be Expensive" (*New York Law Journal*, April 30, 2002) by Daniel Wise; *Race and the Death Penalty in North Carolina, an Empirical Analysis: 1993–1997* (April 2001) by Isaac Unah and John Charles Boger; *The Disposition of Nebraska Capital and Noncapital Homicide Cases (1973–1999): A Legal and Empirical Analysis* (July 2001) by David C. Baldus et al.; *A Broken System: Error Rates in Capital Cases, 1973–1995* (June 2000) by James S. Liebman, Jeffrey Fagan, and Valerie West; "Capital Appeals Revisited" (*Judicature*, vol. 84, no. 2, September–October 2000) by Barry Latzer and James N. G. Cauthen; and *The Fair Defense Report: Analysis of Indigent Defense Practices in Texas* (December 2000) by Texas Appleseed.

David G. Chardavoyne's *A Hanging in Detroit: Stephen Gifford Simmons and the Last Execution under Michigan Law* (2003) provided, among other things, information on the rituals of public executions. *Executions in the United States, 1608–2002: The ESPY File* (2005) by M. Watt Espy and John Ortiz Smykla lists every known execution to have occurred in the North American British colonies and the United States from 1608 to 2002.

The news feature service *Human Rights Features* and Forum 90, an abolitionist group that monitors capital punishment in Japan, provided information on the imposition of the death penalty in Japan—"Japan Hanging on to Death Penalty" (April 2003) and "The Hidden Death Penalty in Japan" (2001), respectively.

Media sources consulted for this book include *Washington Post*, ABC News, CBS News, NBC News, CNN, Fox News, *Wall Street Journal*, *Austin Chronicle*, *Atlanta Journal and Constitution*, and *New York Times*. Polls taken by the Gallup Organization, Field Research Corporation, Pew Research Center, Quinnipiac University Polling Institute, Harris Interactive, and Higher Education Research Institute were also used in preparing this book.

INDEX

Page references in italics refer to photographs. References with the letter t following them indicate the presence of a table. The letter f indicates a figure. If more than one table or figure appears on a particular page, the exact item number for the table or figure being referenced is provided.

A

ABA (American Bar Association), 83, 94–96

Abolition movement
  abolitionist countries, 114–115
  decline of, 4
  DNA testing and, 9
  in Japan, 113–114
  in nineteenth century, 3–4
  in 1960s, 4
  in 1990s, reconsideration of death penalty, 9
  overview of, 3

Abolitionist countries
  commitment of, 114–115
  for ordinary crimes only, 114
  overview of, 114

Acevedo Vilá, Aníbal, 132–133

ACLU (American Civil Liberties Union), 79, 83

Actual Innocence (Scheck), 121

Adams, Chris, 84

Adolescents
  capital punishment for minors, 37–40
  capital punishment of, 7
  juvenile offenders, 54

AEDPA. *See* Antiterrorism and Effective Death Penalty Act

African-Americans
  capital punishment as deterrent, 125
  death penalty, support/opposition for among, 98
  discrimination against in death penalty cases, 131–132
  execution statistics for, 77

executions of, 71
racial bias against, 75
racially biased sentencing against, 47–48

Age
  death penalty, support/opposition for by, 99
  of death row inmates, 61
  minimum for execution, 54–55
  at time of arrest for capital offense/age of prisoners under sentence of death, 63 (*t6.4*)

Aggravating circumstances, 37

AI. *See* Amnesty International

Ake, Glen Burton, 41–42

Ake v. Oklahoma, 42

Alabama
  DPMIP report for death penalty process reform, 95
  judge sentencing in, 19
  lesser charge option in, 16

Alabama, Beck v., 16

Alabama, Harris v., 19

Alabama, Rudolph v., 5

Alabama, Swain v., 49

Albright, Madeleine K., 110

Aldridge, Joyce, 8

Allen, Nancy, 38

Allen, Wanda Jean, 70–71

American Bar Association (ABA), 83, 94–96

American Civil Liberties Union (ACLU), 79, 83

The American Freshman: Forty Year Trends (HERI), 98

American League to Abolish Capital Punishment, 4

American Psychiatric Association (APA), 41, 44

American Society for the Abolition of Capital Punishment, 3

"Americans Closely Divided on Death Penalty Moratorium" (Jones), 105

"Americans Rate the Morality of 16 Social Issues" (Saad), 97

Amicus curiae brief, 41

Amnesty International (AI)
  on capital punishment in China, 112
  on capital punishment in Japan, 113
  "Facts and Figures on the Death Penalty," 11, 115
  on retentionist countries, 108–109

"Analysis of June 6 Department of Justice Report on the Federal Death Penalty" (ACLU), 79

Annan, Kofi, 108

Anti-death penalty jurors, 20–21

Anti-Drug Abuse Act of 1988
  death penalty and, 9
  description of, 28, 55
  Juan Raul Garza, execution of, 10

Antiterrorism and Effective Death Penalty Act (AEDPA)
  challenging, 33–34
  establishment of, 7
  purpose of, 10
  restrictions on appeals of, 58

Antiterrorism legislation, 10

APA (American Psychiatric Association), 41, 44

Appeals
  based on new evidence, 31–33
  death row in Virginia, 28
  federal, limiting, 58
  process, establishment of, 5
  process in capital cases, 56–57
  process in Japan, 113
  state variations in, 57–58

Appellate court, 57–58

Apprendi v. New Jersey, 20, 91

Appropriations for FY2005: Commerce, Justice, State, the Judiciary, and Related Agencies (Fergusson and Epstein), 67

Arellano-Félix, Benjamin, 112

Arellano-Félix, Javier, 112

Argentina, 114

Argersinger v. Hamlin, 82
Arizona
    DPMIP report for death penalty process reform, 95
    jury's death penalty sentencing in, 20–21
Arizona, Miranda v., 41
Arizona, Ring v., 20, 91
Arizona, Tison v., 27
Arizona, Walton v., 20
Arizona v. Fulminante, 30
Arkansas, 17
Armstrong, Jeanette, 26
Armstrong, Ken, 83
Armstrong, Sampson, 26
Ashcroft, John D.
    DNA testing and, 90
    on racial bias in capital cases, 79
    Vicki A. Schieber's testimony on, 128
Atkins, Daryl Renard, 44–45
Atkins v. Virginia, 7, 39, 55
Attorney general
    death penalty costs and, 67
    racial disparity in plea bargaining and, 78–79
    racial/ethnic bias of, 77
Attorneys
    contract, 83
    court-assigned counsel system, 83
    defense, ineffective, 82–83
    district attorneys, racial bias among, 81
    right to effective counsel, 27–29
    See also Legal representation
Avena and Other Mexican Nationals, 111–112
Average number of years under sentence of death, 66 (*t*6.8)

B

Bailey, Brenna, 21
Baldus, David C., 47
    The Disposition of Nebraska Capital and Non-capital Homicide Cases (1973–1999): A Legal and Empirical Analysis, 92
    "Racial Discrimination and the Death Penalty in the Post-*Furman* Era: An Empirical and Legal Analysis with Recent Findings from Philadelphia," 77
    Senate testimony of, 79
Baldus study (Baldus, Pulanski, and Woodworth)
    McCleskey v. Kemp, 76–77
    overview of, 47–48
Barefoot, Thomas, 40–41
Barefoot v. Estelle, 41
Barfield, Margie Velma, 69
Batson v. Kentucky, 49
Beck, Gilbert, 16
Beck v. Alabama, 16
Becker, Gary, 121–122
Bedau, Hugo Adam, 64
Beets, Betty Lou, 70

Belgium, 114
Bell, House v., 32
Bell, Robert Holmes, 68
Benjamin, Charles, 39
Bennett, John A., 11
Berk, Richard, 124
Bethley, Patrick Dewayne, 53
Bias, racial. *See* Race/ethnicity
Bifurcated trial system, 51
Bird, Thomas, 9
Birmingham News, 128
Blackmun, Harry A.
    on failure of death penalty, 128
    on *Herrera v. Collins*, 31–32
    on psychiatric testimony, 41
    on racial prejudice in capital cases, 48
    on right to counsel, 28
Blagojevich, Rod R., 91
Block, Lynda Lyon, 71
Bloodsworth, Kirk, 8
Blume, John, 80–81
Boger, John Charles, 79–80
Bonczar, Thomas P., 59
Booth, John, 46
Booth v. Maryland, 46
Boughton, Evelyn, 17
Bowden, Jerome, 55
Bowers, William, 133
Bradford, William, 3
Branch v. Texas, 13
Bravence, Robert and Cheryl, 22
Brazil, 114
Breaking at the wheel, 2
Breard, Angel Francisco, 109–110
Breard v. Greene, 110
Breard v. Netherland, 110
Bredesen, Phil N., 93
Brennan, William J.
    on Baldus study, 48
    on comparative proportionality, 22
    on death penalty, 13
    on death penalty for minors, 38–39
    on execution of mentally retarded, 43–44
    Rudolph v. Alabama, 5
    on *Tison v. Arizona*, 27
    on *Wainwright v. Witt*, 17
Breyer, Stephen G., 36
Bright, Stephen B., 128–129
A Broken System: Error Rates in Capital Cases 1973–1995 (Liebman, Fagan, and West), 88–89, 133
Brooks, Charles, 59
Brown, Mauriceo, 54
Bruck, David, 10
Bruton v. United States, 30
Bryan, Anthony Braden, 36
Bryan v. Moore, 36
Bryson, William, 71
Buenoano, Judias, 70

Bullock, Cabana v., 26
Bullock, Crawford, 26
Burger, Warren
    on death penalty, 14
    on death penalty for minors, 38
    on *Eberheart v. Georgia*, 25
    on mitigating circumstances, 37
Burnett, Lavinia, 70
Burr, Dick, 10
Bush, George H. W., 9
Bush, George W.
    Innocence Protection Act of 2004, 83
    Garza, Juan Raul, execution of, 10
    military executions and, 11
    Tucker, Karla Faye, execution of, 9
    VCCR and, 112
Bush, Jeb, 36

C

Cabana, Donald, 131
Cabana v. Bullock, 26
Calderon, Arthur, 35
Caldwell, Bobby, 17–18
Caldwell v. Mississippi, 18
California
    death penalty, costs of in, 64–65
    moratoriums in, 90
    racial bias in death sentencing, 80
    Robert Harris, death sentence of, 22
California, Chapman v., 29–30
California Commission on the Fair Administration of Justice (CCFAJ), 90
Campbell, Charles Rodham, 34–35
Campbell, Ward A., 120–121
Campbell v. Wood, 35
Canada
    abolition of death penalty in, 9
    public opinion on death penalty, 117
"Capital Appeals Revisited" (Latzer and Cauthen), 89
Capital Defender Office (New York), 83
Capital offenses, by state, 52*t*
Capital offenses, death penalty laws for, 51
Capital punishment
    costs of, 129
    as deterrent, David B. Muhlhausen on, 124–125
    as deterrent, public opinion on effectiveness of, 106
    economic studies on, 122
    extraditions to U.S. and, 112
    federal in non-death penalty states, 55
    for minors, 37–40
    state laws, 51
    See also Death penalty
Capital punishment, history of
    abolition movement, 3–4
    abolition movement, decline of, 4
    colonial period, 1–3
    constitutional issues, 4–5
    current laws, 6–7

DNA and, 8–9
federal death penalty, 9–10
homicide rate connection, 6
nationwide moratorium, end of, 5–6
overview of, 1
reconsideration of, 9
uniform system, creating, 5
U.S. military, 10–11
worldwide trend, 11
Capital Punishment, 30 Years On: Support, but Ambivalence as Well (Langer), 101
Capital punishment, worldwide
abolitionist countries, 114–115
against minors, 115–116
public opinion, international, 116–117
retentionist countries, 108–114
UN resolutions, 107–108
Capital Punishment 2003 (Bonczar and Snell), 58
Capital Punishment 2005 (Snell), 58, 61
"Capital Punishment Proves to Be Expensive" (Wise), 67
Cardozo, Benjamin N., 133
Carpenter, Pamela, 43
Carrier, Murray v., 32
Carrisalez, Enrique, 31
The Case against the Death Penalty (Bedau), 64
Caucasians
capital punishment deterrent effect on, 125
under death penalty, percentages, 3, 75
homicide statistics for, 75
Cauthen, James N. G., 89
CCFAJ (California Commission on the Fair Administration of Justice), 90
Celia (former slave), 70
Champion, Jane, 1
Chaney, Heckler v., 34
Chapman v. California, 29–30
Chardavoyne, David G., 3
Cherboris, Anthony, 55
Chessman, Caryl, 60
Children
capital punishment against, worldwide, 115–116
juvenile defenders, 54
sexual assault against, death penalty for, 52–53
China, 112–113
"China Quick to Execute Drug Official" (Kahn), 112–113
"Chinese Try Mobile Death Vans" (McDonald), 113
Christopher, Charisse, 46
Clark, Ramsey, 13
Clemency, 56–58
Clinton, Bill
Antiterrorism and Effective Death Penalty Act, 7
Juan Raul Garza, execution of, 10
racial/ethnic bias, DOJ study of, 77–78
Cobb, Raymond Levi, 28–29
Cobb, Texas v., 29

Coerced confessions, 29–30
Coke, Edward, 6
Coker v. Georgia, 25, 52
Cold hit, DNA, 8
Collins, Herrera v., 31–32
Colonies, U.S., 1–3
Colorado, 4
Common crimes, 3–4
Commonwealth v. Martorano, 21
Commutation, 57
Comparative proportionality, 22
"Comparative Review of Death Sentences: An Empirical Study of the Georgia Experience" (Baldus, Pulanski, and Woodworth), 47, 77
Competency standard, 45–46
Confessions, coerced, 29–30
Connecticut, 66–67
Considerations on the Justice and Policy of Punishing Murder by Death (Rush), 3
Constitution Project's Death Penalty Initiative, 83
Constitutional issues, 4–5
Contract lawyers, 83
Cook, Shirley, 39
Cornyn, John, 49
"Cost of Public Defender Services: Cost Attributable to the Death Penalty" (Connecticut), 67
Costs. *See* Death penalty, costs of
Counsel, right to effective, 27–29
Countries that are abolitionist for all crimes, 115t
Countries that are abolitionist for ordinary crimes only, 2007, 116 (t10.6)
Countries that are abolitionist in practice, 114t
Countries that have abolished the death penalty, 1976–2007, 116 (t10.5)
Court cases, 89
Ake v. Oklahoma, 42
Apprendi v. New Jersey, 20, 91
Argersinger v. Hamlin, 82
Arizona v. Fulminante, 30
Atkins v. Virginia, 7, 39, 55
Barefoot v. Estelle, 41
Batson v. Kentucky, 49
Beck v. Alabama, 16
Booth v. Maryland, 46
Branch v. Texas, 13
Breard v. Greene, 110
Breard v. Netherland, 110
Bruton v. United States, 30
Bryan v. Moore, 36
Cabana v. Bullock, 26
Caldwell v. Mississippi, 18
Campbell v. Wood, 35
Chapman v. California, 29–30
Coker v. Georgia, 25, 52
Commonwealth v. Martorano, 21

Eberheart v. Georgia, 25
Eddings v. Oklahoma, 37–38
Enmund v. Florida, 26
Estelle v. Smith, 41, 44
Fierro v. Gomez, 35
Ford v. Georgia, 49
Ford v. Wainwright, 6, 42–43
Foster v. Florida, 36
Furman v. Georgia, 5, 13, 51
Germany v. United States of America, 111
Gideon v. Wainwright, 82
Godfrey v. Georgia, 25–26
Godinez v. Moran, 45–46
Gregg v. Georgia, 14–15, 56
Harris v. Alabama, 19
Heckler v. Chaney, 34
Herrera v. Collins, 31–32, 89
Hill v. McDonough, 36
Hitchcock v. Dugger, 37
House v. Bell, 32
Hynes v. Tomei, 92
Jackson v. Georgia, 13
Jurek v. Texas, 15, 41
Kansas v. Michael Lee Marsh II, 122–123
Kyles v. Whitley, 32–33
Lankford v. Idaho, 22–23
Lockett v. Ohio, 16, 37
Lockhart v. McCree, 17
McCleskey v. Kemp, 48
McFarland v. Scott, 28
Mexico v. United States of America, 111–112
Miranda v. Arizona, 41
Morales v. Tilton, 90
Murray v. Carrier, 32
Murray v. Giarratano, 28, 84
Payne v. Tennessee, 46
Pennsylvania v. Finley, 28
Penry v. Johnson, 44
Penry v. Lynaugh, 40
People v. LaValle, 93
Proffitt v. Florida, 15
Provenzano v. Moore, 36
Pulley v. Harris, 22
Ring v. Arizona, 20, 91
Roberts v. Louisiana, 15
Roper v. Simmons, 7, 39, 54–55, 116
Rudolph v. Alabama, 5
Saldano v. Texas, 49
Sattazahn v. Pennsylvania, 21
Sawyer v. Whitley, 32
Schlup v. Delo, 32
Schriro v. Summerlin, 21
Simmons v. South Carolina, 18
Singleton v. Norris, 43
Spaziano v. Florida, 18–19
Stanford v. Kentucky, 38
State v. Torrence, 58
State v. Wilson, 52–53

Strickland v. Washington, 33, 82
Summerlin v. Stewart, 21
Swain v. Alabama, 49
Texas v. Cobb, 29
Thompson v. Oklahoma, 38
Tison v. Arizona, 27
Trop v. Dulles, 4
Turner v. Murray, 47
United States v. Jackson, 92–93
United States v. Quinones, 120
Wainwright v. Witt, 16–17
Walton v. Arizona, 20
Wiggins v. Smith, 27–28
Wilkins v. Missouri, 38
Williams v. Taylor, 33, 34, 58
Witherspoon v. Illinois, 16
Woodson v. North Carolina, 15, 93
Yates v. Evatt, 30–31
Court-assigned counsel system, 83
Courts of appeals, geographic boundaries of, 57 *f*
Crime in America: Observations on Its Nature, Causes, Prevention, and Control (Clark), 13
Crime laboratories, 90
Crimes
    common, 3–4
    exceptional, 4
    sentence proportionality for, 22–23
    uncharged, right to counsel for, 28–29
Criminal history
    of death row inmates, 62–64
    profile, death row prisoners, 65*t*
Criminal intent, 26–27
Criminal Justice Legal Foundation (CJLF), 82
Crist, Charlie, 91
Cruel and unusual punishment
    death row, extended stays on, 36
    executions methods and, 58–60
Cruse, Jeffrey Alan, 34

D

Dale, Thomas, 2
Darrow, Clarence, 4
Davis, Allen Lee, 35
Davis, Henry, 30–31
Dead Man Walking (film), 9
Deadlock, jury, 93
"Death, Yunnan Style" (Zhang), 113
Death penalty
    advance notice of imposing, 22–23
    advocates on racial bias, 82
    cases, legal errors in, 88–89
    circumstances that do not warrant, 25–26
    crimes warranting, 71–72
    current laws governing, 6–7
    defendants in federal death penalty process, stages in, 77*t*
    as deterrent, 106, 124–125

in European Union, abolition of, 131
excessive frequency of use question, 102
fairness of, 102
innocence and, 102
vs. life imprisonment with no parole, 101–102
mandatory in North Carolina/Louisiana, 15
morality of, 97
moratorium on, 105–106
plea bargaining and, 78
racial bias in, 75
status of prisoners sentenced to, 67 *f*
support for, 97–100
support/opposition, reasons for, 100–101
Supreme Court on proper imposition of, 14–15
uniform system, creating, 5
See also Capital punishment
"The Death Penalty" (ACLU), 83
Death penalty, costs of
    Acevedo Vilá, Aníbal, on, 133
    in California, 64–65
    in Connecticut, 66–67
    federal, 67–69
    Fagan, Jeffrey, on, 129
    in Kansas, 65–66
    in New York, 67
    overview of, 64
    in Washington, 65
Death Penalty and Sentencing Information in the United States (Sharp), 82
Death penalty debate, argument against
    Acevedo Vilá, Aníbal, 132–133
    Bright, Stephen B., 128–129
    Fagan, Jeffrey, 129–130
    Feingold, Russ, 130–131
    Green River Killer plea bargain, 94
    Schieber, Vicki A., 127–128
    Shelton, Hilary O., 131–132
Death penalty debate, argument for
    McAdams, John, 120–121
    Muhlhausen, David B., 124–125
    Otis, William G., 123
    Rubin, Paul H., 121–122
    Scalia, Antonin, 122–123
    Scott, Ann, 119–120
"The Death Penalty for Child Rape: Why Texas May Help Louisiana" (Gershowitz), 53
Death Penalty for Female Offenders: January 1, 1973, through June 30, 2007 (Streib), 61
Death Penalty Information Center (DPIC)
    on clemencies, 57
    "The Federal Death Penalty," 9
    Innocents list, 89, 120
    on juvenile executions, 54
Death penalty laws
    appeals process in capital cases, 56–58
    capital offenses, 51

death penalty methods, 58–60
federal capital punishment in non-death penalty states, 55
mentally retarded people, executing, 55
minimum age for execution, 54–55
sexual crimes, 52–53
terrorism, 51–52
Texas "law of parties," 53–54
witnesses to executions, 60
See also Legislation and international treaties
Death penalty methods
    electrocution, 59
    hanging, 59–60
    lethal gas, 59
    lethal injection, 59
    overview of, 58–59
Death Penalty Moratorium Implementation Project (DPMIP), 94–96
Death penalty opponents
    Green River Killer plea bargain, 94
    on ineffective defense counsel, 82–83
    on racial bias in death sentencing, 75
"Death Penalty Poll Highlights" (AP/Ipsos poll), 97–98, 117
Death Penalty Sentencing: Research Indicates Pattern of Racial Disparities (GAO), 77
"Death Penalty Unequal" (Welsh-Huggins), 81
Death row, extended stays on, 36
Death row inmates
    characteristics of, 61
    criminal history of, 62–64
    exonerations of, 85–88
    gender of, 61
    long waits of, 64
    numbers of, 61
    race of, 61
    removed from death row, 64
"Death Row Often Means a Long Life" (Tempest), 64
Death Row USA: Winter 2007 (LDF), 71
Death without Justice: A Guide for Examining the Administration of the Death Penalty in the United States (ABA), 94–96
Death-qualified jury, 17
Defense. *See* Legal representation
Defense attorneys, 82–83
Del Papa, Frankie Sue, 88–89
Delo, Schlup v., 32
Deoxyribonucleic acid (DNA) testing
    Acevedo Vilá, Aníbal, on, 133
    backlog, 90
    convictions/executions via, 8
    inmates freed by, 8
    laws, expanding, 9
    as new evidence, 89
    overview of, 8
    postconviction, 90

science of, 89
in wrongful convictions, 89
Dezhbakhsh, Hashem, 125
Diaz, Angel, 90–91
DiCamillo, Mark, 100
Dickson, Mark, 26
Direct appeal, 56
The Disposition of Nebraska Capital and Non-capital Homicide Cases (1973–1999): A Legal and Empirical Analysis (Baldus et al.), 92
District attorneys, 81
District courts, geographic boundaries of, 57 *f*
DNA Analysis Backlog Reduction Act of 2000, 90
DNA testing. *See* Deoxyribonucleic acid (DNA) testing
DOJ (U.S. Department of Justice), 77–78, 79
Double jeopardy, 21–22
Douglas, William O.
on death penalty, 13
Rudolph v. Alabama, 5
Douglass, Richard and Mary, 41–42
DPIC. *See* Death Penalty Information Center
DPMIP (Death Penalty Moratorium Implementation Project), 94–96
Due process, advance notice of imposing, 22–23
Dugger, Hitchcock v., 37
Dulles, Trop v., 4

E

Easley, Mike F., 93
Eberhardt, Jennifer, 81–82
Eberheart v. Georgia, 25
Economics of crime, 121–122
Eddings, Monty Lee, 37–38
Eddings v. Oklahoma, 37–38
Education level of death row inmates, 61
Ehrlich, Isaac, 122, 125
Ehrlich, Robert L. Jr., 91, 124
Eichmann, Adolf, 11
Eighth Amendment
description of, 1
mental retardation and, 44
Trop v. Dulles, 4
violation of, 13
Eisenberg, Theodore, 80–81
Ekelund, Robert B., 125
Electrocution
cruel/unusual punishment consideration, 35–36
first use of, 4
overview of, 59
An Empirical Analysis of Maryland's Death Sentencing System with Respect to the Influence of Race and Legal Jurisdiction (Paternoster et al.), 80
English Penal Code, 1
Enmund, Earl, 26
Enmund v. Florida, 26

Epstein, Susan B., 67
Espy, M. Watt, 2
Essa, Yazeed, 112
Estelle, Barefoot v., 41
Estelle v. Smith, 41, 44
Ethnicity. *See* Race/Ethnicity
Europe
abolition of death penalty in, 9
death penalty in, 11
European Union, 131
Evatt, Yates v., 30–31
Evidence
hearings for constitutional claims, 33–34
new, appeals based on, 31–33
suppressed, 32–33
"An Examination of the Death Penalty in the United States" (U.S. Senate hearing)
Bright, Stephen B., testimony of, 128–129
Fagan, Jeffrey, testimony of, 123–130
overview of, 82
Schieber, Vicki A., testimony of, 127–128
Exceptional crimes, 4
Executions
demographics of, 128–129
by electrocution, 4
by hanging, constitutionality of, 34–35
homicide rate/executions, 1960–2005, 8 *f*
of the insane, 42–43
of juveniles, 54–55
by lethal gas, 35
locations of, 69
methods in U.S. colonies, 2–3
methods of, 34–36, 58–60
1930–2006, 6*f*
1973–2005, 69 (*f*6.4)
numbers of, 69
numbers of by method, 72
prisoners under sentence of death/executions, 7(*f*1.3)
public, abolition of, 3
by race/ethnicity, 71
rise of after moratorium, 6
by state/method, 73*t*
2005, 71*t*
witnesses to, 60
of women, 69–71
Executions in the United States, 1608–2002: The ESPY File (Espy and Smykla), 2
Exonerations
Innocence List, criticism of, 87–88
McCarty, Curtis, 87
overview of, 85
Porter, Anthony, 85, 87
"Explaining Death Row's Population and Racial Composition" (Blume, Eisenberg, and Wells), 80–81
Extraditions to the U.S., 112

F

"Facts and Figures on the Death Penalty" (Amnesty International), 11, 108, 115
"Facts on Post Conviction DNA Exonerations" (Cardozo), 133
Fagan, Jeffrey, 88–89, 129–130
"The Failure of the Death Penalty in Illinois" (Armstrong and Mills), 83
Fair Defense Act, Texas, 83
FDA (U.S. Food and Drug Administration), 34
Federal death penalty
costs of, 67–69
expansion of, 9–10
increase in, 10
resumption of in 1990s, 10
"The Federal Death Penalty" (DPIC), 9
The Federal Death Penalty Abolition Act of 2007, 130–131
The Federal Death Penalty Act
Gary Lee Sampson and, 55
prohibiting execution of mentally retarded, 55
See also Violent Crime Control and Law Enforcement Act
Federal Death Penalty Cases: Recommendations Concerning the Cost and Quality of Defense Representation (Subcommittee on Federal Death Penalty Cases of the Judicial Conference Committee on Defender Services), 67
Federal Death Penalty Resource Counsel Project (FDPRCP), 10
The Federal Death Penalty System: A Statistical Survey (1988–2000) (DOJ), 77
The Federal Death Penalty System: Supplemental Data, Analysis, and Revised Protocols for Capital Case Review (DOJ), 79
Federal laws providing for death penalty, 53*t*
Feguer, Victor, 9
Feingold, Russ, 130–131
Fergusson, Ian F., 67
Field, Mark, 100
Fierro, David, 35
Fierro v. Gomez, 35
Fifth Amendment
Double Jeopardy Clause of the, 21
guilty pleas in New York and, 92
psychiatric evaluation and, 41, 44
Finley, Pennsylvania v., 28
Florida
DPMIP report for death penalty process reform, 95
Ford v. Wainwright, 42–43
judge sentencing in, 18–19
moratoriums in, 90–91
Florida, Enmund v., 26
Florida, Foster v., 36
Florida, Proffitt v., 15
Florida, Spaziano v., 18–19

Ford, Alvin, 42–43
Ford, James, 48–49
Ford v. Georgia, 49
Ford v. Wainwright, 6, 42–43
Foreign nationals, 109–110
Foreign nationals executed, 110*t*
Forum 90, 113
Foster, Charles Kenneth, 36
Foster, Kenneth, 54
Foster v. Florida, 36
Fourteenth Amendment
    appeals and, 31
    Furman v. Georgia, 5
    violation of, 13
Fox, James Alan, 75
Franklin, Benjamin, 3
Fulminante, Arizona v., 30
Fulminante, Oreste C., 29–30
Furman v. Georgia, 5, 13, 51

G

Gabrion, Marvin, 55, 68
"Gabrion Defense Costs Taxpayers
    $730,168" (White), 68
Gallup poll
    current on death penalty, 1
    on fairness of death penalty, 102–103
    public opinion on death penalty, 9, 97–99
    reasons for support/opposition of death
        penalty, 100–101
Gang homicides, 82
GAO (U.S. General Accounting Office), 77
Garvin, Dawn Marie, 91
Garza, Juan Raul, 10, 77
Gas, lethal, 35
Gates, Thomas, 2
Gee, Jon, 58
Gender
    breakdown of proponents of death
        penalty, 103 (*f*9.6)
    of death row inmates, 61
    support for death penalty and, 99–100
    women executed, 69
General appeals process for capital cases, 56 *f*
Geographic boundaries, U.S. Courts of
    Appeals/District Courts, 57 *f*
George, Ronald, 65
Georgia
    defender offices in, 84
    DPMIP report for death penalty process
        reform, 95
    executions method in, 36
Georgia, Coker v., 25, 52
Georgia, Eberheart v., 25
Georgia, Ford v., 49
Georgia, Furman v., 5, 13, 51
Georgia, Godfrey v., 25–26
Georgia, Gregg v., 14–15, 56
Georgia, Jackson v., 13

"Georgia Public Defender System on Trial"
    (Jarvie), 84
Germany
    ICJ suit against U.S., 110–111
    Mohammed Ali Hamadi, extradition to
        U.S., 112
Germany v. United States of America, 111
Gershowitz, Adam, 53
Giarratano, Joseph, 28
Giarratano, Murray v., 28, 84
Gideon v. Wainwright, 82
"*Gideon*'s Broken Promise: America's
    Continuing Quest for Equal Justice"
    (ABA), 83
Gilbert, Kristen, 55
Gilmore, Gary, 5–6
Ginsburg, Ruth Bader
    on double-jeopardy protection, 21–22
    "In Pursuit of the Public Good: Lawyers
        Who Care," 84
    on Sixth Amendment rights, 20
Gittings, R. Kaj, 125
Glendening, Parris N., 91, 124, 131
Godfrey, Robert, 25–26
Godfrey v. Georgia, 25–26
Godinez v. Moran, 45–46
Goldberg, Arthur J.
    on capital punishment, 129
    Rudolph v. Alabama, 5
Gomez, Fierro v., 35
Gomez, James, 35
Grand jury, 53
Gray, Ronald, 11
Great Act of 1682, 2
Great Britain
    public opinion on death penalty, 116–117
    public opinion on death penalty, Great
        Britain/Canada/United States, 117 (*f*10.1)
    public opinion on death penalty for
        murder, Great Britain/Canada/United
        States, 117 (*f*10.2)
Greece, 114
Greeley, Horace, 3
The Green Mile (film), 9
Green, Steven, 11
Green River Killer, 94
Greenawalt, Randy, 27
Greene, Breard v., 110
Greenhouse, Linda, 112
Gregg v. Georgia, 14–15, 56
Grigson, James P., 41
Guilty pleas, 92

H

Habeas corpus
    AEDPA restrictions on, 58
    defined, 28
    federal, defined, 56
    relief, AEDPA and, 33
    state, defined, 56

Hakamada, Iwao, 113
Hamadi, Mohammed Ali, 112
Hamlin, Argersinger v., 82
Hanging, 59–60
Harris, Darrel, 67
Harris, Louise, 19
Harris, Pulley v., 22
Harris, Robert, 22
Harris, Robert Alton, 35
Harris v. Alabama, 19
Hatch, Steven, 41–42
Heckler v. Chaney, 34
HERI (Higher Education Research Institute), 98
Herrera, Leonel Torres, 31, 89
Herrera v. Collins, 31–32, 89
The Hidden Death Penalty in Japan (Forum
    90), 113
Higher Education Research Institute
    (HERI), 98
Hill, Clarence E., 36
Hill v. McDonough, 36
Hirasawa, Sadamichi, 113
Hitchcock v. Dugger, 37
Homicide
    circumstances of by race of offender, 77*t*
    death penalty for, public opinion on,
        101–102
    gang related, 82
    offending rate, by race, 76 (*f*7.2)
    by race of offender/victim, 76 (*f*7.4)
    rate, 1900–2002, 7(*f*1.4)
    rate, death penalty connection with, 6
    rate, effects of capital punishment on,
        124–125
    rate/executions, 1960–2005, 8*f*
    statistics, race and, 75
    victimization rate, by race, 76 (*f*7.3)
Homicide Trends in the United States (Fox
    and Zawitz), 75
House, Paul, 32
House v. Bell, 32
Huddleston, Jack, 40
Human Rights Council (UN), 108
Human Rights Research, 109
Hunt, Jeneane Michelle, 29
Hynes v. Tomei, 92

I

ICJ (International Court of Justice),
    109–110, 111, 112
Idaho, Lankford v., 22–23
Illinois, 91
Illinois, Witherspoon v., 16
"The Impact of Legally Inappropriate
    Factors on Death Sentencing for
    California Homicides, 1990–99" (Pierce
    and Radelet), 80
"In Pursuit of the Public Good: Lawyers
    Who Care" (Ginsburg), 84
Income, support for death penalty and,
    99–100

Indiana, 96
Indigent defense systems, 82–83
"Innocence: List of Those Freed from Death Row" (DPIC), 89
Innocence Protection Act of 2004
    description of, 9
    for indigent defendants, 83
    postconviction DNA testing and, 90
Innocents, execution of, 121
Innocents list, 120
Insanity
    execution and, 42–43
    psychiatric testimony as proof of, 41–42
    Supreme Court on, 6–7
International Bill of Human Rights, 107
International community
    countries that are abolitionist for all crimes, 115t
    countries that are abolitionist for ordinary crimes only, 2007, 116 (t10.6)
    countries that are abolitionist in practice, 114t
    countries that have abolished the death penalty, 1976–2007, 116 (t10.5)
International Court of Justice (ICJ), 109–110, 111, 112
International Covenant on Civil and Political Rights, 107
Iowa, 4
Israel, 11

J

Jackson, United States v., 92–93
Jackson v. Georgia, 13
Japan, 113–114
"Japan Hanging on to Death Penalty" (South Asian Human Rights Documentation Center), 113
Jarvie, Jeremy, 84
"Jessica's Laws," 52
Johanns, Mike O., 92
John Paul II, Pope, 9
Johnson, Dorsie Lee, Jr., 40
Johnson, Penry v., 44
Jones, Jeffrey M., 105
Jones, Louis, Jr., 10
Judges
    delay of execution for habeas corpus review, 28
    sentencing by, 18–19
    See also Supreme Court rulings
Jurek v. Texas, 15, 41
Jurisdictions with/without death penalty, 2007, 2t
Jurors
    anti-death penalty, 16–17
    death sentence recommendations of, 17–18
    lesser charge consideration, 16
    parole information, keeping from, 18
    racially based use of peremptory challenges in selection of, 48–49

sentencing by, 20–21
    sentencing hearings responsibilities, 51
"Jurors Dish out Death in Arizona: Sentencing Rate up since Judges Lost Say" (Walsh), 20–21
Jury
    deadlock instructions in New York, 93
    death-qualified, 17
    grand, 53
    selection in capital cases, 68
Justice, miscarriage of, 32
Justice for All, 82
The Juvenile Death Penalty Today: Death Sentences and Executions for Juvenile Crimes, January 1, 1973–December 31, 2004 (Streib), 54
Juvenile offenders, 54
Juveniles executed, January 1, 1973–August 24, 2007, 54t

K

Kahn, Joseph, 112–113
Kansas, 65–66
Kansas v. Michael Lee Marsh II, 122–123
Keller, Morris, Jr., and Mary Elizabeth, 34
Kemmler, William, 4, 58
Kemp, McCleskey v., 48
Kendall, George, 1
Kennedy, Anthony M., 40
Kennedy, Patrick, 53
Kentucky, 77
Kentucky, Batson v., 49
Kentucky, Stanford v., 38
Kersey, Thomas, 26
Kidnapping
    Supreme Court on, 51
    Supreme Court on death penalty for, 25
Kinsella, John J., 91
Kopp, James Charles, 112
Kyles, Curtis Lee, 32–33
Kyles v. Whitley, 32–33

L

LaGrand, Karl, 110
LaGrand, Walter, 110–111
LaHood, Michael Jr., 54
Lane, Charles, 112, 113
Langer, Gary, 101, 105
Lankford, Bryan and Mark, 22–23
Lankford v. Idaho, 22–23
Larranaga, Mark A., 65
Latzer, Barry, 89
Latzer study, 89
LaValle, People v., 93
LaValle, Stephen, 93
Law of parties (Texas), 53–54
Lawes, Lewis E., 4
Lawes Divine, Morall, and Martiall, 2
Layson, Stephen K., 125
LDF (NAACP Legal Defense and Educational Fund), 71

Lebanon, 112
Legal errors, 88–89
Legal representation
    ineffective, 82–84
    overview of, 82
    for postconviction review, 84
Legislation and international treaties
    AEDPA, 7, 10
    AEDPA, challenging, 33–34
    AEDPA, restrictions on, 58
    Anti-Drug Abuse Act, 9, 28, 55
    antiterrorism, 10
    constitutional issues, 4–5
    death penalty in U.S. colonies, 1–3
    DNA Analysis Backlog Reduction Act of 2000, 90
    Federal Death Penalty Abolition Act of 2007, 130
    Federal Death Penalty Act of 1994, 55
    Great Act of 1682, 2
    Innocence Protection Act of 2004, 9, 83
    Lawes Divine, Morall, and Martiall, 2
    Michigan death penalty, 3–4
    The Royal Charter for South New Jersey, 2
    Terrorist Bombings Convention Implementation Act of 2002, 10
    USA Patriot Act, 10
    Violent Crime Control and Law Enforcement Act, 9–10
Lesser charge consideration, 16
Lethal gas, 35, 59
Lethal injection
    numbers of executions by, 72
    overview of, 59
    Russ Feingold on, 131
    states using, 58–59
Liebman, James S., 88–89, 133
Liebman study, 88–89
Life imprisonment with no parole, 101–102
Lockett, Sandra, 37
Lockett v. Ohio, 16, 37
Lockhart v. McCree, 17
"Looking Deathworthy. Perceived Stereotypicality of Black Defendants Predicts Capital-Sentencing Outcome" (Eberhardt et al.), 81–82
Louisiana
    death penalty for rape of minors in, 52–53
    mandatory death sentence in, 15
Louisiana, Roberts v., 15
Loving, Dwight, 11
Lowe, Wesley, 82
Lunsford, Jessica, 52
Lynaugh, Penry v., 40

M

Maguire, Kathleen, 71–72
Maine, 4
Maleng, Norm, 94

Malice, presumption of, 30–31
Malone, Roy, 16
Mandatory death penalty. *See* Death penalty
Mariadason, Thomas, 113
Marshall, Thurgood
    on death penalty, 14
    on execution of the insane, 42–43
    on *Witherspoon*-excludables, 17
Martorano, Commonwealth v., 21
Maryland
    moratorium in, 91–92, 124
    racial bias in death sentencing, study on, 80
Maryland, Booth v., 46
Massachusetts, 55
Massachusetts Bay Colony, 1
McAdams, John
    death penalty, argument for, 120–121
    on racial bias in capital cases, 82
McBride, Tracie Joy, 10
McCarter, Lorenzo, 19
McCarver, Ernest, 55
McCleskey, Warren, 47, 76–77
McCleskey v. Kemp, 48, 77
McCree, Ardia, 17
McCree, Lockhart v., 17
McDonald, Hamish, 113
McDonough, Hill v., 36
McFarland, Frank, 28
McFarland v. Scott, 28
McKimble, Clinton, 71
McNally, Kevin, 10
McVeigh, Timothy, 10, 60, 123
Medellin, Jose, 111–112
Medill School of Journalism, 89
Mental retardation
    executing people with, 43–45, 55
    Supreme Court on, 7
Merritt, Jeralyn, 93
Methods of execution, by state, 59*t*
Mexico v. United States of America, 111–112
Michael Lee Marsh II, Kansas v., 122–123
Michigan
    abolition of death penalty, 3–4
    non-death penalty law of, 55
Mills, Steve, 83
Minimum age for execution, 54–55
Minorities, 77–78
    See also African-Americans; Race/Ethnicity
Minors
    capital punishment for, 37–40
    capital punishment for, worldwide, 115–116
    sexual assault against, death penalty for, 52–53
Miranda v. Arizona, 41
Miscarriage of justice, 32
Mission to the United States of America (Ndiaye), 109

Mississippi, 26
Mississippi, Caldwell v., 18
Missouri, Wilkins v., 38
Mitchell, Alfred Brian, 119–120
Mitigating circumstances, 37
Mocan, H. Naci, 125
"Monitoring and Evaluating Contemporary Death Sentencing Systems: Lessons from Georgia" (Baldus, Pulanski, and Woodworth), 47, 77
Moore, Bryan v., 36
Moore, Provenzano v., 36
Morales, Michael, 90
Morales v. Tilton, 90
Morality
    of death penalty, public opinion on, 97
    opposing death penalty, reasons for, 101
Moran, Godinez v., 45–46
Moran, Richard Allen, 45
Moratorium
    California, 90
    in death penalty states, 90
    Florida, 90–91
    Illinois, 91
    international, UN push for, 108
    Maryland, 91–92
    nationwide, effects of on murders, 122
    nationwide, end of, 5–6
    nationwide, executions following, 69
    nationwide, overview of, 13
    Nebraska, 92
    New Hampshire, 92
    New Jersey, 92
    New York, 92–93
    North Carolina, 93
    Tennessee, 93
    Texas, 93–94
"More Than Two-Thirds of Americans Continue to Support the Death Penalty" (Taylor), 105
Muhlhausen, David B., 124–125
Muncey, Carolyn, 32
Murder. *See* Homicide
Murder Victim's Families for Human Rights (MVFHR), 127
Murray, Turner v., 47
Murray v. Carrier, 32
Murray v. Giarratano, 28, 84
Mustard, Donna, 65

N

NAACP Legal Defense and Educational Fund (LDF), 71
National Association for the Advancement of Colored People (NAACP), 131–132
National Institute of Justice (NIJ)
    Postconviction DNA Testing: Recommendations for Handling Requests, 89
    The Report to the Attorney General on Delays in Forensic DNA Analysis, 90

research into racial bias in capital cases, 79
Research into the Investigation and Prosecution of Homicide: Examining the Federal Death Penalty System, 78
Ndiaye, Bacre Waly, 109
Nebraska
    electrocution execution in, 58
    moratoriums in, 92
Netherland, Breard v., 110
Nevada
    Frankie Sue Del Papa on Liebman study, 88–89
    lethal gas execution in, 58
New Hampshire, 92
New Jersey, 92
New Jersey, Apprendi v., 20, 91
New Jersey Death Penalty Study Commission Report, 92
New York
    Capital Defender Office, 83
    death penalty, costs of in, 67
    death penalty, unconstitutionality of, 106
    moratoriums in, 92–93
    support for death penalty in, 102
Newton, Frances Elaine, 71
Nichols, Brian, 84
Nichols, David A., 94
Nigeria, 108
NIJ. *See* National Institute of Justice
Norris, Singleton v., 43
North Carolina
    mandatory death sentence in, 15
    moratoriums in, 93
    racial bias in death sentencing, study on, 79–80
North Carolina, Woodson v., 15, 93
North Carolina Innocence Inquiry Commission (NCIIC), 93
Number of persons executed, by jurisdiction, 69*t*
Number of prisoners under sentence of death, 62 (*t*6.1)
Number sentenced to death/number of removals, by jurisdiction/reason for removal, 68*t*

O

O'Connor, Sandra Day
    on criminal intent, 26
    on death penalty for minors, 38, 40
    on execution of mentally retarded, 43–44
    on fairness of death penalty, 128, 131
    on indigent defendants, 84
    on *Ring v. Arizona*, 20
    on *Tison v. Arizona*, 27
Oda, Shigenu, 111
Ohio
    DPMIP report for death penalty process reform, 96
    racial bias in death sentencing, study on, 81

Ohio, Lockett v., 16, 37
Ohio Associated Press (AP), 81
Oken, Steven, 91
Oklahoma, Ake v., 42
Oklahoma, Eddings v., 37–38
Oklahoma, Thompson v., 38
Oklahoma City bombing, 10
Olsen, Lise, 83
Optional Protocol to VCCR, 111–112
Ordinary crimes, 3–4
Otis, William G., 123
"Oversight of the Federal Death Penalty"
    Acevedo Vilá, Aníbal, testimony of, 132–133
    Muhlhausen, David B., testimony of, 124–125
    Otis, William G., testimony of, 123
    Shelton, Hilary O., testimony of, 131–132
"An Overview of the Federal Death Penalty Process" (Burr, Bruck, and McNally), 10
Owings, Lindsey, 28–29

P

Paraguay, Republic of, 110
Pardon, 57
Parole
    information, keeping from jury, 18
    life imprisonment without, *vs.* death penalty, 101–102
Pastore, Ann L., 71–72
Patel, Marilyn Hall, 35
Paternoster, Raymond, 80, 124
Patterson, James Earl, 8
Patton, Paul E., 39
Payne, Pervis Tyrone, 46
Payne v. Tennessee, 46
Penitentiaries, 3
Penn, William, 2
Pennsylvania
    Commonwealth v. Martorano, 21
    DPMIP report for death penalty process reform, 96
Pennsylvania, Sattazahn v., 21
Pennsylvania v. Finley, 28
Penry, Johnny Paul, 43–44
Penry v. Johnson, 44
Penry v. Lynaugh, 40
People v. LaValle, 93
Peremptory challenges, 48–49
Performance Audit Report: Costs Incurred for Death Penalty Cases (Kansas), 65
Perry, Rick, 54, 93–94
Persons executed, by race/Hispanic origin, 71*f*
Persons executed, by state, 69 (*f*6.5)
Persons under sentence of death, 1955–2005, 62*f*
Persons under sentence of death, by race/Hispanic origin, 63*f*
Pew Research Center
    Religion and Politics: Contention and Consensus, 99

Trends in Political Values and Core Attitudes: 1987–2007, 98
Pierce, Glenn, 80
Plantz, Marilyn Kay, 70–71
Plea bargaining
    Green River Killer, 94
    racial disparity in, 78
Pleas, guilty, 92
Pokorak, Jeffrey, 81
Political affiliation, support for death penalty and, 99–100
Political philosophy of public who deem death penalty morally acceptable, 98*f*
"Poll: Lock the Doors on Death Row" (Sussman), 105
"Poll: Public Ambivalent about Death Penalty" (Langer), 105
Polls, public opinion, 97
Ponsor, Michael A., 55
Poor defendants
    legal representation for, 75, 81–84
    Texas Fair Defense Act, 93–94
Poore, Barbel, 38
Postconviction DNA Testing: Recommendations for Handling Requests (NIJ), 89
Postconviction review, 84
Powell, Lewis F., Jr.
    on death penalty constitutionality, 14
    on failure of death penalty, 128
    on racial prejudice in capital cases, 47, 48
    on victim impact statements, 46
Power of clemency, 56–57
Presumption of malice, 30–31
Prisoners
    death row, demographic characteristics of, 64*t*
    executed, by offense, 72*f*
    federal death penalty, 55
    federal on death row, 130
    innocent, 121
    rights during psychiatric examination, 41
    under sentence of death/executed, by race, 76 (*f*7.1)
    under sentence of death/executions, 7(*f*1.3)
    sentenced to death, status of, 67*f*
"Probing the Capital Prosecutor's Perspective: Race of the Discretionary Actors" (Pokorak), 81
Proffitt v. Florida, 15
The Prohibition Era
    effects on abolitionist movement, 4
    homicide surge during, 6
Prosecution
    errors, cases involving, 29–30
    racially based use of peremptory challenges, 48–49
Prosecutors Perspective on California's Death Penalty (CJLF), 82
Protess, David, 89
Provenzano, Thomas, 36

Provenzano v. Moore, 36
Psychiatric testimony, 40–42
"Public Defender Chief Quits, Says Courts Should Be 'Told the Truth'" (Rankin), 84
Public defenders, 83
Public opinion
    on morality of social issues, 98*t*
    on preferred sentence for murder, 104 (*t*9.5)
    on whether an innocent has been executed in last five years, 105*f*
Public opinion on death penalty
    current, 1
    death penalty, support for, 97–100
    death penalty *vs.* life imprisonment with no parole, 101–102
    as a deterrent, 106*f*
    deterrent, effectiveness as, 106
    excessive frequency of use question, 102
    fairness of, 102, 105*t*
    frequency of use, 104 (*f*9.8)
    Great Britain/Canada/United States, 117 (*f*10.1)
    innocence and, 102
    international, 116–117
    morality of, 97
    moratorium, 105–106
    for murder, 99*f*
    for murder, Great Britain/Canada/United States, 117 (*f*10.2)
    overview of, 9, 97
    reasons for support/opposition, 100–101
    in states with/without death penalty, 103 (*f*9.7)
    2007, 2*f*
Puerto Rico, 132–133
Pulanski, Charles A., Jr., 47, 76
Pulley v. Harris, 22

Q

Quakers, 2
Quijano, Walter, 49
Quinn, Cynthia, 93
Quinones, United States v., 120

R

Race and the Death Penalty in North Carolina, an Empirical Analysis: 1993–1997 (Unah and Boger), 79–80
Race/Ethnicity
    Baldus study, 76–77
    bias in death penalty, 75
    California study, 80
    in capital cases, 47–49
    death penalty advocates on race, 82
    death penalty and, John McAdams on, 121
    death penalty and, William G. Otis on, 123
    death penalty support and, 98–100

of death row inmates, 61

death row waits by, 64

DOJ study of racial/ethnic bias, first, 77–78

DOJ study of racial/ethnic bias, second, 79

executions by, 71

homicide statistics and, 75

Maryland study, 80

North Carolina study, 79–80

Ohio study, 81

persons under sentence of death, by race/ Hispanic origin, 63f

plea bargaining, disparity in, 78

racial bias, claims of, 81–82

racial justice legislation, 77

support for death penalty and, 99–100

U.S. GAO study, 77

using to obtain death sentence, 49

Racial discrimination

in death penalty cases, David B. Muhlhausen on, 124

in death penalty cases, Hilary O. Shelton on, 131–132

"Racial Discrimination and the Death Penalty in the Post-*Furman* Era: An Empirical and Legal Analysis with Recent Findings from Philadelphia" (Baldus et al.), 77

Racial Justice Act (Kentucky), 77

Racial justice legislation, 77

Radelet, Michael, 80

RAND Corporation, 124

Rankin, Bill, 84

Rape

executions for, 72

of minors, 52–53

Supreme Court on death penalty for, 25

2004 national study, 80–81

Reasons for opposing death penalty, 103 (t9.3)

Reasons for supporting death penalty, 103 (t9.2)

Reckless indifference of human life, 27

Recommendations to Governor Rick Perry (Texas), 93

"Reducing the Risk of Executing the Innocent: The Report of the Illinois Governor's Commission on Capital Punishment," 88

Rehnquist, William H.

on death penalty, 14

on *Eberheart v. Georgia*, 25

on execution of the insane, 43

on *Herrera v. Collins*, 31

on right to counsel, 28

on *Wainwright v. Witt*, 16–17

on *Witherspoon*-excludables, 17

Reid, Willie, 46

Religion and Politics: Contention and Consensus (Pew Research Center), 99

Reno, Janet, 79

Report of the Governor's Commission on Capital Punishment (Illinois), 91

The Report to the Attorney General on Delays in Forensic DNA Analysis (NIJ), 90

Reprieve, 57

Research into the Investigation and Prosecution of Homicide: Examining the Federal Death Penalty System (NIJ), 78

Resendis, Angel Maturino, 109

Resolution 2393 (UN General Assembly), 107–108

Retentionist countries

China, 112–113

Japan, 113–114

overview of, 108–109

United States, 109–112

Ridgway, Gary Leon, 94

Riggs, Christina Marie, 70

Ring, Timothy Stuart, 20

Ring decision, 20–21

Ring v. Arizona, 20, 91

Roberts v. Louisiana, 15

Robertson, Pat, 131

Rodriguez, Alfonso, Jr., 55

Rodriguez, Chipita, 70

Roper, Donald, 7

Roper v. Simmons, 7, 39, 54–55, 116

Rosenbergs, 60

The Royal Charter for South New Jersey, 2

Rubin, Paul H., 121–122, 125

Rucker, David, 31

Rudolph v. Alabama, 5

Ruiz, Alejandro Gilbert, 35

Rush, Benjamin, 3

Ryan, George, 57, 91, 105, 131

S

Saad, Lydia, 97

Saldano, Victor, 49

Saldano v. Texas, 49

Sampson, Gary Lee, 55

Sarivola, Anthony, 29–30

Sattazahn, David, 21

Sattazahn v. Pennsylvania, 21

Sawyer v. Whitley, 32

Scalia, Antonin

death penalty debate, argument for, 122–123

on death penalty for minors, 38–39

on double-jeopardy protection, 21

on execution of mentally retarded, 45

on *Lankford v. Idaho*, 22–23

on mitigating circumstances, 37

on *Ring v. Arizona*, 20

on *Schriro v. Summerlin*, 21

Scheck, Barry, 121, 123

Schieber, Vicki A., 127–128

Schlup, Lloyd, 32

Schlup v. Delo, 32

Schriro v. Summerlin, 21

Schwab, Mark Dean, 91

Schwarzenegger, Arnold

Stanley "Tookie" Williams, execution of, 9

veto of CCFAJ bills by, 90

Scott, Ann, 119–120

Scott, Elaine Marie, 119–120

Scott, McFarland v., 28

Sellers, Sean, 54

Sentencing

comparative proportionality, 22–23

by judge, 18–19

by jury, 20–21

September 11, 2001, 10

Sessions, William, 131

Sexual crimes, 52–53

See also Rape

Shaheen, C. Jeanne, 92

Sharp, Dudley, 82

Shaw, Leander J., Jr., 36

Shelton, Hilary O., 131–132

Shepherd, Joanna M., 122, 125

Shockley, Leonard, 54

Sibley, George, Jr., 71

Simmons, Christopher, 39

Simmons, Jonathan Dale, 18

Simmons, Roper v., 7, 39, 54–55, 116

Simmons v. South Carolina, 18

Singleton, Charles, 43

Singleton v. Norris, 43

Sixth Amendment

Lockhart v. McCree, 16

right to impartial jury, 20

Sjodin, Dru, 55

Slepian, Barnett, 112

Slovik, Edward, 11

Smith, Ernest, 41

Smith, Estelle v., 41, 44

Smith, Frank Lee, 89

Smith, Jordan, 54

Smith, Lois Nadean, 70–71

Smith, W. Jack, 47

Smith, Wiggins v., 27–28

Smykla, John Ortiz, 2

Snell, Tracy L., 58, 59, 61

Sourcebook of Criminal Justice Statistics 2003 (Maguire and Patore), 71–72

Souter, David H.

on presumption of malice, 30–31

racially based use of peremptory challenges, 49

South Asian Human Rights Documentation Center, 113

South Carolina, 30–31

South Carolina, Simmons v., 18

Spaziano, Joseph, 18–19

Spaziano v. Florida, 18–19

Spencer, Timothy, 8

Stanford, Kevin, 38

Stanford Law Review, 122

Stanford v. Kentucky, 38

State v. Torrence, 58

State v. Wilson, 52–53

States

    capital offenses by, 52*t*

    clemencies granted by, 1976–2005, 58*t*

    death penalty laws, constitutionality of, 14–15

    death penalty variations in, 51

    death row inmates in, numbers of, 61

    faults in capital punishment system, 94–96

    lack of death penalty standards in, 5

    with life imprisonment without parole sentencing option, 101–102

    moratoriums in, 90–94

    non-death penalty, federal capital punishment in, 55

    offering life without parole sentence, 104 (*t*9.4)

    powers, death penalty and, 1

    uniform death penalty system for, 5

Statistical information

    age at time of arrest for capital offense/age of prisoners under sentence of death, 63 (*t*6.4)

    average number of years under sentence of death, 66 (*t*6.8)

    capital offenses, by state, 52*t*

    circumstances of homicides, by race, 77*t*

    clemencies granted, by state, 1976–2005, 58*t*

    countries that are abolitionist for all crimes, 115*t*

    countries that are abolitionist for ordinary crimes only, 2007, 116 (*t*10.6)

    countries that are abolitionist in practice, 114*t*

    countries that have abolished the death penalty, 1976–2007, 116 (*t*10.6)

    criminal history profile, death row prisoners, 65*t*

    defendants in federal death penalty process, stages in, 77*t*

    demographic characteristics of death row prisoners, 64*t*

    executions, 1930–2006, 6*f*

    executions, 1973–2005, 69 (*f*6.4)

    executions, by state/method, 73*t*

    executions during 2005, 71*t*

    foreign nationals executed, 110*t*

    gender/age breakdown of proponents of death penalty, 103 (*f*9.6)

    general appeals process for capital cases, 56*f*

    homicide offending rate, by race, 76 (*f*7.2)

    homicide rate/executions, 1960–2005, 8*f*

homicide victimization rate, by race, 76 (*f*7.3)

homicides by race of offender/victim, 76 (*f*7.4)

inmates received under sentence of death, 62 (*t*6.2)

jurisdictions with/without death penalty, 2007, 2*t*

methods of execution, by state, 59*t*

number of persons executed, by jurisdiction, 69*t*

number of prisoners under sentence of death, 62 (*t*6.1)

number sentenced to death/number of removals, by jurisdiction/reason for removal, 68*t*

persons executed, by race/Hispanic origin, 71*f*

persons executed, by state, 69 (*f*6.5)

persons under sentence of death, 1955–2005, 62*f*

persons under sentence of death, by race/Hispanic origin, 63*f*

political philosophy of public who deem death penalty morally acceptable, 98*f*

prisoners under sentence of death/executed, by race, 76 (*f*7.1)

public opinion on death penalty, 2007, 2*f*

public opinion on death penalty, Great Britain/Canada/United States, 117 (*f*10.1)

public opinion on death penalty for murder, 99*f*

public opinion on death penalty for murder, Great Britain/Canada/United States, 117 (*f*10.2)

public opinion on death penalty frequency of use, 104 (*f*9.8)

public opinion on death penalty in states with/without death penalty, 103 (*f*9.7)

public opinion on fairness of death penalty, 105*t*

public opinion on morality of social issues, 98*t*

public opinion on preferred sentence for murder, 104 (*f*9.5)

public opinion on role of death penalty as deterrent to murder, 106*f*

public opinion on whether an innocent has been executed in last five years, 105*f*

reasons for opposing death penalty, 103 (*t*9.3)

reasons for supporting death penalty, 103 (*t*9.2)

states offering life without parole sentence, 104 (*t* 9.4)

status of prisoners sentenced to death, 67*f*

support for death penalty, by race, 101*f*

support for death penalty, by race, 1972–2007, 102*f*

time under sentence of death, by race, 66 (*t*6.7)

U.S. Supreme Court death penalty decisions, 5*t*

    women under sentence of death, by race, 63 (*t*6.3)

Status of prisoners sentenced to death, 67*f*

Statutes, unconstitutionally vague, 25–26

Stevens, John Paul

    death penalty, argument against, 120

    on death penalty for minors, 38

    on execution of mentally retarded, 45

    on *Lankford v. Idaho*, 22–23

    on right to counsel, 28

    on *Spaziano v. Florida*, 19

    on victim impact statements, 46

Stewart, Potter J.

    on death penalty, 13–14

    on *Gregg v. Georgia*, 15

    on *Jurek v. Texas*, 15

Stewart, Summerlin v., 21

Streib, Victor L., 54, 61

Strickland v. Washington, 33, 82

Study Pursuant to Public Act No. 01-151 of the Imposition of the Death Penalty in Connecticut, 66

Summerlin, Schriro v., 21

Summerlin, Warren, 21

Summerlin v. Stewart, 21

Support for death penalty, by race, 101*f*

Support for death penalty, by race, 1972–2007, 102*f*

Suppressed evidence, 32–33

Supreme Court rulings

    anti-death penalty jurors, exclusion of, 16–17

    capital punishment for minors, 37–40

    competency standard, 45–46

    death penalty, proper imposition of, 14–15

    death penalty constitutionality, 13–14

    on double jeopardy, 21–22

    insanity and execution, 42–43

    juror's death sentence recommendation, 17–18

    juror's lesser charge consideration, 16

    mental retardation and execution, 43–45

    mitigating circumstances, 37

    parole information, keeping from jury, 18

    psychiatric testimony, 40–42

    race in capital cases, 47–49

    sentencing by judge, 18–19

    sentencing by jury, 20–21

    sentencing procedures, 22–23

    victim impact statements, 46–47

Sussman, Dalia, 105

Swain v. Alabama, 49

T

Takahashi, Sachiho, 113

Taylor, Humphrey, 105

Taylor, Stephen, 36

Taylor, Williams v., 33, 34, 58

Teenagers. *See* Adolescents

Tempest, Rone, 64
Tennessee
    DPMIP report for death penalty process
        reform, 96
    moratoriums in, 93
Tennessee, Payne v., 46
Terrorism, 51–52
Terrorist Bombings Convention
    Implementation Act of 2002, 10
Tessmer, John, 39
Testimony
    of Acevedo Vilá, Aníbal, 132–133
    of Bright, Stephen B., 128–129
    of Fagan, Jeffrey, 129–130
    of McAdams, John, 120–121
    of Muhlhausen, David B., 124–125
    of Otis, William G., 123
    of Rubin, Paul H., 121–122
    of Schieber, Vicki A., 127–128
    of Scott, Ann, 119–120
    of Shelton, Hilary O., 131–132
Texas
    Fair Defense Act, 83
    "law of parties," 53–54
    moratoriums in, 93–94
Texas, Branch v., 13
Texas, Jurek v., 15, 41
Texas, Saldano v., 49
Texas Appleseed, 93–94
Texas v. Cobb, 29
Thomas, Clarence
    on extended stays on death row, 36
    on *Ring v. Arizona*, 20
Thompson, William, 38
Thompson v. Oklahoma, 38
Thurmond, Strom, 88
Tilton, Morales v., 90
Time under sentence of death, by race, 66
    (*t*6.7)
Timmerman, Rachel, 55, 68
Tison, Gary, 27
Tison v. Arizona, 27
Tomei, Hynes v., 92
Tomiyama, Tsuneki, 113
Torrence, State v., 58
*Trends in Political Values and Core
    Attitudes: 1987–2007* (Pew Research
    Center), 98
Trial system, bifurcated, 51
Trop v. Dulles, 4
Tucker, Karla Faye, 9, 70
Tucker, Ricky, 26
Turner, Willie Lloyd, 47
Turner v. Murray, 47

U
UCMJ (Uniform Code of Military Justice),
    10–11
"The Ultimate Sacrifice" (Nichols), 94

UN Economic and Social Council
    Resolution 1574, 108
Unah, Isaac, 79–80
"Uncertain Justice" (Olsen), 83
Uniform Code of Military Justice (UCMJ),
    10–11
United Kingdom, death penalty abolition in,
    114
United Nations (UN)
    Convention on the Rights of the Child,
        115
    Human Rights Council moratorium on
        executions, 108
    resolutions on capital punishment,
        107–108
United States
    capital punishment in, international
        perspective, 108–109
    defiance of UN in death penalty cases,
        109–110
    extraditions to, 112
    federal death penalty, 9–10
    foreign nationals rights in, 109
    Optional Protocol to the VCCR,
        withdrawal from, 112
    public opinion on death penalty, Great
        Britain/Canada/United States, 117
        (*f*10.1)
    public opinion on death penalty for
        murder, Great Britain/Canada/United
        States, 117 (*f*10.2)
    racial bias in death sentencing, study on,
        80–81
    UN moratorium on executions, response
        to, 108
    vs. Western democratic nations, 11
United States, Bruton v., 30
United States of America, Germany v., 111
United States of America, Mexico v., 111–112
United States v. Jackson, 92–93
United States v. Quinones, 120
U.S. Constitution, 4–5
U.S. Courts of Appeals, geographic
    boundaries of, 57*f*
U.S. Department of Justice (DOJ)
    study of racial/ethnic bias, first, 77–78
    study of racial/ethnic bias, second, 79
U.S. District Courts, geographic boundaries
    of, 57*f*
U.S. Food and Drug Administration
    (FDA), 34
U.S. General Accounting Office (GAO), 77
U.S. Government Accountability Office.
    See U.S. General Accounting Office
U.S. military
    death penalty laws, 10–11
    Edward Slovik, execution of, 11
    John A. Bennett, execution of, 11
"The U.S. Military Death Penalty"
    (DPIC), 11
U.S. penal system, 3

U.S. Supreme Court
    AEDPA, challenging, 33–34
    on Antiterrorism and Effective Death
        Penalty Act, 7
    appeals based on new evidence, 31–33
    Atkins v. Virginia, 7
    on *Breard v. Greene*, 110
    on criminal intent, 26–27
    de facto moratorium of, 91
    death penalty, circumstances that do not
        warrant, 25–26
    death penalty decisions, 5*t*
    on death row, extended stays on, 36
    on execution methods, 34–36
    Ford v. Wainwright, 5
    on prosecution errors, cases involving, 29–30
    on right to effective counsel, 27–29
    Trop v. Dulles, 4
    uniform death penalty system for states, 5
    on Vienna Convention, 111–112
USA Patriot Act, 10
Utah, 5

V
VCCR (Vienna Convention on Consular
    Affairs), 109
Venezuela, 114
Victim impact statements, 46–47
Vienna Convention on Consular Affairs
    (VCCR), 109
Violent Crime Control and Law
    Enforcement Act
    description of, 9–10
    federal prosecutions increase since, 67
Virginia, Atkins v., 7, 39, 55
Virginia Colony, 2

W
Wainwright, Ford v., 6, 42–43
Wainwright, Gideon v., 82
Wainwright v. Witt, 16–17
Walnut Street Jail, 3
Walsh, Jim, 20–21
Walton v. Arizona, 20
Warren, Mark, 109
Washington (state), 65
Washington, Strickland v., 33, 82
*Washington's Death Penalty System: A
    Review of the Costs, Length, and Results
    of Capital Cases in Washington State*
    (Larranaga and Mustard), 65
Wells, Martin T., 80–81
Welsh-Huggins, Andrew, 81
West, Valerie, 88–89
Western democratic nations, 11
White, Byron R.
    on coerced confessions, 30
    on death penalty, 14, 130
    on racial prejudice in capital cases, 47

White, Ed, 68
Whitley, Kyles v., 32–33
Whitley, Sawyer v., 32
"Why Japan Still Has the Death Penalty" (Lane), 113
Wiggins, Kevin Eugene, 27–28
Wiggins v. Smith, 27–28
Wilkins, Heath, 38
Wilkins v. Missouri, 38
Wilkinson, Beth A., 83
Will, George, 131
"'Will This Day Be My Last?' The Death Penalty in Japan" (Amnesty International), 113
Williams, Michael Wayne, 34
Williams, Stanley "Tookie," 9

Williams, Terry, 33
Williams v. Taylor, 33, 34, 58
Wilson, Anthony, 52–53
Wilson, State v., 52–53
Wise, Daniel, 67
Witherspoon v. Illinois, 16
Witnesses to executions, 60
Witt, Wainwright v., 16–17
Women under sentence of death, by race, 63 (*t*6.3)
Wood, Campbell v., 35
Wood, Willie, 30–31
Woodson v. North Carolina, 15, 93
Woodworth, George, 47, 76
Workman, Philip, 93

Worldwide death penalty trend, 11
Writ of certiorari, 56
"Wrong Place, Wrong Time" (Smith), 54
Wuornos, Aileen Carol, 71

Y

Yates, Dale Robert, 30–31
Yates v. Evatt, 30–31
York, Mary Lou, 43

Z

Zawitz, Marianne W., 75
Zhang, Ivy, 113
Zheng Xiaoyu, 112–113
Zimmerman, Paul R., 125